THE HISTORY OF
HIGHER EDUCATION

THE HISTORY OF HIGHER EDUCATION

Major Themes in Education

Edited by
Roy Lowe

Volume III
Universities and the state

Routledge
Taylor & Francis Group

LONDON AND NEW YORK

First published 2009
by Routledge
2 Park Square, Milton Park, Abingdon, Oxon, OX14 4RN, UK

Simultaneously published in the USA and Canada
by Routledge
270 Madison Avenue, New York, NY 10016

Routledge is an imprint of the Taylor & Francis Group, an informa business

Typeset in 10/12pt Times NR MT by Graphicraft Limited, Hong Kong
Printed and bound in Great Britain by
MPG Books Ltd., Bodmin, Cornwall

British Library Cataloguing in Publication Data
A catalogue record for this book is available from the British Library

Library of Congress Cataloging-in-Publication Data
The history of higher education : major themes in education / edited by Roy Lowe.
p. cm.
Includes bibliographical references and index.
ISBN 978-0-415-37854-3 (set) – ISBN 978-0-415-38469-8 (vol. 1, hardback) –
ISBN 978-0-415-38470-4 (vol. 2, hardback) – ISBN 978-0-415-38471-1
(vol. 3, hardback) – ISBN 978-0-415-38472-8 (vol. 4, hardback) –
ISBN 978-0-415-38473-5 (vol. 5, hardback) 1. Education, Higher–History.
I. Lowe, Roy.
LA173.H584 2008
378.09–dc22
2008008884

ISBN10: 0-415-37854-0 (Set)
ISBN10: 0-415-38471-0 (Volume III)

ISBN13: 978-0-415-37854-3 (Set)
ISBN13: 978-0-415-38471-1 (Volume III)

Publisher's Note

References within each chapter are as they appear in the original
complete work.

CONTENTS

v

CONTENTS

ACKNOWLEDGEMENTS

The publishers would like to thank the following for permission to reprint their material:

The University of Chicago Press and Konrad H. Jarausch for permission to reprint Konrad H. Jarausch, 'Higher Education and Social Change: Some Comparative Perspectives', in K. H. Jarausch (ed.), *The Transformation of Higher Learning, 1860–1930*, Klett-Cotta, Stuttgart, 1981, pp. 9–36.

Taylor & Francis for permission to reprint Michael Sanderson, 'Conclusion', from *The Universities and British Industry, 1850–1970*, M. Sanderson, Copyright © 1972 Routledge and Kegan Paul, London. Reproduced by permission of Taylor & Francis Books UK.

Ayer Company Publisher for permission to reprint W. H. G. Armytage, 'Community Service Stations: The Transformation of the Civic Universities, 1898–1930', in W. H. G. Amytage, *Civic Universities*, Arno Press, a New York Times company, New York, 1977, pp. 243–264.

Blackwell Publishing for permission to reprint Roy Pascal, 'The Universities and Social Purpose', *Universities Quarterly* (now *Higher Education Quarterly*), vol. IV, 1949–50, Turnstile Press, London, pp. 37–43.

The Random House Group Ltd. for permission to reprint Sydney Caine, 'Reflections on Policy', from *British Universities: Purposes and Prospects* by Sydney Caine, published by The Bodley Head.

Ayer Company Publisher for permission to reprint Robert O. Berdahl, 'Conclusion', from Robert O. Berdahl, *British Universities and the State*, University of California Press, Berkeley and Cambridge University Press, London, 1959, pp. 183–194.

The Office of Public Sector Information for permission to reprint excerpts from Report of the Committee appointed by the Minister of Education and the Secretary of State for Scotland in June, 1958, Ministry of Education Sottish Education Department, *Grants to Students*, June 1958, HMSO, London, pp. 1–8 and 77–87.

ACKNOWLEDGEMENTS

The Office of Public Sector Information for permission to reprint excerpts from *Higher Education*, Report of the Robbins Committee, 1963, HMSO, London, pp. 4–10 and 365–367.

Taylor & Francis for permission to reprint Harold Silver, 'Pasts and Futures', from *A Higher Education: The Council for National Academic Awards and British Higher Education 1964–89*, Harold Silver, Copyright © 1990 Falmer Press. Reproduced by permission of Taylor & Francis Books UK.

Penguin Books Ltd for permission to reprint E. P. Thompson, 'The Business University', in E. P. Thompson (ed.), *Warwick University Ltd.*, Penguin Books, Harmondsworth, 1970, pp. 13–41.

The Institute of Economic Affairs for permission to reprint H. S. Ferns, *Towards an Independent University*, The Institute of Economic Affairs, 1970, pp. 9–26.

Vincent Carpentier, 'Funding in Higher Education and Economic Growth in France and the United Kingdom, 1921–2003', from *Higher Education Management and Policy*, Volume 18 Issue 3, pp. 1–22, © OECD 2006. This article is a substantially developed version of a paper published as 'Cycles longs et financement universitaire: une perspective historique sur les réformes actuelles au Royaume-Uni', *Économie et Sociétés*, Cahier de l'ISMEA, Hors Série, no. 40 (2005), pp. 1607–1634.

Oxford University Press for permission to reprint Notker Hammerstein, 'National Socialism and the German universities', *History of Universities*, vol. XVIII/I, 2003, Oxford University Press, Oxford, pp. 170–188.

Blackwell Publishing for permission to reprint Lord Lindsay of Birker, 'The Commission on German universities', *Universities Quarterly* (now *Higher Education Quarterly*), vol. IV, 1949–50, Turnstile Press, London, pp. 82–88.

James T. Flynn and The Catholic University of America Press for permission to reprint James T. Flynn, *The University Reform of Tsar Alexander I, 1802–1835*, The Catholic University of America Press, Washington D.C., 1988, pp. 1–25.

Blackwell Publishing for permission to reprint Alexander Kinghorn, 'The American State University Today', *Universities Quarterly* (now *Higher Education Quarterly*), vol. X, 1955–56, Turnstile Press, London, pp. 69–79.

Symposium Books and Sheldon Rothblatt for permission to reprint Sheldon Rothblatt, 'Affirmative Action,' in Sheldon Rothblatt, *Education's Abiding Moral Dilemma: Merit and Worth in the Cross-Atlantic Democracies, 1800–2006*, Oxford Studies in Comparative Education, Symposium Books, Oxford, 2007, 277–300.

ACKNOWLEDGEMENTS

Greenwood Publishing Group for permission to reprint John E. Fleming, 'Blacks in Higher Education to 1954: A Historical Overview', from *Black Students in Higher Education: Conditions and Experiences in the 1970s*, Gail E. Thomas (ed.), Greenwood Press, Westport, Connecticut and London, England, 1981, pp. 11–17. Copyright © 1989 Greenwood Press.

Blackwell Publishing for permission to reprint John Rex, 'Apartheid in the South African Universities', *Universities Quarterly* (now *Higher Education Quarterly*), vol. VIII, 1953–54, Turnstile Press. London, pp. 333–340.

Disclaimer

INTRODUCTION

The third volume deals with the relationship of the universities and higher education with the state. For this purpose, the term 'state' is interpreted loosely, so that although most of the extracts chosen are concerned with the ways in which higher education and the polity interact, some of the others deal with the ways that educational developments impinge on economic and social progress more broadly.

The collection begins with two extracts that deal with general issues. Thirty years ago, Konrad Jarausch was the instigator of a very significant collaboration between scholars from Europe and America which was concerned with the linkages between developing systems of higher education and the professionalisation of society. His introductory essay, which is reproduced here as Chapter 51, examined changing recruitment to higher education in four countries to establish ways in which the diversification of higher education and the increase in enrolments related to the modernisation of society and its professionalisation. Alongside this, Guy Neave, another widely known commentator on trends in higher education, reflected in his address to the 1983 conference of to the Society for Research into Higher Education on the ways in which universities across Europe were becoming accountable to their societies in ways they had not previously been (Chapter 52). He speculated on the intensification of this trend and reflected on its likely significance into the twenty-first century.

There follow a number of essays looking at aspects of the relationships between universities in Britain and wider society. First, in Chapter 53 Michael Sanderson, author of a magisterial and exhaustive account of the links between the universities and economic development, summarises his argument that, during the late nineteenth and early twentieth centuries, there was a rapprochement between the universities and industry which enabled institutions of higher education to become one of the dynamos of economic and social change. His argument ran counter to much that was being written when he published in the 1970s and is a significant counterpoint to some of the other essays included in this collection. In the same decade, W. H. G. Armytage's major study of the rise of the civic universities (Chapter 54) appeared. He too was an incisive and respected commentator on developments in higher education, and in the extract selected from this book he identified the ways in which the emergent redbrick universities had become 'community service stations' by the mid-twentieth century.

Another commentator on the early twentieth-century university scene was Lord Curzon of Kedleston. In 1909, during his period as Chancellor of the University of Oxford, Curzon, a former Viceroy of India and leading politician, offered his views on the reform of the university. The extract chosen here from his book *Principles and Methods of University Reform* deals with the admission of 'poor men' to the university (Chapter 55). It provides a fascinating insight into the thinking of a leading Conservative politician into the twin challenges posed to Oxford by the appearance of the WEA and Ruskin College.

Another period of ferment for universities in Britain was the years following the Second World War. Roy Pascal, a Professor of German at the University of Birmingham and a leading Communist commentator on trends in higher education, reflected on the need for the universities to enshrine a social purpose at the heart of their work in his article in the *Universities Quarterly* published in 1949 (Chapter 56). Not many years later, Sir Sydney Caine was identifying the postwar expansion and questions of funding as posing the most critical challenges for the universities. Chapter 57, extracted from his book, gives one view of the prospects for a 'binary system' raised by Anthony Crosland in his famous speech at Woolwich in 1965. Robert O. Berdahl, in his book on the universities and the state published in 1959 (Chapter 58), looked towards the achievement of a uniquely British balance, with academics retaining some degree of autonomy within a state-controlled system.

By the late 1950s the practice of awarding financial grants to students was becoming increasingly widespread. The extract selected to reflect this process is the Scottish governmental report on *Grants to Students*, presented in 1958 (Chapter 59). This Scottish report was mirrored elsewhere in the United Kingdom, but had the advantage that it not only reflects the trend towards universality, but has interesting insights and detail on the contrasts in practice which existed in different parts of the United Kingdom. It was chosen for this reason. Even more portentious was the 1963 Robbins Report, which might be seen as fixing the moment historically when government began to treat higher education in the United Kingdom as a system. The axiom which appears in this extract (Chapter 60), that courses should be available for all those who were qualified and who wished to pursue a course in higher education – the famous 'Robbins principle' – was to prove one of the most potent influences on the planning of higher education in Britain in the years that followed. Following this, in Chapter 61, the extract from John Carswell's book *Government and the Universities in Britain* offers a thoughtful critique of the planning process which Robbins and the coming of universal grant aid to students had begun. It would be wrong to conclude this overview of postwar developments without some consideration of the binary system. Harold Silver's account of the workings of the CNAA (Chapter 62) provides a telling commentary on what the binary system meant in practice for those involved day to day.

During the 1960s thinking around the universities in Britain became heavily politicised, and two publications in 1970 captured both sides of the debate. E. P. Thompson, who had been appointed to a post at the newly opened University of Warwick and was alarmed at the close rapprochement between the university and local industrial interests, produced *Warwick University Ltd.* as a polemic on the dangers which he thought were inherent in current trends (Chapter 63). Conversely, Harry Ferns was one of a very vocal group of academics arguing that what the universities needed was greater freedom from government and a closer involvement with non-governmental financial interests (Chapter 64). His call for an independent university was to result, a few years later, in the foundation of the University of Buckingham as an entirely private institution. Issues around governmental investment in higher education are explored in Chapter 65 from an entirely different perspective by Vincent Carpentier, a notable economic historian whose work throws light on the cyclical nature of funding and expansion during the twentieth century, suggesting significant new ways of analysing change in higher education.

Next, three essays explore relationships between the German universities and their social context. In Chapter 66 Charles McClelland examines the ways in which the challenge of preparing students for work in the growing professional sector led to tensions between those who supported theoretical study and those in favour of the expansion of technical subjects at the start of the twentieth century. This was a tension which also raised issues around the funding of universities. Notker Hammerstein, in Chapter 67, deals with the sensitive issue of the ways in which the universities responded to the challenge of National Socialism. How did Nazi policy towards academic research develop? What was the response of the universities to National Socialism? How far did they become a part of the problem rather than of the solution? These are some of the questions at the heart of his analysis. In contrast, Lord Lindsay of Birker placed an article in the *Universities Quarterly* in 1949 detailing the work of the Commission appointed by the British military Government immediately after the Second World War to plan the reconstruction of the German universities in the British Zone (Chapter 68). This was to become a template for university reform far more widely, and his article is of significance for that reason as well as for its insights into a very early example of postwar planning.

Chapter 69, extracted from James T. Flynn's book on university reform in Russia, reminds us that there are other societies in Europe which have a much longer tradition of the planning of university reform. Tsar Alexander II involved himself in this issue during the early years of the nineteenth century. The following two extracts reflect on American trends. In Chapter 70

Alexander Kinghorn offers a gloomy view of relations between the American States and their universities during the mid-1950s, while in Chapter 71 Sheldon Rothblatt reflects on the ways in which 'affirmative action' impinged on practice on American campuses. Alongside this, in Chapter 72 John E. Fleming offers an overview of the recruitment of black students to higher education in North America through the nineteenth and early twentieth centuries. Finally, in Chapter 73 John Rex reports on one of the most vexed political issues of the twentieth century in his account of the impact of South African apartheid on the universities.

HIGHER EDUCATION AND SOCIAL CHANGE

Some comparative perspectives

Konrad H. Jarausch

Source: K. H. Jarausch, *The Transformation of Higher Learning, 1860–1930*, Stuttgart: Klett-Cotta, 1981, pp. 9–36.

Seemingly self-evident, the relationship between higher education and social change has proven elusive. Social scientists have tended to focus on the practical reform of both according to some normative conception, often oblivious to the disappointments of the past. Historians who dared address that numinous monstrosity called "modernization" have usually ignored education or treated it as a dependent variable despite the insistence of many 19th century observers that it was a significant promoter of change.[1] Those who have taken a closer look have been disappointed in their effort to determine the general contribution of schooling to industrial development, unless they have focused more specifically on technical training. Others who have pondered the transmission of values have stressed the "actively incongruent" role of higher learning in social upheavals based upon the largely traditional content of the curriculum.[2] Part of this confusion results from an excessively narrow view of social change, limited by and large to industrialization. From a broader Weberian perspective, which includes rationalization, bureaucratization and professionalization as key processes, the role of education in the transformation of traditional society looms much larger. Instead of a simplistic alternative which defines schooling as either the passive product of society or the active motor of progress, the relationship between higher education and social change is circular and interdependent with both transforming each other. Not a deductive theoretical approach (be it functionalist or Marxist), but an inductive empirical study of one phase of their interaction is therefore likely to yield clearer insights, as long as it is sufficiently systematic and general.[3]

One such "seismic shift" is the emergence of "modern" higher education between the middle of the 19th and the first third of the 20th centuries. During the development of a mature industrial society, a small, homogenous, elite and pre-professional university turned into a large, diversified, middle-class and professional system of higher learning. While its antecedents in the late 18th century involve practical enlightenment as well as idealist neohumanist reforms, the major alterations in size, institutional structure, social composition and career pattern of graduates took place after initial industrialization before they were interrupted by the Great Depression and the Second World War. But from the perspective of mass higher education during the middle of the 20th century, these changes in higher learning were still limited by institutional tradition and social constraints.[4] Because the sequence, intensity and manner of this central transformation differed in various highly industrial countries of the West, a comparison can help isolate the relative importance of various causes. The British experience of industrialization preceding educational mobilization contrasts sharply with the German pattern of higher learning before economic growth, with the Russian sequence of both developments imported in the Central European mold and with the American way of both coinciding in time. Despite considerable differences in cultural style, institutional tradition and educational policies, certain developments, such as increases in size and complexity of institutions, cut across national frontiers and modernized higher learning in all countries of the West. Hence it is imperative to distinguish the common pattern from national peculiarities and vice versa.[5]

In order to gain greater explanatory depth, such an analysis has to be limited in several respects. The focus on higher education, defined loosely as post-secondary schooling beginning at age 18, provides a distinctive subject matter with clear boundaries. The common social approach to scientific research, liberal education or training contributes greater cohesion, even if the methods vary from intellectual to quantitative history. Interdisciplinary perspective produces a methodological tension between historicist attention to the particular and social scientist penchant for generalization or modeling.[6] Among the variety of issues, four themes seem to represent crucial aspects of the transformation. First, the absolute and relative expansion of enrollments provides a basic numerical indicator of the spread of higher learning and of the growth of its social importance. Second, institutional diversification approaches the internal differentiation of universities in terms of teaching subjects and research institutes as well as the proliferation of institutions in the technical and commercial fields. Third, the opening of recruitment raises the question of educational elitism or mobility during the second half of the 19th century and examines the university in terms of its societal clientele. Finally, the process of professionalization analyzes the relationship between institutionalized learning and the spread of the professions in terms of their scientific bases, practical training or state credentialling. While any number

6

of other problems, such as scientific progress, educational finances or university governance, could also have been discussed, these four dynamic processes emphasize change and facilitate comparison.[7]

Although American academics are sometimes defensive and hesitate to investigate their own institutions, their continental colleagues at the turn of the century were convinced of their own importance:

> The greatly admired level of civilization in Germany is living proof of the immeasurable value of the universities. Did not the culture which has now spread through every stratum of society issue chiefly from this primary and most copious source? More importantly this is where the great discoveries in the natural sciences were made, to whose practical application communication and commerce owe their progress. Here the principles of the rule of law were developed and taught. Here the moving ideas of economic progress were conceived, which public life struggles to implement. Here the spirits have matured who have succeeded in grasping the great truths of present and past reality and by teaching have made them the intellectual property of the people. Did not the universities nurture the spark of patriotism and of political honor in the darkest hours? Did not the salvation of the fatherland proceed from the universities in the hour of greatest need?

Somewhat exaggerating the active impact of higher education on society, contemporary self-consciousness demonstrates that for professors and students alike higher learning involved the spread of civilization, the advancement of science and the propagation of modern nationalism.[8] Seen in a broader context, the history of higher education is too important to be left to the vagaries of anniversary tributes to yet another illustrious alma mater. Instead it needs to be firmly integrated into the general discussion of social change in order to determine the university's contribution to "modernization" as well as to the perpetuation of traditional elites, values and styles.[9] Although the "most important questions" concerning not only arrangements but also purposes deal mostly with intangibles, a comparative framework for the study of higher learning requires, whenever possible, quantitative answers, marrying social, as it were, to intellectual history.[10]

The dynamics of expansion

A basic index of the internal structure and external influence of a system of higher education is its enrollment. "Major changes in the size of the student body are the structural pivots around which the history of the university has to be built," since large scale swings of attendance "not only have obvious and far-reaching effects on the economics, the architecture and the teaching arrangements of the university, they also have profound repercussions on its intellectual life." Because institutional figures and government statistics are often inflated, a first task is the reconstruction of the pattern of expansion in each of the four countries concerned. Previous attempts to measure absolute or relative growth have encountered three particular difficulties: Comparisons based on highly aggregated figures tend to be unreliable, if not misleading, because of varying degrees of inaccuracy and incompleteness of the numbers on which they are based. More sophisticated efforts have been frustrated by the unit of measurement problem of which institutions (and consequently students) should or should not be included in "higher education." Finally, cross-national comparisons built on age-cohort representation indices have found it difficult to focus on comparable spans of years among the population as base.[11] Fortunately these obstacles can be partially overcome by reaggregating data in individual settings from below, by defining higher learning not only legally (according to government practice) but also functionally (as post-secondary) and temporarily (18-year-olds and above) and by calculating the index of inclusiveness on the basis of empirically determined average length of study which is then compared to the relevant age group. The fragmentary evidence suggests three overriding questions: What was the absolute growth in student numbers? Which types of institutions contributed to it? How did the expansion of higher learning relate to population increase?

In all four countries student numbers rose so dramatically during the three-quarter century that higher learning multiplied at an average of ten times (Table 1).[12] The most rapid decades of growth were the 1870s and 1880s as well as the last pre-war years and once again the 1920s. While the German universities, with the highest level of initial attendance, expanded more slowly, Russian and British institutions grew strongly, and American colleges increased astoundingly since their students were younger and academic standards were less rigorous. Despite this considerable increase in the traditional university sector, the newer forms of higher education mushroomed even more quickly, 13–17 times in relatively restrictive Britain and Germany, and 36–66 times in the more inclusive American and Russian systems (Table 2). Much of this dynamism was due to the explosion of higher technical education and to the expansion of teacher training, which slowly reached equality with older disciplines and institutions. Even relative to the population (which doubled in this period) the expansion was still so substantial that one is tempted to call it an educational mobilization, since it not only reflects demographic growth but goes considerably beyond it (Table 3). The century-long contraction of higher education was arrested in the first decades of the 19th century; but only after 1850 did this reversal turn into sustained educational growth. Not surprisingly the most limited system was the British with only about 1.9% of the 20- to 24-year-old cohort enrolled in higher education. By 1930 the Germans were still somewhat

Table 1 Absolute University Enrollment.

country: year:	Britain		Germany		Russia		United States	
	stud.	univ.	stud.	univ.	stud.	univ.	stud.	univ./col.
1860/1	3,385	5	12,188	20	5,000	9	22,464	
1870/1	5,560		13,206		6,538		31,900	560
1880/1	10,560		21,209		8,045		49,300	
1890/1	16,013		28,621		13,169		72,250	
1900/1	17,839		33,739		16,357		100,000	
1910/1	26,414		53,364		37,901		144,800	
1920/1	34,591		86,367		109,200		251,750	
1930/1	37,255	16	97,692	23	43,600	21	489,500	1,400
growth:	11 times		8 times		9–22 times		22 times	

Note: British figures include both Old Universities and New Provincial Universities. German figures are for the Empire (less Strassburg after World War One) and include only universities. Russian figures include Warsaw and Dorpat until World War One. Because there is no precise American equivalent to the European university sector, an approximate estimate of U.S. dynamics was based on one half of the enrollment in colleges and universities together with the entire enrollment in the professional schools, since these were clearly of university-like status and function. The U.S. figures were computed from informed estimates of the college/ university, professional school, and normal school/teacher's college enrollment, provided by C. B. Burke. Since they were for males in 1860 and for both males and females thereafter, they somewhat overstate expansion.

more inclusive at 2.61% of the same age span, while the Russian spurt after the 1905 revolution and then again in the early and late 1920s raised the levels of inclusiveness to 4.3% of the age group in 1939. With the most open and varied structure, the United States was clearly ahead of all other developed nations with 11.25% of a 5-year age cohort going to college, graduate or professional school. Hence the German and British rates of increase were the lowest (five to six times), the American, starting at a higher level, somewhere in the middle (6.5) and the Soviet, calculated in terms of proportion among 10,000 of the population, the most dramatic (14), since they had the furthest to go. This substantial, but still limited, expansion beyond population growth made higher education accessible to a considerably larger segment of the relevant age group.[13]

Contemporaries already speculated about the causes of "this rapid increase in the number of our students." While academic boosters invoked "progress" or "democratization," statisticians offered "the high social esteem" of college graduates, "the universal spread of classical culture" and the "commercial depression" as reasons.[14] Although their relative weight differed according to context, about a handful of direct and indirect factors seems to have been involved. (1) While in Germany growth mainly occured in already existing institutions, in Britain (trebling), Russia (doubling) and the United States (more than doubling) a considerable part of the expansion

Table 2 Non-University Higher Education Enrollment.

country/ year	Britain			Germany			Russia			United States		
	Tech.	Teach.	Tot.	Tech.	Teach.	Tot.	Tech.	Teach.	Tot.	Coll/Un.	Teach.	Tot.
1860/1		2,129		2,187	(3,610)		(3,750 est.)			8,300	2,000	10,300
1870/1		2,527		3,957	(5,008)					20,000	9,900	29,900
1880/1		3,002		4,822	(9,892)		7,120			27,000	41,000	68,000
1890/1		3,126		6,594	(10,553)					39,750	45,500	85,250
1900/1		6,951		13,970	(11,648)		9,538			52,000	76,000	128,000
1910/1	3,024	12,257		14,884	(17,854)		30,990			78,800	131,300	210,100
1920/1	5,434	21,882		23,089	(9,039)	40,433	180,800			184,750	161,500	364,250
1930/1	8,030	20,924	28,954	22,890	3,200	37,199	247,300		247,300	391,300	293,600	684,900
			13 times			17 times			66 times			66 times

Note: British figures include technical training in day institutes which eventually turned into colleges and teacher education. German figures are based mainly on technical colleges but include all other *Hochschulen* officially recognized as such, while the teacher number is for pedagogical academies and the 1930/1 total also includes art and music schools. Figures in parentheses, compiled by H. Titze, include students in primary teacher training seminaries in Prussia which achieved recognition as higher education only in 1925. The Russian figure is for institutes, i.e. higher technical training, with the 1860 number estimated according to the 10% of schools classified as higher and the 1920 and 1930 numbers estimated by subtracting university enrollment from total higher education enrollment. The United States figures are for one half of the college and university students as well as all of the students in normal schools and teacher's colleges, on the assumption that roughly half of the college/university curriculum was equivalent to non-university instruction (such as in engineering and nursing) in Europe and that normal schools and teacher's colleges were definitely part of the non-university sector in Europe.

Table 3 Relative Enrollment in Higher Education.

country/ year	Britain		Germany				Russia	United States		
	R	K	L	R	K	J	A	R	K	B
1860/1			.30			.50	.14			3.1
1870/1			.40	.6		.63				2.3
1880/1			.58			.77	.17	1–2.0		3.4
1890/1		.41	.73	1.0	.67	.93		1.5–2.5	1.79	3.5
1900/1	1.2	.41	.79	1.2	.94	1.12	.20	1.5–3.5	2.29	5.0
1910/1	1.2	.58	1.31	1.5	1.26	1.63	.80	2.0–4.0	2.89	5.6
1920/1	2.7	1.60	1.96	2.7	1.97	2.47	1.20	2.5–5.0	4.66	9.0
1930/1	2.7	1.60	1.89	2.7	1.98	2.61	4.30	6.0–7.5	7.20	15.0
per five year age cohort:			1.89			2.61	4.30			11.25

Note: R=Ringer, K=Kaelble, L=Lowe, J=Jarausch, A=Alston, B=Burke. Ringer's British figures include all postsecondary education, while Kaelble's numbers are related to 20- to 24-year-olds. Lowe's more precise figures comprise universities, teacher training and technical education in colleges. Ringer's German figures include universities and technical colleges but exclude teacher training and are based on the 20–23 year cohort in contrast to Kaelble who uses the above sources but compares to 20- to 24-year olds. Jarausch employs rather the 19- to 23-year-olds and includes teacher training in his student numbers for the 1910s to 1930s. Alston's column, for which there are no comparable figures, rests on calculations of students compared to 20- or 24-year-olds. Ringer's U.S. figures register the range of college graduates. Kaelble's U.S. data are based on the same age span as before, clearly inappropriate for U.S. students. Burke's figures compare rather to 18- to 21year-olds (a shorter span) and are self-aggregated. His 1860 figure is only for males, while the 1870 ff index is based both on males and females.

was due to the foundation of new colleges and universities. (2) Especially important for the increase beyond population growth was the lowering of admissions barriers which allowed women (from 1/5 to 1/2 of the system by 1930), graduates of modern high schools (such as the *Realgymnasia* and *Oberrealschulen* in Germany after 1900), minorities (like the Jews in Russia after 1905) and foreigners access to higher learning which had previously been denied. (3) Moreover, this emergence of a "compensatory" sector of higher education of lower prestige and also lower prerequisites in applied technology (the Russian special institutes) and teacher education (the normal schools etc.) provided "soft" options unavailable before. (4) Similarly, the cooptation of new curricula into extant institutions (such as commercial training in Germany or home economics in the United States) made their offerings more attractive and vocationally relevant than the older prestige professions. (5) Finally, once begun, rapid expansion fed upon itself, since higher education, acting as lead sector, absorbed the majority of its own graduates to sustain the growth in secondary schools, universities and non-university institutions.[15]

Among the broader, indirect reasons, increasing demand appears to have been as important as rising supply. (1) Although often invoked, population growth seems at best to have been a necessary but not sufficient precondition, since it did not always translate directly into expansion of higher learning (as in the second half of the 18th century), unless first channeled through a secondary education system. (2) Despite occasional short-range negative correlations with the business cycle, economic growth seems to have been imperative as an underlying condition both as a consumption good (more affordable with the spread of prosperity) and as an increasingly necessary job prerequisite because of the academization of business and the standardization of careers. Though difficult to measure, rising demand for educated manpower (apparent as favorable career prospects for academic professions) exerted a powerful attraction for secondary school graduates. (3) The pull of social prestige operated somewhat more nebulously since many scholars presuppose a desire for upward mobility without explaining how it comes about. Higher education became a coveted avenue of social mobility when status was no longer ascribed (as in an estate society) but attained by individual effort (as in a liberal class system). (4) Although educational policies tried to foster economic growth, the state, in Russia and Germany suspicious of oversupply, often affected the labor market more by expanding the higher civil service. Only after World War One did conscious attempts to create equality of educational opportunity begin to have an impact on enrollments (as in Russia in the 1920s). (5) Finally, the reversal of cultural attitudes after the enlightenment in favor of neohumanism and scientific research seems to have translated only hesitantly into greater student numbers although it no doubt contributed in the long run to the vitality of the arts and sciences (in the U.S., Britain and Germany). A comparison of causes of enrollment expansion therefore does not suggest a tight model, but rather a diffuse set of internal and external factors, generally related to modernization, which need to be proven more explicitly.[16]

Often treated only in passing, the implications of the enrollment expansion for the emergence of the modern system were considerable. When it was allowed to operate unchecked (unlike in Russia where it was bureaucratically controlled to eliminate dissent), the dynamism of attendance resulted in liberal-capitalist market cycles of varying length. In each major field or faculty, growth would produce "an excess of educated men" in a career which would discourage students and eventually make numbers decline absolutely or relatively until the demand for graduates was restored, when the whole cycle (with some delay) would be set into motion again. For instance, in Germany this mechanism produced academic unemployment crises in the 1790s, 1830s, 1890s and 1920s. The consequences of expansion for institutional structure, social access and professional training, therefore, need further consideration. Not only in the U.S. did self-sustained system's growth create the first mass universities and a near chaos of hierarchically ranked, but competing, centers of higher learning. The persistence of inequality of educational opportunity which both helped and hindered the

12

enrollment expansion also requires more debate. Whereas aspirations for mobility pulled many lower middle class youths into higher education during favorable prospects, oversupply crises discouraged lower class pupils from continuing their education while only deflecting privileged sons from one attractive career to another. Nevertheless the overall growth in student numbers eventually produced more graduate professionals which furthered the academization of government and business. Educational expansion should, therefore, not be taken for granted, since its pattern, causes and consequences pose a number of unresolved questions, such as the continued growth in liberal education in the U.S.[17]

The diversification of institutions

A second major aspect of the transformation of higher learning is the process of institutional diversification. Around the turn of this century academic observers began to discuss the emergence of *Großwissenschaft* or of the *Großbetrieb der Wissenschaft* as scientific "counterpart to large scale industrial enterprise" and to big government.[18] In contrast to the small, intimate, semi-monastic institutions of earlier times, the large, impersonal scholarly factories were animated by a new spirit and developed novel complex structures. For instance, the universities of Berlin and Moscow enrolled about 10,000 students on the eve of the war. Although one dimension of this growing diversity is the proliferation of research disciplines investigated by J. Ben-David, the process is broader and more encompassing, since it also includes the emergence of new types of higher learning, which differ in prestige, and the establishment of new teaching specialties, which only sometimes coincide with fields of knowledge and include higher and lower training levels. A broader taxonomy suggested by B. R. Clark defines "differentiation" as occurring *among* institutions in horizontal (various sectors) or vertical (hierarchical) directions or as taking place *within* institutions along horizontal (scholarly sections) or vertical (tiers of training) lines. In this framework the central comparative questions become: How much differentiation did the expansion of institutional size produce in contrast to earlier decades? Along which of the four axes did the transformation diversify the character of higher learning most dynamically? Did differentiation operate unchecked or was there not also a countervailing tendency towards institutional convergence on the pure research model? Because national, cultural and administrative peculiarities render quantitative comparisons difficult, the discussion of differentiation remains somewhat impressionistic, although within individual countries it can and must be based on hard numerical evidence.[19]

Because "differentiation is then in part an accumulation of historical deposits," its elusive processes can be most easily identified on the external level between institutions. The fundamental mechanisms in all four countries

Table 4 The Non-University Share of Higher Education.

	England	Germany	Russia	United States
1860	38.6	15.2		32.4
1870	31.2	23.0		48.4
1880	22.1	18.5	20.0	58.0
1890	16.3	18.7		54.0
1900	28.0	29.3	26.0	53.8
1910	36.6	21.8	36.0	59.2
1920	44.1	31.9	24.0	60.9
1930	43.7	27.6	73.0	58.3

Note: These percentages for non-university enrollments were calculated for Britain and Germany by dividing the figures in Table 2 by those in Table 1. The Russian figures are taken from Table 3 of J. McClelland, "Diversification in Russian-Soviet Education." Although there is no clearly definable university sector in America, the non-university share for the U.S. was estimated by taking one half of the college and university enrollment together with the normal school and teacher's college figures from C. B. Burke. The high point of university dominance in each country is indicated by a ___, whereas the zenith of non-university enrollment is marked by a . . . .

appear to be the adding-on of new types, the upgrading of existing secondary institutions and the transformation of their function towards the traditional university ideal. Since cloning of universities themselves was relatively slow and their size could not be stretched indefinitely, the simplest response to growth pressures was the addition of new sectors such as the commercial colleges and administrative or pedagogical academies in Germany after the turn of the century (Table 4). Rarely, if ever, were they completely new, but rather built like the *Technische Hochschulen* on older secondary polytechnics, which were raised to tertiary rank in 1875, and after a protracted struggle received formal equality in 1900 so that they are today known as technical universities. However the price of legal and social recognition was often the adoption of the traditional university ethos or governance and the transformation of the curriculum towards pure rather than applied research and towards the humanities. Some institutions, like the British redbricks, altered their entire mission from higher technical training towards the traditional university function. This horizontal differentiation was accompanied by vertical diversification as well, since relatively homogenous systems developed an elaborate set of formal and informal hierarchies. Even after the achievement of legal parity, the older core universities such as Oxbridge continued to overshadow the new civic universities, who in turn lorded it over the teacher's colleges and technical colleges. Only in Russia did the technological institutes triumph completely over university *nauka*. But everywhere the applied institutions of higher learning began to threaten the numerical predominance of their elder scientific sisters. In the United States this vertical differentiation led to the establishment of recognized successive tiers of higher education, with high school diplomas becoming a college entrance requirement and undergraduate preparing for professional and graduate study.[20] By the first third of the present century the institutional matrix had diversified to an extent that, except for Germany, higher education was hardly any longer synonymous with the university.

Since the internal differentiation within institutions of higher learning is less clearly understood, it might help to conceptualize developments as suggested by the German evidence.[21]. First, the personnel structure of universities appears to have shifted from full professors (over half in Berlin 1810) towards assistant professors (51% by 1909). Senior scholars had less and less student contact (the ratio deteriorated from 21 to 64 students per professor) so that three quarters of all courses were taught by untenured faculty. Below them a whole new category of *Assistenten* (research and teaching assistants, often with a Ph.D.) emerged to staff proseminars and laboratories, whose labor was often exploited and who were denied participation in academic self-government. Second, the number of teaching fields and subfields continued to multiply, since the same course was not simply subdivided into sections, but rather new variants of basic lectures were developed together with novel subspecialities (which sometimes proved ephemeral). While the total number of offerings tripled in Berlin from 571 in 1860 to 1677 in 1909, modern history, which had been taught by the legendary L. von Ranke in 1871, fragmented into five courses (by Sternfeld, Breysig, Schmitt, Schiemann and Hintze) in 1914, a specialization which was even more thorough in the technical subjects. Not only did earlier innovations spread through the entire national system, but the center of instruction shifted from lectures to seminars (their ratio changed 6.1 to 1 towards 2.9 to 1 at Berlin). Third, in research, the seminar and the institute proliferated as the focus of activity, especially in the humanities, sciences, medicine and even more so in technology. In Heidelberg the three original seminars were joined by 23 others before World War One and the natural science institutes doubled in number and expanded in size so that research shifted out of the individual scholarly study or home laboratory into a large, well financed facility. Although this proliferation of junior faculty, teaching specialities and research disciplines continued the impetus of the early 19th century, its intensification and spread to lesser institutions created the modern diversified university.

Only a tentative list of factors commonly advanced as explanations can be offered at this point. (1) While the explosion of student numbers in some areas justified diversification (like in the humanities), it failed to produce this effect in others (such as law, which handled them with only a few faculty members). (2) Although the professional research imperative created numerous subfields within established disciplines such as medicine, it had apparently somewhat less effect on the natural sciences and can therefore not simply be used as general cause without further qualification. (3) Undoubtedly the academic labor market influenced the differential rates of diversification of faculties or institutions, but demand for graduates was often fickle and unpredictable. While established professions (such as medical doctors) could manipulate it, "scientification" was less successful in the natural sciences where professionals (industrial chemists) were weaker. (4) Donors and philanthropists, as in the celebrated case of the Cavendish laboratory, facilitated the establishment of new institutions (University of Chicago, Stanford) or institutes. But their impact was heaviest in capital intensive fields (such as technology) and in countries with private higher education (such as in the United States and Russia). (5) Similarly academic, professional, business or political groups might speed the foundation of a new chair or the granting of parity for the technical colleges (like the German VdI, association of engineers), but as often as not they failed to convince the public and the government to grant university admission as to the Prussian primary schools teachers (DLV). (6) Obviously government policy, whether as general willingness to fund (as Prussia under Friedrich Althoff) or in specific targeting of growth (as Russia in the non-subversive institutes) played an enormous role. But students were not always willing to follow so that some heavily supported sectors like engineering and agriculture in the U.S. differentiated professionally without adequate audience among academic youth. (7) Finally, the structure of the scientific community seems to have been important in slowing down fragmentation in older, more theoretical disciplines and allowing greater latitude in newer, largely applied fields of uncertain cognitive boundaries. These ambiguities and ironies indicate that causes of differentiation should be less confidently postulated than cautiously documented in each particular instance.[22]

The dynamics of diversification also had some important consequences. Internal institutional differentiation furthered the emergence of the academic career as a sequential profession with restricted room at the top, which on the continent created the *Ordinarienuniversität*, controlled and run for the chairholders. Moreover disciplinary specialization led to the loss of philosophical unity and the increasing erosion of "liberal education" in favor of research training or professional preparation. At the same time the traditional fusion of *Forschung und Lehre* began to break down, since the gap between teaching and research widened to such an extent that much scientific innovation was carried on in semi-autonomous institutes, supported by foundations like the Kaiser Wilhelm Gesellschaft. External differentiation between institutions began to threaten the autonomy of higher education, since the necessary increase of state funding allowed the educational bureaucracy to exert greater policy control even in those countries like England and the U.S. where formal governmental interference was minimal. Moreover, the establishment of scientific institutes and more so independent technological institutions linked higher learning more closely to the mature industrial economy. In some sectors, like electronics, chemicals or machine building, industry began to rely not only on basic but also applied research at the *Technische Hochschulen* or Russian institutes. Finally the emergence of competing centers of higher learning with somewhat different educational missions created a status hierarchy of institutional types, which offered compensatory social access but also condemned the more "modern" sectors to continuing inferiority unless they conformed to the older neo-classical mold. As a counterpoint these centrifugal forces created centripetal trends like informal research networks, formal scholarly associations (American Historical Association) and regional accrediting associations (North Central) which unified specialities, disciplines and institutions in an academic community. Ironically the dialectical result of this double differentiation was therefore a growing convergence on the new type of a modernized, diversified higher education conglomerate.[23]

The opening of recruitment

Another important dimension of the transformation of higher learning was the broadening of social recruitment of students and, thereby ultimately, also of professors. While turn-of-the-century apologists of the university claimed that "the possessors of academic culture . . . come from all classes of society", critics charged that "higher education is a right, reserved for the rich, but inaccessible for the great mass of the people". Statistically documenting the existence of such inequality, some well-known social scientists as R. Dahrendorf, P. Bourdieu and Ch. Jencks have debated the reasons for discrimination and argued vigorously for compensatory policies, favoring working class children, religious minorities, rural youths, women and blacks.[24] Since in the 19th century the liberal principle of equality of opportunity became generally accepted, the discussion largely revolves around evaluative perspectives of time and place. Viewed against the backdrop of earlier elitism, almost any broadening of access seems progressive; seen in terms of more recent egalitarian advances, earlier openings appear insignificant. Part of the difficulty also lies in the problem of measuring the relative "social openness" of higher learning in contrast to other time periods and countries. While published government figures are often designed to cover up important analytical distinctions, social classification schemes are largely incompatible, especially when applied across boundaries or temporal eras. In order to compare at all the historian is forced to run the double risk of employing categories whose internal meaning changes over time and varies in different countries, consoling himself with the notion of functional equivalence. Fortunately the procedures of measurement, such as indices of representation, are less controversial and can be refined by focusing on the youth-population at risk.[25] Therefore questions about the recruitment of higher education abound: Did educational opportunities increase or decrease with industrialization? What were the national or continental patterns of access? What were the causes and consequences of the partial social opening?

The fragmentary comparative evidence from 1860 to 1930 suggests that the social recruitment of higher learning altered significantly in all four countries (Table 5).[26] Although partly a definitional artifact (landed elites are no longer identifiable in the 20th century), the nobility and the traditional agrarian upper class all but disappeared from higher education, both relatively and somewhat less so absolutely. Similarly the educated professionals, half of which had, in the middle of the 19th century, recruited themselves, declined in importance to about 1/5 of the student body. Their place was taken in the 1890s by the new commercial and entrepreneurial elite (with between 1/5 and 2/5 of all students) as logical alternative stratum with sufficient means to afford post-secondary training. After the turn of the century, the entire upper middle class was outstripped by students from lower-middle-class homes, who, with the spread of prosperity, began to supply about half of the students. Although in the mid-19th century the traditional callings of artisan, shopkeeper and peasant had made up the bulk of petit bourgeois representation, by the 1930s the newer service pursuits such as white collar employees, middling and lower officials, schoolteachers, etc. overshadowed them (in Germany by 2-to-1). Initially almost totally excluded, the working class breached the educational barrier after the First World War, especially in Russia, but also to some extent in Britain and in non-elite U.S. institutions like Temple. While the German pattern reveals this sequence first, the English figures follow it (especially when one assumes a less elitist cast for the redbricks) and exceed it in terms of working class access by 1930. In the Russian case an educated middle class first had to be created out of the nobility before the lower middle class could emerge as the strongest parent stratum, and the astounding 38.4 lower class proportion in 1927/28 is a result of the conscious proletarianization policy of the Bolsheviks. While the Penn figures for the U.S. demonstrate both the breakthrough of "ordinary" sons after 1890 and the tenacity of the elite after 1910, the multi-college 1925 sample shows a preponderance of business (50%) over professional or service (ca. 42%) clientele and a respectable but restricted working class representation. Finally, institutional differentiation also produced a remarkable pattern of access differences. Within universities some units (such as catholic theology) tended to be more accessible than others (such as law); some tiers, such as undergraduate instruction, were more open than others, such as professional schools (medical). Among institutions the applied (vocational) training centers were likely to be more lower middle class than the theoretical research combines, thereby creating a prestige hierarchy which was justified by claimed functional differences. But despite variations over time, nationality and institution, the basic thrust of expansion and differentiation led to the emergence of the middle class university.[27]

The causes of the broadening of access to higher learning are as vigorously disputed as its extent. (1) The economic discussion revolves largely

Table 5 The Social Origin of Students in Percent.

	1870				1890				1910				1930			
	Brit.	Germ.	Russ.	U.S.	Brit.	Germ.	Russ.	U.S.	Brit.	Germ.	Russ.	U.S.	Brit.	Germ.	Russ.	U.S.
upper class	40	?	60	9.7	21	?	23	8.5	15	?	8	3.8			11.9	18.9
upper middle profess:	49	41.7	17	27.5	54	31.1	43	22.1	48	22	29.3	20.1	47.0	22		24.2
busines:	7	22.9	4		19	38.0	9		21	17	10.3			13		
lower middle old:	2	35.1	5	7.3	6	30.0	11	3.1	7	28	24.3	3.4	30.1	18		24.7
new:	0			12.8	2			12.5	2	27		15.9	17.6	37	49.2	22.9
lower class:	0	.3	3	12.8	0	.1	3	5.1	1	3	14.5	8.9	5.1	4	20.2	
unknown	2		3	29.8	1			49.5	5	2	4	47.7		6	18.2	6.8

Note: The classification scheme is based on Jarausch, "Occupation and Social Structure in Modern Central Europe," *Historical Social Research*, 11 (1979), 10–19. The "upper class" includes the nobility, the landed gentry and the urban patriciate. The "upper middle class" is divided into professionals (with higher learning) and businessmen (entrepreneurs, bankers, etc.). The "lower middle class" distinguishes the older (artisan, shopkeeper, peasant) from the newer (white collar employee, teacher, government official) elements. The "lower class" is a catchall for the proletariat and the lower layers of society. Since it generally received some form of higher education, the clergy was grouped with the academic professions (even in England and Russia where it is usually listed separately). On the assumption that peasants' sons were not from the landless laborer families but from prosperous households, farmers' children appear under "old middle class," except for Russia where they were the estate from which sprang the industrial proletariat, separated out in the 1930 figure. The British figures for 1870 to 1910 are based on Oxford and the 1930 numbers on a random sample of British adults born before that year. The German figures for 1870 and 1890 are based on Berlin, Leipzig, Wurttemberg and Bonn and the 1910 and 1930 numbers pertain to the country as a whole. The Russian 1870 (1865), 1890 (1880) and 1910 (1914) figures include all universities, while the 1930 (1927/8) number refers to all of higher education. The U.S. figures between 1870 and 1910 (1873–1898) are based on the University of Pennsylvania, while the 1930 (1925) number includes a sample of 55 colleges and universities.

around the emergence of a mature industrial economy which augments certain strata (like plutocratic entrepreneurs) and diminishes others (like the landed gentry and, because of agricultural rents in Britain, also the clergy). Moreover it involves the spread of prosperity which made education available as a consumption good to larger groups. Similarly, it focuses on the growth of science based and technological industries like electronics and chemicals, which created a demand for trained manpower such as engineers, chemists and the like. Finally, it also touches on the rise of big business which required a new layer of salaried and college educated employees to administer its far-flung concerns. (2) While conceding the significance of academic self-recruitment, the social debate emphasizes on the one hand popular aspirations for mobility, especially for those members of the new middle class who were emulating their workplace superiors. On the other hand it stresses the importance of the preservation of status through educational means, starting with the nobility and its endangered birth prerogatives and descending through the plutocracy (for younger sons who could not inherit) to the old middle class which tried to transform its meager possessions into educational certificates. (3) The political argumentation centers on state policy towards certain strata (like the Russian nobility in the 1850s or the proletariat in the 1920s) since admissions favored particular groups or discriminated against others (antisemitic quotas for instance). However it also underscores the expansion of government bureaucracy in the direction of the welfare state which created an intermittent but generally growing demand for graduates as in Germany. (4) Taking for granted the attractiveness of the ideal of the educated man, cultural explanations address the astounding popular hunger for self-improvement which often transcendend any functional justification. While the effects of secularization on the cultural elite have been widely discussed, the importance of the deauthorization of religion for the middle and lower classes and the emergence of a pro-educational scientism need to be probed further.[28] Incorporating many aspects of the general transformation of society, these causative factors nevertheless found very real limits in resources, aspirations, institutional policies and cultural styles which preserved the continued exclusivity of much higher learning.

What were the consequences of the emergence of the middle class university? During mature industrial society the traditional elite system, mitigated by charity and patronage, gave way to a modern, competitive pattern, characterized by the struggle of previously uninterested (such as the wealthy middle class) or excluded (such as the new middle class) strata for access to higher learning. A comparison of the fragmentary indices of recruitment (Table 6)[29] indicates a gradual decline of the over-representation of the elite and upper middle class and therefore a reduction in the disparity between upper and lower classes, as well as a gradual convergence towards a common distribution.[30] But the gains were not duplicated to the same degree

Table 6 Social Access to Higher Education: Index of Recruitment and Dissimilarity.

	England			Germany			Russia			United States
	Cambri.	Oxford	sample	Heid&Kiel	Prussia	Germany	all higher ed. students			55 college sample
	1850–99	1910	bef.1930	1847–57	1911/2	1930	1914	1923/4	1927/8	1925
elite				35.3			21.6			
profs.				79.2			25.0			
up. mid.	57.0	48.0	6.6		7.0	3.7				3.5
busin.	2.2	6.4		5.8	2.0	1.4	12.8			3.0
old mc.				0.6		0.9		5.6	6.3	0.9
lowerm.			1.5							
new mc.		0.02			2.2	2.5	2.6			1.2
lower	0.0		0.3	0.006	0.03	0.08	0.2	0.32	0.42	0.12
dissim.			22	5883		46	108		15	21

Note: The Index of Recruitment is calculated by dividing the percentage of students from a certain stratum by the percentage of professionals in the population. Hence values above 1 indicate over-representation and values below 1 under-representation. The Index of Dissimilarity is calculated by dividing the index of representation for the highest by that of the lowest stratum in the table. As values decrease toward 1, the disparity of representation of different social groups diminishes. In order to minimize distortions due to the difficulty of matching social categories for students and the population, combined figures have been presented wherever separation proved analytically impossible.

by working-class children, farmers' sons, the offspring of minorities, etc. They began to make considerable progress in Russia and Britain, but still remained substantially under-represented everywhere. Moreover much of the new equality was rhetorical rather than real, compensatory more than substantive, since cooptation into the outer layers of learning, the applied institutions, technological subject areas, or open faculties like theology and philosophy, permitted the perpetuation of elitism in the more prestigious professions such as law and medicine. By raising expectations while only partially fulfilling them, this limited opening of higher education increased social tensions within institutions. It also created political pressures which prompted the first measures to reduce inequality and eventually led to a new era of welfare opportunities in the middle of the 20th century. Ironically the influx from the lower middle class and the limited inclusion of the working class helped to stabilize the system. When the children of these education-ally mobile children entered the university, they contributed to "academic" self-recruitment, keeping its share at about 1/5 of the student body from then on. Finally the partial broadening of recruitment also furthered the importance of educational qualifications over job performance in govern-ment and business. Hence the middle-class complexion of the university served to legitimate its increasingly important selection function by blend-ing cultured self-perpetuation and status preservation with a degree of mobility based on meritocracy.[31]

The process of professionalization

The newest focus of the debate about the transformation of higher learning is the emergence of the professions. Rescuing the "forgotten middle class," i. e. the non-capitalist bourgeoisie, from oblivion, this concept draws atten-tion to the social product of higher education, the academics, and to their impact upon society. Since contemporaries talked about *Berufsstand* (occu-pational estate), in Central and Eastern Europe the very term was a Western import, although its implications were very much in evidence. If one accepts B. Bledstein's definition as a basis for discussion ("a full time occupation in which a person earned the principal source of an income . . . mastered an esoteric but useful body of systematic knowledge, completed theoretical training before entering a practice or apprenticeship, and received a degree or license from a recognized institution"), the crucial role of higher learning for the emergence of "the culture of professionalism" is obvious. Because of the slipperiness of the concept, which is embroiled in an interminable dis-cussion about a finite set of ideal-typical traits, this analysis must be limited to its connection with higher education, whose importance can hardly be overestimated for professionalization. In order to reduce the confusion, three preliminary clarifications are in order. (1) Although the development of the professorial research ethic is central to the rise of the academic profession, the professionalization of the callings of university graduates is distinctive, broader and sometimes independent of higher learning. (2) Both processes within and without the university take place in an interactive triangle composed of the profession (with its practitioners and organizations), the state (as regulator and certifier) and institutionalized higher education (as training ground). (3) While expansion, differentiation and recruitment condition their interplay, higher learning affects professionalization primarily in terms of admission (selection), curriculum (knowledge) and examination (credentialling).[32]

The relationship between professionalization and higher learning is, therefore, more complex than assumed in static sociological theory or historical analysis, proclaiming it a dominant principle of contemporary society. Although "professional" training had, in the Middle Ages, taken place in the universities, by the middle of the 19th century liberal education and pure research had pushed much professional preparation outside, e.g. in England. Only in the present century was it gradually reabsorbed by higher learning. Moreover the "old professions", usually defined as the clergy, lawyers, doctors (that is problematic especially in the U.S.) and professors, already flourished by 1850 and therefore only expanded in size, increased in scientific character, and somewhat opened their recruitment thereafter. The emerging "new professions", such as high-school teachers, engineers, chemists, etc. were more intimately involved, since their victories in gaining university admission, in obtaining scientific standing for their disciplines and in achieving a standardized and recognized set of examinations were both cause and consequence of enrollment expansion, differentiation and social opening. At times the resistance of the state bureaucracy and of university professors to organizational pressures could defeat the aspiration of an upwardly mobile occupation which carefully imitated the model of the older professions. At other times they were deflected into less prestigious units, tiers or types of institutions, even if they occasionally shared the same function as in Tsarist Russia. Finally, the interaction between higher learning and professionalization also varied by social/cultural tradition. The liberal Anglo-American model was characterized by vigorous professional organization and autonomy (even in professional training). In contrast the bureaucratic German-Russian pattern depended heavily on state regulation and licensing, since all three corners of the triangle (professionals, officials and professors) revolved around government.[33]

Although some university spokesmen claimed to pursue only science (*Wissenschaft, nauka*), higher education, by also providing professional training, influenced professionalization in three fundamental ways. First, formal admission requirements and informal pressures of habit and expectation combined to create a clearly indentifiable pattern of social selection among fields of study and institutions, which channeled certain social strata into specific professions. Everywhere law was the most prestigious faculty, attracting the nobility or the wealthy patriciate as well as some children of academics. Medicine was somewhat more diverse with doctors' or apothecaries' offspring, wealthy sons and some lower-middle-class children able to afford its considerable costs. Favored by sons of clergymen, Protestant and Orthodox theology drew upon teachers' and peasants' children because of its numerous stipends, while Catholic theology was even more lower middle and lower class. Finally, the arts and science subjects were the true melting pot of the university, blending a few academic children with sons of the plutocracy and especially of the old and new lower middle class. The less prestigious institutes, specialized schools, etc., aside from their practitioners' children, attracted an even less distinguished clientele except for some special Russian institutes and high technology institutions. Second, the curriculum provided an aura of scientific theory, so important to the professional's claim to superior expertise. However in practice the gulf between professorial research interests, the students' learning of the "scientific method" and the later needs of the practitioner seemed to be widening, except in industrial research. Hence the universities were less successful than the technical colleges and institutes in imparting practical skills which might be applied upon graduation without subsequent internship. Though less directly identifiable, liberal education also added an important command of culture and that social veneer which made the graduate acceptable as a member of the professional class. Third, the examination system, whether entirely academic (as for German chemists), bureaucratic (as for Russian doctors) or independent (such as the English bar examination), provided that essential proof of competence upon which the professional based his claim to market monopoly. The clash between the academic's insistence on intellectual attainment and the practitioner's emphasis on applicable skill, either divided the internal content of the examination as in the West or established two successive theoretical and practical stages as on the Continent.[34]

Since the numerical parameters of professionalization are somewhat indistinct, there is little agreement on the reasons for the interaction between profession and higher education. Focused on "the provision of an esoteric, evanescent, fiduciary service" Western literature generally argues that "the professions were called forth by the free market." Hence the collective manipulation of demand by organized practitioners who persuaded the public to grant them a monopoly in exchange for certain standards of expertise and skill became the central cause. However this liberal reconciliation of free competition with economic security was predicated upon the victory of the academically trained occupational elite over other practitioners, and therefore involved higher learning at least as an important political tool. In contrast, continental scholarship stresses "the close association of many professions with the authority and prestige of the state" which was the chief employer of older professionals, controlled educational requirements or testing procedures and regulated the practice of the liberal professions. The ascendancy of the old professions like doctors over nonacademic competitors like surgeons, midwives, witches, etc. (in 1852 in Germany) may well have been a matter of the status policy of university graduates who persuaded the government to disenfranchise the others even before medical science had a higher cure rate than traditional folk healing. But once again the crucial argument that convinced the bureaucracy rested on the higher learning of the true professional. Because it was often used to gain power (such as by one professional faction over another), studies of professionalization ought to probe the educational dimension more thoroughly than hitherto. The coincidence between the rise of the new professions and the transformation of higher learning is not entirely accidental. Universities and especially technical colleges produced novel careers through scholarly specialization while aspiring practitioners time and again tried to legitimate their claim to professional status through higher learning. Ultimately professionalization and academization therefore fed on each other by continually upgrading entrance requirements (i.e. demanding more formal secondary schooling), making the curriculum content and teaching style more scientific (even trying to transform legal instruction from memorizing rules into legal research) and by increasing academic demands for the various certifying examinations.[35]

The implications of professionalization therefore involve not only higher learning, but also society and polity. Although the process began during the first half of the 19th century, in the subsequent decades the academic career emerged as full-fledged profession in its own right, structured into successive steps from *Assistentur* to *Ordinariat*, from tutorship to professorship. This process was accompanied by an increasing tension between professional training and liberal education. Expansion, diversification and social opening brought growing masses of vocational students into academe, but not only in Britain was the hold of neohumanism so strong that any number of technical colleges reverted to the arts curriculum and the collegiate model. Although in Russia technical training clearly won out by the 1920s, elsewhere the liberal arts (especially in the U.S.) showed a surprising resilience and popularity with students. Hence it would be incorrect to assert that professional training had triumphed completely. The very sequence of undergraduate study followed by a professional school, which emerged during this period, represents a compromise between both demands. In a broader sense, the professionalization of academe also led to a professionalization of society, since, however they were defined, the "professions" multiplied more quickly than the population at large (Table 7).[36] The older professions academized, organized and grew moderately, thereby gaining and maintaining an upper-middle-class position by combining a market monopoly with meritocratic educational credentials. The new professions strove mightily

Table 7 The Professions in the Workforce in Percent.

	Britain		Germany		Russia	United States	
	Prof & Serv.	*Prof & Tech.*	*Acad. Profs.*	*Prof & Serv.*		*Grads*	*Prof & Serv.*
1852			0.64	2.9		.69	
1871	3.9			3.0		.84	1.78
1890	4.4			3.5		.92	3.96
1910	4.1		1.16	4.6	.19		5.4
1930	6.1		2.56	7.9	.31		8.0

Note: The categorization of the British census figures changed during World War One from "professional occupations and their subordinate services" to "professional and technical occupations." The last entry is for 1951. The first German figures attempt to include only presumptive graduates of higher education. In contrast the second German figures, according to census practice, include government officials and free professionals (except for the military) irrespective of academic qualification. The first Russian figure is from the 1897 census which indicates that 133,600 received some kind of higher education out of a workforce of 69,148,022 males and females. The second figure from the 1926 census (when it was dangerous to be regarded as a professional) is 233,000 (while another one of 280,000 also appears). Both were averaged to about 250,000 and compared to a workforce of 80,453,000 (including all 15–60 year olds). The figures were compiled by P. Alston. The first U.S. figures represent college graduates as proportion of all males over the age of 20. They were compiled by A. Creutz and presented in a paper called "College Graduates and the Professions in Nineteenth Century America" (MS Dearborn, 1980). The second U.S. figures describe the percentage of the professional service category among total American employment in 1870, 1900, 1920 and 1940. They were computed from D. Bell, *The Coming of Post-Industrial Society* (New York, 1973), 130.

to follow this pattern through admission to some form of higher learning, recognition of the scientific nature of their expertise and establishment of certifying examinations based on knowledge and skill. However many aspiring groups remained quasi-professions, because their subjects were not academically recognized, their low pay consigned them to the lower middle class, and their associations were too weak to wrest autonomy from the public or the state. In creating professional status politics, professionalization contributed both to the spread of Liberalism in Central and Eastern Europe and to its internal division between a commercial-entrepreneurial bourgeoisie and a cultural-academic *Bildungsbürgertum*.[37]

Higher education and "modernization"

The emergence of the large, diverse, middle-class and professional system of higher learning between 1850 and 1930 casts a new light on the relationship between education and social change. Sociological theories stressing "educational mobilization" explain only the enrollment expansion and not even that very well. Since higher learning does not necessarily grow directly with population, the spread of literacy and the diffusion of primary schooling precede, but also sometimes follow, the expansion of the universities, as in Russia. The "partial modernization" approach seems more attuned to the contradictions in the differentiation process between scientific progress and academic traditionalism. It reconciles the proliferation of non-university institutions with the continued magnetism of the most elitist (Oxbridge) styles of higher learning. But its relevance for the other three topics is limited. The historical thesis of the active incongruence of higher learning with change helps to highlight the dichotomy between the commercial-industrial and the educational-bureaucratic middle class and points out the obstacles to mobility for the proletariat and other discriminated groups. But it overstates "the perpetuation of tradition" because "outlooks more or less explicitly at odds with their time" were not so prevalent in the technical and other non-university sectors and largely absent among scientists and doctors as well. Instead, professionalization with its mixture of modern (science, skill, examination) elements with traditional (organization, auto-nomy, ethos) traits suggests as an alternative the ambivalence of modern-ization. The ambiguity of the relationship between education and social change emphasizes the dynamics of growth, diversification, social opening and professionalization while at the same time indicating their very real limits. The adjective "ambivalent" also describes the academics' conflict of emotions over the transformation of higher learning. While many enthusias-tically welcomed its research advances, at the same time they pessimistically struggled against its decivilizing dangers.[38]

The ambivalence of this transition is evident in the different path followed by each country. Starting with comparatively low relative enrollment, Eng-land expanded vigorously by adding a host of new university, technical and teaching institutions which no longer conformed to the collegiate ideal. The social elitism of Oxbridge therefore gradually gave way to a still somewhat narrow but accessible system, especially for the lower class, since the hold of liberal education was broken by compensatory vocationalism. Beginning with higher enrollments, Germany increased more slowly, pioneering the model of scholarly specialization and higher technical or business educa-tion, but was more reluctant to include primary teacher training and other subjects. Its upper-class recruitment broadened only to include the new and old lower middle class while keeping out the proletariat. In contrast to English distrust between the professions and the universities, the association of state, higher education and professionals became even more intimate with *Bildung* giving way to *Ausbildung* (cultivation to professional training). With the lowest original enrollment, Russia made the most dramatic gains, less by expanding its universities than by creating numerous higher insti-tutes, especially from the 1890s to the 1930s. Thereby the most elitist (noble) system was transformed into the most open (at least for the proletariat and peasantry) at the price of legal discrimination against the educated and propertied middle class. Instead of being content with democratizing the universities, the Bolsheviks rather promoted the training of proletarian cadres, immediately useful for the production process of the first Five Year Plan. Having the highest enrollment, because of the secondary role of much of undergraduate collegiate education, the United States experienced further growth and continued to lead the other three countries by 1930. The staggering diversity of religious, regional, social and academic characteristics of institutions persisted, although a graduate university sector in the European sense of the word emerged out of the traditional colleges after the Civil War. Because of its greatest initial egalitarianism (making some kind of educational certificate available to almost everyone who wanted it), there was less subsequent broadening of social access than in other countries. Curiously enough, professional education did not displace the liberal arts, but in a characteristic compromise, was added onto the undergraduate sequence for the most prestigious occupations while vocational training became a lower class token alternative.[39]

The causes of the transformation are ambiguous as well. In contrast to contemporary rhetoric about the contribution of higher learning to economic growth, it has been difficult to substantiate this connection beyond the effect of higher technical and managerial training. Instead, the spread of higher education seems to coincide with general "cultural and material progress" as a consumption good, afforded by more parents of modest means. Despite the covariation of enrollment and industrial production curves, predictions of demand have proved baffling for government statisticians while the market cycles of deficit and oversupply seem impervious to bureaucratic manipulation. The role of education in the emergence of class society is similarly contradictory. The shift from birth and wealth to expertise as a job requirement opened the doors for some meritocratic competition, but continued to favor the older elites. The formalization of legal entitlements (first on the Continent, but eventually also in the West) represented a typical liberal compromise between aspirations for mobility and self-perpetuation of the educated. Nevertheless the "social-aristocratic" tone of the cultured created one of the crucial status divisions of modern society. Despite the late 19th century belief in the progress of science and technology, the humanism inherent in liberal education continued to be attractive to students who craved its social distinctions. While the rationality of higher learning contributed to secularization, the classical content of cultivation sometimes turned academics away from the cacophony of the machine and the masses, making them profoundly uneasy about modernity. But exaggerated faith in rational knowledge and popular scientism fueled the expansion of scientific and technological subjects as social cure-alls as well. The rhetoric about academic freedom notwithstanding, the expansion of state funding also led to increased bureaucratic control which decided who got educated where and in what field. Though supporting science and technology, governments often tried to muzzle criticism coming from the universities.[40] Economic growth, social aspirations, cultural values and state policy, therefore served as essential motors of the transformation of higher learning across national frontiers. But their particular strength varied in each context, their force was buffered by the relative autonomy of educational institutions, and their impact was mediated by the conflicting decisions of corporate groups and individual actors.[41]

The implications of the transformation of the university into "an expression of the age, as well as an influence operating upon both present and future" also raise a host of puzzling questions. In the transition from traditional elite higher learning to modern mass higher education the large, diverse, middle-class, professional system which emerged around the turn of the century represents an intermediary stage. Still echoing earlier ideals, higher learning performed by 1930 a far broader mission in society than a three-quarter century before. Although resented by a cultured minority, the expansion of enrollment beyond population growth moved universities from the periphery into the center of cultural life. Through incorporating "secondary, technical, vocational, and popular education", the diversified modern institutions played a crucial economic role in providing technological innovation and trained manpower. The cooptation of the lower middle class increased the chances for mobility or status preservation, and therefore helped legitimate the continuation of privilege as meritocratic. Finally, the political "adulteration and dilution" of the curriculum to include business, journalism, home economics, etc., contributed to the rise of ever new "professions". Nevertheless the emergence of "modern" higher learning before 1930 also encountered definite limits. No country outside of America enrolled more than 10% of the age cohort. Especially in the traditional British and German systems scientific differentiation did not mean the abandonment of the chair/institute system which restricted subjects to those deemed sufficiently "academic". Only in Russia were more than 10% of the students recruited from the bottom half of the population. Finally, even in the newest system the professionalization of vocational training did not include every new pretender to academic status such as "hair-dressing". The unresolved tension between modernity and tradition in this intermediary stage of higher learning contributed to those pressures which led to the next transformation, the emergence of mass higher education. In 1930 Abraham Flexner, in his grand comparison of American, English and German universities, could still cling to a vanishing ideal:

> A modern university would then address itself whole-heartedly and unreservedly to the advancement of knowledge, the study of problems, from what ever source they come, and the training of men—all at the highest level of possible effort.[42]

Notes

1 R. G. Paulston, "Social and Educational Change: Conceptual Frameworks," *Comparative Education Review*, 21 (1977), 370–395; H. U. Wehler, *Modernisierungstheorie und Geschichte* (Göttingen, 1975); P. N. Stearns, *European Society in Upheaval* (New York, 1975), 2nd ed.

2 P. Lundgreen, *Bildung und Wirtschaftswachstum im Industrialisierungsprozeß des 19. Jahrhunderts* (Berlin, 1973); F. K. Ringer, *Education and Society in Modern Europe* (Bloomington, 1979).

3 P. V. Meyers, *The Modernization of Education in 19th Century Europe* (St. Louis, 1977) is but a brief sketch; H. U. Wehler, "Vorüberlegungen zu einer modernen deutschen Gesellschafts-geschichte," in *Industrielle Gesellschaft und politisches System* (Bonn, 1978), for M. Weber's view of modernization; H. Gerth and C. W. Mills, *From Max Weber: Essays on Sociology* (New York, 1958).

4 L. Stone, "Introduction," in his *The University in Society* (Princeton, 1974) 2 vols. and the successor collection on *Schooling and Society* (Baltimore, 1976); for a similar periodization Stearns, *European Society*, 179 ff; Ringer, *Education*, 52 ff. The mid-19th century offers a convenient starting point also because statistics become more available and reliable while the Second World War disrupted time series or changed their units drastically.

5 France was excluded for reasons of space and dissimilarity of institutions (i.e., no universities until the late 19th century), A. Prost, *Histoire de l'enseignment en France 1800–1967* (Paris, 1969). For similar comparative attempts, P. Flora, *Quantitative Historical Sociology* (The Hague, 1977); H. Kaelble, *Historische Mobilitätsforschung* (Darmstadt, 1978); Ringer, *Education and Society*, passim.

6 For the social history of education, E. Rury, "Elements of a 'New' Comparative History of Education," *Comparative Education Review*, 21 (1977), 342–51; H. Graff, "'The New Math,' Quantification the 'New' History and the History of Education," *Urban Education*, 11 (1977), 403–40 and the discussion at the History of Education Society Meeting at Washington in November 1979.

7 The topics emerged out of K. H. Jarausch, "The Social Transformation of the University: The Case of Prussia, 1865–1914," *Journal of Social History*, 12 (1979), 609–636; "Frequenz und Struktur. Zur Sozialgeschichte der Studenten im Kaiserreich," in P. Baumgart, ed., *Bildungspolitik in Preußen zur Zeit des Kaiserreichs* (Stuttgart, 1980), 119–149.

8 A. Langguth, "Bilanz der akademischen Bildung," *Burschenschaftliche Bücherei* (Berlin, 1901), 1, 303–64; C. E. McClelland, *State, Society and University in Germany, 1700–1914* (Cambridge, 1980).

9 M. Steinmetz, "Laufende Arbeiten zur Geschichte der Universitäten und Hochschulen auf dem Territorium der DDR," paper delivered at the meeting of the International Commission on the History of Universities at the XV. International Congress of Historical Sciences in Bucharest, August 11–12, 1980; for the disparate state of the field see the 19 resumes of the communications by the participants at the congress, printed in *Rapports* (Bucharest, 1980), 3: 323–360.

10 K. H. Jarausch, ed., *Quantifizierung in der Geschichtswissenschaft. Probleme und Möglichkeiten* (Düsseldorf, 1976); M. Kaplan, "The Most Important Questions," *Oxford Review of Education*, 3 (1977), 87–94; G. Iggers, *New Directions in European Historiography* (Middletown, 1975); J. Kocka, *Sozialgeschichte* (Göttingen, 1977); J. Henretta, "Social History as Lived and Written," *American Historical Review*, 84 (1979), 1293–1333.

11 Stone, "The Size and Composition of the Oxford Student Body 1580–1909," *University in Society*, 1: 22 ff; C. E. McClelland, "A Step Forward in the Study

of Universities," *Minerva*, 14 (1976), 150–161; F. K. Ringer, "Problems in the History of Higher Education," *Comparative Studies in Society and History*, 19 (1977), 239 ff; Flora, *Quantitative Historical Sociology*, 56 ff; Ringer, *Education and Society, passim*; H. Kaelble, "Educational Opportunities and Government Policies: Postprimary European Education before 1914," in P. Flora and A. J. Heidenheimer, eds., *The Development of the Welfare State in Europe* (New Brunswick, 1981).

12 Tables 1 to 3 are based on the essays of R. Lowe, H. Titze, P. Alston and C. Burke as well as on Ringer and Kaelble, cited in N. 11; the German figures are from R. Riese, *Die Hochschule auf dem Wege zum wissenschaftlichen Großbetrieb* (Stuttgart, 1977), 339 ff; C. Quetsch, *The Numerical Record of University Attendance in Germany in the Last Fifty Years* (Berlin, 1961), 51; K. H. Manegold, *Universität, Technische Hochschule und Industrie* (Berlin, 1970), 320 f; W. Hoffmann, *Das Wachstum der deutschen Wirtschaft* (Berlin, 1965), 172 ff.

13 Since the British indices of Kaelble and Lowe dovetail, they seem credible (except for Kaelble's sudden jump between 1910 and 1920, which is likely to be based on a difference in inclusion of institutions). Ringer's, Kaelble's and Jarausch's German figures roughly coincide (when one makes allowance for the differential age-spans), but Jarausch's emphasize greater dynamism. Although there are no comparable figures for Russia from other authors, the index compiled by P. Alston rests on a comparison of students with 20–24 year olds. While widely used, the proportion of students per 10,000 of population tends to be misleading, since the composition of various populations is likely to differ in age and therefore the comparable cohort is not always the same size. The trend direction of all U.S. figures is similar; Burke's are the most inclusive, consistent over time, self-compiled and also reliable.

14 H. von Petersdorff, "Der Zudrang zu den Deutschen Hochschulen," *Akademische Blätter*, 4 (1888/9), 3f; J. Conrad, *German Universities during the Last Fifty Years* (Glasgow, 1885), 19 ff; F. Eulenburg, *Die Frequenz der deutschen Universitäten von ihrer Gründung bis zur Gegenwart (Leipzig, 1906)*, 250 ff.

15 R. A. Lowe, *The English School: Its Architecture and Organization* (Birmingham, 1977); H. Titze, *Die Politisierung der Erziehung. Untersuchungen über die soziale und die politische Funktion der Erziehung von der Aufklärung bis zum Hochkapitalismus* (Frankfurt, 1973); P. L. Alston, *Education and the State in Tsarist Russia* (Stanford, 1969); C. B. Burke, *American Collegiate Populations* (New York, 1982).

16 For a somewhat more ambitious approach see J. E. Craig and N. Spear, "The Dynamics of Educational Expansion: A Methodological and Conceptual Framework," paper presented at the Comparative and International Education Society Conference (Vancouver, 1980); C. A. Anderson and M. J. Bowman, "Education and Economic Modernization in Perspective," in L. Stone, *Schooling and Society* (Baltimore, 1976), 3–19.

17 D. K. Müller, *Sozialstruktur und Schulsystem. Aspekte zum Strukturwandel des Schulwesens im 19. Jahrhundert* (Göttingen, 1977) and "Modellentwicklung zur Analyse von Krisenphasen im Verhältnis von Schulsystem und staatlichem Beschäftigungssystem," *Zeitschrift für Pädagogik*, 14. *Beiheft* (Weinheim, 1977), 37–77; U. Hermann and G. Friedrich, "Qualifikationskrise und Schulreform. Berechtigungswesen, Überfüllungsdiskussion und Lehrerschwemme," *ibid.*, 13 (1977), 309–325.

18 T. Mommsen, "Antwort an Harnack, den 3. Juli, 1890," *Reden und Aufsätze* (Berlin, 1905), 209 f; A. Wagner, *Die Entwicklung der Universität Berlin, 1810–1896* (Berlin, 1896); A. Harnack, "Vom Großbetrieb der Wissenschaft," *Preußische Jahrbücher*, 119 (1905), 193–201.

19 J. Ben-David, *The Scientist's Role in Society: A Comparative Study* (Engelwood Cliffs, 1971); B. R. Clark, "Academic Differentiation in National Systems of Higher Education," *Comparative Education Review*, 22 (1978), 242–258; introductory comments by J. Herbst on diversification at the "Education and Social Change" conference, March 1980.

20 Clark, "Academic Differentiation," 250 ff; S. Rothblatt, *The Revolution of the Dons: Cambridge and Society in Victorian England* (New York, 1968); P. Lundgreen, *Techniker in Preußen während der frühen Industrialisierung. Ausbildung und Berufsfeld einer entstehenden sozialen Gruppe* (Berlin, 1975); J. A. McClelland, *Autocrats and Academics: Education, Culture and Society in Tsarist Russia* (Chicago, 1979); J. A. McLachlan, "The American College in the Nineteenth Century: Toward a Reappraisal," *Teacher's College Record*, 80 (1978), 287–306.

21 R. Riese, *Die Hochschule auf dem Wege zum wissenschaftlichen Großbetrieb*, 94 ff; K. D. Bock, *Strukturgeschichte der Assistentur. Personalgefüge, Wert- und Zielvorstellungen in der deutschen Universität des 19. und 20. Jahrhunderts* (Düsseldorf, 1972); R. Rürup, ed., *Wissenschaft und Gesellschaft: Beiträge zur Geschichte der Technischen Universität Berlin* (Berlin, 1979).

22 The generational element, mentioned by Sheldon Rothblatt, also comes into play, but in itself is rarely enough to explain the process, since age tension may lead to conformity as well as to innovation. Cf. A. Spitzer, "The Historical Problem of Generations," *American Historical Review*, 78 (1973), 1353–85.

23 S. Rothblatt, *Tradition and Change in English Liberal Education* (London, 1976); F. Pfetsch, *Zur Entwicklung der Wissenschaftspolitik in Deutschland* (Berlin, 1974); R. R. Locke, "The End of Practical Man: Higher Education and the Institutionalization of Entrepreneurial Performance in France, Germany and Great Britain, 1880–1940" (MS Hawaii, 1981); J. A. McClelland, "The Mystique of *Nauka*: Science and Scholarship in the Service of the People," appearing in a volume edited by T. G. Stavrou (1981).

24 F. Paulsen, *The German Universities: Their Character and Historical Development* (New York, 1895), 110 ff; the Socialist deputies Strobel and Liebknecht in the Prussian Landtag on April 25, 27 and June 13, 1910, *Stenographische Berichte des Abgeordnetenhauses*, vol. 544; R. Dahrendorf, *Society and Democracy in Germany* (Garden City, 1967); P. Bourdieu and J. C. Passeron, *Les Heritiers. Les étudiants et la culture* (Paris, 1966); Ch. Jencks, *Inequality: A Reassessment of the Effect of Family and Schooling in America* (New York, 1972).

25 Ringer, *Education and Society*, 22 ff; H. Kaelble, "Educational Opportunities and Government Policies," *passim*; R. Boudon, *Education, Opportunity and Social Inequality* (New York, 1975); C. A. Anderson, "The Social Status of University Students in Relation to the Type of Economy," *Transactions of the Third World Congress of Sociology*, 5 (1956), 51–63.

26 For the sources of Table 5 see L. Stone, "The Size and Composition of the Oxford Student Body," 103; J. Floud, "The Educational Experience of the Adult Population in England," in: D. Glass, ed., *Social Mobility in Britain* (London, 1954), 137 f; K. H. Jarausch, "The Social Transformation of the University," 625; H. Kaelble, *Historische Mobilitätsforschung*, 102; A. Rashin, "Gramatnost' i narodnoe obresovanie v Rossii," *Istoricheskie zapiski*, 37 (1951), 78; V. R. Leikina-Svirskaia, *Intelligentsiia v Rossii* (Moscow, 1971), 62–4; J. McClelland, "Proletarianizing the Student Body: The Soviet Experience," *Past and Present*, 80 (1978), 134–5; R. Angelo, "The Students at the University of Pennsylvania and the Temple College of Philadelphia," *History of Education Quarterly*, 19 (1979), 186; E. O. Reynolds, *The Social and Economic Status of Students* (New York, 1927).

27 H. Perkin, *Key Profession: The History of the Association of University Teachers* (London, 1969) and *The Origins of Modern English Society* (London, 1969); J. E. Craig, *Scholarship and Nation-Building: The Universities of Strasbourg and Alsatian Society, 1870–1914* (Chicago, 1983); D. R. Brower, *Training the Nihilists: Education and Radicalism in Tsarist Russia* (Ithaca, 1975); R. Angelo, "The Students at the University of Pennsylvania," 179–205. Cf. also B. R. Clark, "Problems of Access in the Context of Academic Structures," *Yale Higher Education Working Paper*, 16 (New Haven, 1977).

28 H. Kaelble, "Educational Opportunities in Europe, 1900–1970: The Emergence of a Pattern?" (paper delivered at the "Education and Social Change" conference, 1980); P. Lundgreen, "Besitz und Bildung. Einheit und Inkongruenz in der europäischen Sozialgeschichte?" *Geschichte und Gesellschaft*, 7 (1981), 262–75; J. McClelland, "Proletarianizing the Student Body," 122–146. Cf. Ringer, *Education and Society*, 71 ff, 157 ff.

29 The Cambridge and Oxford figures are from Kaelble, "Educational Opportunities," Tables 4 and 5 with a lower class figure added for Oxford on the assumption that about 50% of the British population in 1910 fell into that category. The pre-1930 sample is recalculated from J. Floud, "The Educational Experience," 137 f. The Heidelberg and Kiel figures are from Jarausch, "Die neuhumanistische Universität und die bürgerliche Gesellschaft," *Darstellungen und Quellen zur Geschichte der deutschen Einheitsbewegung*, Table 9; The German figures for 1930 are recalculated from Kaelble, *Historische Mobilitätsforschung*, Table 12 and Ringer, *Education and Society*, 315. The Russian 1914 figures are from D. Brower, "Social Stratification," Table 2; the Soviet figures for 1923/4 and 1927/8 are from J. McClelland, "Proletarianizing the Student Body," Table 4. The U.S. 1925 sample is calculated once again from Reynolds, *Social and Economic Status*.

30 Some national pecularities in Table 5 deserve notice. Although virtually non-existent in Oxbridge in the middle of the 19th century, the working-class had made considerable gains in England by the 1930s. In Germany the opening was a victory of the new middle class (2.5 times over-represented) which means that Central Europe was most elitist by 1930, although it had started out more openly. In Russia the change was most rapid and complete, so that the proletariat was over-represented (1.6) by the late 1920s. In America business representation was particularly strong and the service occupations also exceeded the old middle class, whereas the system appears more accessible for workers in individual institutions such as Temple than as a whole.

31 The concepts of charity, competitive and welfare opportunities are from H. Kaelble, "Educational Opportunities and Government Policies," part one; Cf. Jarausch, "The Social Transformation of the University," 60 ff, and "Die neuhumanistische Universität," *passim*.

32 B. J. Bledstein, *The Culture of Professionalism: The Middle Class and the Development of Higher Education in America* (New York, 1976), 86 f; A. LaVopa, "The Language of Profession: Germany in the Late 18th Century" (MS, Princeton, 1980); D. Rüschemeyer, "Professionalisierung: Theoretische Probleme für die vergleichende Geschichtsforschung," *Geschichte und Gesellschaft*, 6 (1980), 311–325; K. H. Jarausch, "Higher Education and Professionalization" (comment on a session on "Careers, Profession and Nineteenth Century Higher Education" at the 1979 SSHA meeting at Cambridge).

33 M. S. Larson, *The Rise of Professionalism: A Sociological Analysis* (Berkeley, 1977); H. Perkin, "Professionalization and English Society Since 1880" (MS Princeton, 1979); R. Spree, "The Impact of the Professionalization of Physicians on Social Change in Germany During the Late 19th and Early 20th Centuries,"

Historical Social Research, 15 (1980), 24–39; A. LaVopa, *Prussian Schoolteachers: Profession and Office, 1763–1848* (Chapel Hill, 1980); A. Engel, "Emerging Concepts of the Academic Profession at Oxford 1800–1845," in L. Stone, *The University in Society*, 1: 322–338.

34 A. Engel, *From Clergyman to Don: The Rise of the Academic Profession in 19th Century Oxford* (New York, 1982); C. E. McClelland, *State, Society and University in Germany 1700–1914* (Cambridge, 1980); C. E. Timberlake, *Essays on Russian Liberalism* (Columbia, 1972); D. Light, "Introduction: The Structure of the Academic Professions," *Sociology of Education*, 47 (1974), 2–28. Cf. K. H. Jarausch, "Professional Education at German Universities," (paper delivered at the Western Association for German Studies meeting at Wichita State University, 1980).

35 H. Perkin, "Professionalization," *passim*; Nancy M. Frieden, *The Russian Physician, 1830–1905: Professional, Reformer, Radical* (Princeton, 1981), especially chapter 5; C. Huerkamp, "Ärzte und Professionalisierung in Deutschland: Überlegungen zum Wandel des Arztberufs im 19. Jahrhundert," *Geschichte und Gesellschaft*, 6 (1980), 349–382; D. Rüschemeyer, *Lawyers and their Society* (Cambridge, Mass., 1973).

36 For the sources of Table 7 see B. R. Mitchell and P. Deane, *Abstract of British Historical Statistics* (Cambridge, 1962), 60 f. The first sets of German figures (1852 and 1907) is from Jarausch, *Students, Society*, Table 2–3 as well as from T. Geiger, *Die soziale Schichtung des deutschen Volkes* (Stuttgart, 1932), 20 ff (for 1925). The other numbers are from W. G. Hoffmann, *Das Wachstum der deutschen Wirtschaft*, 204 ff.

37 D. R. Skopp, "Auf der untersten Sprosse: Der Volksschullehrer als 'Semi-Professional' im Deutschland des 19. Jahrhunderts," *Geschichte und Gesellschaft*, 6 (1980), 383–402; R. S. Turner, "Social Mobility and the Traditional Professions in Prussia, 1770–1848" (MS, New Brunswick, 1979); P. Stearns, "The Middle Class: Towards a Precise Definition," *Comparative Studies in Society and History*, 21 (1979), 377–396. The non-economic sector of the upper and middle class has been consistently ignored by social historians preoccupied with industrialization.

38 W. Rüegg, "Bildungssoziologische Ansätze zur Erforschung des Bildungswesens im 19. Jahrhundert," in his and O. Neuloh, eds., *Zur soziologischen Theorie und Analyse des 19. Jahrhunderts* (Göttingen, 1971); D. Rüschemeyer, "Modernisierung und die Gebildeten im Kaiserlichen Deutschland," *Kölner Zeitschrift für Soziologie und Sozialpsychologie, Sonderheft* 16 (1973), 515–29; Ringer, *Education and Society*, 6 ff, 18 ff. For the ambivalence of the educated cf. K. H. Jarausch, "Liberal Education as Illiberal Socialization: The Case of Students in Imperial Germany," *Journal of Modern History*, 50 (1979), 609–36.

39 The extant data in Ringer, *Education and Society* and the above tables are too fragmentary to support anything but these preliminary impressions. According to issue, alignments of countries differ. In terms of expansion the established British and German institutions grew less dramatically than the emerging Russian and American systems. In terms of diversity the American and German systems seem to have held the lead, at least initially. In terms of social access Russia and Britain seem to have been the most open for the lower class by 1930. Finally in terms of professionalization the Anglo-American association-autonomy model appears to differ basically from the Continental (German-Russian) state-education model.

40 P. Lundgreen, "Educational Expansion and Economic Growth in Nineteenth Century Germany," in Stone, ed., *Schooling and Society* (Baltimore, 1976);

W. G. Hoffmann, "Erziehungs- und Forschungsausgaben im wirtschaftlichen Wachstumsprozeß," in: G. Hess, ed., *Eine Freundesgabe der Wissenschaft für E. H. Vits* (Frankfurt, 1963), 101–33; R. Meyer "Das Berechtigungswesen in seiner Bedeutung für Schule und Gesellschaft im 19. Jahrhundert," *Zeitschrift für die gesamte Staatswissenschaft*, 12 (1968), 763 ff; L. O'Boyle, "Education and Social Structure: The Humanist Tradition Reexamined," *Internationales Archiv für Geschichte der deutschen Literatur*, 1 (1976), 246 ff; K. Vondung, ed., *Das Wilhelminische Bildungsbürgertum* (Göttingen, 1976).

41 M. S. Archer, *Social Origins of Educational Systems* (London, 1979) and J. E. Craig, "On the Development of Educational Systems," *American Journal of Education*, 89 (1981), 189–211. Rather than nominalist abstractions, the intermediary linkages are crucial.

42 A. Flexner, *Universities: American, English, German* (London, 1930), 3–218. In 1967 Clark Kerr wrote in his introduction to the new edition with all the arrogance of the prophet of the "multiversity" before the student revolution: "The universities did all the wrong things—undergraduate instruction, professional schools (other than law and medicine), service activities, vocational courses, extension work. They did all the wrong things—and they entered the Golden Age." For the ideological reversal of the educated accompanying the social transformation see Jarausch, *Students, Society and Politics in Imperial Germany: The Rise of Academic Illiberalism* (Princetown, 1982).

52

THE UNIVERSITY AND THE STATE IN WESTERN EUROPE

Guy Neave

Source: D. Jaques and J. T. E. Richardson (eds) *The Future for Higher Education*, Proceedings of the 19th annual conference of the Society for Research into Higher Education, 1983, Guildford: SRHE and NFER-Nelson, 1985, pp. 27–40.

There are few arts more hazardous than prediction, and predicting what will be the state of the university in ten to fifteen years time, no less so. Nor is it by any means sure that those timid trends emerging from certain higher education systems in Western Europe will, inevitably, take the same direction in Britain. Though all countries in Western Europe, with the possible exception of Ireland, are facing the prospect of a dramatic drop in the size of the age cohorts entering higher education, and though all are faced with economic difficulties, the way governments respond to this is very different. Much depends on what one might call the ideological constellation which underlines government thinking and the way in which higher education is perceived.

It is, I think, very important to underline this sea change in the intellectual climate. There are several reasons for this. In the first place, the rise in certain countries of Economic Libertarianism or the theories of the Chicago school, has brought about a totally different concept of the role and place of the university in society. Second, the advent of the new utilitarianism represents not just a break up of the consensus that underlay higher education's development from the early sixties. It represents the break up of an international consensus as well. Thus, most Western European policies towards higher education in the sixties and seventies were broadly similar both in their strategic purpose and in the way they emerged. With hindsight, this period may be seen as harnessing higher education to the broad purpose of the welfare state to advance equality of opportunity, to remove the structural and financial obstacles to access to higher education, and, in certain instances, to provide second chance education for those who had missed out in their earlier careers. There are, to be sure, still countries that adhere to this neo-Keynesian consensus: France is one (though for how long is a different matter), Sweden is another, and Greece, with the current reforms of higher education, may constitute a third. At the other extreme of this same dimension stands the United Kingdom where the social model contained in supply side economics is very rapidly being applied in the determination of higher education development. In between these two extremes, one can locate the majority of European countries, their policies having in common the need to reduce expenditure, to place limits on student numbers in certain fields. But generally speaking these cuts are pragmatic rather than being a wider attempt to operate a major shift in social values.

It is, not unnaturally, difficult to foresee just how far those countries such as the Netherlands or the Federal Republic of Germany might not move over to a more hard-nosed approach. This said, how the university will evolve in future depends, to a high degree, on the place that the conflicting ideologies assign to it as a prime instrument of social and economic change – which is the Keynesian thesis – or as an ancillary vehicle acting in support of the broader goal of stimulating private enterprise, individual initiative and the nation's industrial performance. In short, we stand at a very crucial period in the history as well as the development of higher education. The role of higher education is changing from being an instrument for broad range collectivist and interventionist strategies for social change based on the concept of social justice and instead, it appears to be moving, in certain countries at least, towards being a supplementary institution whose actions are based on what may be termed the individualist, competitive ethic.[1]

The future of the university is governed by the coincidence of three crises: the demographic downturn, reduction in public expenditure and the ideological redefinition of its role in the nation. And, if the latter may appear somewhat far fetched, one has only to remember how far expansion twenty years ago was affected by what today is known as the neo-Keynesian consensus.

This said, there are four areas which, if current developments in Europe are the shape of things to come, will be profoundly affected and, perhaps for that reason, profoundly different in the university system of ten to twenty years ahead. These are: the structure of studies and the student clientele; the status of academic staff; the research relationship; and university funding patterns. If one were to resume these four themes under a single heading, what they all point towards is an increasing and more detailed intervention by the state to regulate, fine tune or profile areas which, hitherto, have either been in the hands of academia or subject to joint negotiation between academia and the relevant state administration. In short, the shift in the balance of power between the university, higher education and the state will most firmly be in favour of the latter.

In many ways this shift has already begun. Over the past ten years there has scarcely been any of these four fields that has not been subject to increasing scrutiny and legislative enactment, whether this takes the form of the Hochschulrahmengesetz of 1976 in Western Germany, the Loi d'Orientation of 1968 and its successor currently under debate in France or the 1977 Higher Education Reform Act in Sweden.

Let us take these by turn.

Structure of studies and student clientele

Between 1983 and the end of the decade, most European systems of higher education will have had to cope with the arrival of the demographic hump of the largest age cohort born in the sixties. From the end of the 1980s on to the turn of the century the size of the age groups will diminish radically.[2]

In terms of sheer volume, disregarding such factors as age qualification rates and age participation rates, the decrease from the hump to the bottom of the trough will be in the order of 45 per cent for the Federal Republic of Germany, 39 per cent in the case of Italy and Denmark, and 35 per cent for Austria, Switzerland and the United Kingdom.

If we look at the situation in five countries for which projections about student numbers are available – Austria, the Federal Republic of Germany, Denmark, the Netherlands and the United Kingdom – the peak as far as numbers qualified to enter higher education is reached in 1985 for the Federal Republic, Denmark and the United Kingdom, and in 1990 for Austria and the Netherlands. To some extent, the fall in the overall size of the age cohorts may be offset by an increase in the age qualification rate, details of which are set out in Table 1 for those countries having made projections in this area. Against this is the fact that, in a large number of Western European states, the proportion of those qualifying and taking up places in higher education is steadily falling.

The prospect of spare capacity during the last decade of this century has led many observers to suggest that one solution is to diversify the student

Table 1 Projections in the Age Qualification Rate for Certain Western European Countries: expressed as percentages.

	1985	1990	1995	2000
Austria		26.4	27.1	26.9
Finland		40.0	39.6	39.7
Federal Republic of Germany	30.0	33.0	38.0	
Denmark		40.0	40.0	
Netherlands		14.7	14.9	14.9
United Kingdom		16.7	17.9	17.8

Source: See Note 2.

clientele, to place added emphasis upon adult students, to expand short courses and to expand the permanent education function as a makeweight.[3]

This, of course, is not a novel solution. Rather it is a continuation of a trend which was already emerging in the course of the seventies and most visible with the reforms undertaken in Sweden in 1977. Recently, for instance, the Dutch universities have begun to turn their attention to this potential.[4]

However, it has to be said that if diversification is rational from the standpoint of higher education, much depends here on whether governments are prepared to underwrite a latter-day edition of the biblical instruction 'Go ye forth into the highways and byways and compel them to come in that My house may be full.' It is an option entertainable so long as governments do not see the demographic downturn as an opportunity further to reduce higher education's budget in line with falling demand. In short, the decision to increase the number of part-time, adult students is not an inevitable development. It is, in effect, a decision that does not depend on the internal development of the institution of higher education so much as on the role ascribed to higher education by government policy.

Far more significant, from a long-term point of view, is the tendency for governments increasingly to intervene, either to restructure the length of undergraduate courses, to change what may be called the curricular pathways and subject combinations in them, and thus to win a closer oversight of such matters as the subject profile and balance. Restructuring of studies has, broadly speaking, assumed two forms – the first negative, the second positive. The negative form of intervention is familiar to all in higher education, though not necessarily seen from this particular angle. It is the drastic reduction in the number of places in the field of teacher training, the closure of certain institutes specializing in this area in the United Kingdom, the Netherlands, the Federal Republic of Germany and Denmark.[5]

Similar measures are taken in other fields, for example the decision to cut back the number of medical students in France in 1972 – a measure currently under discussion in the Netherlands and also in Denmark.[6,7]

The positive form of intervention is best seen in the Swedish University Reform of 1977, and, more recently, in the proposals contained in the French higher education Guideline Bill. These are remarkably similar to one another. They involve replacing the traditional discipline structure of undergraduate courses with a series of tracks, broadly corresponding to particular sectors of the national labour market. In the case of the Swedes, these were:

- The technical sector
- The administrative, economic and social welfare sector
- The medical and paramedical sector
- The teaching sector
- The cultural and information sector

For some, the importance of these developments lies in the explicit linkage of a curricular nature between the university and the labour market. For others, for whom the university may primarily stand as a scholarly community, they are examples of intolerable interference in the university's fundamental task, that of the free acquisition and transmission of knowledge. A third group may take another view on the matter and see in these examples a redefinition of the university's task towards the 'professionalization' of higher education: in short, a shift in the type of knowledge held necessary for a post-industrial society.

It is of course a historical anachronism to see anything particularly new-fangled in the notion of professionalization. Medicine, law and theology, the heart of the medieval university, corresponded to well defined parts of the medieval equivalent of 'high level manpower' in the occupational structure of that time. Far more important is the change this represents in terms of what may be called the vehicular disciplines, through which the eternally important qualities of creativity, originality, capacity to synthesize, to draw relevant conclusions and to maintain a critical frame of mind, are fostered and perpetuated. The basic issue beneath the contemporary debate over 'professionalization' higher education studies is twofold: on the one hand, to have a greater part assigned to those disciplines held to reflect the culture of industrial society – the sciences of organization, administration, human comportment, the organization, distribution and creation of wealth; and on the other a move beyond those historical vehicular disciplines which, in the past, formed what Montaigne called 'L'honnête homme'. Essentially, as all know, these were the study of the classics and the humanities.

Attempts to redefine and recombine the 'vehicular disciplines' are many. Indeed the French 1968 Guideline law placed particular importance on 'interdisciplinarity'. But it was a discretionary principle and fell on stony ground. No more than four per cent of students followed formally inter-disciplinary courses in 1972.[7] The major difference between the rise of this notion in the early seventies and the gathering drive to consolidate it today lies in the fact that governments are less prepared to leave the redefinition in the hands of academia. Intervention by public authorities to 'profile' the disciplines in higher education, to place greater weight on some and less on others is a tendency that is gathering force. There are, of course, various stages in this development, ranging from the specific intervention designed to accelerate the development of those disciplines associated with 'high technology' – biology, computing and those disciplines associated with information technology – measures which can be seen at undergraduate level in Denmark and France, among others, in informatics and technical subjects, and in the Netherlands in the proposal to boost agronomic and administrative sciences.[8] And, at the other end of the spectrum, there is the wholesale intervention and re-profiling at systems level which may be seen in Sweden and in France and in the current reforms being introduced in the Greek system of higher education.

The status of academic staff

Personally, I believe this trend will be strengthened in the coming years as a result of the continued pressure to contain public expenditure on the one hand and on the other the relatively poor bargaining position higher education will face once the demographic downturn begins to bite. This has equally far ranging implications for academic personnel, their career structure and the relative standing of teaching personnel as compared to those acting as the professional intermediaries between institution and public authorities – namely the administrative estate.

Over the past decade, the academic constituency grew considerably: by around a third in the Federal Republic of Germany, by some 83 per cent in Spain, by some 75 per cent between 1965 and 1975 in the Netherlands, and in France more than doubled between 1966 and 1978 from 20,373 to 41,987.[9] This growth was accompanied by wide-ranging shifts in power inside academia, principally in the diminution in professorial power, the recognition of the right of middle and junior staff levels to take part in decision-making. Irrespective of the particular country involved, academia, in contrast to the situation ten years ago when expansion was, in Europe at least, largely born on the backs of growing numbers of young, part-time auxiliary staff, is now an ageing profession. Promotions are blocked and the difficulties that are likely to result from this, in terms of the research capacity of higher education, are a source of constant worry to most governments.[10]

Whether the academic profession is becoming more precarious in the security afforded to its members is largely a matter of the constitutional, legal and administrative status afforded to its members. In certain countries, such as France, Italy and the Federal Republic of Germany, the status of civil servant is a considerable protection – the equivalent of tenure, though with far more weighty guarantees in constitutional and administrative law than is the case in Britain. This means, in effect, that direct government intervention to accelerate departures can only operate at two particular levels: at the upper level by reducing the age of retirement from 70 to 65, for instance, or at the bottom level by dismissing, or by non-renewal of contract for, part-timers without civil servant status.

Looked at from a general European perspective, the most important factors that will bear down upon the academic profession over the next ten to fifteen years are two: first the effects in terms of advancement and funding that will flow from the trend towards 're-profiling' the disciplinary line-up; second, the shift in the balance of power towards university administration, seen less as the handmaiden to academia than the secular arm of financial accountability for central or local administration.

As regards the first, the consequence of assigning greater priority to some fields of study is the inevitable withdrawal of recognition from others. If pushed to the extreme, it may well be that the combined effects of 're-profiling' with the drive to harness higher education's research capacity to the perceived requirements of national competitiveness will create a highly stratified profession – stratified perhaps between research-oriented high technology fields and policy-oriented areas of the administrative sciences on the one hand and on the other hand the teaching areas revolving primarily around the humanities and some of the more esoteric of the social sciences.[11]

As regards the second, the press for financial accountability plus the growing trend to have outsiders, representatives of national or regional interests, whether political, commercial or industrial, on the various decision-making organs of the university (a development particularly evident in Sweden, Norway, and currently under hot debate in France and Greece) could well increase the power of university administration as the main co-ordinating instance between the institution and its increasingly complex ties with the outside world.[12]

How drastic this shift may be is difficult to determine, for if there is one thing that governments – whether reforming or merely pragmatic – have found to their cost, it is the power of the academic profession to resist change. But, taken together, these two developments suggest that the area over which the collegium will be able to operate in future may well be considerably more restricted than it is now. Whether this will lead to a strengthening of the managerial approach inside academia as an extension of its increasing role outside strictly academic affairs, is again difficult to foresee.

The research relationship

Despite the ideological differences that colour the place higher education is assigned in the social fabric, it is clear that all governments, whether left or right, have, over the past few years, paid closer attention to the role of research and the capacity of the university to contribute to the national effort in this area. Some countries, for instance France and Sweden, see university research as a way of priming the industrial pump, as a crucial part in accelerating economic recovery.[13]

Some of the administrative changes that have taken place in order to 'lock' higher education in with government research priorities have been remarkable. In 1981, shortly after the French Socialists had come to power, responsibility for the national research strategy was moved from the Ministry of Education to the then Ministry of Technology and Research. Similarly, the Social Democrat administration in Sweden took further measures to strengthen the dialogue between researchers and government. The deputy premier was placed at the head of a secretariat for co-ordinating research policy whilst a new forum for discussion between government and the universities was created, with the prime minister chairing.

These are perhaps extreme examples of a more general trend towards harnessing research to national priorities. Greater control over research priorities springs from several considerations. First, the need to optimize and at the same time to rationalize investment at a time when public expenditure is being strictly limited. Second, the need to operate within the research area a similar strategy to the 're-profiling' done at the level of undergraduate study. Third, the necessity to make sure that sufficient able students are attracted into research. And, finally, to counter the possible decline in research capacity as a result of the ageing of academia.

Amongst efforts to strengthen the graduate research base one can, of course, point to the increased powers assigned to the Italian National Research Council[14] and the marked shift in new posts away from the arts and social sciences, with a concomitant reinforcement of science appointments.[15] In West Germany, the use of Heissenberg Fellowships – awarded for six years to post-doctoral students to continue high level research – was recently strengthened by increasing the amount of financial support for fundamental research and affording more 'favour' financing for students destined for research in fields deemed of national significance.[16]

These particular examples can be interpreted in a variety of ways. However, whatever the interpretation, they are pointers to the fact that 'driven' or 'sectoral' research – inquiry specifically undertaken in response to the demands of outside bodies, whether government agencies or private enterprise (the customer/contractor principle) – would appear to be on the increase. If this situation might be satisfactory insofar as it brings into academia the competitive instinct – that pygmy-killer dynamism which some feel is the driving force of business – there are other concomitants that follow the rise of such research. First, there is the fact that it also entails a change in the balance of power away from the universities and towards those funding or commissioning bodies from whence manna and half-roasted quails do flow. Driven or sectoral research is less the result of granting public funds to free inquiry than of applying a specifically tailored remit, with the power to determine what shall be investigated and what shall not lying in the hands of research councils, ministries, industry. Second, the incentives to move over to this contract research are considerable – additional posts, growth of consultancies and, for those countries where tenure remains unprotected by constitutional or administrative fiat, a lesser degree of insecurity.

But it also follows from this that the more links are laid down with outside agencies, the greater the possibility of further fragmentation within the academic profession. Such fragmentation might emerge in four strata:

- Those involved in fundamental, long-term research in priority areas backed by government.

- Those involved in short/medium-term contract research backed by the private sector.
- Those involved in research related to teaching on small personal grants.
- Those involved in teaching alone.

Some will point out that this is nothing new. And that the academic profession can always be divided between the research-oriented and the teaching-oriented. But, taken in combination with the rise of sectoral research on the one hand and the demographic decline on the other, the penalties of being in those fields which do not easily lend themselves to activities falling into the first two categories are likely to be rather unenviable. Disparities in terms of the type of resources, internal as well as external, research as well as consultancy, between the different academic fields are likely to grow.

There are many other possibilities which could affect the development of the research relationship over the next fifteen years. One is for increasing institutional stratification and the emergence of a particular category of 'research universities' on the American model, centres of excellence in regular receipt of earmarked research funding. Since the status hierarchy between institutes of higher education in many Western European countries tends to be less pronounced than it is in Britain or the United States – if, indeed it exists at all – this particular development poses rather a more radical change than it may in Britain. The second possibility is for research on a contract basis to move out of university and, increasingly, to be located in specialized institutes half way between academia and government. This pattern of research institute already occupies a considerable place in France[17], whilst the pattern of specialized research agencies closely associated with, but not directly part of, university life has long been a characteristic in Germany.[18]

There are several reasons for thinking this pattern might develop further elsewhere. First, the halt in recruitment to the academic profession has left a large number of highly qualified young people with the relevant skills but often without the opportunity to employ them. Second, the development of a para-academic diaspora may gain considerable impetus from the potential derived from the so called 'new information technologies'. Third, such institutes, seen from the standpoint of prospective commissioning bodies, whether government or private sector, may appear to be more responsive because less engaged in the multifarious other responsibilities of academia.

University funding patterns

The more specific point about the way research is funded raises the fourth and final topic which, I feel, will assume greater significance in the current range of issues that will affect the future of the university. If I were to hazard a guess, the university of the 1990s and the year 2000 will depend far more on multi-source funding than it does at present. It is, of course, a matter of record that the expansion of higher education in Western Europe was born on the coffers of central government. And it is equally apparent when one comes to look at recent developments and proposals in the domain of higher education financing which have been rather more gentle in Europe than they have been, for instance, in Britain.

The first question is whether university financing in the future will be directly related to student numbers. In 1977 the French authorities moved away from this criterion, and replaced it by a formula of such complexity that it can only have been devised by a polytechnician and thus understood only by others of that ilk.[19]

The abandonment of this yardstick has certain advantages, particularly if a country's higher education policy is to rise on the crest of the demographic wave rather than dive through it. The second question is whether, in the event of per capita funding being maintained, central government will not step in to fix an annual quota of places available in the *whole of the higher education system*. If this strategy seems somewhat unusual in the British context, there are nevertheless certain countries, amongst which Sweden and Denmark, where this is current practice. In the case of the former, the number of places is set by the Ministry of Education and in the case of the latter, it is set by parliamentary vote along with the higher education budget.

As for the matter of diversifying funding sources, here two trends appear to be developing at present. The first is to diminish the amount of financial support from central government and instead to increase the contribution from local or regional authorities. To be sure, the change in the source is not a shift from the principle of funding from the public purse. But it does mean that in certain areas higher education is more beholden to its immediate geographical region. This innovation was one of the main features of the 1977 reform of the Swedish university, partly to ensure that regional and local interests were possessed of financial teeth, partly too, as a means of giving substance to the policy of regional devolution and participation.[20] In France, a similar consideration emerged in the Freville Report on university finance.[21] Strangely, this issue, first broached during the dying days of the Giscardien regime, was taken up and given a new lease of life by the government of M. Mitterrand. And, though first conceived as a way of giving universities that lean and hungry look that apparently inspires initiative and entrepreneurship, the same proposal is now launched forth as part of a wider exercise to strengthen the regional tier of administration and to reduce that of Paris.

The second trend in funding patterns is to place greater reliance on private industry, either in the form of research contracts or by setting up short courses for retraining personnel at mid-career. The rise of contract research has been discussed in the previous section. And, though it has always been present, the development of 'science parks', whether in the Netherlands, in Belgium around Louvain la Neuve or in France at Grenoble, shows that the linkage between university and industry is becoming increasingly institutionalized and of growing significance. Contract training courses are seen as a major part of the current higher education reform in France, both as a means of diversifying funding, and as helping mid-level and senior management acquire those skills required by the development of high level technology.

Conclusion

If current trends in the Western European university *are* the shape of things to come, then the university of the future will be under even greater pressure for financial, political and performance accountability. Not only will those instances to which it will have to give account be more complex and greater in number. They will also be largely external to the higher education system. This means, essentially, that whatever the criteria used to denote, define and measure 'efficiency', they will tend to an increasing extent not to be those of the university itself. How far academia will be capable of resolving at best, or reconciling at worst, the potential conflict between internal academic values and those imposed from outside is largely a matter of guess work. Academia's power of accommodation to change from outside is, of course, considerable. Even so, it has been the burden of this paper to suggest that those areas over which academia has power, appear themselves to be shrinking. External control over student numbers, growing intervention, either through the differential allocation of posts and resources between those fields of academic activity deemed vital to the national interest, or through the outright reduction of others, all point to the very real possibility that those matters over which academia is seen as having legitimate predominance are becoming increasingly limited to the act of teaching, student evaluation and the appointment or advancement of colleagues within confines strictly determined by the state.

Over the past few years, the number of external bodies representing public interests, whether at local or regional level, has increased in number. And their voice inside academia has increased as well. In the area of the public funding of research, commissioning agencies, whether research councils or ministries, appear to be less the funding arms of academia than instruments of government policy. Indeed, the rise of the subfield of science policy and research policy within economics in some countries, higher education studies in others,[22] may be seen as a reflection of this alteration and a recognition of its importance for academia.

Some may care to see in these possibilities a very real threat to academic autonomy. Others may argue that by transforming higher education into the symbol of a competitive society, the system of higher education itself is becoming more closely linked to the political ideologies of the hour. And more subject to them. It may well be so. But even assuming that autonomy is conceived as the same thing from one country to another, which often it is not, it is no less obvious that the reality of such autonomy is that it is a changing concept, dependent on whether the state or representatives of the public are prepared to uphold a self-denying ordinance of non-intervention in those areas they recognize as essential to *Lehr- und Lernfreiheit*.[23]

Just how this will be agreed upon depends to a high degree on the policies governments will adopt to meet the forthcoming fall in student numbers, to meet the shift of public expenditure away from the dwindling numbers of young people in the population and towards the growing numbers of the old. It also depends on which ideological construct is placed on the role of higher education in society. The future of the university, no less than the nature and the extent of the autonomy accorded to academia, hang upon these three factors. No soothsayer worth his salt would dare to make any utterance as to their outcome!

Acknowledgement

This paper was prepared using material gathered by EURYDICE, the Education Information Network of the European Communities. I acknowledge here the help of all EURYDICE Central Unit staff.

Notes

1 Neave, Guy (1982a) On the edge of the abyss *European Journal of Education* 17 (2) 124–126.
2 *Child and Family: Demographic Developments in the OECD Countries* (1979) Paris: Organisation for Economic Cooperation and Development. Neave, Guy (1983a) Demographic trends and higher education: or, is fewer really better *Memorandum to the Standing Conference of Presidents, Rectors and Vice-Chancellors of the European Universities* Bruxelles, November 1983 (typewritten) Table II.
3 See Cerych, Ladislav (1983) in *Response to Adversity* Guildford: Society for Research into Higher Education.
4 Open universiteit mengt zich in slag om studenten *NRC Handelsblad* 3 March 1983.
5 *The Impact of Demographic Change upon the Education Systems of the European Community* (1981) Bruxelles: EURYDICE.
   Measures taken by Member states in response to the demographic crisis *Note to the Members of the Education Committee, Document VI713/83-EN (123/en)* (1983) Bruxelles: Commission of the European Communities.
   Berlingske Tidende 17–18 February 1983.
6 Neave, Guy (1978) Foreign student mobility in France. In Burn, Barbara B. (Editor) *Higher Education Reform: implications for foreign students* New York: International Institute for Educational Exchange.
7 Stop bepleit op toeloop geneeskunde *NRC Handelsblad* 19 March 1983.
   Berlingske Tidende op. cit.
8 *Faits Nouveaux 2/83* Strasbourg: Council of Europe.

9 Neave, Guy (1983b) The changing face of the academic profession in Western Europe *European Journal of Education* 18 (3) (forthcoming).

10 Skoie, Hans, (1976) *Ageing University Staff* Oslo: Institute for Studies in Research and Higher Education.
Teichler, Ulrich (1982) Recent developments in the Federal Republic of Germany *European Journal of Education* 17 (2) 167
SOU 1981:29 *Forskningens Framtid* Stockholm: The Report of the Andren Committee on the Future of Research
Neave, Guy (1982b) Mobility is the key to France's future *Times Higher Education Supplement* 29 January 1982.

11 Role and function of universities *Discussion Paper (83) 8* (1983) Paris: Organisation for Economic Cooperation and Development.

12 *Projet de Loi: Loi d'orientation de l'enseignement superieur* (1983) Paris: Ministere de l'Education Nationale (xerox).
For Greece see *On the Structure and Function of Higher Education Institutes. Law No 1268/82, 1982* Athens: Ministry of Education and Religious Affairs (xerox) (English translation).
Neave, Guy (1983c) The regional dimension: some considerations from a European perspective. In Shattock, Michael (Editor) *The Structure and Governance of Higher Education* Guildford: Society for Research into Higher Education.

13 Interview with Dr Hans Landberg, Director General, Swedish Council for the Coordination of Research, Stockholm, 2 November 1982.
Neave (1982b) *op. cit.*

14 *Times Higher Education Supplement* 21 January 1983.

15 *Corriere della Serra* 9 July 1983.

16 Federal Republic of Germany: educational policy of the new government *Council of Europe Newsletter 5/82* (1982) p.19.
Teichler (1982) *op. cit.*

17 Machin, Howard (1982) *The CNRS and Social Science Research in France* London: London School of Economics (xerox) p.13.

18 ben David, Joseph (1979) *Centres of Learning: Britain, France, Germany and the USA* New York.

19 Goldberg, Lucien (1979) University financing in France. In Lyman, J. Glenny (Editor) *Funding Higher Education: A Six Nation Analysis* New York: Praeger.

20 Neave (1983c) *op. cit.*

21 *La Réforme du Financement des Universités (1981)* Paris: La Documentation Francaise.

22 Neave, Guy and Jenkinson, Sally (1983) *Research on Higher Education in Sweden. An Analysis and an Evaluation* Stockholm: Almqvist Wiksell International.

23 Neave, Guy (1982c) La notion de limites comme modèle des liens existant entre l'université et l'Etat *CRE Bulletin* 58.

53

CONCLUSION

Michael Sanderson

Source: M. Sanderson, *The Universities and British Industry, 1850–1970*, London: Routledge and Kegan Paul, 1972, pp. 389–97.

This study has tried to show that various pressures arose in the nineteenth century which induced the universities and industry to turn towards each other. The fear of French and then German competition, the increasingly scientific nature of innovation, the emergence of the large firm and the rise of special skills like accountancy all created a need for the graduate in industry. Oxford and Cambridge were not suited to supply this need though the latter reformed and removed some of the institutional barriers impeding the scientific education of the secular potential businessman. The origin of the appointments boards in both universities created an important new device for a closer linking of the universities and industry which others soon copied. Because of the defects of the ancient universities, new civic universities in the North and Midlands arose, directly financed by industry and business and frequently owing their existence to them. Accordingly all developed industrial specialisms in their research and teaching which served local and national industry, while a large proportion of their graduates, unlike those of the ancient universities, went into industrial careers. Parallel with these technological developments there were later moves from the 1890s to develop economics as a suitable university training for businessmen in which Cambridge, Birmingham, and LSE took a lead that others followed.

The Welsh and Scottish traditions underwent a somewhat different experience. The Welsh university colleges arose largely as an expression of Welsh national culture. They received little support from industry, save that of south Lancashire, their studies had little industrial relevance and their output to Welsh industry was slight. They presented a pathological example of a university movement largely disengaged from industry and greatly weakened thereby. The Scottish case was more complicated. Their problem was to modify an old university system based on assumptions of giving a rather general mixed arts and science education to large numbers of students destined for the ministry and teaching. Increasing scientific education and increasing permitted specialism seemed to them the way to adjust to the demands of industry. At the same time, in their research, Scottish professors in engineering, electrical physics, and shipbuilding presented an example of close involvement in industry that was a model to the English professoriate.

The First World War was seen as a very important phase in this development in that it presented a number of challenging problems in the field of drugs, explosives, aeronautics, and so forth which university personnel tackled with striking and well publicized success. Moreover, at that time the universities were almost unique in containing the scientists with the ability to handle such problems. The war also created a 'cult' of science and brought direct government sponsorship of it. Moreover, the pressures of war-time and the collaboration of university personnel with firms brought formal contacts between the universities and industry on a greater scale than had existed hitherto. The war also showed the worth of women graduates in industry as welfare officers, and also had the effect of turning many servicemen's thoughts to higher education and future careers in science and technology after the war.

In the inter-war years, in spite of depression, the progressive connection of the universities and industry continued in several areas. The rise of research within the firm, especially in the 1920s, created a new and most important entree for the graduate into the firm. Also the increase of 'functionalism' in management and problems of management succession created by war-time losses inclined more firms to turn to the graduate. Many of the 'new' industries by their scientific nature required men with a higher scientific education, while for the non-scientific graduate new developments in economics and commercial education created new courses in industrial administration. For women, still forced into careers by their excess in the population, new fields opened in advertising, stores, welfare management, and light electrical engineering which brought the woman graduate into industry virtually for the first time.

It was no surprise that in the Second World War the universities should have been at the very heart of the war-time science for the production of radar and the atomic bomb, both in close contact with industry. After the war and up to the late 1950s, the graduate was never so much in demand from industry, as not only the traditional chemist and physicist but also the mathematician was avidly absorbed into the firm. The arts graduate, too, was turned to more than before to fill in the gaps of industry's needs which even the contemporary urgent concern about increasing technological manpower had failed fully to meet. In this situation, and faced with the coming to university age of children born in the immediate post-war years, the country embarked on a major expansion of the universities, creating 'new' ones whose involvement with industry tended not to be great, and upgrading former colleges of technology into 'technological' universities the basis of whose existence was their connection with industry.

The increasing involvement of the universities with industry is perhaps the most important single development in the history of the British universities over the last hundred years. It will be stressed, however, that it is far from the only important connection. Indeed, such parallel themes as the connection of the universities with agriculture, with medicine, with teacher training, or the Civil Service would well merit thorough investigation which is not the purpose of this study to pursue. While this is not a study of the whole history of British universities in general but of one vital theme in their modern development, we believe this connection to have been of special importance. It has created a situation in which it would be virtually impossible for a university to return purely to that liberal education envisaged by Mill and Newman, to studies, in Newman's words 'independent of sequel' and not 'informed by any end'. To engage totally in such studies would almost inevitably entail cutting off such an institution from industrial support and the precedents for that in the last hundred years have been almost uniformly gloomy—Cambridge before the 1890s, Dundee after the 1890s, and the Welsh colleges before 1914. It has frequently been stressed how essential industrial support has been for the vitality, health, and very existence of the universities. This has not only been so most obviously at the financial level, but because the testing of their research and of their graduate products in subsequent work situations has given a beneficially astringent effect to studies, which those without practical application cannot have. Also the requirements of industry have opened up a whole range of new subjects and cross connections which would not necessarily have come about without those demands—the chemistry of glass, the mathematics of flight, the biology of the food fishes, for example. Finally, the favourable regard of the local business community, as in Birmingham, Liverpool, or Manchester, has provided a climate powerfully conducive to the healthy growth of universities as its lack elsewhere has retarded it.

Reciprocally, if the industrial and business connection has been vital for the universities so has it been for industry. This has been so through the original knowledge that the universities have provided of which ample evidence has been given in this study. Much of the expertise for the electrical industry before the 1920s came from the universities, while others like fisheries, canning, mining, marine engineering, leather, dyes, and so forth have been highly dependent on university work for their developing science. Indeed, universities virtually created many of them. It is the exceptions like motor car engineering and cotton textiles which stand out as unusual in owing little to the universities. This reliance was probably relatively greater before the 1920s than after. Then, with the rise of research laboratories within the firm, the universities became merely one of a number of agencies producing new industrial science, and in the case of dyes and electricals, for example, the chief locus of innovation moved from the university to the firm. But for most others the university, with the research association and the firm laboratory, remained a major fount of new ideas. Second, even where the universities were not innovating, their consultancy services often had a widespread and profound effect in improving the scientific efficiency of firms even in routine matters, as was seen, for example, in Roscoe's advisory work in chemistry from Manchester University and Arnold's in metallurgy from Sheffield. Third, and most obvious, the universities have been increasingly suppliers of personnel with as much as one-third of their output going into these fields. In the nineteenth century it was the chemist and the engineer, and then successively with a widening range of occupations, the economist, welfare worker, physicist, and latterly the mathematician and the arts graduate. Indeed, in those areas where from time to time the universities have conspicuously failed to produce certain types of labour —metallurgists, geologists, and mechanical engineers in the thirties, for example—then industry was loud to complain of the serious deleterious effects this lack of supply was having.

This close and progressive enmeshment of industrial considerations in the very fabric of British universities that has taken place over the last hundred years has posed a number of problems and dilemmas for the present and the future. First, there is the conflict of criteria about the optimum size of the university population. On the one hand is the belief that the numbers of students ought to be related to and even restricted by the demands of society, including industry, for their future services as graduates. The obvious drawbacks of this approach are that it is extremely difficult to forecast with precision future demand for certain types of labour, partly because of the difficulty of predicting future economic performance and partly because of the impossibility of foretelling technical change. Thus predictions about future requirements of types of skills may be as awry as those about amounts of skill. If this criterion is a dubious one—and we have seen various examples of shortfalls and overproductions in the past—then the other is to base estimates of proposed university populations on numbers of people qualified and willing to attend a university, rather than on estimates of their subsequent job prospects. Indeed, much of the expansion of the 1960s was argued in terms of social justice for qualified school leavers as much as on the need for technical manpower. The activities of the 'new' universities are largely catering for the former considerations rather than the latter. This distinction is an important one here because after a period of rapid expansion the early 1970s began with a period of recession and fears of graduate unemployment which led easily to arguments about 'overexpansion'. The point we would wish to stress is that a too close consideration of supposed immediate industrial needs in response to temporary and fluctuating circumstances could lead to the acceptance of criteria about university numbers not only socially unjust, but also against the best interests of industry itself, which can have no wish to return to the scramble for graduates in short supply that characterized the late 1940s and 1950s. The concept that young people who are so qualified may attend a university as a right is an important innovation and it would be retrograde if the close involvement universities have with industry should cause it to be abandoned in favour of criteria based on manpower planning, were these latter more restrictive.

The second dilemma posed by the involvement of the universities and industry is the nature of the education to be provided. We have seen ample evidence of the power of industrial needs to change and amplify the content of university teaching, and these effects have generally been beneficial and enriching for the universities. But on the other hand, two kinds of conflicts may arise over the content of education where the interests of industry may not be those of the university as a centre of excellence in scholarship. The first of these centres around the problem of specialism and generalism. To say that industry has preferred more or less specialization would be too crude. Historically it has sometimes called for more and sometimes less. For example, the changes in the Scottish universities' curricula were a move towards specialism for the benefit of industry as were the demands for specialist geology and metallurgy in the inter-war years. But, conversely, at other times it has been in the interests of industry to require a widening of the context of certain subjects. This was so with the widening of the Mathematical Tripos in the 1900s to include applied subjects, the creation of chemical engineering out of two specialisms in the 1920s, and the placing of economics in successively wider contexts to produce commerce courses in the 1900s and industrial administration programmes in the 1930s. It is frequently argued that such is the pace of technical change that any science or technology studied by students so rapidly becomes obsolete that there is consequently little point in studying anything to much degree of specialist depth. This lends weight to arguments in favour of broadly based multidisciplinary general degrees which would purport to give a certain 'flexibility' to cope with future change. Were this to become widely followed, and especially if science degrees were much diluted with arts, the dangers of producing graduates having a broad smattering of most things in general and mentally equipped for nothing in particular would be considerable. This is not an English tradition, but the nearest approach was the old Scottish unreformed university education which even in the nineteenth century became increasingly unsuitable as an education for an industrial society, and which could only survive because almost all its science professors had had a supplementary education at Cambridge in mathematics, the stronghold of specialized high excellence. We have noted that the Eaborn report made an unfashionable stand against this generalist approach on behalf of chemical education and the chemical industry. If industry came to believe that a lower level general education best served its purpose there may be a conflict of duty presented to the universities who would prefer to continue teaching at the highest level, holding out to the student the possibility of achieving excellence and depth of grasp in some coherent, if limited, area of scholarship.

The second potential area of conflict of interest about the whole content of education is that over the type of student required by industry. Here there is a long standing clash between the demands of scholarship and notions of a wider 'rounded' non-academic education. At Oxford and Cambridge in the nineteenth century there were plenty of men whose purpose in being there was not learning but the social and sporting life; indeed this disturbed several witnesses to the Royal Commissions on the two universities in the 1850s. However, the evidence of the early appointments officers of the two universities suggested that before 1914 firms were taking graduates with the highest degrees they could get. They certainly took academic attainment into account and believed it relevant as a predictor of ability and future success. Evidence from Imperial College for the 1930s also suggests the same. In the inter-war years, however, there arose the concept of the 'right type', the paragon of appointments office and industrial literature, who represented a balanced ideal of academic work, sport, travel, and so forth. This in itself was admirable, but by the late 1940s some industrial opinion seemed to have toppled over to an extreme. In particular some of the comments at contemporary FBI conferences denigrating academic excellence and condemning 'studiousness' as a danger to the universities strongly suggested that the ideals of businessmen and the ideals to which universities ought to cling had sharply diverged. The humorous retort, 'we cannot put on courses on running the rugger club', well characterized the fatuousness of some of the statements to which it was reacting. Similarly the Acton Society Trust found that 'ability to fit in' was far more highly valued by firms than intellectual curiosity and originality of thought as a characteristic of its graduate recruits. This divergence of values between the universities and industry is a serious point. It may well be that for many students the essentially academic education of universities would be a less suitable training for business than some kind of mixed educational-cum-adventure, outward bound, initiative-testing kind of post-school experience. The Army is very properly making a strong case in its advertising for short service commissions in arguing their future value for potential industrial entrants. It might have been a bold stroke if instead of financing one or two of the new universities, the government had experimented with a form of residential college providing this kind of initiative training but without any pretensions to undertake academic work to a high level. This would be preferable to a situation in which universities take on more and more non-academic and non-intellectual functions to which their students divert increasing amounts of time, knowing well that industry has less interest in the class of their degree than in their other activities. If there is a divergence of values between the scholar and the business man, universities should make quite clear both to students and to industry which values they are primarily concerned to foster.

Occasionally we have noted in the past instances of industrial interference in university affairs or clashes between university and industrial interests —as with the restrictions on Arnold's publishing, Pope's interference in economics at Bristol, Webb's resignation, the clash of Mackay and Alsop and Brunner at Liverpool, and the Warwick incident. And yet in spite of the considerable stir such suspicions about business raised in the 1930s, we do not regard them as truly deep and serious threats to the university system. More dangerous than these surface scandals is the insidious assumption that the activity of universities ought to be, and can be, measured in terms of some rate of return on expenditure. Such assumptions are understandably attendant upon the great increase in public expenditure on higher education in the 1960s and owe much to the contemporary rise of the economics of education as a study. But at the root is the close relation that the universities and industry now bear towards each other. It would be deplorable if these three factors, all good in themselves, created an attitude of mind in which the only education that was valued was that which apparently gave this measurable return and which served the economy in a quantifiable manner. The most crude form of this attitude was seen in some remarkable attacks on the Open University in the summer of 1971 on the grounds that it had not been able to show such a return. This may be the most adverse effect of the whole movement of the *rapprochement* of the universities and industry if it coarsens the public view of the purposes of education to a crudely measurable vocationalism. This drifting change should be seen in its historical context.

Before the drawing together of the universities and industry, we have seen that attitudes to the functions of universities were dominated by the old liberal anti-vocational education ideal. It has been one of the virtues of this drawing together greatly to enrich university activity and to widen its scope beyond the narrowness of curriculum envisaged by the liberal education ideal. This created universities with a healthy mixture of vocational and liberal education as the civic universities espoused the pure arts—which they were obliged to do to gain entrance to Victoria and to become chartered universities—and as Oxford and Cambridge improved their sciences and accepted technology. It would be an undesirable reversal if this balance of liberal and vocational education were then tilted to the other extreme in which only vocational and chiefly industrial subjects capable of yielding a measurable return became regarded as worthwhile objects of university study. There are certain rapidly developing areas of higher education where such justifications are manifestly absent. In particular the Open University, dealing with the middle-aged, ought to have no need to justify itself on such grounds. The same is true of the education of women. Some of the chief beneficiaries of the expansion of the 1960s have been middle-class girls and they are precisely the people who find it most difficult to obtain employment on graduating and who with early marriage are least likely to remain long in any employment they eventually obtain. But to recognize this is in no way to invalidate the extending of higher education to the second-chance middle-aged or to girls, the beneficial effects of which in social and personal terms are likely to prove great though totally outside the realms of calculation. Whereas before the engagement with industry too much university education was of a consumption rather than a productive character, there is a danger with the close involvement of the universities and industry of swinging to an equally unbalanced opposite extreme of denying the validity of consumption education, of the widening and disciplining of the mind for its own sake, and seeking to test such education by the criteria of 'investment' in 'human capital'. This is one of the risks attendant upon greatly increased public expenditure in a higher education system whose recent tradition has been so closely geared to industry.

At the beginning of the period with which this study deals university men were chiefly destined for the learned professions. Throughout the period we have been concerned with, they have filtered increasingly into a widening range of industrial and business employments in the circumstances we have considered. For the future, with continued expansion, graduates will continue to filter into a whole range of occupations in which they have not formerly been greatly involved—into junior and infant teaching, the police, secretarial posts, the management of cinemas, grocery stores, and football clubs and all manner of occupations calling for the absorption and ordering of information and the taking of decisions and initiative. Although graduate status will lose slightly whatever 'special' character it bestowed on its holder in the 1900s or the 1930s, yet it would be wrong to regard such future occupational change as a 'waste' of graduates or as evidence of 'overexpansion'. The small minority with the self-igniting desire for scholarship will continue to be stimulated by university life as before. The bulk of the rest, merely as intelligent and moderately hard working as their predecessors ever were, will transmit at least something of university values a little more widely in a society that can only benefit from them.

The universities have been able to retain those values and standards whilst absorbing the stimulus and adapting to the needs of industry over the last hundred years. To continue to do so in the face of further democratization presents the next immediate challenge from which, compared with their response to industrial involvement, they have rather less to fear but rather less to gain.

54

COMMUNITY SERVICE STATIONS

The transformation of the civic universities, 1898–1930

W. H. G. Armytage

Source: W. H. G. Armytage, *Civic Universities*, New York: Arno Press, 1977, pp. 243–64.

1

It is not your wonderful machinery, not even your unequalled supplies of minerals, which we have most cause to envy. It is something worth both of these combined, the class of scientific young experts you have to manage every department of your works. *We have no corresponding class in England.*

So an English steel magnate lamented to Andrew Carnegie who, amongst his many other generosities to this country, offered to give £50,000 to help the City of Birmingham to establish a university on the American model where such young experts could be trained. That he did so was largely due to the dynamic parliamentary representative of Birmingham, Joseph Chamberlain, who became the first president of the newly incorporated Mason University College in 1898. Chamberlain had first made his name as an advocate of efficient primary education: now he worked to crown the many civic schools with a civic university. At a luncheon before the first meeting of the Court of Governors of Mason University College on 13 January 1898 he said:

> To place a university in the middle of a great industrial and manufacturing population is to do something to leaven the whole mass with higher aims and higher intellectual ambitions than would otherwise be possible to people engaged entirely in trading and commercial pursuits.

He appealed for an endowment of a quarter of a million pounds, additional to the existing endowment of £235,000, so that application could be made for a charter. Birmingham responded by convening a meeting on 1 July 1898 to appoint the requisite executive, canvassing, finance, and management committees. By February of the following year the target figure was passed by £76,500. So Birmingham applied for a charter, which was sealed on 24 March 1900. It was only right and proper that Joseph Chamberlain should be the first chancellor. One of his first acts in that office was to appeal for yet another quarter of a million pounds with which to erect new buildings.

American influence was strong in the new foundation. Professors J. F. Poynting and F. W. Burstall with G. H. Kenrick, a city father, had made a special trip to the United States to investigate the teaching of applied science. Carnegie confirmed their observations that the existing buildings and apparatus of Mason College were quite inadequate as a nucleus for the new university. So Chamberlain secured from Lord Calthorpe an initial tract of twenty-five acres on the Bournbrook side of the Edgbaston Estate where the new scientific departments were to be planned. Chamberlain selected as Vice-chancellor Oliver Lodge, then Professor of Physics at Liverpool. He also chose the architect of the new buildings.

Aptly enough, the first building ready for use was the power station, where an engine was in motion by 1904. Burstall and the architect, in conjunction with the professors of mining and metallurgy, planned the layout, and captured the sympathy of Sir James Chance, a local industrialist, who endowed a chair of engineering. R. A. S. Redmayne, the Professor of Mining, conceived the idea of establishing a model coal mine within the vicinity of the main university buildings.

The marriage of university and region, so happily consummated, bred a number of new university studies, which in turn led to new faculties. Thus a degree in commerce was inaugurated under the guidance of W. J. Ashley, who was much influenced by German and American examples, and pioneer studies in economic history, public finance, accounting, and commercial law flourished under his wing. New subjects, like the biochemistry of fermentation, stemmed from the needs of the brewing industry, and these, under the capable direction of Professors Adrian J. Brown and A. R. Ling, subsequently expanded to include malting, brewing, and other fermentation processes.

Not all the studies fell into such banausic categories however. Music was stimulated by the establishment of a chair in 1904—held successively by Sir Edward Elgar and Sir Granville Bantock; philosophy by the presence of J. H. Muirhead and Walter Moberly; History by J. H. B. Masterman and C. R. Beazley; English Literature by Macneile Dixon, Churton Collins and E. de Sélincourt. Thus the Faculty of Arts grew. Thus Birmingham University set the pattern of a scientific and cultural service station, as it catered for the two million inhabitants of its area.[1]

2

The tricuspid Victoria University of Manchester fell apart under similar strains. Sympathetic detonations in Liverpool were set off by the shock of Birmingham's success. Such explosions might have been foretold as early as 1890, when Leeds and Liverpool quarrelled violently over the proposal that a chair of theology should be established, and Manchester, as the senior partner, was much offended. There were other combustible elements which accumulated over the years. Continual travelling to Manchester for meetings of examiners and of the Court of Governors was a perennial exacerbation, especially since the lay members of court felt that they were assisting the growth of Manchester rather than their own local colleges.

Liverpool was the first to move. Ramsay Muir published *A Plea for a Liverpool University* in 1901, stressing the menace of foreign competition and reiterating

> the university is the only possible vitalising force in general education, which aims at producing intelligence; it is the only possible vitalising force also for technical education, which aims at developing capacity for a particular profession.

England, he continued, had fewer universities in proportion to her population than any other civilised country except Turkey. He urged the conscious imitation of America, Germany, and Scotland and proudly advanced the claims of Liverpool to enjoy a university of the same status as Munich or Leipzig. He pointed to its existing achievements:

> the first to treat architecture as on a level with other professions by devising a university curriculum for it; one of the first to bring primary teachers under university influence; the first to attempt high commercial education; the first to bring modern science systematically to bear upon the plagues which hinder trade in tropical regions.

But Leeds, which had greatly benefited from the federal connection, did not feel strong enough to stand alone, and was therefore as anxious to continue the relationship as Liverpool was to end it. Manchester's attitude would turn the scale, and Manchester declared for abolition. So in October 1903 Manchester and Liverpool received charters, leaving Leeds as the sole member of the Victoria University. Leeds, anxious to secure the title of Yorkshire University, met opposition once more, this time from University College, Sheffield, formerly an unsuccessful applicant for inclusion in the federal scheme. Sheffield's rejection by the Victoria University, and Leeds' determination to secure a Yorkshire title, fired the leading citizens of Sheffield to emulate Birmingham, Liverpool, and Manchester, and obtain a civic university of their own. So, a year after Leeds received its charter in 1904, Sheffield too became a university.[2]

A fifth new university also won its charter in this decade. A committee of Bristol citizens was formed to obtain a charter for their university college, and the Colston Society was formed in 1899 to collect funds for it. At a governors' meeting in 1901 Percival spoke on the subject. R. B. Haldane, addressing the University College Colston Society in 1902 pointed to the rich western area which such a university could serve, and sketched the possible constitution of a West of England university on the Victoria pattern, with a court at Bristol and units at Southampton, Exeter, and Reading. The Professor of Chemistry, M. W. Travers, added his voice, pointing out that Bristol was the largest city in England without a university.

The agitation was not without effect, and in 1908 the Colston Society were informed that Henry Overton Wills, member of the tobacco family, offered £100,000 if a charter could be obtained in two years. A royal visit provided the opportunity to supplicate, and on 24 May 1909, with Henry Overton Wills as Chancellor, the University of Bristol was chartered. A link with the north was provided by the appointment of Isambard Owen, formerly principal at Newcastle, as Vice-Chancellor. But the university had been launched in troubled waters. In the years before the first world war it suffered greatly, and was saved by timely assistance from the Wills family.

Bristol, in addition to encouraging civic and industrial technologies, cultivated rural sciences. It became responsible for the administration of the Agricultural and Horticultural Research Station at Long Ashton (founded in 1903 by the National Fruit and Cider Institute) where research was carried out on problems of fruit culture, and problems of pest control were investigated. Another research station at Chipping Campden was associated with the University after 1921 and became the research centre of the fruit and vegetable canning industry in England.[3]

So discredited was the federal principle, that two emerging civic colleges at Southampton and Exeter preferred to remain autonomous.[3] Exeter Extension College was founded in 1901, and in the following year, thanks to the efforts of the Rev. Edmund Kell, the Hartley University College at Southampton was incorporated and recognised by the Treasury as worthy to receive a grant.

3

The promoters of these civic universities also played a great part in securing treasury assistance for them. In 1901 Sidney Webb, an architect of London's integrated educational system, urged

> Nothing would be more widely popular at the present time, certainly nothing is more calculated to promote National Efficiency,

than a large policy of Government aid to the highest technical colleges and universities. The statesman who first summons up courage enough to cut himself loose from official pedantries on this point, and demand a grant of half a million a year with which to establish in the United Kingdom, a dozen perfectly equipped faculties of science, engineering, economics, and modern languages would score a permanent success.[4]

Sidney Webb's advice can be best appreciated when one considers the actual amount then given by the State to the universities, £25,000, as compared to his suggested £500,000.

The volume of support for his suggestions grew steadily. Joseph Chamberlain remarked, in a trenchant letter to *The Times* on 6 November 1902, that 'university competition between states is as potent as competition in building battleships, and it is on that ground that our university conditions become of the highest possible national concern'. And when at the same time Germany was giving to one university more than the British were giving to all their universities, Chamberlain's arguments were pointed enough to hurt. Politicians like A. J. Balfour, scientists like Sir Norman Lockyer, and the university colleges themselves all combined their forces to present the case for increased subventions. University grants, they argued, were investments, since universities were agents of economic progress. The examples of America and Japan were conjured up to reinforce their case, and stimulate action.[5]

The response came in 1904, when, by a Treasury minute dated 30 March, the university grant was doubled from £27,000 to £54,000, and its allocation referred to a committee of four. This committee was to consider the necessity of 'stimulating private benevolence in the locality' and to confine its assistance to those bodies which afforded 'education of a University standard in the large centres of population'.

The most prominent member of this committee was R. B. Haldane. Not only did he coin the adjective 'civic' for the newly chartered universities, but he was constantly on guard against the proliferation of technical high schools unconnected with them. 'You cannot, without danger of partial starvation,' he told an audience, 'separate science from literature and philosophy. Each grows best in the presence of the other.'[6] And the civic universities which he so carefully nourished responded by inviting him to open their buildings and preside over some of their most important functions.

4

Three other factors worked to entangle universities with the state.[7] The first of these was the pressure of the population upon existing food supplies. By special acts of parliament in 1909 and 1910, £2,900,000 was set aside to develop agriculture, rural industries and fisheries, and a Development Commission of eight members was established to allocate these funds after consultation with the appropriate ministries.

University College, Reading (whose new buildings Haldane opened in 1906), showed the way by sending a deputation to visit three leading agricultural colleges in Canada and two in America. Expenses were defrayed by L. Sutton, a seed merchant, and Alfred Palmer, a biscuit manufacturer. The report of this deputation, published in 1910, was a challenging testament of the lead which a college could and should give in the improvement of agriculture. Though only eighteen years old at the time, this department of agriculture at Reading was the largest in any civic university, and the largest in England and Wales with the exception of Cambridge. The members of the deputation urged from their transatlantic experience that it should become 'the aggressive distributor of the best ideas and methods of agriculture', serving the 14,925 farmers in the Reading area. They continued:

> The true aim and ambition should be to build up a Department which should in effect become an Agricultural University, providing first and foremost for the needs of the great agricultural community around it.

They called for more effective co-operation with county councils, and the institution of an extension section to deal with the external work of the agricultural department. With shrewd insight, they pointed to the difficulty with which a new university in an old social order was faced. For Society, inured to neglect, was suspicious of theory and clung to the traditional ways. Looming with ever-increasing significance on the horizon were the energetic examples of the United States and Canada where a university was regarded

> as a lever to be used in numerous ways to advance the interests of civilisation. Because the University in Canada and the United States is so conspicuous a unit in the intellectual organisation of society, and because its work ministers so directly to public needs, there is far less hesitation in Canada and in the United States about the propriety of liberal State aid.[8]

The Development Commissioners caught on. A survey of the existing facilities for agricultural education and research in the United Kingdom was made and in 1911 a plan was adopted with two main objects: to create well-equipped and well-staffed institutions for prosecuting specialised research, to link these research institutes with agricultural schools on one side and farmers on the other. Both objects involved the universities. Five original research institutes for plant breeding (Cambridge), plant nutrition (Rothamsted), animal breeding (Edinburgh), animal nutrition (Cambridge and Aberdeen), and economics (Oxford) expanded to twenty-five, mostly connected with universities and under their own governing bodies. By 1931 they were receiving £185,000 a year from the Development Fund. The second object of linking these research institutes with agricultural schools involved the training of chemists, mycologists, entomologists, economists, and veterinary surgeons both for schools and for advisory centres. By 1931 the advisory centres alone were costing £85,000 a year—also from the Development Fund. And these advisory centres were divided into seventeen 'provinces'; regional needs were at last recognised. In addition to this a training scheme was adopted whereby twelve students a year were selected for special post-graduate training. So great became this organisation for the scientific study of agriculture that in 1931 an Agricultural Research Council was created by Royal Charter under the Lord President of the Council, and held its first meeting on 9 July of that year.[9]

Having planned the improvement of agriculture, the Development Commissioners turned to fisheries. Here the problem was vastly different for there was no tradition of recorded observations to be handed on. True, the *Beagle* and the *Challenger* had sailed, but they were voyagers in uncharted waters. So the Development Commission encouraged free research to build up a 'complete knowledge of the sea and the life in it'. While the Marine Biological Associations Laboratory at Plymouth, the Ministry Laboratory at Lowestoft, and two Scottish Laboratories were the main centres of such research, three civic university laboratories were also assisted: Port Erin (Liverpool), Cullercoats (Armstrong College), and Hull. The stimulating effect of these opportunities upon the biologists, and the impetus they gave towards the study of marine biology, was considerable.[10]

5

A sense of imperial responsibility undoubtedly stimulated the convening in 1912 of a Congress of the Universities of the British Empire. This congress established the Universities Bureau of the British Empire, a body intended to provide a centre of university information, and to serve as a link between the imperial universities. This developed into the Association of Universities of the British Commonwealth, and began to publish the *Universities Yearbook*. One of the results of its work has been the institution of quinquennial congresses, at which various problems are discussed. As far as Great Britain is concerned, the staff of the association act as the secretariat to the Committee of Vice-Chancellors and Principals of the Universities of Great Britain and Ireland.

At the first of these congresses, held in 1912, a suggestion was made that British universities should institute the post-graduate degree of doctor of philosophy in order to attract research students who were flocking to America and Germany. The Foreign Office strongly urged the adoption of this degree, and in 1917 the five civic universities of Manchester, Liverpool, Leeds, Sheffield, and Birmingham held a conference on the subject and agreed on a common course of action. They agreed that it would be preferable to adopt the Ph.D. as the degree desired, rather than to lower the standard of the D.Litt. or the D.Sc. A year later, their resolution was adopted by all universities except Cambridge.

The institution of the Ph.D. has enabled the civic universities to build up strong reputations in particular fields, not all of them concerned with science and technology. Perhaps the most notable example was Manchester, where under the able and energetic direction of Professor Tout, a powerful school of medieval history was created.

The Ph.D. degree did not succeed in fulfilling the hopes of its promoters. As the University Grants Committee reported in 1930:

> It is true that the institution of the Ph.D. degree has had less effect than was originally expected in the way of attracting to our Universities students from other countries, but it is perhaps not wholly to be regretted that our Universities have not had among their other serious preoccupations to improvise arrangements for dealing with a large and sudden influx of foreign students in search of some particular academic label.[11]

In the sciences, this was not surprising, in view of the intensive programme of State aid to research which other countries had been adopting since the first world war. But in the arts it was. And perhaps a reason for that might have been found in the melancholy fact that in 1925–6 all the grant-aided Universities and Colleges of Great Britain put together did not spend as much on books as the four American Universities of Illinois, Michigan, Minnesota, and North Carolina, and only a little more than Harvard and Yale.

6

We have seen how national concern for the utilitarian aspects of higher education prompted an increase in State grants to universities, how the pressure of population compelled State action to stimulate agricultural education and fisheries research, and how the growing sense of responsibility for the welfare of backward races generated a pooling of imperial university experience. But these three aspects of State assistance were completely overshadowed in 1914 by a fourth: the dominant needs of national defence.

With Germany as the national enemy, the nation found itself immediately deprived of the very materials needed to fight the war: optical glass, khaki dye, magnetos, drugs, tungsten, and zinc, so a committee was appointed under Lord Haldane to consider ways and means of supplying them.

The universities branch of the Board of Education prepared a memorandum pointing out the failure of the universities to train a sufficient number of research workers and suggesting means by which the weakness of native industries could be remedied. This memorandum was referred to a small committee presided over by Sir William M'Cormick, then chairman of the Advisory Committee on grants to universities. In 1915, when the Royal Society and other bodies waited on the Presidents of the Boards of Trade and Education, asking for 'government assistance for scientific research for industrial purposes, the establishment of closer relations between the manufacturers and scientific workers, and teachers, and the establishment of a National Chemical Advisory Committee for these purposes', the government acted boldly. A month later they established the Department of Scientific and Industrial Research, and constituted it as a Committee of the Privy Council.

The Department of Scientific and Industrial Research, designed to 'operate over the Kingdom as a whole with as little regard as possible to the Tweed or the Irish Channel', proved a very real help to the civic universities. For the Department's small advisory committee was placed under the chairmanship of Sir William M'Cormick, who had already been acting as chairman of the committee which had been advising the Board of Education since 1909, on the distribution of university grants. As chairman of both the Advisory Council of D.S.I.R. and the Committee on University Grants, he was in a position to exercise a powerful influence on university development.

For, as the White Paper (Cmd. 8005), dated 23 July 1915, declared when it established D.S.I.R.:

> it is obvious that the organisation and development of research is a matter which greatly affects the public educational systems of the Kingdom. A great part of all research will necessarily be done in Universities and Colleges which are already aided by the State, and the supply and training of a sufficient number of young persons competent to undertake research can only be secured through the public system of education.

This the Advisory Council did in three ways: by proposals for specific researches; by proposals for developing special institutions and by establishing research studentships and fellowships. Working in intimate collaboration with the Royal Society and the principal scientific and professional institutions as well as with the universities, the D.S.I.R. established a system whereby suggestions could be initiated for consideration. Some measure of public surveillance was secured by the obligation to present an annual report.[12]

At the same time, in 1916, the Consultative Committee of the Board of Education reported on the need for enlarging the output of the universities. The Committee under Sir William M'Cormick, which had been distributing grants under the aegis of the Board of Education, was now retransferred to the Treasury, and in 1919 was charged

> to enquire into the financial needs of university education in the United Kingdom and to advise the Government as to the application of any grants that may be made by Parliament towards meeting them.

And, symbolising both the insufficiency of private endowments to meet the tasks ahead and the need for a national stimulus of scientific research in all available universities, Oxford and Cambridge accepted grants from the University Grants Committee.

The choice of Sir William M'Cormick to chair both the University Grants Committee and the Advisory Council of D.S.I.R. until his death in 1930 was significant, for the work of the latter bore enormously upon the universities.

Fundamental research under the creative guidance of professors was encouraged, especially by Sir George Beilby. This policy was implemented in three main directions: first by the distribution of maintenance grants to young researchers; secondly by the award of more senior grants, which in 1928–9 were consolidated into Senior Research Awards, equivalent to university fellowships in status and tenure; lastly, by direct grants to heads of departments and senior lecturers for research with an immediate application, but needing assistance from outside.

The Advisory Council of D.S.I.R. were also responsible for the consideration of the need of special institutions. Since both the National Physical Laboratory and the Geological Survey came under its control after 1920, it was in a special position to co-ordinate scientific research. It advised the creation of a Fuel Research Board, established in 1917 with Sir George Beilby as Director, and a Fuel Research Station, established at Greenwich a year later. In 1918 too the Food Investigation Board was established under W. B. Hardy, and in 1919 a Low Temperature Research Station was established at the University of Cambridge to study problems of refrigeration. In 1920 a Building Research Board was established, in 1921 a Forest Products Research Board, in 1922 a Chemistry Research Board, and in 1927 a Water Pollution Research Board. These boards, though they possessed their own laboratories, stimulated collateral research in a number of universities. Forestry at Oxford, the Imperial College, and St. Andrews; and the colloids of sewage by University College, London, were notable cases in point.

Like a beneficent deity, D.S.I.R. moved in a mysterious way its wonders to perform. Sometimes it co-operated with a specialist body, like the

Institute of Metals (founded in 1908) in order to finance research into a particular problem such as the corrosion of aluminium and other non-ferrous metals. Sometimes it relinquished control of a specific technology to a university. This was notably the case in Glass Technology, which it encouraged Sheffield to develop as a speciality.

Following the channels it created was the fount of charity controlled by the Livery Companies of London, who were anxious to stimulate industrial expertise. To the new Department of Glass Technology at Sheffield, the Worshipful Company of Glaziers contributed; while the Clothworkers having already built and equipped the Department of Textiles and Colour Dyeing at the University of Leeds, continued to give an annual endowment of £10,000. The latter also gave a further £7,000 a year to the City and Guilds Engineering College and other sums to technical colleges all over the country. The Drapers, by numerous gifts to universities throughout the country, were responsible amongst other things, for the buildings of the Applied Science Laboratories at Sheffield University and those of Queen Mary College in the University of London. Both University and King's College in the same university received substantial aid from them. The Fishmongers helped, amongst other bodies, the University College of Hull. The Goldsmiths endowed both the Library and the college which bear their name at the University of London. The Ironmongers founded fellowships and scholarships at Sheffield University. The Skinners helped to endow the Leather Department of the University of Leeds. The Armourers and Brasiers offered prizes and certificates for technical students at Sheffield University. The Founders endowed research and study, chiefly at King's College, London. The Paviours founded in 1928 a part-time professorship of Highway Engineering at the Imperial College in 1928. The Cutlers, amongst their numerous benefactions, have maintained scholarships and exhibitions at Oxford and Cambridge.[13]

The flow of students and research workers to the universities was also materially sustained by the cumulative charity of a number of public bodies. The Board of Education, by its award of grants for further education and training to ex-service men, made 26,000 awards in the immediate post-war years to enable students to resume their university courses. In addition, a system of State scholarships was established in 1921 enabling the more promising pupils of grammar schools to proceed to universities with their fees paid and a generous maintenance allowance. The Local Education Authorities also co-operated by instituting a similar system of awards.

7

There was yet another service for which the universities were paid by the State—Medical Research. As a result of the Insurance Act of 1911 the Medical Research Committee was established in 1913 from funds derived from the contributions of insured persons. This source of revenue sustained it for six years until 1919 when it was reorganised as the Medical Research Council and placed, like D.S.I.R., under the Privy Council with funds voted directly by Parliament. These funds have been supplemented from time to time by grants from public bodies and private benefactors, and a third of its income is devoted to the National Institute for Medical Research at Hampstead.

The other two-thirds of its funds sustain various researches conducted in hospitals and universities throughout the country. Pathology, Bacteriology, Optics, Microphotography, Biochemistry, Pharmacology, Applied Physiology, and Hygiene have all benefited from the grants so received from the Medical Research Council. It also awards travelling fellowships.

Sub-committees, composed of medical and scientific workers from all over the country, have been set up to examine specific problems of nutrition, mental disorders, tuberculosis, radiology, anaesthetics, epidemics, and many others, while special attention is devoted, through an Industrial Health Research Board, to the problems of working conditions in modern factories. As the Prince of Wales truly said in his presidential address to the British Association in 1926:

> There can surely be no plainer duty, for a State charged with the health of an industrial civilisation, than to promote with all its resources the search for such knowledge as this, as well as to provide for its application when obtained.

8

'I have sometimes thought,' wrote Sidney Webb in 1904, 'that the dwindling Arts faculty would be saved, even without its reform, by the inrush of teachers.'[14] He was right. The 1902 Act, of which he was so efficient, if invisible, an architect, created both a demand for qualified teachers for the new secondary schools which the universities alone could satisfy, and a reservoir of talent upon which the universities were to draw so much that the very curricula of those schools were oriented towards their matriculation requirements. In 1902 36 per cent. of existing teachers had never passed the examination for the teachers' certificate and 55 per cent. had never been to a training college of any kind.

All the civic university colleges had possessed 'day training colleges' since 1890. These were designed to help primary school teachers acquire degrees, and survived until 1911. They were superseded because they combined professional training and the degree course to the detriment of the degree course. After 1911 a four-year course was instituted in which the intending teacher took three years for a degree and one for professional training. This professional year was tested by the award of a Board of Education certificate. A third change gave more responsibility to the universities when in 1926 the Board allowed diplomates of the education departments to obtain their certificate without a further examination. In that year too, the universities were endowed with representation on the newly created Regional Boards, set up to examine non-university trained teachers from the training colleges, and thus to influence their curriculum as well. Some results of this latter relationship meant yet more university students, for where the training colleges were near enough to be affiliated to their regional universities, students were allowed to become undergraduates. Durham was notable in this respect, recruiting students from Bede College, St. Hild's, and Neville's Cross. London University also incorporated Goldsmiths' College for a similar purpose.

The low financial status of teachers, who always struggled against inadequate salaries, proved a deterrent to many aspirants for university courses. As late as 1914 a male certificated teacher received only £129 per annum and his woman counterpart £96. In 1917, however, H. A. L. Fisher, called from the Vice-Chancellorship of the University of Sheffield to be President of the Board of Education, obtained an increased exchequer contribution towards the cost of teachers' salaries. Two years later in 1919, he established a committee under Lord Burnham which established national scales of remuneration for primary teachers. Other committees did similarly for secondary and technical teachers till by 1921 a series of scales was in operation. These scales, together with the increasing amenities offered by the schools, did much to attract university students to accept what was informally known as the 'pledge', i.e. they undertook a university degree course, financed by the Board of Education, under the obligation of accepting appointments at the end of their course.

The economic troubles of 1926 and the further crisis of 1931 tended to divert even more of the secondary school pupils towards universities, since other avenues were closed. The attraction of an established superannuation system, established in 1918 and 1925, and based on a pension proportionate to length of service and status, did much to create a feeling that in an insecure economic world, the teacher was at least insured.

Indeed it is not too much to say that the civic universities in their struggling years, and the university colleges all along, owed the very existence of their arts faculties and in many cases their pure science faculties to the presence of a large body of intending teachers whose attendance at degree courses was almost guaranteed by the state.

9

With such stimuli, the growth of the civic universities was remarkable. London became almost the embodiment of Haldane's dream: a great imperial university covering every aspect of human knowledge. Though the Davey

Commissioners had not included the four schools of music, nor the four Inns of Court, they had reconstituted twenty-four other colleges as schools of the University of London. These were University College, King's College, six colleges in the Faculty of Theology, two women's colleges (Holloway and Bedford), the Royal College of Science, the South East Agricultural College, the ten medical schools of the great London Hospitals, the Central Technical College, and the London School of Economics.

To these twenty-four were added another eleven during the period 1902–25: Westfield (1902), the London School of Tropical Medicine (1905), the East London College (1909), University College Hospital Medical School (1909), the London Day Training College (1910), the Royal Dental Hospital School (1911), Birkbeck College (1920), and the School of Pharmacy (1925). The Royal Army Medical College and the Royal Naval Medical School were admitted to the Faculty of Medicine in 1908 and 1913 respectively.

Haldane's vision of a great metropolitan university, offering advanced instruction to students in every field of human endeavour seemed to materialise at last. Research Institutions like the Lister (1905), the School of Oriental Studies (1918), the Institute of Historical Research (1921), the Maudsley Hospital and Bethlem Royal Hospital (1924), the Cancer Hospital (1927), grew up under its wing. New degrees were established in Engineering and Economics (1903), Agriculture (1905), Commerce (1919), Horticulture (1918), Household and Social Science (1920), and Estate Management (1921). Diplomas in a yet wider range of subjects were offered in Education, Geography, Theology, Anthropology, Archaeology, Bacteriology, Biology, Fine Art, Journalism, Librarianship, Psychology, Public Administration, Slavonic Studies, Sociology, Town Planning and Civic Architecture, and the network of extension classes covered every field of human endeavour.

To administer this vast congeries of colleges, research institutions, and classes, a central administrative building was needed, and in 1920 the government offered the university $11(\frac{1}{2})$ acres of land in Bloomsbury, on condition that King's College moved there and sold their site to the Government. King's refused, so the Government sold the land back to the vendor. Seven years later, thanks to a grant from the Rockefeller trustees, the university were able to buy the land on their own terms, and throw up the functional crag that now towers over the British Museum and Russell Square. That it should face Boyle's house in Southampton Row, and Cavendish's on the corner of Montague Street and Gower Street, was apt acknowledgement of its intellectual patrimony.

Yet the most difficult institution for the University of London to digest was the Imperial College of Science. This, an amalgamation of the former Royal College of Science, the Royal School of Mines, and the Central Technical College, was intended for advanced teaching and research in technology. Architect of the scheme was Sidney Webb's spiritual agent in politics: R. B. Haldane. He not only induced the L.C.C. to promise an annual grant of £20,000, but chaired a Departmental Committee of the Board of Education appointed in 1904 whose report suggested the amalgamation. Its establishment was accelerated by the will of Alfred Beit, which provided some £60,000 for the purpose. Chartered in 1907, the Imperial College of Science and Technology developed a strong antagonism to the University of London, and many of the teachers and students campaigned for a separate university. So a Royal Commission was appointed under Haldane, which sat from 1909 until 1913. In the latter year a Departmental Committee was established to execute its recommendations. But the War put an end to its activity, and it was not until 1924 that another Departmental Committee was appointed, after a controversy that raged through the correspondence columns of *The Times*. This in turn reported in 1926, recommending the now familiar engine of a statutory commission. This, established by the University of London Act of that year, drafted new statutes which came into operation on 21 March 1929.

These statutes welded the University of London into an administrative whole under a Court, to whom the grant-giving bodies like the University Grants Committee and the London County Council made block grants for subsequent distribution to individual institutions. And one of the first and most important tasks of this newly established Court was to concentrate the University around Bloomsbury, where a self-contained estate had been secured by the financial assistance of the Rockefeller Foundation (which gave £400,000 for the purpose in 1927) and the administrative assistance of the London County Council (which allowed certain roadways to be enclosed).

10

As London University tended to nucleate around Bloomsbury, so the provincial universities and university colleges tended to develop communities, usually, however, on the periphery of the towns which nourished them. This removal, as it were, from the traffic of busy cities was accompanied by a corresponding widening of intellectual perspectives. Birmingham seemed to have set the example in 1900 by its Edgbaston estate which more than doubled in size throughout the period by adding in the decade after the war, new buildings to accommodate departments of Botany, Brewing, Zoology, and Oil Engineering. Thanks to a generous gift by the Anstruther-Gough-Calthorpe family, another 41 acres was added to this estate, and plans were drawn for the transfer of the two main Birmingham Hospitals to an adjacent site. Leeds also embarked in 1924 on the rehousing of their entire university, and, in response to a public appeal, obtained a magnificent endowment for a new library from Sir Edward Brotherton. Reading, which received its charter in 1926, acquired a further 20 acres of land.

And when, in 1926, the University of Reading received its charter, it became the ninth degree-giving university. Since its inspection by the

Treasury Commissioners in 1901, Reading had held the status of a university college. Four years later after moving into a new and extensive site, it developed two characteristic features under its persevering and energetic principal W. M. Childs. The first was its department of Agriculture which was expanded to embrace Horticulture in 1907, and elevated to the status of a faculty in 1913. The second was its early and steady development of halls of residence—a new thing in the civic universities.

University Colleges followed suit. Exeter acquired a hundred acres of land on the outskirts of the city to which they planned to transfer their existing urban departments. Southampton built itself into the framework of Wessex, establishing a chair of music amongst other things, and acquiring a fine old house, once the property of the Sloane family, as a men's hostel. For Nottingham, Jesse Boot did what the Wills family had done for Bristol: building a magnificent group of new departments at Highfields, three miles from the city. These three became, in a very real sense, regional service stations, even though their degrees were awarded by the University of London.

In 1922 a fourth university college was founded for Leicestershire and Rutland, and rechristened University College, Leicester, in 1927. A fifth college was promoted in 1926 at Hull, and formally incorporated under the Companies Act of 1929 as 'an institution for the promotion, in all their branches, of higher learning, science, the arts and knowledge in general'. Its governing body consisted of representatives of the Royal Society, the British Association, the Law Society, the Dental Association, the Royal Institute of British Architects, the Pharmaceutical Society, the Trades Council, the Co-operative Movement, the Free Churches, the Urban Districts and County Councils. So comprehensive were the professional and political needs which new universities were supposed to satisfy! In their articles of association, the promoters frankly acknowledged that their purpose was

> To establish, organise and maintain classes and lectures . . . for the purpose of promoting education and research, and to provide instruction in such branches of education as shall be required for the training of entrants to the learned, teaching and technical professions, industry and commerce, and in such other branches of education as shall from time to time be directed by the managing Body or Bodies.
>
> To grant diplomas of merit and efficiency.
>
> To act in conjunction with, and to receive grants from, and co-operate with any University, Institute, College, School, Society or Association whose objects are altogether or in part similar to those of the Association.
>
> To co-operate with and receive grants from and make arrangements with County Councils, City and Borough Councils, Educational Societies and Committees, Railway Companies, and other

public bodies, with a view to promoting and forwarding all or any of the objects of the Association.

No better definition of a community service station could have been conceived at that time.

This University College, endowed with a quarter of a million pounds by T. R. Ferens (who had also presented an Institute of Otology to the University of London) also received £150,000 from the Corporation of Kingston-upon-Hull and a site of 18½ acres. Foundations were formally laid on 28 April 1928, and plans were envisaged for a university of nearly two thousand students. But the immediate advances were, in their way, solid. For by collaboration with the local technical college, a diploma in aeronautics for aircraft designers was developed, and, with government help, a special scheme of fisheries research was inaugurated.

11

Though the nine universities and five university colleges developed during this period into vital cores of their respective regions, there was a strong current of feeling that they should and could develop even more. Patrick Geddes called for a great renewal along Baconian lines, in which 'the university militant, affirmative, selective, predictive' was to play a leading rôle:

> the reawakening movement of the universities has been slow, timid, blindfold, because lacking in civic vision. Now, therefore is urgent an arousal of the universities to their spiritual responsibilities for the fullness of life in all its phases, individual and social. In every region is needed a comprehensive working together of city and university on each plane of the ascending spiral from home to humanity.[15]

Geddes saw clearly that the domination of English universities by the Germanic idea of complete objectivity should be overthrown. To him, regional capitals each had responsibilities to their respective regions: Newcastle to North England, Manchester and Liverpool to Lancashire, Leeds to Yorkshire, Sheffield to Peakdon, Birmingham to the Severn area, Nottingham to Trent, Southampton to Wessex, Norwich to East Anglia, Oxford to Central England, Plymouth to Devon, and London and Bristol to their own environs. Response to the specialised needs of each of these areas would, he argued, revitalise the curricula of the universities in these capitals. And to enable the regions to be adequately served in this respect, he proposed further universities at Plymouth, Norwich, and Northampton.

Geddes and his disciples wrote before the foundation of Hull or Leicester University Colleges, and their views, tinged by admiration of mid-western universities in Wisconsin and Michigan, provoked derision in more orthodox academic circles. Yet there were some, even among the orthodox, who agreed that the march of American mind had far outpaced anything accomplished in England. Ramsay Muir, for instance, cited the example of Iowa, which, with a population of two millions, sustained as many universities as all England: the State University being larger than both Oxford and Cambridge combined. Ramsay Muir commented on the respect for scientific methods of enquiry which pervaded all branches of American life, the 'immense facilities for research in every subject bearing upon industry', and the sustained output of great numbers of employable university graduates.[16]

All this, Ramsay Muir regretfully concluded, had a most important social consequence: 'the absence of that acute class feeling which is today one of the chief obstacles to progress in England.' But he lamented in vain. The liberalism of his own youth had lost the power to animate, much less to endow, similar institutions in England; while his own warnings were derided by the disillusioned generation of the late twenties. This generation's viewpoint was well expressed by Aldous Huxley in *Point Counterpoint*, where the 'easiness' of a life devoted to erudition, scientific research, philosophy, or criticism was mocked:

> It's the substitution of simple intellectual schemata for the complexities of reality: of still and formal death for the bewildering movements of life. . . . The intellectual's life is child's play; which is why intellectuals tend to become children—and then imbeciles and finally, as the political and industrial history of the last few centuries clearly demonstrates, homicidal lunatics and wild beasts.

Mark Rampion, one of the vocal ideologues of the novel, was a graduate of Sheffield University, who by marrying above his class, emancipates himself from what he regards as the fate of most of his fellow students. 'Teaching, teaching,' he exclaims to his wife-to-be, 'does it surprise you that I should feel depressed?' His talents lead him into art and journalism, and one of Huxley's most expressive satires on the contemporary world emerges in a description of Rampion's drawing 'Fossils of the Past and Fossils of the future'. In this, J. J. Thomson and other intellectual leaders of the time, are depicted as marching towards extinction. 'And a damned good thing too,' Rampion comments, 'only the trouble is they're marching the rest of the world along with them.'[17]

12

It was during this very period that the University of Manchester was fostering the most significant scientific research of modern times: the concept of the nucleus of the atom. The pioneer in this field was Ernest Rutherford, a brilliant New Zealander and the first postgraduate student to work at the Cavendish Laboratory in 1895. After experiments there with another old Manchester student, J. J. Thomson, on the ionisation of gases he was elected to the chair of physics at McGill University, Montreal, where he put forward the theory of spontaneous atomic disintegration leading to the discovery of isotopes.

Rutherford's election to the Langworthy chair of physics at Manchester, which he held from 1907 to 1919, marked another step forward in atomic research: that of the nucleus of the atom, which stemmed from his experiments on the scattering of α particles (doubly ionised helium ions). By utilising these particles to bombard nitrogen and thereby change it into an isotope of oxygen, he made the wildest dream of the alchemists come true.

By so doing, Rutherford opened vast and illimitable vistas. Not only did he help to endow mankind with a new prime mover, destined to react as powerfully on society as electricity had done in the previous century, but he helped to fashion another powerful inquisitor of nature. He stood at the gates of a new era, just as Faraday did a century before him. And it was but fitting that when, in 1930, the chairmanship of the Advisory Council of the Department of Scientific and Industrial Research fell vacant, he should be appointed to the post.[18]

References

1. AMERY, Julian, *Life of Joseph Chamberlain* (London, 1951), iv, 209–21.
    VINCENT, Eric W. and HINTON, Percival, *The University of Birmingham* (Birmingham, 1947), 29. For the influence of America in Educational circles see R. H. Heindel, *The American Impact on Great Britain* (Philadelphia, 1940), 273–98; and *Special Reports on Educational Subjects* (H.M.S.O., 1902), ii, 419–32.
2. See *Case for the Liverpool University Committee* and *Case and Appendix of the Yorkshire College, Leeds.* R. B. Haldane, on p. 78 of the former petition, argued that Leeds and Sheffield should constitute a Yorkshire University. It is interesting that soon afterwards, in 1906, W. H. Owen should present detailed proposals to the city council for the establishment of a university at Hull. For insights into the ideals of civic university teachers at this time see A. Smithells, *From a Modern University* (Oxford, 1921), and Ramsay Muir, *An Autobiography and Some Essays* (London, 1943).
3. COTTLE, B., and SHERBORNE, J. W., *The Life of a University* (Bristol, 1951), 1–36.
4. Fabian Tract No. 108, also published in the *Nineteenth Century* for September, 1901.
5. For Lockyer's efforts, and those of the British Science Guild, see T. M. Lockyer, *Life and Work of Sir Norman Lockyer* (London, 1928), 184–93.
6. *Education and Empire* (1902), 32–3, 85. See also *An Autobiography* (London, 1929), in which Haldane wrote (p. 90): 'By this time [1902] I had come to see that what we needed badly in our own country was more universities and universities of the civic type, in different parts of these islands. Turning to these matters, one of the first of the new university movements on which I set to work

was that in Liverpool. . . . I addressed the men of business of the city in a speech . . . warning them of their peril from German rivalry if they continued to neglect science and education. Liverpool made a splendid response. I also worked hard at London and at Bristol, where the university was ultimately founded of which I am now Chancellor.'

Haldane was elected Chancellor of the University of Bristol in 1912, and his inaugural address emphasises this theme.

7. The precedent was set by the establishment of the National Physical Laboratory in 1902, which grew out of the work of the British Association's Committee on Standards, formed to provide industries with accurate methods of measurement and grading. This played an important part in the evolution of mass-production. The then Prince of Wales said at its opening: 'I believe that in the National Physical Laboratory we have almost the first instance of the State taking part in scientific research . . . to bring scientific knowledge to bear practically upon our everyday industrial and commercial life, to break down the barrier between theory and practice, to effect a union between science and commerce.'

8. *The Problem of Agricultural Education in America and England with Special Reference to a Policy of Developing the work . . . at University College, Reading* (Reading, 1910).

9. COMBES, N. M., *Agricultural Education in Great Britain* (London, 1948).

10. See the Reports of the Development Commission.

11. *Report of the University Grants Committee* (1930).

12. HEATH, H. F., and HETHERINGTON, A. L., *Industrial Research and Development in the United Kingdom* (London, 1946), 251–6. In fairness to the champions of the humanities, it must be said that they were most active at this time. On 4 May 1916 a letter appeared in *The Times*, replying to that of the scientist's on 2 February, under the title 'Educational Aims and Methods', and urging a proper balance in the curriculum. The Classical, English, Geographical, Historical, and Modern Language Associations took up the matter, and with the co-operation of the British Academy, formed the Council for Humanistic Studies which met the representatives of the scientific bodies to draft seven resolutions in January 1917. For a detailed account of these discussions see I. L. Kandel, *Education in Great Britain and Ireland*, U.S. Bureau of Education, Bulletin (1919), 47ff.

13. HEATH and HETHERINGTON, *op. cit.*, 307–10.

14. WEBB, Sidney, *London Education* (London, 1904), 81.

15. GEDDES, P., and BRANFORD, V., *The Coming Polity* (London, 1917, 2nd ed., 1919), 214–15, 343, and C. B. Fawcett, *The Provinces of England* (London, 1919).

16. MUIR, Ramsay, *America the Golden: An Englishman's Notes and Comparisons* (London, 1927), 27–31. This should be contrasted with the judicious endorsement of the 'structural efficiency' of English universities to be found in William S. Learned, *The Quality of the Educational Process in the United States and in Europe* (New York, 1927).

17. Aldous Huxley was thinking of D. H. Lawrence, a former student of Nottingham who died in 1930. He published an edition of Lawrence's letters in 1932.

18. EVE, A. S., *Rutherford* (1939), 163–266.

55

THE ADMISSION OF POOR MEN

Lord Curzon of Kedleston

Source: Lord Curzon of Kedleston, *Principles and Methods of University Reform*, Oxford: Clarendon Press, 1909, pp. 42–75.

ints
ass-
tion
rd
ty.

Constitutional questions, however, are of greater moment to the inner world of Oxford, which realizes their importance, than they can be to the outside public, which is less concerned with machinery than with results. Of all the criticisms passed upon modern Oxford, none can compare in the earnestness, amounting often to vehemence, with which it is urged, or in the interest which it excites, than the complaint that neither the education, the endowments, nor the social advantages of the University are sufficiently open to the man of humble means. This charge is often couched in somewhat rhetorical language. We are told that Oxford is a place where the standard of living is high, and that of learning low; that it is the resort of idlers and loafers; that its endowments, intended for the poor, are wasted upon those who do not require them; that it is out of touch with the main system of national education, of which it ought to be the apex and crown; and that it is, in fact, the University of the leisured classes instead of the nation. Even Bishop Gore did not shrink from describing it in the House of Lords as 'a playground for the sons of the wealthier classes', and as 'not in any serious sense a place of study at all'. I have quoted the above phrases all of which are taken from recent speeches or writings on the subject, because they condense in picturesque form impressions which are widely and, no doubt, honestly held on the subject, and because neither shall we convince our critics unless we close with their charges, nor shall we be able to amend ourselves unless we know of what it is that we are accused.

me
on
o.

It is an illustration both of the vitality and the complexity of the problem that precisely the same complaints were before the Commissioners of 1850, and that many pages of their Report, and no small number of their recommendations, were devoted to its solution. The fact that the charge still survives is no proof that their diagnosis was wrong or that their remedies have failed. On the contrary, it will be easy to show that in many directions conspicuous progress has been made in opening the resources of Oxford to the classes referred to; while any one familiar with recent history will know that there is at the present time a preponderance of opinion in the University in favour of such further advance as may be required. A comparison of the present situation with that of 1850 will be useful rather as indicating how the problem has itself changed, in consequence of the immense political and intellectual upheaval that has marked the last half-century, and perhaps also as reminding us that we are dealing with social and economic conditions that will not invariably or mutely yield to paper reforms.

Views and proposals of the Commission of 1850. The Commissioners of 1850 deliberately declined to cater for the poor as such. The poor man for whom they sought to provide must satisfy two conditions before he could profit by their sympathy. He must 'have received the previous training indispensable for an academic career'; and his education must be such as would qualify him for the service of 'the State or the Church'. In other words, they contemplated enabling the poor man, who had the requisite ability, to become a clergyman or to fill any public or professional office; but they were more concerned in helping real ability than they were in compensating real poverty. The remedial measures proposed by them—notably the argument for open Scholarships—bore the impress of this idea. Indeed, in abolishing the limitation imposed upon many Scholarships in respect of particular schools or localities or of founder's kin, they indirectly legislated against the poorer classes, preferring the advantage of a higher standard of scholastic attainment to the mitigation of poverty as such. Now that Oxford has ceased to be a training ground mainly for the Anglican Church, and that social classes are knocking at the door who were then content to remain outside, the question of the admission of the poor has assumed a very different aspect. The other remedial measures discussed or proposed by the Commissioners of 1850 either failed of their object or were not attended with the desired results, in some cases because academic opinion was half-hearted or divided upon them, in others because no action was taken on those sections of the Report. Thus the Commission advised

Affiliated Halls, Independent Halls, Lodgings. against the experiment of Affiliated Halls conducted on cheaper terms (a scheme which again finds favour with some modern reformers), partly because of the cost of building, but mainly because they dreaded the revival of social distinctions in the University based on wealth and poverty. They were also distrustful of the plan of Independent Halls, though willing that the experiment should be tried. They thought that life in lodgings connected with the Colleges, as widely practised at Cambridge, was worthy of trial but would not materially reduce the cost of living. They recommended, however, that students should be allowed to become members of the University without becoming members of a College or Hall, but living in private houses under the superintendence either of Colleges or of responsible individuals—at a cost which they estimated at £200 for a four years' course—a suggestion which was the direct parent of the Non-Collegiate system, though it did not take practical shape till many years later, in 1868. Thus the action of the Commission of 1850, while useful to us in indicating the permanent difficulties of the question, leaves us with the general impression that it has now to be examined afresh, in the light of more modern experience.

For a time after the events of 1850–54 the subject would appear to have languished. Mark Pattison frankly criticized the system of open Scholarships on the ground that they had become mere educational prizes and did not provide for the poor man; but he was averse from creating a class of poor men holding special Exhibitions with a poverty qualification, His solution was the Non-Collegiate, or, as he called it, the 'lodging-out' system; but he attached more importance to raising the character and reputation of the teachers—as a means of widening the circle to which Oxford should appeal—than to any expedients for recruiting a larger number of students. When Jowett wrote his Memorandum in 1874, the problem of the poor was identified by him with the problem of University Extension—as the phrase afterwards came to be employed—i. e. with the foundation of colleges and lectureships in the large towns. The Commission of 1877–82—apart from the organization created for Non-Collegiate students—did not deal with the matter directly at all. Views of later reformers.

In more recent times the discussion of the question has suffered from the defect that little or no attempt has been made to distinguish between the various classes to whom the term 'poor' has been generically applied. All sections of the community below the richer middle classes—all sections, in fact, who require some assistance to enable their sons to partake of an Oxford education—have been lumped together under a single designation; and the failure of many of the plans proposed has been due to the fact that measures suitable to one section have been wholly unsuited to another. Further, the economic changes in modern society necessitate a more scientific distinction; for the middle and professional classes who could legitimately be called poor half a century ago are now much wealthier, and adopt a higher standard of living; while the classes who may now fairly be described as poor did not at that time aspire to a University course. Present aspect of the problem.

Before, however, we proceed to analyse the needs of the present day, there are certain anterior propositions for which I should like to claim acceptance, and the neglect of which appears to me to have been a source of very common error. The first is this. In opening the University to the poor, we do not wish to close it to the rich. In providing assistance to the man who cannot come without it, we must equally consider the man who requires no such aid. Indeed, in a sense he is indispensable to the former, for without his pecuniary contribution to the University there would not be that surplus, without which the University and Colleges in combination could not pay their way. Oxford is not now, and never has been, a purely eleemosynary institution. It exists not merely for the purpose of helping the poor to make their way in the world, but for giving that broad and liberal Claims of the well-to-do as well as the poor.

79

education, which has always been associated with its name, to rich and poor alike. It is from the free and happy mingling of both classes in a society than which there is none in the world more exempt from aristocratic temper or prejudice, that the glory and the benefit of Oxford spring. Without the amenities with which the wealth of earlier benefactors has endowed it, and which some portion of its existing means are required to maintain, without the refinement that springs from the enjoyment of those resources, and without the good fellowship and mutual respect that are born of contact between men of different stations and upbringing, not merely in the lecture room or examination hall, but in the quadrangle, the college garden, the debating society, the playing field, and on the river, Oxford could never have fulfilled its mission and could not now fulfil it to the nation. If by some ukase the doors of the University were to be closed to-morrow to the prosperous and well-to-do, and were to be opened only to those of humble means, two results would inevitably ensue. Firstly, the intellectual standard would be lowered; and secondly, the University would in truth become the University not of the nation but of a section of it, and the first to discover and to lament this fact would be the poorer classes themselves.

Duty of Oxford to the leisured classes.   Further, in educating the so-called upper classes, may we not claim that Oxford is fulfilling a duty every whit as national and as imperial as in stretching her resources to the uttermost for the assistance of the poor? Much denunciation has been heaped, ever since Mark Pattison's day, upon the wealthy pass-man, who is supposed to devote to sport all the time that he can spare from the neglect of learning. In so far as he is convicted of idleness let him be taken in hand and reformed. There will be more to be said upon that head later on. But in so far as he represents a particular stratum in the national life it is important that he too should not be denied the advantages of a University course. It is as desirable that Oxford should educate the future country squire, or nobleman, or banker, or member of Parliament, or even the guardsman, as it is that it should sharpen the wits of the schoolmaster or the cultivated artisan. Without endorsing the popular cant about the 'governing classes', we know that the former type may be, and often is, called upon to take a prominent part in public life, and he is immeasurably better fitted to do so by the experience that he has undergone and the equipment that he has received at Oxford or at Cambridge. Such men do not impede the real work of the University, they do not prevent a single scholar or a single poor man from matriculating; they are better situated under a relatively strict discipline at Oxford than if they were let loose upon the world. Indeed, we have only to look to foreign countries, where the sons of the richer classes are in too many cases leading lives of irresponsible frivolity or dissipation, but where many an envious eye is cast upon the system that is here so frequently assailed, to realize that we have in our old Universities a mechanism for training the well-to-do to a sense of responsibility and a capacity for public affairs which it would be the height of folly to throw away.

The second proposition upon which I would venture is that the standard of living at Oxford, and indeed at any academic institution, is primarily created by the majority of the students who frequent it. It may be that economies are possible in College management and administration, and this too is a subject that will call for discussion; for extravagance is as unnecessary in the case of the well-to-do as it is oppressive in the case of the poor. But no curtailment of expenditure that is capable of being effected, no redistribution of wealth that might take place, can permanently bring down the Collegiate system of living at Oxford, differing as it does *toto coelo* from the practice of Scotch or German Universities, to the level of economy that is possible in those places. The inestimable advantages of the College system, with its associations of mingled tenderness and pride, and the moral influence of its society and training, cannot be had without paying a certain price for them. Even the plant, in use for six months of the year alone, requires to be maintained. But it is not the University or the Colleges in the main that fix this standard. It is determined even more by the pocket-money furnished by the parent to his son, by the atmosphere of comfort from which he proceeds at home, and to which he returns for his vacation, and by the tone of clubs and societies, in the formation of which the University, as an academic institution, plays no part. The University can do two things to alleviate the incidence of what is sometimes felt as a burden by the poorer classes. It can create special opportunities or facilities (by the use of its endowments and otherwise) for enabling them to participate to the fullest extent in the advantages that are more easily accessible to the well-to-do; and it can wage war against superfluous luxury. But as long as the community at large becomes wealthier and more prosperous—as it is doing from day to day—so long is it certain that its scale of living will be reflected in those Universities and public schools which enlist its confidence; and the extreme critics might more fairly preach their crusade in the drawing-rooms of society than in the common-rooms of Oxford.

Subject to these reservations, which I think should be present in our minds, and which the experience of the past, in spite of half a century of reformatory efforts, is sufficient to establish, I hope that we may, in again considering the claims of the poor, do so with the most earnest desire to extend and amplify the work of our predecessors, and, if necessary, to build upon new foundations.

We may differentiate between the social strata with whom we are now called upon to deal according to their occupation or their earlier education. If we adopt the former test we shall place in one category the industrial or wage-earning or artisan class, popularly known as the 'working-man', and in another category the professional class in its many ramifications. The distinction between these two may be otherwise expressed (with substantial

[margin note: Standard of living.]

[margin note: Duty of Oxford to the poor.]

[margin note: Different classes of the poor.]

accuracy) as that between the men who wish to remain in their order, but desire a University education as a means of raising themselves within it, and the men who hope by means of a University education to rise in the social as well as in the intellectual scale. If we apply the educational test, we shall place on the one side those who, owing to the necessities of a wage-earning life, have probably had no education since they left the Elementary School; on the other side those who have passed through both the Primary and Secondary Schools and have come to Oxford assisted by the many Exhibitions and Scholarships which are open to students in those circumstances. In either case the distinction between the two classes is fundamental. The University, in my judgment, will fail in its duty to the nation—of which both are powerful and indispensable elements—if it does not endeavour to provide with equal anxiety and liberality for both; but it will require to provide for them by different means.

Needs of the working-classes

The Working-Classes. I will begin with the case of the wage-earning classes; and herein my task is much simplified by the labours of the Joint Committee of representatives of the University and of working-class organizations which sat last year, and whose singularly able and attractive report was issued in December, 1908. They deal with one facet only of the problem which we are here discussing, but it is perhaps the most important.

Nature of their appeal to Oxford. It is clear that for the first time since their appearance as a political force, and largely in consequence of it, many of the working-classes of this country are looking with eager eyes to Oxford to assist them in the task of preparation for their new and arduous responsibilities. Their feeling towards the older Universities is no longer one of hostility, though some suspicion, which it is fortunately in our power to disperse, may here and there exist; the cry to disestablish and disendow is not loudly heard. They turn to Oxford, not because they are enamoured of its beauty or romance— although those of them who have already entered into residence are far from being indifferent to these attractions—but because they associate its name with that liberal and humane scheme of mental training which no modern or provincial University can give to them, but which they regard as indispensable for the part that they desire to play in the national life; and perhaps still more because they think that they have an indefeasible right to share in a great national inheritance.

The nature of the service which they ask of Oxford is equally clear. They are under no illusion as to their own shortcomings. The extension of the franchise, participation in local government, and the increasing influence of trade organizations have given them power, but power unaccompanied by knowledge. This knowledge, which an education arrested at the primary stage is unable to furnish, can alone enable them to wield their power for

in Oxford society and are seldom seen in College rooms. The fact is that the attempt to furnish them with a College organization cannot compensate for the absence of College buildings and the exclusion from College life. The endurance of the collegiate ideal is indeed one of the most remarkable and the most eloquent features of modern Oxford. For it reveals to us the real secret of the Oxford spell, and shows us the lines upon which the treatment either of the poor or of any other branch of the Oxford-seeking community must be handled if it is to be attended with success.

It is probably for these reasons in the main that the maximum number of Non-Collegiate undergraduates in residence, which in the four years 1878–1881 averaged 202 per annum, has in the last two years been not more than 166 and 172 respectively. But this decline in numbers has also been due to the introduction of stricter regulations; while it is consoling to learn that, although some of the best students seek to join Colleges where they can, the percentage of migrations has greatly diminished. This is a testimony to the advance which has been made in tuition. The system now fills a definite and exceedingly useful place in the organization of Oxford life and teaching: it deserves a wider publicity and greater financial support. Under different conditions it might one day play a more conspicuous part; and I commend its interests to the attention of Council. But it is clear that we shall not find in it a comprehensive solution of the problem of the poor, though it may afford one method by which the students of institutions such as Ruskin College might be admitted to the University if it were so desired.

Desirability of greater encouragement.

The University Extension system

The term University Extension has been used in the last half-century with two very different connotations. In the sense in which it was employed by the first Commission and by Mark Pattison, it meant, to quote the latter's words, 'not merely an addition to the numbers attending Oxford, but the admission to its benefits of a class which has been hitherto excluded by social position or income'; and hence all the earlier suggestions which were made under this title were directed to providing more opportunities *at Oxford itself* for the admission and teaching of poor men. Then came Jowett and others preaching that Oxford should go out, as Cambridge, under the impulse of Professor James Stuart, had begun to do, into the large towns and cities, providing examinations and teachers, and planting colleges in the great centres of population. This movement took effect in the schemes started at both Universities for Extension lectures, which subsequently developed into the present imposing system of classes, and lectures, and examinations, managed at Oxford by a Delegacy, which has been one of the most successful instruments in popularizing Higher Education in the last quarter of a century. The title has thus been appropriated to a more literal interpretation of the words, and is now generally used to signify University work *outside*

History of University Extension.

the University. It has in fact been the first step in a movement of which we are now approaching the second. Hitherto Oxford has been going out to furnish its help, and by so doing has encouraged the desire which is everywhere finding such articulate expression among those whom it has reached, to come to Oxford and complete the process of education within the walls of the University. Apart from this, the Extension movement, by the local interest which it has aroused, has been the direct parent of the Colleges that have been started, in connexion with the two older Universities, in some provincial towns, and has powerfully stimulated the demand which has led to the creation of Provincial Universities.

Alleged failure to reach the industrial classes.

The financial necessities, however, of a system which had to be self-supporting (for the only charge directly imposed upon the University has been the cost of the Central Office and Secretary[1]) have prevented its feelers—though nearly half a million students have been reached—from stretching out to the industrial classes, whose needs we are now examining; and it is therefore not surprising that the recent Working-Class Education Committee in their Report should have frankly pointed out the reasons for this failure. They are contained on pp. 36–9 of the Report and are thus summarized in the Table of Contents: (*a*) it is too expensive; (*b*) it necessitates the attracting of large audiences; (*c*) the teaching is not systematic; (*d*) it is too much withdrawn from the University.

Proposals of the Working-Class Education Committee

Proposals of Working-Class Education Committee.

The Committee then proceed to formulate their proposals, which are: That Tutorial Classes of not more than thirty students should be established in selected industrial towns, the plan of study, lasting for at least two years, to be drawn up by the work-people and the University in consultation, the teachers to be appointed and half paid by the University, and to receive the status of University lecturers, so as to give them an official rank in Oxford and to maintain a connexion between the two branches of the alliance that will benefit both. At the end of two years it is proposed that a certificate should be awarded by the Extension Delegacy, of a character to satisfy the requirements of the Committee for Economics (or other similar Committees) for the admission of students, not being members of the University, to Diploma courses; and that a new Diploma course be established in Political Science (for which the Trustees of the University Re-endowment Fund have already offered to create a Lectureship), perhaps ultimately to develop into a School of Politics and Economics, with suitable Chairs attached to it.

Artisan students at the University.

I have merely summarized these recommendations, because they deal principally with the case at a stage anterior to that with which I am concerned, and will be considered on their own merits by the University. Indeed, Tutorial Classes have already been held during the present winter at eight industrial towns, and steps have been taken to deal with the Economic and Political Science Diplomas in the manner proposed. I am here more directly interested in the measures to be adopted *at the University*, for accommodating these working-men students when they arrive in Oxford to complete the course for which their provincial studies in the classes will have prepared them. The work at earlier stages is a voluntary addition to the responsibilities of the University—just as is the task which it has elsewhere undertaken in the examination and inspection of Public and Secondary Schools. As such, it is admirable; but it is no part of the life of Oxford itself.

The artisan students may of course enter any College or Hall; or they may join the Non-Collegiate body, requiring in either case the assistance of Scholarships or Exhibitions for the purpose. These endowments may be created for them either by the Labour organizations or the Local Education Authorities in the parts of the country from which they come; or they may be provided by the University or Colleges; or they may be awarded by the two in combination. What Oxford can do in this respect will be more clear when I deal with the subject of Scholarships and Exhibitions in a separate chapter. For the moment it is sufficient to recognize (1) that the cost of living, under whatever system they reside, must be cut down as low as possible; (2) that even so, some pecuniary assistance will be required to enable them to meet it. The working-man will in some cases be married, and will leave a wife and family behind him who must be maintained in his absence; at Oxford he will be drawing no wages, and he will be of a class to whom the term pocket-money is almost unknown.

Ruskin College[2]

At this stage it seems desirable to allude to the one institution already existing at Oxford, which has hitherto to a large extent supplied the needs of resident working-men. Ruskin College was founded about nine years ago; and although it has no formal connexion with the University, it has received every encouragement, while retaining the support of the trade societies and organizations by whom it was founded and is endowed. The broad facts are well known that it provides for some fifty or sixty students of the working-classes, between the ages of twenty and thirty, drawn for the most part from the North of England and from Wales, that these are all or mostly engaged in trades (miners, weavers, cotton spinners, blacksmiths, painters, compositors, joiners, are among those who have passed through), that they receive teaching and write papers and essays, and are examined on subjects of political, social, and economic science, some staying for a two years' course, but the majority for only one, and that the cost of their board, lodging, and education for the entire year (for, unlike the ordinary University student, they cannot afford to take vacations) is only £52. At the end of their time these men go back to their towns and trades; but my own inquiries among

Ruskin College.

87

them convinced me—and the conclusion is honourable to them—that with the desire to improve themselves is associated the desire to rise, and that many aspire to qualify for such posts as Secretaries of Trades Unions and Councils, or of Friendly and Co-operative Societies, as members of Local or Municipal bodies, or, in the last resort, as Labour M.P.'s.

Character of tuition.

Oxford has extended a warm welcome to the new-comers. University men of the highest standing serve on the College Council; College tutors and lecturers place their services at the disposal of the students; the latter are at liberty to attend all University lectures; and they are invited to take part in the debates of the Oxford Union. The title 'College' might lead the ignorant to suppose that the inmates are accommodated in a structure of some size or importance. This is far from being the case, the house in which they reside being on the same scale of modesty as their entire scale of living, and the men themselves do the service of their rooms. The friends of the College have, however, obtained a site for a new building, and are endeavouring to raise £20,000 for that object.

Connexion with the University.

Some well-wishers of this institution have suggested that a closer connexion between it and the University might be established by making it a licensed lodging-house or hostel or by converting it into a Private or Public Hall. The Committee before referred to have made no such recommendation, and have confined their suggestions on this point to the hope that more money may be provided for Scholarships and Exhibitions at Ruskin College, both by Colleges and by external bodies. It is not certain that the College itself desires incorporation with the University, since neither its studies nor its students, as they at present exist, harmonize with the University courses or degrees. Should individual members of the College wish to become regular members of the University on the basis of Non-Collegiate students, or to proceed to a degree, it is improbable that the University would place any obstacle in their path. Should the College, however, prefer to remain outside the University, its independence will continue to be respected, and the encouragement hitherto given to it will, I am sure, be in no degree modified or withdrawn.

Admission of working-men to ordinary Colleges.

The Committee, however, have themselves pointed out that the effect of restricting working-class students to Ruskin College would be to give rise to a false impression that it is the wish of Oxford to put them off with some kind of unofficial recognition, and to confine the ordinary Colleges to men of other social classes. Such a misunderstanding would, they add, be most lamentable.[3] From this they proceed to argue that special arrangements should be made for admitting working-class students to the ordinary Colleges. There is nothing in theory to be said against such a proposal, and much in its favour; and an attempt is already made by some Colleges to meet these or analogous requirements by providing rooms on a very modest scale of furniture and rent. But it would, I think, be a mistake to suppose that the standard or cost of living at the ordinary College can be brought down to a point which will enable working-men (except with a larger assistance in each case from Scholarships than is likely to be forthcoming) to enter them in any great numbers; besides which, there will always remain the difficulty of equating the educational, wholly apart from the social, position and requirements of the man who has enjoyed little education since he was twelve or thirteen, and the man who has come to Oxford as the result of an educational process that has lasted till he was eighteen or nineteen. If therefore we limit ourselves to the anticipation above referred to, we shall, I fear, court disappointment; nor will the University, in my judgment, have dealt in a sufficiently broad or generous spirit with the claim that is presented to it. There is the further practical difficulty that while the Colleges are in vacation for six months of the year, the working-man is compelled, for the reasons that I have given, to be in residence for the whole, or nearly the whole; a difficulty which does not appear to me to be solved by the suggestions of the Committee, that the working-class students should all be congregated in a single College during vacation, and that they should then be lectured to at Ruskin College or by teachers from outside.[4] I am afraid that the first suggestion is not practicable, and that the second, even if practicable, might involve a serious dislocation of studies.

Hostels or halls

Other suggestions that have been made are that Colleges should build *Aedes* Hostels.
annexae or Hostels attached to themselves for the special accommodation of poorer men, including working-men; or that such Hostels should be created independently of the Colleges, whether of the academical type or under private supervision. If they are to be effective, these institutions would in practice require to be cheap corporate lodging-houses, with a common table, under competent supervision: they would in fact be a direct reversion to the practice of the Middle Ages.

The College Hostel idea possesses the initial advantage that funds might in some cases be available for the purpose, and that Colleges could build and control the Hostel, if the ground were forthcoming, of their own initiative and responsibility. If a Hostel not attached to a particular College were started, it should probably be placed for economy's sake in some less expensive and less highly-rated portion of the town—for which purpose the statutory one and a half mile limit of residence would have to be extended. In both cases, and particularly in that of the independent Hostel, the difficulties of discipline and control would be considerable; and there would remain the danger, which led the Commission of 1850 to regard all these proposals with suspicion, that a distinct line of social cleavage might be created between the well-to-do man and the poor man, the College student and the Hostel student, and that in endeavouring to subsidize poverty we might in reality penalize it. It does not appear to me, however, that any prognostications, whether favourable or the reverse, are of much value unless supplemented by experience: and a single Hostel, started upon these or similar lines, would do more to answer the question than have done the *a priori* disputations of fifty years.

Public and Private Halls. As regards Public and Private Halls, it is notorious that the movement of the past half-century has been in the direction of gradually eliminating the former, so much so that only one now survives,[5] namely, St. Edmund Hall, upon which sentence of ultimate absorption was passed by the last Commission, although an effort is now being made to save its independent existence, and there are many who think that, with some improvement, it might be rendered of great advantage to poor men. Private Halls do not appear in modern times to have attracted much favour. There are at present only three of them, and their united muster of undergraduates is not much over fifty. Neither their constitution nor their character qualifies them to provide a comprehensive solution of the Working-class or indeed of the Poor problem.[6]

A Working-men's College

Suggestion of a Working-men's or Poor men's College. I am inclined to take a wider outlook, and to hope that the University may itself, with outside assistance, attempt a solution. Given the unquestioned desire of the working-classes to come to Oxford, and not merely to hang, so to speak, upon the outskirts, but to penetrate to the sanctuary of University life, it seems to me that the satisfaction of the need should not be left to private enterprise or to a necessarily somewhat precarious combination between academical and external interests, but that it should be recognized and regulated by no less a body than the University itself. There is always a danger that a Working-men's College, outside the University, and subject neither to its influences nor its discipline, may develop into a club dominated by the narrow views of particular political or economic schools, recruiting itself solely from one party, and out of touch with many of the best elements in academic life. As has been well said, we do not want merely to attract to Oxford the 'Hot-heads' or the 'Hot-hearts' of Labour. My own idea is that instead of, or in addition to, utilizing the existing machinery of the Collegiate and Non-Collegiate systems, we should found at Oxford a University Workingmen's College, not confined to artisans alone but embracing—according to its size and capabilities—the members of all those classes who are too poor, even with financial assistance, to enter the ordinary Colleges, or to spend half the year in vacations. Such a College should have a fixed scale of cost, if possible not more than £60 per annum; a large number of maintenance Scholarships or Exhibitions should be attached to it, which I would appeal to the richer Colleges to contribute. But the education should not be given for nothing, since a purely gratuitous benefaction would sap the sense of self-respect; and a University education is deserving of some sacrifice, if not on the part of the individual (who may be too poor to afford it), at least on the part of those from whom he comes. I would similarly ask the Colleges to elect or to lend Fellows who would constitute the staff and conduct the tuition. The Principal would be appointed by the University.

The members of the College would be matriculated, and subject to academic discipline, but the conditions of their study and residence would differ from those of other undergraduates. They would not as a rule proceed to a degree, since they would not have the requisite leisure for a three years' course. The normal course should be one of two years, leading to one of the Diplomas already granted or hereafter to be created by the University; but it should not be confined exclusively to Sociology and Economics, since it is doubtful if of themselves these are capable of ensuring a liberal education. There should be an admixture of History and Geography and English Literature and Natural Science. The working-man or the poor man whom we wish to encourage is not the man who comes to Oxford merely in order to obtain a sketchy acquaintance with political problems, or to practise the arts of the popular speaker. I do not think that Oxford is a proper palaestra for such exercises. The type that we desire to assist is the man, however humble his origin, who comes as a genuine learner and student, anxious to acquire not so much superficial attainments as a sound and solid education. [*Its courses, tuition, and mode of life.*]

If any student, after receiving his Diploma, wished to stay on and to take a degree, he should be at liberty to do so. Some of the Diploma subjects are already included in the degree course, so that the holder of a Diploma is already some distance on his way to a degree. The College would remain in session throughout the vacation, special arrangements being made for lectures and tuition. A connexion would be maintained between the College and the country by means of the enlarged activities about to be undertaken by the University Extension Delegacy. Indeed, I would go further than recent suggestions have done. For I would ask the Colleges from time to time to grant Fellowships to the teachers who were thus spreading the influence of the University outside; and I would make them the means through their classes of sending up the picked pupils of the year to the Oxford Working-men's College, in order to carry their training to its logical conclusion. The taint of poverty would not cling to the College any more than it does to Keble College, which claims at a somewhat higher cost to provide 'sober living and high culture of the mind' for a particular class of students whose training is to be a 'Christian training, based upon the principles of the Church of England'. In Keble also the tutorships and lectureships have not infrequently been held by Fellows of other Colleges.

The students of our hypothetical College would enjoy all the intra-mural and extra-mural advantages of the Colleges and the University in combination; all would not be drawn from the same class, and the tradesman's, the business man's, and even the poor gentleman's son, would mingle with the artisan. The link between them would be humble means and the needs of frugal subsistence; and the indescribable glamour of College society would soon hold them in its thrall and leave its mark upon them for life. The College could exist side by side, and without risk of competition, with Ruskin College, since there would always remain a large class of working-people who would prefer to be detached from the University, and exclusively to manage their own affairs. Those who aspired to College life (and the Committee have reported that there is a genuine and widely spread desire to this effect) would go to the one: those who demanded complete independence would remain faithful to the other.

Appeal to
an outside
benefactor. For the creation of such an institution, the land and the buildings, as well as the endowments, are required; and we must look for these in the main to external help. Fain would I hope that these words may fall under the eye of some public-spirited benefactor, to whom the idea may appeal of thus opening the doors of England's oldest University to the new applicants for its bounty. He might fill a conspicuous gap in the educational equipment of the nation; he might open a new vista of public usefulness and fame to Oxford; and his name would worthily be added to that long and illustrious list, beginning with Humfrey Duke of Gloucester and ending with Martha Combe, widow, that is read out by the preacher of the University sermon upon Sundays in the Bidding Prayer in St. Mary's Church. The scheme itself may be susceptible of much improvement, and I have not ventured beyond outlines; elaboration would be for a later stage. But with such a benefactor, if he were forthcoming, both University and Colleges would surely join hands in the endeavour to translate the conception into reality.

The poor of other classes

The poor
of other
classes. From the artisan poor I pass to the poor of other classes. These may be subdivided according to their occupations, into the sons of persons of humble means, such as the tradesman, the farmer (the yeoman class who formerly provided the great bulk of the provincial students who flocked to Oxford has now wellnigh disappeared), the teacher in Primary and Secondary Schools, the poor clergyman; and the small professional man, the solicitor, lawyer, land agent, doctor, &c., who desire to enter their sons for their own professions, or aspire to give them access to the public services of the country.

The schools
from which
they come. Or, as before indicated, we may distinguish between the pupil who comes to Oxford from the superior Secondary Schools and Grammar Schools, organized on Public school lines, and the pupil educated after leaving the elementary school in schools of the Municipal and County Council type, dependent mainly on Government grants and public money, and preparing their students principally for business avocations. Of the former class a considerable number come to Oxford, and it is important that we should retain our hold upon them, since they form the core of the respectable professional middle classes. Hitherto they have looked to the older Universities for the education of their sons; but with the growth of public grants to Secondary Schools, followed by popular control, there will be a tendency to divert this current to the Provincial Universities, such as Birmingham, Manchester, and Leeds. Its loss would be a great injury to Oxford.

Of the second class the number that comes to Oxford is small. But we must strive to attract the best, for they will be the leaders in the upward movement of the lower middle classes that is the distinguishing mark of contemporaneous social evolution; and it is therefore of great importance that their early training should be conducted on liberal rather than utilitarian lines, and that they should meet their more fortunate contemporaries on equal terms and should understand their point of view. A worse disaster could hardly befall English education than that the seven new Provincial Universities should become the exclusive resort of the poor and unpolished man, and that Oxford and Cambridge should be reserved for the rich and cultured.

In respect of special endowments, this class is well provided for. The provision made, firstly by Scholarships from Elementary or Secondary Schools, and later on by Town or County Council Scholarships,[7] by College or City Company Exhibitions, and by private generosity, is very considerable. It does not happen to be extensively advertised, and its range and liberality are imperfectly known even in Oxford. As a matter of fact the boy coming from a County Council School is often better endowed than the son of a professional man from Marlborough or Clifton. I know of one rich College in which eleven poor men hold Scholarships and Exhibitions averaging £133 per annum. The opportunities open to this class are indeed so generous that the standard of attainment is sometimes with difficulty maintained; and while the columns of the newspapers are open to denunciations of the idle rich, the phenomenon of the idle but well-endowed poor passes unnoticed and unashamed. *Endowments for these classes.*

One class of the struggling poor is extremely well provided for—a relic of the times when Oxford existed almost wholly as a training-ground for the Church. These are the poor clergy. In many Colleges there are Scholarships and Exhibitions reserved for the sons of the clergy, sometimes with a limitation of locality, generally with no geographical limitation at all, and as a rule with a poverty qualification. Similar provision exists for candidates for Holy Orders, irrespective of parentage. In this respect the University needs to make no addition to its bounty. *The poor clergy.*

There is another class for whose assistance something has been done, but to encourage whom it seems to me that a further and special effort ought to be made. I speak of the Teachers in Elementary and Secondary Schools. A Day Training College has been founded at Oxford for the preparation of Elementary Teachers, and support is given to this institution both by the *Teachers in Elementary and Secondary schools.*

University and the Colleges. The University has established a Delegacy which is recognized by the Education Department as the Committee of the College, so that the students, who are required to matriculate and thus to become members of the University, can earn their Government allowance of £25 or £40 for residence in Oxford during three years. The support from the Colleges takes the form of Exhibitions or grants in aid. For Secondary Teachers there is a special course culminating in a Diploma; and the interests of this class are also supervised by a special Delegacy. But the work has suffered much in point both of numbers and finance by the uncertain policy of H. M. Government in abolishing the Register of Teachers, the existence of which acted as an incentive to teachers to qualify. The Elementary Teachers and many of the Secondary Teachers belong to the class of persons of humble means. The University can undertake no more honourable duty than the education of those who will mould the thought of the future. More encouragement might be given to both grades by Scholarships or Exhibitions, but the real obstacle in the path of teacher-students who are proceeding to a degree is compulsory Greek in Responsions.

Alleged obstacles in Oxford system. With regard to all the classes, however, of whom I have been speaking— i. e. the poor of every grade—the existence or the liberality of endowments will not compensate those who are not so fortunate as to obtain them; and it may be that even in spite of subsidies in pecuniary or other shape there are features in the Oxford system which act as a deterrent to the entry of poor students or prevent their multiplication, and which it might be possible to alleviate or remove. Whether these relate to the cost of living in Colleges, to the incidence of University and College Fees and Dues, to the distribution of endowments, or to the nature and subjects of Examinations—and they fall as a rule under one or other of these headings—it is incumbent upon us to give them our serious attention.

Cost of living in colleges

Cost of living in Colleges. This is one of the oldest of complaints. The Commission of 1850 in solemn tones deplored the excessive cost of residence at the University, which they said varied at that time from £370 to £450 for the full four years' course (excluding caution-money, travelling, clothes, wine, and amusements). All included, they thought that a son cost his father £600 in four years, or at the rate of £150 per annum. Since those days the outlay has been in many ways reduced by the superior arrangements now made by the Colleges,[8] and by the vigilant efforts at reduction inspired quite as much by the volition of the College authorities, as by pressure from outside. On the other hand there has been the steady rise in the material well-being and standards of the classes frequenting Oxford, to which I have before referred, and which pulls in the opposite direction.

I have previously given the figures for the Non-Collegiate system. Keble (where all meals are in common) makes a fixed annual charge of £85. From a detailed inquiry in all the Colleges, I have ascertained that the minimum outlay for which a careful undergraduate can reside in the majority of Colleges is £100 per annum, though in some it will be less, that the average outlay is about £120–£130, and that rich men spend more. To these totals a sum of from £8 to £12 per annum—for a four years' course—should be added, for clubs, fees and dues, and tips to servants.

These estimates exclude the cost of living in vacations, and that of travelling, clothes, books, pocket-money, wine, and tobacco. It must be remembered that in the University and College Dues, in the Tuition Fund, and in the maintenance of Establishment, there is an irreducible minimum of cost, no small part of which is paid for the advantage of residence inside the College walls.

Many proposals have been made for curtailing the expenditure thereby imposed upon poor men. It has been suggested that two or three Colleges might be thrown into one, with the result of a considerable saving in respect of College officers and servants; or that existing Colleges should be remodelled so as to provide single rooms, instead of sets of rooms, for the average undergraduate; or that the less wealthy Colleges should deliberately shut their doors against well-to-do students and cater exclusively for the men of modest means. No one of these suggestions would, I think, command confidence as a general panacea, and any too radical revolution in College internal economy or the College fabric might be attended with consequences at which even the most intrepid of reformers would stand dismayed. More fruitful appears to me to be the suggestion that there should be a conference of College Domestic Bursars, to discuss the management of College kitchens, maintenance charges in general, and the purchase of supplies. An examination of the published College Accounts is sufficient to show that there is a wide diversity of systems, and that what is a source of profit to one College is accepted as a loss by another. A searching examination (with the aid of some expert external assistance) might result in valuable economies; it would certainly introduce greater system; and it might mitigate the ill effects of competition in local markets.

Fees and dues

An even more favourable ground of inquiry is suggested by the system of Fees and Dues paid to the University and Colleges. For an undergraduate pursuing the ordinary course to a B.A. followed by a M.A. degree, these are as follows:—

(a) University Fees.

	£	s.	d.
Admission Fee, paid at Matriculation.	3	10	0
Average Fees for all examinations leading to			
degree or diploma. £8 to 9		0	0
Admission to B.A. degree.	7	10	0
Admission to M.A. degree.	12	0	0
	£31 to £32	0	0

(b) University Dues (paid through Colleges).

	£	s.	d.
12/6 per quarter or £2 10s. per annum for a four years' course (though less for a shorter course).		10	0

(c) College Fees.[9]

	£	s.	d.
Admission Fee,[10] usually.	5	0	0
Admission to B.A. degree, average[11].	3	14	6
Admission to M.A. degree, average[12].	4	9	6

(d) Life Membership.

	£	s.	d.
(i) University Dues: per annum.	1	0	0
or Composition charge, according to age, from.	15	15	0
Recovery of right of voting in Convocation, after removal of name from College Books[13].	10	0	0
(ii) College Dues: per annum. 14s. to	1	0	0
Composition charge, according to age, from about.	15	15	0[14]

Fees and Dues are one of the main sources of income of the University. From this source (which includes many fees, such as Lodging Fees, Proctorial Fines, Research degree Fees, &c., not mentioned above) the University received in 1906 an income of £37,892, in 1907 an income of £38,954, and in 1908 an income of £40,678. From Admission and Degree Fees the nineteen Colleges whose accounts are published annually by the University (Keble is not included) derived in 1907 an income of £6,900.

Suggested reduction. An examination of the charges here summarized will I think lead to the conclusion that in some cases a reduction may reasonably be considered, and that the University and Colleges have it in their power, by a joint reduction, to lighten a burden that cannot generally fail to weigh heavily on the poor man. The two in co-operation might find it possible to reduce the combined fee for M.A., if not for B.A., and the combined Composition Fee. The Colleges are of course at liberty to charge what Degree Fees they may please, for, although the University confers the degree, it is by College tuition in the main that it has been won, but a somewhat greater uniformity of charge might be introduced. The University Fee of £12 for the M.A. degree would appear to be excessive, and it is not difficult to comprehend why so many men, having taken the B.A. degree, at an average cost of

96

£7 10s. to the University plus £3 14s. 6d. to the College, i. e. a total of £11 4s. 6d., remove their names from the books at this stage, partly because they are tempted by the recovery of the caution-money (which in all probability had been paid by their fathers four years earlier), partly because they are deterred by the £12 to the University plus an average of £4 9s. 6d. to the College, i.e. a total of £16 9s. 6d., which is the additional fine before they become M.A.'s and members of Convocation. Similarly the charge for re-entry, in the case where a man does not compound, seems to be unduly high, and within my own knowledge has chilled the penitence of many who regretted having taken their names off the books, and contemplated a return. On the other hand, if the University were seriously to consider a material loss of income by any reductions of the above character, there are certain respects in which it might fairly recoup a portion, at any rate, of the sacrifice. The idea has been mooted, and appears to be well worthy of examination, that all *resident* graduates should pay an annual fee for the use of the privileges and institutions of the University, which they now enjoy for no higher payment than the non-resident, who is unable to make any use of them at all. A slight increase in the very moderate charge for University Dues might also not unreasonably be asked from those who would profit so materially by a reduction of Degree Fees, if this were decided upon.

Before leaving this branch of the subject I should mention that I have encountered an opposite school of thought, who argue that the fees at present charged by the University err on the side of moderation, and that they ought to be raised all round. They contend that the University is in the position of a club which has rebuilt and greatly enlarged its premises, thereby offering increased advantages to its members; and that it is entitled, therefore, to demand an enhanced entrance fee and annual subscription. There may be plausibility in the argument, but at a moment when we are considering how to open an Oxford career to larger numbers, and to induce more students who have completed it to keep alive their connexion with the University, it might be ill-timed and unwise. Nor should we forget that half a century ago the Commissioners of 1850 pointed to a reduction of fees as a means of opening the University to larger and poorer classes than those from whom the majority of students were even then drawn. *Opposite school of thought.*

The case has so far been mainly considered from the point of view of its effect upon the University. But the College standpoint must not be disregarded. Just as the University Fees and Dues are a large source of income to the University, so, though in a less degree, are the College Fees one of the means by which the Colleges are enabled to give an education to their undergraduate members.[15] If it were not for the endowments possessed by them, they could not educate their students, as they now do, under cost price. Since the newer Schools have been established, e. g. in Natural Science, English Literature, and Modern Languages, for which many Colleges cannot provide teaching of their own, they find themselves compelled *Effect of College Fees.*

to pay out nearly the whole of the Tuition fees received from their students in these subjects to outside teachers. This is a tendency which is likely to increase; and it may well be that ultimately a College will not be able to carry on its tuition without subsidizing the Tuition Fund from corporate revenues or raising its Tuition fees. College Fees and Dues may be regarded from this point of view as a deferred contribution to the expenses of tuition; and unless the lowering of fees were to lead to a considerable increase in the number of men paying them, Colleges might have to draw more heavily upon their corporate revenues in the future.

Two other subjects of paramount importance are raised by the consideration of increased opportunities for the admission of the poor to Oxford. These are the use that is made of Scholarships and Exhibitions, and the impediment that is alleged to exist in the compulsory requirement of Greek at the initial stage of any University course leading up to a degree. The former of these questions is a portion of the larger problem of administration of the endowments enjoyed by the Colleges for the advancement of learning; the second raises the issue of the University examinations as a whole. I propose accordingly to treat them in separate chapters, although both of these will be in direct logical sequence to the subject hitherto under discussion.

Information Bureau. A suggestion has been made by the Tutors' Conference that a Bureau should be established at Oxford for the special information of parents and others with regard to the facilities offered by the University for the admission and education of the poor. Such an office might be started independently, or in connexion with the reorganization of the central office of the University which I shall propose later on.

Notes

1 On the other hand, it must not be forgotten that the Colleges have lent substantial assistance, in some cases by contributions to the Delegacy Fund, in others (Balliol and Christ Church) by the appointment of a specially selected Fellow or Senior Student for the purpose.

2 These paragraphs were in print before the recent events that have brought about the temporary closure of Ruskin College. The incidents referred to appear to have been the result of an attempt to utilize the institution for the purposes of a particular propaganda, and they are of importance as indicating the risks that may attend a movement which though to some extent connected with the University is yet outside of it, and is unaffected by University traditions or discipline. I have decided to leave the paragraphs unaltered, because no friend of the working-classes can wish that this temporary set-back should permanently arrest either the desire of the industrial classes to profit by an Oxford course, or the willingness of the University, subject to reasonable guarantees, to provide it.

3 Report, p. 77.

4 Report, p. 81.

5 As late as 1872 there were five: St. Alban Hall, since united with Merton; St. Mary Hall, since united with Oriel; Magdalen Hall, which became the nucleus of

Hertford; New Inn Hall, since united with Balliol; and St. Edmund Hall, which still survives.

6 The number of students in a Private Hall, and in any *Aedes annexae* attached to it, taken together, is limited by Statute to twenty.

7 The number of County or Borough Council Scholarships held by Oxford students appears to be in excess of fifty.

8 E. g., rooms are now, as a rule, let furnished, in place of the old and costly system of buying furniture at a valuation. Where this survives the amount is sometimes lent by the College. A similar arrangement is applied to linen, crockery, and plate. Rooms are let on a carefully graduated scale of rents. Many Colleges have established Common Room Stores where groceries, wines, and fruit can be bought at a fixed tariff. In many cases there is a limit to the expenditure in buttery or kitchen. College Clubs are consolidated, and a subscription, covering the whole, can be paid through the College.

9 I have not included in these caution-money, usually about £30, of which part is commonly returned upon taking a degree, and the remainder upon the removal of a name from the College books; nor Tuition charges, as a rule from £22 to £25 per annum, because neither of these affords a reasonable ground of reduction.

10 One very poor College charges £8 5s., one £5 5s., thirteen £5, one £4, one £2, one £1 10s., and two 0. These charges are in a few Colleges somewhat reduced in the case of Scholars and Exhibitioners.

11 and 12 These vary so greatly that it seems best to give the figures:—

	B.A.			M.A.				B.A.			M.A.		
	£	s.	d.	£	s.	d.		£	s.	d.	£	s.	d.
Balliol	4	4	0	6	6	0	Merton	2	0	0	2	0	0
B.N.C.	5	0	0	8	0	0	New	2	2	0	2	2	0
Ch. Ch.	3	3	0	3	3	0	Oriel	4	10	0	5	10	0
C.C.C.	2	10	0	5	0	0	Pembroke	7	0	0	5	0	0
Exeter	4	12	6	4	0	0	Queen's	5	5	0	3	6	0
Hertford	5	5	0	5	5	0	St. John's	6	7	0	6	13	0
Jesus	3	11	0	3	1	0	Trinity	3	16	0	6	1	0
Keble	1	0	0	1	0	0	University	5	0	0	6	0	0
Lincoln	1	1	0	1	1	0	Wadham	4	4	0	8	4	0
Magdalen	0	17	6	1	5	0	Worcester	3	1	0	6	3	0

13 This is not paid by any one who compounds.

14 The College Composition charge varies in different cases from half the University fee to the same fee.

15 The majority of the larger Colleges derive from this source an annual income of from £400 to £600.

56

THE UNIVERSITIES &
SOCIAL PURPOSE

Roy Pascal

Source: *Universities Quarterly* IV (1949–50): 37–43.

The ferment of thought about the universities, during and immediately after the war, was provoked by the threat to our national existence and institutions, and by our realization of the immense importance of the universities in the national life. Their practical contribution was great, not only in the sphere of technical achievement, but also in all branches of administration, of economic and political warfare. Studies normally considered to be "purely academic" suddenly uncovered a practical use. There was a clearer appreciation of the social value of university education in developing personal qualities of intelligence, initiative, and adaptability, and the universities' shortcomings in this respect were justifiably criticized.

At the same time, the war brought home a lesson of still wider bearing, that a nation and society can survive only if its members find in it a worthy social purpose, and are willing to devote themselves energetically to this purpose: a lesson as true, we know, in peace as in war. The universities were called upon to help to formulate this purpose and carry it to the mass of the people outside their walls. So the underlying principle of all the reports, articles and books on the universities in this period was to formulate the universities' responsibilities to society. The Vice-Chancellor of Birmingham University summed up this trend when he said: "If the nation fails to save its soul alive, we are so delicately poised on the see-saw of world economics and world politics that reputation, prosperity, employment and standard of living are likely to crash. . . . All our educational institutions have a decisive part to play in the attainment of the objective. . . . The universities must scoop into their net all in whom character and intellect are combined in greater than average degree. They must study to provide an environment in which their students can live the best possible and fullest community life. They must give a balanced education related directly to Man's history and destiny, to the environment in which he has to live, and to the ends and aims that alone make life worth while."[1]

Universities and Government have worked together towards the practical realization of these principles. As a result the tasks and problems of society are more directly mirrored in the universities than ever before; if there is a "crisis" in the world, then there must be a "crisis in the university". Sir Walter Moberly has done us a great service in posing the question thus, and one must meet him on his own ground. He has already been sharply challenged by Michael Oakeshott in his long review, and I wish to set out from these two interpretations.[2]

The technical and economic revolution of our time has brought, in Moberly's view, a complete breakdown of established values and convictions. The universities must accept their responsibilities to modern society—he finds no moral grounds for refusing to contribute in greater measure to the advancement of scientific knowledge and technical skills or the solution of social problems; and, in a more democratic age, the universities must be made available for social classes for whom they have, in the main, been out of reach. The universities have expanded but, in his view, have failed to respond to the spiritual needs of the times. They teach as if the world outside were still as secure, materially and spiritually, as it seemed to be fifty years ago; the traditional principles of research and education are out of contact with a society in crisis, and leave our students without guidance in a puzzling world. The universities must break through their limited departmentalistic purposes and give students through religion a consciousness of personal value and divine purpose.

I cannot here analyse the meaning of religion for Moberly. He does not discuss the question of the validity of his desire for a sense of supermundane certainty. Sometimes he expresses it as a purely subjective feeling, and sometimes it appears in an ecclesiastical form, as order or humility or theology. In both forms it contrasts strangely with the liberal and humane spirit in which he outlines certain reforms he considers desirable; and at times he opens the door to a religious zealotry which would play havoc with the universities—as for instance when he approves Pusey on p. 265. The important thing is that, despite his advocacy of practical reforms with which most of us would agree, he appears inwardly unconvinced of their value, since his essential concern is the introduction of something totally different into university life, a new spirit, a new attitude, a belief: an ideology plastered on the top of alien and incorrigible behaviour. During the war we were mainly concerned with the secular social and personal purpose of the university; here we find a transcendental objective. And this objective produces a distorted picture of the universities. The worse things appear, the more necessary seems the "metanoia" for which he calls. His description of students on p. 207, his statement that "many a student's life is dominated by Angst," his cursory condemnation of Arts Faculties on p. 184—they are well-nigh caricatures. Such distortions undermine the value of much of his criticism, which is frequently solid and pertinent. He fails, with his unique opportunity as former Chairman of the University Grants Committee, to give an adequate picture of the changes actually going on in the universities and of the spiritual and practical forces which *are* responding to the "needs of the times" and seeking to revitalize our university tradition.

Oakeshott[3] has drawn attention to the contradictions in Moberly's approach and to the resulting incoherence. He suggests—and in my opinion rightly—that the psychological distress postulated by Moberly is a distress felt not by a younger generation but by one cradled in the pseudo-certainties of Victorian England:

> Was ihr den Geist der Zeiten nennt,
> Das ist im Grund der Herren eigner Geist,
> In dem die Zeiten sich bespiegeln.

But Oakeshott plunges us into an even deeper gulf. Shedding the religious or humanistic illusions of the religious or humane Moberly, he considers the present state of the world to be a chaos, in which all moral and cultural values are swallowed by "the plausible ethics of productivity". To save its soul the university must cut itself off as far as possible from the values ruling the world, it must hold fast to tried practices, and resist the insidious and overt attacks of the "men of power" with their principles of social welfare and efficiency. Planning is not a good; it indicates "our absence of direction and our loss of dependable habits of behaviour". The war can give us no inspiration; it was a period in which "laws were suspended and the balance of society disturbed". "The contemporary world offers no desirable model for a university." "The leaders of the rising class are consumed with a contempt for everything which does not spring from their own desires, they are convinced in advance that they have nothing to learn and everything to teach, and consequently their aim is loot."

In such a situation, the university can "preserve its identity" only by as radical a resistance to external influences as possible. Oakeshott's Burkism leads him to burke the issue.

> Wo so ein Köpfchen keinen Ausgang sieht,
> Stellt er sich gleich das Ende vor.

Admitting reluctantly that the universities must reflect the world in which they exist, he stresses only the means by which they may shut out the external world as far as possible. Thus his account of the development of the universities in the past ignores the social sources of change and emphasizes only the discrimination exerted by the universities. Thus he can ridicule the concept of "social" justice and allow himself the extravagant statement

that we all "know it to be an illusion that there was any large untapped reserve of men and women who could make use of this kind of university"
—the increase of student numbers is seen only as a disturbance. Thus he
would define the university purely formalistically as an "interim", a definition which tells us nothing about the content and character of studies, their
origin and their social purpose. Moberly, he says, by accepting the principle
of social responsibility must necessarily accelerate the disintegration of
values and deepen a crisis which no ideology can overcome.

Both Moberly and Oakeshott, then, interpret the problem of the university in terms of a social development which in varying degrees they abhor.
They join a vast body of opinion which watches with something akin to
despair the rise to power of a social class which creates new demands and
new standards. The rapid and violent development of society during the last
four hundred years has led to a series of revolutions which have repeatedly
provoked similar reactions in men attached to forms in which they were
cradled. This is not the place to discuss this problem directly; the question
is, is this diagnosis of a social cataclysm borne out by our experience in the
universities, and by the perspective ahead?

No doubt the task of re-orientation is far more difficult for Oxford and
Cambridge which (or rather, certain aspects of which) provide the background for Oakeshott's gloom, than for the modern universities, which have
never shared in certain of their privileges. But it would be easy to make out
a case, based on the experience of the latter, to prove the beneficent results
of the new times. In the past starved of funds, short of departments and
staff, without adequate buildings, limited in the material bases of a healthy
student life, these universities are now more in a position to fulfil the functions of a true university. The increase of student demand has, despite some
drawbacks, given a real existence to some departments and allows many
the power of selection of students. Full employment lessens the pressure of
utilitarian considerations on our students; a larger staff has allowed us to
develop more intimate and personal education. The association of "town"
and "gown" informs us that outside, in the larger world, a high value is
placed on the general ability and personality that we can encourage in our
pupils. The contrast between a governing "élite" and a subordinate mass
has become meaningless in our society; at all levels efficiency is needed
combined with consciousness of social purpose and personal quality.

Do these and similar developments mean a distortion of the true purpose
of a university, loss of its "identity"? The recent history of any university
would, I am convinced, show that its growth has brought an enriching of
the true university tradition. I am best acquainted with my own university
and best acquainted with its shortcomings; I am sure it would stand a
stern test. There has been a great development of departments, of research
some of which is the direct outcome of technical or social problems. Are the
principles of university life or study perverted or degraded by such work?

Are the staff or students or syllabuses unfit? Consider the development of Extra-mural studies, of Physical Education, of the Institute of Education; examine (if you can) the mentality or temperament of the much increased student body. What different conclusions would be forced upon an investigator from those of Moberly, how totally unlike Oakeshott's assertions they would be! Consider the experiments being made in encouraging students to think and discuss matters outside their degree courses. Not that all is good or that amazing changes have been made; there is too, in Faculties and Senate, a great variety of opinion. But the atmosphere of such a university is totally different from that postulated by Moberly or Oakeshott; there is here vigorous life which, though it rarely finds general philosophical formulation, is a truer reflection of the opportunities and reality of our times than the anxieties of those who cling to old habits of mind. Take for example the new University College of North Staffordshire, as direct a product of the time as can be found. In its novel form, in the shape of its curriculum, does it pervert the "identity" of the university? Or is it not rather a hopeful sign of the creativeness of a tradition which can find a new form appropriate to a particular setting and a new time?

The relationship of the university to the world is complex and the conditions governing this "interim" period are not the same as those governing men in their adult work. But this period is a preparation for later life, and must be fruitful in it. The consciousness of meaning, of value, can arise only if the life of its members (that is, their studies and their extra-curricular activities) is purposefully linked up with the society which it serves and fertilizes. This was the case in Oxford and Cambridge, and I suggest still is so, despite Oakeshott's interpretation; but if his attitude to the outside world were to prevail, the old academic spirit would not be preserved, it would lose all substance and vitality. Nor can meaning be injected from an extraneous source, if the actual forms of university life do not provide it. The religious feeling that Moberly advocates might become, in spite of his wishes, a dogmatic imposition at loggerheads with all intellectual and social practice, introduced out of political expediency; or, more probably, it would take the form of the savage and arrogant misanthropy of Kierkegaard, not a balm in Gilead but the symptom of acute distress.

I would maintain, then, that the new demands made on our universities, and the new opportunities given them, have given a new vitality to our academic tradition. In all cases, essential decisions have been in the hands of the universities themselves and they have been able to assure themselves that the fundamental conditions of academic work are preserved; if mistakes are made, they can be rectified in the same way. I agree, however, with Moberly that in many respects we shrink from consciously formulating our responsibilities, and because of this lag behind them. The urgency of these responsibilities can be measured only by the seriousness of the material and social crisis around us, and it is significant that both Moberly and Oakeshott do not plumb the depths of the crisis in Britain; we have the form of an empire without the power, we talk of social justice but rule colonial peoples, we live on credit, we cling to privileges and blind ourselves to their hollowness. The universities share the moral and material responsibility for cutting through illusions and eliminating these contradictions; if they fail, our culture and our ethos will become a mockery. We should start by giving our students the opportunity of examining the social and philosophical bases of their studies, by encouraging them—and ourselves—to enquire into the *ratio* of each separate discipline. They should be encouraged to ask what is the social relevance of their work, even if the answer be, as it must, highly complex. No one would say that students in the highly vocational departments, such as Medicine or the Applied Sciences, are essentially different from those let us say in departments of English or History; but it is necessary to define the links between them, and to find a remedy for shortcomings in our syllabuses which at present are palliated only by the common foundations of student life. Experiments along such lines are going on, in the form of general courses or of new methods within specialist departments; we need information and criticism, which might be a suitable task for research in our Education Departments, which on the whole resolutely ignore university problems.

Our universities exist in a developing society which has shaped them, which they influence. If they are worth anything, they will play that active part in society which Moberly defines. If society is in turmoil and full of conflicts, our students must know about it. They must acquire at the universities that intellectual discipline which will enable them to discriminate; they should learn that no knowledge is without its presuppositions, without a social origin and a social relevance, so that they themselves will be morally prepared to apply what they have acquired in vigorous action in the social situation awaiting them. In their studies and their communal life they acquire the habit of personal effort and co-operation. These are principles and objectives already implicit in our universities; their urgency demands effort, but not dismay.

Notes

1 Presidential Address to the Union of Educational Institutions, December, 1945.
2 *The Cambridge Journal*, June, 1949.
3 *The Cambridge Journal*, June, 1949, p. 520.

57

REFLECTIONS ON POLICY

Sydney Caine

Source: Sydney Caine, *British Universities: Purposes and Prospects*, London: Bodley Head, 1969, pp. 246–66.

What emerges from the previous chapters is inevitably confusing. There are great elements of diversity but significant uniformities; many cross-currents but some main trends. In trying to distinguish the most important features the risk must be run of apparent inaccuracy through the ignoring of exceptions and shades of emphasis.

We began by noting how in modern times, the vast extension of the range of knowledge had widened the scope of university activity and lengthened the time needed to master a subject; how the same extension of knowledge had increased the need for highly educated people if full advantage was to be taken of it for technical purposes; and how the increase of affluence had made it possible for society to maintain far more people in full-time education up to university level. We noted further the consequential increase both in number and in social prestige of the academic profession. We went on to examine the various purposes traditionally attributed to university activity: the simple maintenance and dissemination of knowledge, mind and character training; preparation for the 'learned' professions; and research; and we particularly noted certain continuing ambiguities about the issues of 'élite' versus 'general' education, 'academic' versus 'vocational' and teaching versus research. Among other things it has been shown that the universities have a somewhat varying and unsystematic relationship to the various professions; the claim of the universities to be the dominant centres of research and sources of new discoveries has been critically discussed; and the wide extent of higher or post-school educational activities outside the universities has been emphasised.

Of all the changes in ideas about the purpose of a university, the most important if the least discussed is the decline in the significance attached to character training. In a sense this began with the release of universities from dominance by the church, whether one dates that from the final abolition of religious tests in Oxford and Cambridge in 1871 or the forming of the 'atheist' University College in London in 1828; but for some generations the universities continued to be inspired by inherited ideas of morality and ethical purpose, if not by theological dogma. Today such moral and ethical standards are very largely eroded; attempts to enforce traditional standards are condemned as intolerable interference with freedom; even the mention of such standards is derided and opposed by members of staff as well as students; and increasingly in the more speculative branches of knowledge, especially in the social sciences and philosophy the criterion of approval of ideas tends more and more to be simply their novelty, because there is no other standard by which they can be judged. In this final development character-training merges with mind-training and the latter also is in danger of being dangerously softened by the tendency of so much modern philosophy to fight shy of any criterion other than the most formal of logical rules by which the validity of thought-processes may be judged. There is need to lay less emphasis on bright ideas and facile 'solutions' of intricate social problems and far more on the testing of ideas against facts and experience and simultaneously the testing of one set of facts against another. The right approach is still that indicated in the quotation already made (Chapter 2) from Arnold Nash in which he said how he had learned from Morris Ginsberg that 'not even the clearest thinking can atone for failure to begin with the facts' and from Karl Mannheim that 'the facts are never what they seem to be'.

In all this the universities are no more than participants in a far wider social process involving in a much deeper sense a loss of real purpose; and we cannot expect any full reestablishment of what must, however abhorrent the term to progressive thought, be called a moral sense in the universities if it cannot also be re-established in society at large. Nonetheless anything which helps the universities to a clearer view of their own purposes and helps individual members of universities to a clearer view of their own functions should contribute to making the universities leaders in the process of moral regeneration. And the restoration of intellectual standards is something central to the essential purposes of the universities themselves and something in which they should be the natural leaders.

The tendency of British universities, despite their very different origins to move towards a common pattern of activity and organisation has been noted and the present pattern of degree structure and teaching organisation has been summarised, emphasis being placed on the rigidities which are still so much a feature of the pattern. Great stress has been laid on the extent of the financial dependence of the universities on the state; on the powers that puts in the hands of state organs to direct or influence university activity; and on the way those powers are increasingly used, adding substantially on balance to the forces making for uniformity. Reference has been made in several connections to the problems arising from the gap between the number of university places and the number of 'qualified' candidates; to the failure of the universities to do anything substantial to narrow that gap by modification of their traditional practices; and to the anxieties and frustrations of school-leavers hunting for places and assisted in the hunt by a system of state grants whose generosity is not adequately matched by the level of state assistance to the running costs of the universities or the provision of student residences.

These frustrations and the necessarily impersonal relationship in the large universities of today have been noted among the causes of the very obvious malaise of the student population. Nonetheless, it would seem that much the most important cause of that malaise is the widespread intellectual dissatisfaction with modern society which has grown so rapidly among young people and which is intimately connected with the erosion of the sense of moral purpose already noted. It has been suggested that some changes in the university world, especially changes encouraging a feeling of personal responsibility in the individual student, could help to meet this malaise, but little faith has been indicated in any good which might result from concessions to demands for student participation in fundamental university decisions. So far as the effective government of the universities is concerned, it has been suggested that the balance is likely to lie between the providers of finance (at present the state) and the teachers who are the most essential of all the resources needed by a university.

Looking to the universities proper, not to higher education in total, I suggest that in spite of the great variety in the detailed practice of individual institutions, the crucial characteristics are rigidity in structure on the one hand and confusion of purpose on the other. Let us look first at the rigidities.

Perhaps the first rigidity is the one least often commented on, that is the fixed time-scheme of undergraduate courses – still overwhelmingly the main item of university activity. It is, for practical purposes, impossible for anyone to get a first degree in less than three years, in some subjects four or five. The speed at which men and women can learn varies very widely; so does the previous preparation, the degree of knowledge from which they start. But for university purposes all are treated as equal and as capable of proceeding at the same pace, the quick learner who might master the course in two years and the slower of apprehension who would feel more comfortable if allowed four. At school level it is common enough for the brighter pupils to be pushed on and be taking their O levels at 15, but it is not impossible and not counted as failure if they are not ready till 16 or 17. That a university course must be of fixed duration is so universally accepted that one feels very strange in asking the question 'Why?' The only answer which readily occurs is that it is an inheritance from the tradition of apprenticeship; and that does not help very much in the case of non-professional degrees. The most obvious and more rational alternative is that, granted the fallibility of examinations in ascertaining the extent of a candidate's knowledge, the fixed term of study is useful as giving a supplementary guarantee that the candidate has really learned something. Yet this explanation is difficult to reconcile on the one side with the inadequacy of arrangements to ensure that the prescribed period genuinely is spent in study and on the other with the almost exclusive reliance on the terminal examination as the test of achievement.

A second clear aspect of rigidity is the firm tying of students to one place of study, which has already been discussed in Chapters 5 and 6. This rigidity of place is, in fact, closely linked with the rigidity of time because of the normal requirement of a fixed period of study in the university which awards a student's degree, and has been just as little discussed. Associated with it also is the difficulty of changing the subject of study which we may call the rigidity of subject. And fourthly there is still widely prevalent rigidity of form in the still overwhelmingly common specialised honours degree. It is true that real efforts are being made to breach the uniformities of subject and of form but they are as yet only marginally effective.

In the main it remains true that a young man or woman entering a university as an undergraduate is embarking on a course from which little deviation is possible. He, or she, will almost certainly have to remain in the university where he starts for precisely three years and to stick to the limited field which he has initially chosen. It will be impossible to shorten the course and very difficult to lengthen it; and if for any reason he fails to complete it, he will be stamped as a failure and any time he has spent on the course will, so far as formal qualifications or conventional reputation are concerned, have been wasted.

The causes of these rigidities are partly the rules of the universities and partly the working of the system of public financial support. It is the university rules which determine the minimum time to be spent in working for a first degree and the pattern of the degree, but reliance on public support would, apart from any other reasons, make it difficult for a student to prolong that minimum period except in case of illness or other acceptable excuse. In the final analysis it is also public policy which has created the situation of pressure on university accommodation which itself leads to the reluctance of university authorities to let students stay beyond their standard periods of study. Public policy on the one hand encourages many more young people to seek university entry by holding out the promise of a maintenance grant if admission is secured and on the other effectively limits the number of admissions by rationing the financial grants to universities.

Unquestionably rigidity is also encouraged by the growing control of the University Grants Committee and the Department of Education and Science. The imposed uniformity of salary scales, the common standards of building provision, the common level of fees and other specific limitations on freedom of action have already been discussed; but in more intangible ways the growth of central government interest slows up innovation and experimentation, as does the parallel and still more intangible growth in the mechanisms of voluntary co-operation between the universities through the Vice-Chancellors' Committee and other common organs. The constant watchfulness of the Association of University Teachers and the National Union of Students add further weight to the trend towards uniformity of practice and the difficulties of breaking away from it.

The second main characteristic mentioned was confusion of purpose. It is appropriate here to refer back to what has been said about the varieties of higher education. Statistics quoted in Chapter 3 show that the universities account for only a fraction of those receiving post-school or 'higher' education, full-time or part-time. Of course that includes a great deal of study at an intellectual level clearly below that normally associated with universities; but it also includes a fair amount of study at first degree level or not markedly different from it. Professional training in particular is very mixed; some is done very largely within the universities, e.g., medicine, social administration and engineering; some in institutions similar to and associated with universities but not fully assimilated, e.g., teaching; other professional training may be done in universities but is more commonly done outside, e.g., in law, accountancy and architecture. There is certainly no clear set of criteria as to what is proper to university study and what is not.

There are those who would solve the problem of the border-line by moving it so as to include as wide as possible a range of activities. Dr Clark Kerr, the former head of the University of California, in his book on *The Uses of the University* has christened the new form of omni-competent institution the 'multiversity' and has written with apparent approval of the many centres of the University of California, its extension work and numerous research centres, its '10,000 courses', its 'contact with nearly every industry, nearly every level of government, nearly every person in its region', the variation in age, marital status, etc., of its students, the variety of its staff and so on. Kerr accepts that a 'multiversity' may provide at the same time the most advanced research facilities and opportunities for purely scholarly research and courses of instruction both severely practical and pretty elementary. He quotes as illustrative of the opposite view what another distinguished American, Abraham Flexner, wrote of the 'genuine university': 'The heart of a university is the graduate school of arts and sciences, the solidly professional schools and certain research institutes'; and adds that that concept was already dead when Flexner wrote, in 1938.

Kerr goes on further to quote from Allan Nevins: 'Observers of higher education can now foresee the inexorable emergence of an entirely new landscape. It will no longer show us a nation dotted by high academic peaks with lesser hills between; it will be a landscape dominated by mountain ranges.' One such mountain range runs from Boston to Washington and contains nearly half of the American Nobel Prize winners. Another is to be found on the Pacific Coast. (The significance of the two combined is emphasised by Lord Snow's estimate that 80% of the pure science in western countries is to be found in the U.S.A.) What Clark Kerr sees for the future is a 'City of Intellect', a university city with its satellite suburbs which may be viewed as 'encompassing all the intellectual resources of a society' or, wider still, its soul.

This is a glorious conception but we must not be blinded by its glory. The concepts of the multiversity and of the city of the intellect are not by any means identical. It is by no means certain that an institution which attempts to comprise everything within itself will give preference to what is intellectually highest; Flexner might equally well, and perhaps more justifiably, have claimed that his 'genuine university' was the true seed of the City of Intellect. Furthermore any attempt to bring into one organisation 'all the intellectual resources of a society' must raise the spectre of illiberal exclusivity, because that concept leads easily to the idea that whatever is *not* included in the single organisation is unworthy of intellectual consideration. It is the process which leads logically from the idealism of Plato to the rigid thought-moulds of the Politbureau. Clark Kerr himself writes: 'The external view is that the University is radical; the internal reality is that it is conservative'.

Administratively, the attempt to bring every kind of intellectual activity under one cover must lead to enormous and growing difficulties. An institution which covers education in every field from the narrowly vocational to the most abstract academic and at levels varying from what in Britain would be pre-University instruction to post-doctoral research must be faced with almost insoluble problems of allocation of resources; its staff and students must be constantly troubled by uncertainties of loyalty. If the institution is to retain a minimum sense of unity there must be some co-ordination of its multifarious activities. Given California's ten thousand courses, there must be some machinery for deciding whether or not to lay on the ten thousand and first, some authority which directs which teachers provide it and some system of organisation which fits the students who attend it into a a general structure. The machinery of decision can be either authoritarian, concentrated in the hands of professional administrators, or democratic, providing for more or less participation by the whole academic body. So far as it leans to the authoritarian, the sense of community is lessened as the teachers feel more and more a 'We-They' relationship with the administration. So far as it leans to the democratic, the attempt to involve large numbers of academics in every decision must lead both to great slowness and conservatism and to the absorption in committee work of a great deal of academic time which could be better devoted to teaching or research. As to students, we have already seen that the size and impersonality of institutions is a probable contributary cause of current student discontents; widening the area of activity can only increase the feeling of lack of contact by making it more difficult for the individual student to identify the particular unit to which he can feel himself to belong.

The multiversity is likely to meet internally many of the difficulties which have already been noted as affecting United Kingdom universities in their relations with government. Indeed the multiversity is more like an attempt to bring within one system nearly all the varieties of higher education which were referred to in Chapter 3. It is tempting, from the point of view of one popular school of thought, to think that 'co-ordination' of all those activities by a single authority, whether the state Department of Education, as could happen in the United Kingdom, or a 'multiversity', is the best way of resolving their differences and conflicting claims on resources. The great difficulty in any such resolution by some overall decision-making apparatus is the absence of any obvious criteria of decision. We have seen in Chapter 10, how hard it is to find calculable criteria for decisions about allocation of resources to and within universities of the British pattern; the task would be harder still in institutions of even wider and more varied scope and functions. In practice still more would tend to be left to the pulls and pushes of pressure groups and the private consultations of administrators.

The desirability of catering somehow for a wide range of aspects of higher education is not for a moment disputed; nor is the enormous advantage of contact between people working in different institutions on facets of the same intellectual problems – the City of Intellect of Nevins and Kerr or the 'ecological centre' of Ben David which was referred to in Chapter 4. What is suggested is that it would be better to attempt this variety of tasks through a corresponding variety of genuinely independent institutions rather than trying to deal with them all as integral parts of very large multipurpose institutions. It is pertinent to note that in the fundamental re-examination of the French University system now in process, following the disturbances of May 1968, very serious thought is being given to the breaking up of the University of Paris and other large units.

We have to provide for traditional university courses leading to straightforward first degrees in arts and sciences, for high level professional courses, for post-school technical education partly at, and partly ranking below, professional standard and for post-graduate courses; for opportunities of individual research of the Ph.D. type, and for higher level or more systematic research in organised units or institutes; for full-time students and for part-timers, including both part-time study aiming at a degree or diploma and part-time study of a less formal kind; in other words for all the variety of studies and researches contained within the statistics which were summarised in Chapter 3. British Universities have gone less far than some American in the extent of their activities within this range. Some previous passages of this essay may have appeared to argue that they ought to go further in broadening their activities. The point of the previous discussion has, however, rather been that the boundary lines at present drawn seem to have little logical basis. On balance I would conclude that while some of the boundary lines between the U (what is appropriate to a university) and the non-U (what is not) are too sharp, the solution does not lie in developing institutions which, as individual organs will cover everything, U and non-U, but rather in giving narrower definitions to the spheres of action of individual institutions while at the same time seeking to bring about a redistribution of functions between institutions and – in certain respects – reducing the differences of prestige between the U and the non-U.

The same general conclusion emerges from another line of approach. In Chapter 3, reference was made to the 'mainstream' of education, comprising a series of stages: primary or preparatory; secondary up to O level standards; Sixth Form; undergraduate; post-graduate; and post-doctoral. Of these stages, the last three are all at present assumed to lie within the sphere of the University, and I suspect that the attempt to cater for all those three stages in one institution is responsible for a good many current difficulties. Traditionally the university has provided the final stage of formal education or tuition as well as providing opportunities for the first steps in individual discovery or research. Until a few decades ago the last stage of systematic education for the vast majority of students was the undergraduate course. That is no longer true; increasingly the final stages of tuition take place at the post-graduate level. It therefore becomes questionable whether all that is now contained in undergraduate work ought still to be included in the university range and linked with post-graduate work as it is today.

The tradition of British universities has leaned very definitely to the 'élite' concept of the university rather than to the 'general'; that is to the view that a university is a place of study for the very best, not a place to which anyone may claim admission. That tradition has been somewhat eroded by the current expansionist mood and by both the greatly enlarged demand and the apparent social need for education at the traditional university level; but basically it is the right tradition. Universities have been and should continue to be concerned first of all with excellence not with universality in the sense of providing something for everyone. But excellence is now to be sought at a higher level. What the élite tradition needs now is reinterpretation in the modern conditions of knowledge in which the highest level, to which the élite concept is fully applicable, has acquired a different meaning. It is no longer acceptable to treat everything which has formerly fallen within the scope of universities as reserved to an élite; but it is an even worse mistake to assume that therefore everything which now falls within the scope of a university ought to be available to everyone. Clark Kerr's multiversity would need to provide special high-level institutes for the élite, as indeed is so successfully done in the University of California and other large American universities. What is argued here is that, organisationally it is better to recognise the need for such provision in separate institutions rather than confusing them with more general provision.

There is yet another strand of thought to add to this general discussion. A great many people in Britain have come to believe that, at secondary level, the old practice of providing different types of education in separate institutions sought to be replaced by a 'comprehensive' system in which all types of secondary education are grouped in unified institutions. Much of the argument about this has been political and inspired by somewhat naïve expectations about the effects of such a change on class structure; but there are academic and wider social arguments for it also which I believe to be convincing. It is natural then to ask why the objective should not be to extend the comprehensive principle into the higher education sphere as well. More pointedly, there seems to be a prima facie case for a charge of inconsistency against the government which, while pressing its policy of comprehensive secondary education almost brutally on reluctant local education authorities, has explicitly proposed a 'Binary' policy in higher education. Maturer consideration may, however, persuade us that the inconsistency is only superficial. An essential difference between the secondary and tertiary levels is that secondary education is now as near as makes no difference a universal service, compulsory for everyone up to the age of 15 and de facto available for everyone who chooses to take it up to much higher ages, whereas tertiary or higher education is still provided, in any of its varied forms, for only a minority. It is not implausible that just as primary education, once it became a universal public service, acquired a common pattern, so secondary education should now move in the same direction at least to the extent of being provided in institutions of common pattern, whereas tertiary education, precisely because it is nothing like a universal service, can maintain a far more varied pattern. This is not an argument to be pressed to extremes; certainly it is not in the least urged that the actual content of secondary education should be wholly uniform. It is a matter of balance of advantage and what is suggested is that the modern developments both in the growth of knowledge and the enlargement of the general provision of education tilt the balance at secondary level against specialisation and towards comprehensive institutions, but that at the tertiary level the balance remain in favour of greater specialisation both in curricula and in institutions.

The clearest practical outcome of all this so far as universities are concerned is that we need a new look at the point where pre-university work ends and full university work starts. It is right for that break still to come normally at the age of 18 or 19? In times past it was common for boys to matriculate at the age of 14 or so (Cardinal Wolsey is said to have graduated B.A. at 15). Nearly fifty years ago, in 1919, I went up to the university when I was just turned 17 and felt nothing strange about it. Today it is still possible under university statutes for a student to enter at 17 but it is a rare occurrence. The age of entry has gradually risen, not, I imagine, because people mature intellectually later and later but because, with the growth of knowledge, the period over which systematic education can usefully extend has constantly lengthened and the age at which the last stage of that systematic education should start has correspondingly receded.

The student who follows the mainstream all the way is likely to end his full-time organised education at least with a Master's degree, and probably with a Ph.D., at the age of 23 or 24. It would thus be more reasonable that he should start on his final stage at 20 than at 18.

At the same time the present structure offers inadequate opportunity to the young man or woman who may want to go on with an academic-type education beyond the standard of A level but may not really be anxious to stay in full-time education to the age of 21 or 22 or to take the still normal specialised honours degree type of course. Looking purely to the resources problem we might be able to provide a post A level education for appreciably more young people if we did not insist that they must go on for a further three years or not at all. The best use of our resources might be to provide an education falling short of honours level for a larger number than at present get to a university, plus an education up to post-graduate level for a good many more than now get it, rather than to fall between two stools by struggling to get the current numbers up to honours level and then being short of resources to take a sufficient number to the post-graduate level.

If therefore we were now starting from scratch and designing an educational structure related to the present range of knowledge and the present scale of available resources the best structure might well be seen to be secondary schools ending normally with one year of Sixth Form work, i.e., at about age 17; colleges offering two and three year courses which would take over the top layer of current Sixth Form work but extend into what is now done in the first year or two of undergraduate work; and universities which would admit students at about the level normally now attained at the commencement of the final undergraduate year and take them up to and beyond the level now aimed at in the 'taught' master's degrees. This would largely be a systematisation of the situation which effectively prevails in the U.S.A., where children leave the High Schools with a standard of attainment probably a year behind that of good English secondary schools, where the Junior Colleges or Liberal Arts Colleges and many indeed of the lesser-known universities perform the function envisaged for the second stage without aspiring to post-graduate and research activity, and where that activity is in the main concentrated in a minority of universities, including of course those with international reputations, which normally have highly organised separate Graduate Schools and in some cases undertake only graduate activity. Many of the colleges at the second level maintain, at their appropriate level, a very high standard.

A powerful additional argument for such a structure is that it would facilitate the postponement of specialisation and leave more time for much more general education in basic science in combination with literary subjects. It would thus serve the purposes in mind in Professor Pippard's proposal (see Chapter 5) to remodel science degrees more thoroughly and, I venture to think, more effectively. It would also, I believe, afford a better means of giving students a wider view of current affairs combined with real depth of study of special disciplines than the somewhat artificially grouped combinations of the joint first degrees developed in the newer universities.

Obviously there are many side issues to any such radical transformation. If Liberal Arts Colleges come into existence, how far should they be residential? (I would hope that they would not, for reasons already given, fall into the mistake of encouraging students to leave home unless they were going into a genuinely collegiate atmosphere.) How would they be related to existing Colleges of Education, and to Technical Colleges, etc? (It might be hoped that a new structure would help to lessen the distinctions now drawn between university and non-university institutions at the lower age levels). Would entry to a full university be possible only after completing a 'College' course or would promising students be able to make the transition earlier? Professional degrees would presumably become in a sense post-graduate, as they are in America, by being provided only at Universities after completion of appropriate preliminary studies at a 'Junior College'.

Unfortunately we are not starting from scratch but from a very firmly based and rigid system. British undergraduate education and British first degrees can properly be claimed as among the best in the world – for the conditions in which they attained their present form, a generation or so ago. Their virtues and high quality have given them a very precise form and a very firm hold. Because the hold of the present pattern is so firm and so universally established in British universities it is particularly difficult to see how any process of gradual change can be brought about. They appear now, like other organisms which have developed a high degree of adaptation to particular circumstances, to have lost the power of further evolution. This may, however, be too pessimistic a conclusion. It is clearly not sensible to think of a new pattern being created by a grand decision by the common will of the universities or by a single edict of the state. But there may still be ways of moving by gradual and partial steps to a different pattern, a different way of breaking up the time-states of higher education. Two lines of development immediately suggest themselves.

First, 'Liberal Arts Colleges' overlapping both the most advanced work of secondary schools and the earlier years of undergraduate work as now conceived at the universities could emerge from the growth of Sixth Form Colleges and County Colleges and from the development of work in the humanities and pure science at Colleges of Technology. Bases already exist for such developments and the more deliberate creation of 'Liberal Arts Colleges' could follow experiments in such existing institutions. Secondly existing university institutions might initiate new kinds of degrees designed deliberately for the age-group 20 to 23 rather than the age-group 18 to 21. This would be a more radical and deliberate innovation; but it is something which might suit particularly well the resources and circumstances of certain of the more specialised institutions of the University of London such as the Imperial College of Science and Technology, the London School of Economics and the School of Oriental and African Studies. As has been noted earlier the London School of Economics in late years has repeatedly felt uneasy about its present distribution of effort between undergraduate and post-graduate work, at times being tempted to abandon undergraduate activity altogether because its facilities are more appropriate to more advanced work but at the same time feeling reluctant to commit itself wholly to post-graduate work of the older pattern. Traditions and present conventions apart, the logical answer for the London School of Economics would be to offer as is its normal 'first' course a course starting at about the level of the present third year student and going on to at least the level of the present taught Master's degree; and the same might equally suit some other colleges and schools in London and more embryonic units which might develop as semi-independent schools in other universities. It is a pattern, too, which might well prove on examination more attractive than the present two-year Master's degree to the new Business Schools in London and Manchester.

Of course there would be many problems. One would be nomenclature; should the holder of such a new degree be called a Bachelor or a Master? Granted the acceptance of the basic idea there can be little doubt that academic ingenuity would find an answer to that. More difficult might be the basis of admission of students. Some might be taken direct from 'Liberal Arts Colleges' if they develop as suggested but initially most must come from university students of the current type, especially if intellectual quality is to be maintained. Institutions offering the new kind of degrees might be prepared to take students on the basis of their performance at some half-way stage of orthodox university courses, but would students be content to abandon such courses without attaining the degrees they had originally had in mind, and would other universities be happy about the loss of possibly their more enterprising students at that half-way stage?

I do not pretend to see all the answers to these and other problems with any precision but I do believe that they could be worked out in process of time if the experiment could once be initiated. Perhaps the greatest single obstacle to such experimentation is the difficulty of any institution initiating such an experiment within the present rigid pattern of financial and other controls. One thing that might be necessary if the London institutions mentioned were to be free to make such experiments would be the removal of the remaining controls of the University of London over the form of degree for which the constituent Colleges teach; and perhaps their complete independence of the University. Most important of all, however, is likely to be freedom from the restrictions imposed by the whole existing structure of state financing of university education, both direct and via student grants.

Three kinds of change are needed to put institutions of higher education in a freer position to experiment; the reduction of the part played in university finance by direct grants from the state and particularly an increase in the part played by fees paid by students, even if a substantial part of the fees are paid in the first place out of state-provided assistance; the introduction of a loan scheme to cover at least part of the fees and maintenance payable by students so as to give them a stronger individual interest in the value of courses of study; and a reversal of the discouragement, through taxation, of private benefactions. The advantages of establishing a more varied basis for the main finance of universities have been discussed in Chapter 11 and need not be repeated here except to emphasise the openings which that would give to more varied kinds of development. As to the possibility of such changes, it has already been noted that student loan schemes have come increasingly under discussion in recent years; it is more and more realised that the principal direct beneficiary from the provision of higher education is the individual who receives it and that, so long as it is not feasible to provide it for everyone or even for all who have the intelligence and basic education to benefit from it, social justice points rather to some system of ultimate payment by the beneficiaries than towards the provision of higher education as a (nearly) free service. Reviving the habit of private benefactions is a good deal more difficult because it depends largely on both the reduction of the general burden of direct taxation (which, desirable as it is, must depend on wider considerations than policy with regard to university finance) and greater generosity in the allowance of deductions for charitable, etc., gifts. The mere substitution on a significant scale of fee income for direct state grants might, however, have some effect in persuading potential donors that private gifts would not automatically be offset by reduction in state assistance.

Looking again at the situation which would be created if the developments sketched above were undertaken, it would not merely provide more varied opportunities for those who want to go on to a stage beyond G.C.E. 'A' levels but not necessarily to full honours degree standard and a better dividing up of the stages of higher education; it might do several other things. First it might meet in a more satisfactory way the dissatisfactions which led Mr Crosland to make his famous 'Binary System' proposal. That suffered from the defect of appearing to envisage two rival systems running in parallel with different purposes and different systems of control and, by their very grouping into *two* systems, to exaggerate their rivalry and potential opposition. The ideas suggested here envisage rather a multiple system, with not merely two but many varieties of institution, but with no break in the essential unity of purpose of the academically most advanced institutions, the post-graduate schools. Within such a varied system, there would still be room for individual institutions to change their character, to develop and, as in the past, to move up in the academic scale; but those that remained concerned with levels below the highest could still feel, as good secondary schools do today, that they were discharging an essential task in

118

the total educational structure without any suggestion of inferiority because they belonged to the wrong half of a 'Binary' system.

Secondly, such a new system would perhaps help to solve some of the present unease about the relation of teaching and research. Inevitably the present assumption of a natural interest by every university teacher in research would be transferred far more to the 'full university' or post-graduate school than to the 'Liberal Arts College'. Teachers in the former would be dealing with students either at or near the borders of knowledge and approaching the stage of original research; those in the latter with students still some way off it. This would not mean that teachers at the college level would be debarred from personal research activities; many might do very valuable work just as teachers at school level have done in the past. But they would not be expected automatically to be involved in research. That alone would go some way to meet the difficulty already referred to that, under the present system, it is difficult to buy more teaching (if the community wants it) without automatically buying more research (which it may not want so much or in the same subjects). This would not however be the whole answer to the problems arising from the confusion of the teaching and the research function. A further contribution to that would be made if funds for the assistance of research were more explicitly separated from the general grants to universities and if – contrary to general practice today – academic staff were paid specifically both for participation in organised research and for teaching over and above a basic minimum so that a personal choice could be made on a more explicitly calculated basis.

This would, I believe be better than the proposal of the Prices and Incomes Board in 1968, that extra awards should be made to teachers of special competence. Initially it might be even more shocking to some academic opinion because it would involve an even more thorough recognition of the distinctness of the teaching and the research functions. It would not, however carry any implication, such as was in the P.I.B. proposal, that teaching was to be preferred to research and on further thought I hope it might be recognised that both better teaching and better research could result if each were explicitly rewarded. Whatever academic idealists may dream of, academic behaviour is still greatly influenced by material incentives, as was the impression formed long ago by Adam Smith which led him to his famous exposition, in *The Wealth of Nations* (Book V, Chapter 1.), of the advantages of paying university teachers according to the amount of teaching they did rather than on a basis of fixed emoluments. Adam Smith expressed the essence of his view in the sentence: 'The proper performance of every service seems to require that its pay or recompense should be as exactly as possible proportional to the nature of the service'.

I do not suggest a general reversion to the older practice, existing in Scottish universities until a generation or two ago and still to be found in Germany, in which Professors enjoyed a life-term tenure with a stipend assured irrespective of any duties, and collected fees from every student who attended any lectures they chose to give (though such an arrangement has something to commend it on a strictly limited scale as a means of attracting distinguished scholars in the closing years of their active life). It would however be possible to devise various intermediate salary structures in which remuneration depended in part on the actual amount of teaching given.

A third advantage of a more varied structure would be that it would make it easier to make experiments in other directions which have been suggested in earlier chapters, including more 'open' degree structures, great possibilities of transfers from institution to institution, new kinds of examination technique, etc.

Most important of all, however, is the possibility that a real shake-up in the university system seems to be the only way in which openings could be created for the revival of a sense of moral purpose, with which one might expect to see the revival in the strength of real scholarship as opposed to sophisticated theorising. Superficially it might be supposed that the increasing influence exercised by the state might be used to reintroduce the fading sense of purpose; but, given the political structure of this country, it is highly unlikely that state interventions will be inspired by anything deeper than efficiency, economy and the serving of short-term political ends. Universities have best served their most basic purposes of being, as in Clark Kerr's description, the 'soul' of the country and when they have been independent of government and inspired by some vital and independent philosophy. One cannot synthesise a new philosophy which might again make the university world the true soul of the country but one can seek to change the system on which it operates so as to restore its independence and at least give a soil in which a new philosophy might grow.

58

CONCLUSION

Robert O. Berdahl

Source: R. O. Berdahl, *British Universities and the State*, Berkeley: University of California Press and London: Cambridge University Press, 1959, pp. 183–94.

The problem of relations between universities and the state is becoming increasingly significant in most democratic countries. Growing state involvement in university finances is everywhere present or impending;[1] and the Sputnik era has tended to magnify even further the universities' importance to the nation. Although the university-state relations described in this study relate primarily to the unique British circumstances in which all the universities are *de jure* private institutions, many of the theoretical and *de facto* political problems remain the same whether the universities are public or private. The central question which forms the background of most of these problems is: "What may a community legitimately ask of its universities?"

At a conference held on this general topic in 1933, Dr. Ernest Wilkins, President of Oberlin College, offered one answer. A university, he said, must not only, like other private corporations, ensure that its wares are sound, fairly priced, and of the quality represented; it must also sense "a deeper obligation . . . to be responsive to . . . [and] to work and plan with constant reference to social needs and opportunities, present and future."[2]

Such a prospect is abhorrent, however, to people like Michael Oakeshott, Professor of Political Science at the London School of Economics, who see as its logical consequence the egalitarian demand ". . . that the university should move step for step with the world, at the same speed, and partaking in every eccentricity of the world's fashion, refusing nothing that is offered, responsive to every suggestion." Oakeshott concedes that "in the long run" the universities will always more or less reflect the world in which they exist; but he insists that they not yield to outside pressures which would entail for them "a loss of identity."[3]

To Sir William Hamilton, the nineteenth-century exponent of university reform,[4] state interference with the universities appeared less as a threat to their sense of identity than as a means of helping them to help themselves:

A university is a trust confided by the state to certain hands for the common interest of the nation; nor has it ever heretofore been denied that a university may, and ought, by the state to be from time to time corrected, reformed, or recast, in conformity to accidental changes of relation, and looking towards an improved accomplishment of its essential ends.[5]

A much less favorable view of the role of the state in university affairs was taken by John MacMurray, Professor of Philosophy at St. Andrews University. According to him, since knowledge and learning are inherently human and international in scope, "a university can only serve its community by serving humanity. . . . If it were to adopt an exclusively national outlook or to become the servant of a merely national policy, it would betray the nation it thought to serve."[6]

In writing on the general problem of the state and private associations, Lord Lindsay of Birker has offered one theoretical answer to the question of the respective rights of the state and the universities. Distinguishing between "society" and the "state," Lord Lindsay envisages the latter as merely one of many social institutions serving the former; however, because it is the most powerful and one of the most inclusive of the social institutions, the state is assigned the function which Bosanquet has termed "operative criticism"—namely, the general scrutiny of society for the purpose of resolving disharmonies and conflicts which result when men with limited perspectives and loyalties work in groups with limited purposes.[7] According to this analysis, then, the state is not a higher type of institution than a university, but it does have the right to see that university policies are in general harmony with the basic needs of society.

J. D. Mabbott, in a closely reasoned work entitled *The State and the Citizen*, has attempted to delineate more detailed criteria for valid state intervention. He contends that, aside from essential state control in matters of criminal and civil law and the maintenance of peace and order, private associations should be autonomous in all instances except those in which *only* state regulation can achieve the desired ends. This seems satisfactorily definite, but then Mabbott opens a veritable Pandora's box of qualifications by adding: "unless it is shown in any particular case that state action achieves a certain end better than voluntary combination."[8] This clause—and particularly the word "better"—so oversimplifies the complex relationship between state and university that the yardstick he has given is robbed of most of its value. At the very least, the statement should be expanded to read: "unless it is shown . . . that state action achieves a certain end *so much better than voluntary combination that the damage to the private associations involved is more than compensated for by the increased general good.*" This concept, if amended, would imply that state intervention in university affairs would be legitimate either (1) when only state action could accomplish the goal, or (2) when national intervention could produce results that seemed to justify the inevitable damage to university autonomy.

The foregoing analysis suggests that theoretical approaches to the central question do not lead to any clear-cut or automatic directives on the proper times for, or amount of, national interference with universities. On the contrary, the evolution of university-state relations over the past century indicates that governments have increasingly been guided in such matters by material imperatives rather than by abstract principles. A kind of geopolitical law, by which highly planned states tend to "drive out" less planned ones,[9] has made internal conditions in most states more subject than ever before to the pressures of external movements and events, thus limiting the choices in such domestic matters as education. Even in the nineteenth century, the intrinsic desirability of lessening poverty, ignorance, and disease had already prompted many democratic states to move a considerable distance away from the laissez-faire pole; but the trend toward state planning was given its greatest impetus by the immense problems of a series of economic depressions and World War I, and was finally capped by the climactic struggle of World War II and its uneasy aftermath. Such a vast increase in state power could have come only at the expense of many of the private associations which had earlier enjoyed relative freedom in their respective spheres of operation. The "pluralist state"—though by no means yet "singular"—has become much less "plural."

Of the state's changing relations with various private associations, none have become more complex than those with the universities. For although the government has had an equal or even greater interest in the conduct of various associations within, for instance, industry, labor, and agriculture, none of these can maintain with as much justification as the universities that continuing state regulation is antipathetic to their true functioning.

Admittedly, institutions like the churches and the press can attach equal urgency to their demands for freedom from state domination,[10] but they nevertheless do not have the same direct bearing on national survival and prosperity as do the universities. It is, thus, a paradox that in the case of the universities, the state is dealing with an extremely sensitive type of association which must not be too closely supervised, but whose work is so vital to the nation that it must somehow be harmonized with the over-all objectives of national planning.[11] This, then, is the general context in which the British governmental actions affecting the universities must be judged.

The historical sections of this study have indicated that in earlier centuries, before the rise of scientific warfare or totalitarian opponents,[12] the British state could and did allow a very high degree of autonomy to the universities—especially since the universities then had no monopoly, as they now seem to have, on the production of advanced thinkers in the field of science. A number of commentators have noted that in the universities' "worst century," the eighteenth, many of the foremost men of science, and of letters as well, functioned outside the universities.

Before the eighteenth century the state had, of course, felt constrained to intervene occasionally in some aspects of university life, particularly those relating to religious orthodoxy. But these interventions had never assumed the character of continuing supervision, and since the religious and political settlement of 1689, the universities had enjoyed a century and a half of almost absolute liberty. That is why, when the government in the nineteenth century tried to correct the abuses which had meanwhile gained a foothold in the universities, the latter made such an outcry against alleged state trespasses on private rights. But the mid-century Royal Commissions on Oxford and Cambridge Universities clearly established the fact that the universities were "national institutions," in the sense that they had certain minimum obligations to the state which the state had a right to compel them to meet, by *force majeure* if necessary.

Since that time the issue has become mainly one of redefining the content of these minimum obligations and of refining the techniques for ensuring their fulfillment. The inception in 1889 of small state grants to the modern English and Welsh universities, the subsequent increase in the scale of these awards, the formation in 1919 of the University Grants Committee, and the inclusion of Oxford and Cambridge on the grant list in 1923—all these things merely tended to bring the universities to the state's continuing attention sooner than might otherwise have been the case; for the grants were the occasion and not the cause of the state's increased concern with the universities. One might say that if the grants had not been needed they would have had to be invented, for no one can seriously contend that even if the universities were at this moment independently wealthy, the contemporary state would be able to forego efforts to integrate their activities into the framework of national planning.

The U.G.C. has been, therefore, merely the felicitous instrument whereby government planning could be effectively coördinated with state aid to universities. There is little doubt but that the universities' "coöperation" has been somewhat accelerated by the U.G.C.'s financial sanction, but were this weapon not there, some political sanction would surely have replaced it. Such an interpretation naturally raises the question, "Would some other type of state policy toward the universities have been better than the one employed, which leaned so heavily on the U.G.C.?"

It is widely acknowledged that "academic freedom, like virtue, is the permanent object of appreciative and solicitous clichés." It may therefore be permissible for me to contribute a slightly distorted one in asserting that the present system of university-state relations is, to paraphrase Dr. Pangloss, "the best of all possible systems" in the British world as it is today. It is important to stress the qualification "possible," for under other conditions, one could have proposed a more appealing ideal than the present tenuous balance of forces described in preceding chapters. However, given the universities' relative poverty and the state's need to mobilize vital resources to maintain economic and military strength, no other system could have done what the present system has accomplished—namely, integrated university operations into the framework of national planning without damaging the essential attributes of university autonomy.[13]

Some people had hoped that the universities themselves could undertake the task of coördinating their policies with those of the nation. For example, Sir John Anderson (now Lord Waverly), Churchill's Chancellor of the Exchequer in 1944–45, after admonishing the universities to "regard themselves no longer as isolated units, but rather as parts of an articulated whole [whose] activities must be coördinated in the interests of efficiency and economy of effort," stated that "the responsibility for this coördination should be placed upon the universities themselves through the appropriate organs of collaboration."[14]

However, although "the voluntary way is the British way," and although the British universities have, on their own initiative, taken many forward steps (in particular, the enhancement of the coördinating role of the Committee of Vice-Chancellors and Principals[15]), nearly everyone will now agree that the major task of coördination belongs to the state. This is particularly true as long as the state acts primarily through the U.G.C., with its predominantly academic membership. As was seen in earlier pages, the Vice-Chancellors' Committee itself issued a Note in 1946 welcoming more definite state guidance channeled through the U.G.C.;[16] and later, members of the Committee of Vice-Chancellors and Principals testified before the Select Committee on Estimates that they did not consider themselves, as representatives of the various universities, to be the proper persons to sit on a national coördinating committee with public powers.[17]

Furthermore, it is perhaps expecting too much to ask the universities to engage voluntarily in continuous self-examination and self-reform, since academicians seem to share the normal human frailties:

> It is . . . too true that the possessors of vested interests in knowledge, as in material things, tend to fight furiously against those who would introduce a new order. Anyone who has considered the history of universities must have come to the conclusion that in these matters they are no exceptions to the general rule.[18]

Therefore, the University Grants Committee appears to have been the best possible means of reconciling the conflicting claims of national needs and university autonomy. That the U.G.C. could not itself have treated the universities more liberally than it has is indicated by the heavy pressure brought to bear by the Public Accounts Committee for closer governmental supervision of university expenditures.[19]

One of the chief values of the U.G.C. is its self-restraint; it tries not to invoke more than the minimum power necessary to accomplish its goals, and it relies as much as possible on university efforts. Sir Walter Moberly spoke of this quality in reference to the U.G.C.'s role as catalyst to long-range planning within the universities: "[The Grants Committee] is a stimulating influence, always inciting the universities to plan for themselves somewhat more fully than they might do if they were left to themselves."[20]

The U.G.C. as an administrative device is not without its faults, but these are not crucial, and must, as was stated earlier, be judged against the background of the possible. Two substantial criticisms which might be made of the Grants Committee concern its potential rigidity in the face of situations requiring unorthodox responses, and its availability as an instrument of possible future abuse, should conditions force a change for the worse in university-state relations.

Regarding the first point, a writer in the *Times Educational Supplement* raised the following queries:

> How does a strong committee of the academically orthodox come to a state of mind when it is willing to commit large sums of public money to support an experiment which at the time is academically unorthodox? . . . If Lord Lindsay of Birker had not been a power in the Labour Party, would the University College of North Stafford-shire, with its original curriculum, ever have come to the light of day? And if Lord Cherwell had not had the ear of Sir Winston Churchill, would so great a sum have been now devoted to the development of the Imperial College of Science and Technology?[21]

On the basis of its recent policies, one may doubt whether the U.G.C. does in fact suffer from this much rigidity. However, just as in the case of the centralization of funds and hence of power in the Arts Council, which distributes state subsidies to the fine arts,[22] one may nevertheless regret the decline in the number of private sources of financial support for proposals which seem to offer less "safety" than others. The spectre of the Public Accounts Committee demanding its pound of flesh for a costly educational gamble gone wrong is enough to make any public figure think twice.[23] But given the lessening role of private benefactions in university finances and the necessity to keep university tuition fees low so as not to drive away those students who have no scholarships, there seems to be no alternative to the U.G.C. and its subsidies.

The second possible criticism of the U.G.C. is more significant, for although nearly all the commentators, including myself, stand in admiration of the Grants Committee's present enlightened personnel and practices, the danger must be faced that it has acquired a formidable *potentiality* for power which could be abused in less happy times. The U.G.C.'s broad terms of reference (see above, p. 76) have occasioned both abstract[24] and concrete[25] criticisms since 1945. Sir Walter Moberly has commented on this problem, and his conclusions are in the best tradition of British empiricism:

> Undoubtedly the machinery exists by which the State could, if it were so minded, apply almost irresistible financial pressure to the Universities. The basis of confidence is the conviction not that the State cannot but that the State will not want to do so; it rests, in other words, not upon law but upon the convention of the Constitution.
>
> ....
>
> In so far as the actual operation of grants now or later gives cause for anxiety, that is a serious matter, but in so far as forms of words give rise to theoretical questions, I do not think that is a very serious matter.[26]

However, Sir Walter has elsewhere related the problem of possible state abuse of the universities to the broader issue of an informed public interest in academic freedom in the universities—which is a very different issue, by the way, from the matter of public indifference toward internal university policies (see p. 169). According to Sir Walter, "the tacit understanding that has hitherto existed between the universities and the governing class must now be extended to a much wider public."[27] He sees the increasingly representative selection of university students from all grades of society and the universities' extramural education programs as hopeful harbingers of that more widespread understanding of university objectives.

Dr. D. W. Logan, Principal of the University of London, is not so optimistic on this point:

> In the outside world there is, I fear, a great lack of understanding of what the University is, what it stands for and what it does. The responsibility for this sad state of affairs rests largely on the University itself which could justly be accused of going out of its way to hide its light under a bushel. It is vitally necessary that the problems with which the University is faced—and they are many and complex—should be more fully comprehended and the points at issue more clearly grasped than is at present the case.[28]

It is perhaps not necessary to dwell further on this need to interest a wider segment of public opinion than has hitherto been approached, in the broad values of academic freedom; this is one area of the possible, however, where it seems obvious that more could be done in Britain.

Having said this, one must acknowledge that in nearly all other respects the British have done exceedingly well in reconciling the principles of central planning, accountability of public funds, and university autonomy. One cannot but be impressed with the tremendous vitality of contemporary British universities; surely the state leadership of recent decades cannot have been too oppressive.

The question now remains to be answered: "How much of the British pattern is applicable elsewhere?" As was stated in the Introduction, the particular conditions which have contributed to the success of the British system are recognized to be essentially indigenous to the British Isles. However, a conference of European rectors and vice-chancellors found that while the British system would not be appropriate in some nations, the over-all principles of the University Grants Committee constitute "a model which could be followed in many countries."[29] President Dodds of Princeton University has placed the United States among the nations in which the U.G.C. system would not be suitable; the main reasons he gives for this conclusion, over and above the general difference between the dual American system of public and private universities and the unitary system found in Britain,[30] are:

1 the wide differences between [Britain and the United States] in respect to popular views as to both the scope and function of the universities; and
2 the radical differences between the Treasury and Exchequer systems of the two countries, and the legislative and administrative habits which the two systems reflect.[31]

President Dodds is certainly well qualified to speak on this subject; however, I respectfully suggest that the growing financial problems of most private colleges and universities in the United States may invite attempts to adapt some of the general principles of the British system to the American context—at the state, if not at the national, level.

The general principles in Britain which may serve as guides wherever democracies are required to face similar problems appear to be as follows: The state has a legitimate interest in the over-all policies of the universities, whether these are public or private institutions and whether or not public funds are involved. The universities should form their educational policies with sensitivity for national needs, and, if subsidized by public funds, after consultation with the appropriate governmental offices. In case of disagreement over ends or means between the state and the universities, the universities' judgment should prevail, with the understanding that they have the responsibility of demonstrating the wisdom of their decisions within a reasonable time, and subject always to ultimate political intervention in the face of a major breakdown in higher education. The execution of the subsidized policies should be entirely free from the close state supervision which normally accompanies grants of public funds. And, finally, the state organ which links the universities to the government should be composed primarily—but not exclusively—of university men who are not only thoroughly familiar with the work and ideals of the universities but also cognizant of the state's broader domestic problems and external responsibilities.

Although the social institutions and traditions of other democracies may preclude their creating exact replicas of the University Grants Committee with its peculiarly informal modes of operation, the general applicability of the principles enumerated above could lead to Britain's ultimately being regarded not only as the home of the Mother of Parliaments, but also as the progenitor of the most enlightened principles of state conduct toward universities.

Notes

1 "Because of the nature of our contemporary world and society, the inevitable trend in most countries . . . has been towards a greater dependence on and participation by government in respect of university finances and revenues. . . . This dependence is likely to continue." Dr. N. A. M. MacKenzie, President of the University of British Columbia, in "Government and the Universities," in Seventh Congress of the Universities of the Commonwealth, *Report of the Proceedings* (1953), p. 23.
2 New York University, Conference of Universities, *The Obligations of Universities to the Social Order* (1933), pp. 84–86.
3 Michael Oakeshott, "The Universities," *Cambridge Journal*, 2 (1949), 523.
4 See above, p. 27.
5 Sir William Hamilton, *Discussions on Philosophy and Literature, Education and University Reform* (2d ed., 1853), p. 538.
6 John MacMurray, "The Functions of a University," *Political Quarterly*, 15 (1944), 277. Dr. Julian Huxley of UNESCO has called attention to other supranational problems of universities: those connected with religious universities (such as the Islamic University in Cairo, Egypt) and with universities controlled by groups outside the national borders (such as the American University in Beirut, Lebanon). In "Relations of the State and the Universities," in Sixth Congress of the Universities of the Commonwealth, *Report of the Proceedings* (1948), p. 40.
7 A. D. Lindsay, *The Modern Democratic State* (1943), p. 245.
8 J. D. Mabbott, *The State and the Citizen* (1952), p. 126.
9 Critics of the totally planned state claim, of course, that in the long run the power of spiritual values and creative liberties in pluralist states will prevail over "efficient tyranny"; but this study must recognize the fact that the short-run danger of economic decline and/or military defeat has forced the Western democracies to accept a compromise between planning and laissez faire which is much closer to the former than it would otherwise have been. See, for example, E. H. Carr, *The Soviet Impact on the Western World* (1947).
10 See, for example, J. N. Figgis' classic study, *Churches in the Modern State* (1913).
11 It is interesting to note that two prominent figures in Britain have both advanced analogies of university-state relations, neither of which embodies satisfactorily the paradox described above. (To be fair, neither was probably intended to be examined too critically.) Sir Walter Moberly, chairman of the University Grants Committee during the crucial years between 1935 and 1949, has written that university-state relations resemble less those between consumer and producer

than those between patron and artist. "The cogency of the maxim [He who pays the piper calls the tune] varies with the piper. If you are engaging Toscanini and his orchestra, you will do well to leave to him the major voice in deciding the programme." Moberly, *The Crisis in the University* (1949), pp. 239, 229.

R. A. Butler, Chancellor of the Exchequer between 1951 and 1955 and well known for his penchant for analogies, called attention to the need "for a garden of learning . . . where thought is uninhibited and all orthodoxies are strictly questioned. . . . The university's task is to cultivate its own garden, and the state's to supply the manure in useful form and quantities and to ask for the fruits in due season, not to pull up the plants by the root before they flower." In "Government and the Universities," in Seventh Congress of the Universities of the Commonwealth, *Report of the Proceedings* (1953), p. 28.

While Sir Walter's use of the Toscanini analogy correctly stresses that the best results in creative spheres usually emerge in the absence of outside coercion, its musical context does not adequately express the urgency of the state's interest in the universities. After all, no lasting damage would result if a "patron" were forced to listen to Schoenberg when he would prefer to hear Brahms, whereas a state getting a stream of historians when it wanted scientists might feel compelled to take remedial action.

On the other hand, while Mr. Butler's gardening analogy reflects more accurately, perhaps, the universities' importance in a nation that must import more than half of its food, his conclusion that the state could rid itself of all concern for the type, quality, and quantity of "fruit" produced is not justified by the facts.

12 Frederick I and Napoleon, to be sure, made wide use of "planning," but neither had at his disposal the total means which have been available to more recent autocrats.

13 "The universities are being nationalised in the sense that they must operate within the frame of reference of national planning. So far there is much evidence of the power of the State, but virtually none that it has been misused." *The Times*, November 6, 1952.

14 Sir John Anderson, "Universities and the State," *Universities Quarterly*, 1 (1946), 13.

15 See above, p. 90.

16 See above, p. 76.

17 See above, p. 137.

18 Albert Mansbridge, *The Older Universities of England—Oxford and Cambridge* (1923), pp. 172–173. More recently, a fellow university administrator who was envious of Lord Lindsay's freedom to establish a new type program at North Staffordshire, told him, "Of course, we all want to do that, but you will find that your Professors won't let you." To which Lord Lindsay replied, "Yes, but if you can start with a staff who believe in the experiment, you won't have all those vested interests to grapple with." Letter from Lord Lindsay to W. H. G. Armytage, as quoted in Armytage, *Civic Universities* (1955), p. 292.

19 See chapter viii, above.

20 Sir Walter Moberly, in "Relations of the State and the Universities," in Sixth Congress of the Universities of the Commonwealth, *Report of the Proceedings* (1948), p. 16.

21 *Times Educational Supplement*, February 10, 1956, p. 154.

22 The Arts Council, which was created after World War II, attempts to do for the realm of the fine arts what the U.G.C. does for the universities, that is, to distribute national grants to institutions (opera companies, symphony orchestras,

legitimate theaters, ballet companies) whose clientele is unable to pay the growing costs involved, and which may now no longer rely on wealthy private benefactors to make up the resulting deficits. There are interesting questions of state control in this area which are not entirely dissimilar to those relating to universities. However, in the case of the fine arts, it is even more difficult to determine "national needs" but perhaps less urgent to do so. The Select Committee on Estimates has given some attention to the Arts Council; see above, p. 128, n. 49, and S.C.E. 1948–49, *Nineteenth Report*, H.C. 315.

23 Raised here is an issue which deserves more extended consideration than can be given within the scope of this study. It concerns the price which may have to be paid in creative spheres (e.g., learning and the fine arts) for the seemingly necessary replacement of "irresponsible" patrons (that is, either wealthy individuals or political regimes which have not had to account publicly for their expenditures) by responsible state support with its utilitarian standards. Let it quickly be stated that the political "irresponsibility" which permitted the creation of such great works of art as the Pyramids and the Palace of Versailles would be completely unacceptable today; on the other hand, one must admit that enlightened millionaires have generally made more desirable patrons than do contemporary democratic states, for with the former, there has been no worry about having to justify an "extravagance" to a practical-minded state legislature. If the state must, out of general necessity, become more and more the major source of support for various endeavors in learning and the arts (currently more true in Europe than in the United States), it must guard against applying too strictly the flat utilitarian criteria of its other areas of operation.

Albert Mansbridge, a member of the Royal Commission on Oxford and Cambridge Universities in 1922, has written poignantly of this danger as it relates to higher education: "Though the feature of the later years (at Oxford and Cambridge) has been improved organisation, yet 'the Spirit bloweth where it listeth.' It may fail to flow through the conscientiously organised College where every penny is meticulously accounted for, in which there is no waste, and the Fellows are irreproachably correct in all their ways. That, indeed, is the dread of the reformer who is not devoid of imagination. He is full of constant fear that he may fill up the valleys at the expense of the mountain-tops." Mansbridge, *op. cit.*, p. 283.

24 Sir James Mountford, Vice-Chancellor of Liverpool University, quoted the expanded terms of reference of the U.G.C. concerning ". . . the preparation and execution of such plans . . . as may . . . be required in order to ensure that they are fully adequate to national needs," and asked uneasily, "Required by whom?" In "Relations of the State and the Universities," in Sixth Congress of the Universities of the Commonwealth, *Report of the Proceedings* (1948), pp. 17–18.

25 Two members of the Royal Free Hospital of the University of London wrote to *The Times* as follows: "In the [U.G.C.'s] vetoing of the new medical curriculum of the University of London, financial sanctions were used to forbid a policy on academic grounds after it had been authorised by the University Senate and Court and expenditure had been incurred. . . . We urge that [the Grant Committee's] terms of reference be reconsidered and revised." A. St. George Huggett and E. M. Killick, *The Times*, April 18, 1953.

26 Moberly, in "Relations of the State and the Universities" (cited in n. 20, above), pp. 17 and 44.

27 The Rede Lecture, Cambridge University, November 18, 1948. *The Times* expressed a variation of this same theme: "Academic freedom depends on an informed public opinion which believes that for universities to be left free is

right in principle and justified at the same time by the strictest canons of utility."
November 6, 1952.

28 University of London, *Report by the Principal*, 1956–57, p. 3.

29 Conference of European University Rectors and Vice-Chancellors, *Report of the Conference* (1955), p. 179.

30 It might now be argued, on the evidence of the foregoing pages, that the unitary British tradition of *private* universities has been subtly altered, through the University Grants Committee, into a new unitary tradition of *public* universities. In either case, however, the contrast with the dual American system remains.

31 H. W. Dodds, in "Government and the Universities," in Seventh Congress of the Universities of the Commonwealth, *Report of the Proceedings* (1953), p. 34.

59

Excerpts from
GRANTS TO STUDENTS

Ministry of Education and Scottish Education Department

Source: Report of the Committee appointed by the Minister of Education and the Secretary for Scotland in June 1958, *Grants to Students*, London: HMSO, 1958, pp. 1–8 and 77–87.

PART ONE

Chapter 1 The general background

6. Before we attempt to discuss and define the general principles on which we think our own more detailed recommendations should rest, we want to set out the main features of the background. We must first take account of the general differences between the educational systems of England and Wales on the one hand and of Scotland on the other, with special reference to their awards systems. As far as we know, no committee of this kind dealing with education in recent years has had a remit covering all three countries.

Differences between the English and Welsh and the Scottish systems

7. There are marked differences between the two educational systems. Perhaps the crucial difference, from our point of view, is that in England and Wales the G.C.E. "A" level examination is normally taken at about 18, whereas the Scottish Leaving Certificate examination is normally taken at about 17; so that boys and girls usually go from Scottish schools to the university or other higher education a year earlier than in England and Wales. But there are other significant differences. The universities of Scotland are all ancient foundations in or near the main centres of population, and no one of them attracts Scottish students more than the rest. This is quite unlike England and Wales, where the two ancient universities of Oxford and Cambridge still have a greater attraction for many students than the modern universities. Again, higher education outside the universities has

developed differently. Nevertheless we have found no reason why there should not be a very close assimilation of the public awards systems of the three countries, and many of our recommendations are simply for the general adoption throughout Great Britain of the features of one or other of the present systems which we consider to be preferable.

The growth of the universities

8. One of the most striking post-war developments in education, which, like so many others, had its origin in the nation's wartime experience, has been the development of university education and the plans for extending it still further. Before the war, the number of full-time students in the universities of England, Wales and Scotland was about 50,000. In 1959–60, it is over 100,000. Firm plans to increase this number to about 135,000 are being put into effect and serious thought is being given to the possibility of a later increase of another 35,000 or 40,000 beyond that figure. Thus, on decisions already taken, the university population will, within the next five years, be roughly two and a half times as big as it was in 1939; and, if the further possibilities now being discussed come to finality, it will eventually be more than three times as large.

The growth of higher technical education

9. Increased importance is now also being given to all forms of technical education because it is recognised to be vital to the nation's prosperity. The designation of major establishments of further education in England and Wales as colleges of advanced technology, parallel developments in Scotland, the recent introduction of a new qualification, the Diploma in Technology, equivalent in standard to an honours degree, and the growth of sandwich courses are all signs of this recognition. In higher technical education, as in the universities, large scale expansion is certain; but it is even more difficult to predict its ultimate scope.

The growth in the number of awards

10. To be effective, all these improved educational facilities must be available to those who can profit from them. The importance of this was recognised by Sections 81 and 100 of the Education Act, 1944 (for England and Wales) and Sections 43 and 70 of the Education (Scotland) Act, 1946 (see Appendix 2), and by the regulations made under them.[1] As a result, the rapid rise in the number of students qualified for the various types of higher education has been accompanied by the development of extensive systems of awards from public funds, which are often studied with admiration by visitors from overseas. In England and Wales, the Ministry of Education

has increased the number of ordinary state scholarships, awarded annually on the results of the examination for the General Certificate of Education, from 360 in 1939 to 1,850 in 1952, at which figure it has since remained, and the total of university and college scholarships supplemented from public funds has risen to about 1,600 a year. Although the number of holders of state scholarships in England and Wales has risen from about 3,000 in 1948–49 to about 12,000 in 1958–59, the great burden of the growing number of awards necessitated by university expansion during the last decade has fallen on the local authorities. In 1948–49 the number of local authority university awards held by English and Welsh students was about 11,000 and the number held by Scottish students was about 4,000. By 1958–59 the number for England and Wales had risen to about 47,000 and for Scotland to nearly 7,000. Details of the figures for the latter year are given in Appendix 3.

The growth in the scope and cost of awards

11. Another important development since 1946 has been the acceptance of the principle that, subject to need, award-holders should be paid the assessed cost of their maintenance and expenses at the university. This, added to the expansion in numbers, has inevitably led to a substantial rise in the national expenditure on awards. The total cost of university awards in Great Britain in 1951–52 was £5.6m.; in 1958–59 it was £21.6m. In Chapter 13, we give our estimates of the cost of our proposals. We are satisfied that the relatively modest increase in expenditure on awards which we are recommending is essential to enable the country to get full value from the costly expansion of the universities and of the improved facilities now in hand for higher technical education.

Chapter 2 Some general principles

The nation's needs

12. The nation urgently needs the greatest possible number of highly educated men and women. It is true that greater public emphasis is at present laid on the shortage of particular categories such as mathematicians, engineers, scientists and teachers in these fields. But, while we would not attempt to dispute their importance, we would not agree that this should be allowed to distort the system of awards so as to favour one branch of learning above another. We are convinced that the nation should not depart from the ancient and sound tradition that young men and women go to the university to become all-round citizens and not merely to learn a special skill. It is this principle that we have tried to express in our proposals and which should be the foundation of any system of granting awards from public funds.

Men and women students

13. For similar reasons we have, in writing our report and in framing our recommendations, drawn no distinction between men and women students. We believe the public interest is in the award-holder as a student and that it would be wrong to vary the amount or the conditions of an award according to the sex of its holder. At the same time, we know that some families are more ready to encourage or allow their sons than their daughters to go to a university or to take a comparable course, on the ground that, while a boy will probably gain lasting benefit from doing so, a girl may well marry in a few years and her time at university will consequently be "wasted". We take a broader view; in the national interest we want all potential talent to be given its chance to develop and this is the aim behind all our recommendations. Full-time paid employment is not the only means of enriching the national life; nor are the benefits that a university or comparable form of education can confer on the individual or the community measurable only in terms of later earning capacity. A sustained increase in the number of highly educated mothers, as well as fathers, would benefit the nation to an extent that is not yet generally appreciated.

The limitations of our proposals

14. It is important that we should recognise and define the intended scope of our recommendations. It might be possible to use a system of awards, which makes its impact at the point of a student's transition from school to university, so as to influence or limit the freedom of both. Although our proposals can hardly avoid having some effect on both schools and universities, we have no such intention. On the contrary, we have taken full account of the views stated in Chapter 26 of the Crowther report, that in the present competition for university places there is no case for duplicate selection procedures which add to the complexities of administration and the strain on school pupils. But, by the mere fact of making recommendations to remove the difficulties which fall within our field, we cannot avoid isolating or bringing into relief those other difficulties which are not within our scope. The universities themselves, or the individual colleges in them, remain responsible for their admission requirements and selection procedures; and in proposing that award-making bodies should accept certain university decisions more unreservedly than they have done hitherto in disbursing public money to students, we have in effect placed greater responsibility on the universities and colleges, which is where we think it should rest.

The need for uniformity in the treatment of applicants

15. But although we recognise, and accept as right, these limitations on the influence we can or should try to exert, we have been greatly impressed by the opinion, expressed so generally by those we have consulted, that applications by prospective students for awards should be treated uniformly and in accordance with accepted principles. We ourselves share this view and have given much thought to how it can best be put into effect. The kind of uniformity we seek will not be achieved through a system based solely on a code of regulations. Our proposals will introduce a new element in the form of a Standing Advisory Committee, capable of dealing with the practical and human problems that will inevitably present themselves. Examples of the problems which we think such an advisory committee should deal with are mentioned in various chapters of the report (see para. 277).

The importance of interviews

16. The recommendations we are making about selection for awards would not only attach to acceptance by a university or a comparable institution a greater importance than it has had hitherto; they would also dispel the anxiety which many students at present inevitably feel while waiting to hear whether they will get the grant without which they cannot take up the place they have been offered. In particular, for the great majority of applicants, our recommendations would remove the need for an interview by the award-making body designed to discover whether they were suitable for an award from public funds. But in saying this we do not want to suggest that, in the whole process of transition from school to university, there is no place for an interview of any kind. We hope that universities, in addition to making more uniform the present procedures and conditions of admission, will extend as far as possible the practice of interviewing candidates before acceptance. They will need to have as much information as possible to enable them to judge between the large number of candidates who will be competing for a limited number of places. School records and full reports are already of great help to them, and we are sure that schools will continue to give all the help of this kind they can. This should lead to a still closer relationship between schools and universities. For some students, their performance in the school-leaving examination and the reports of their schools will make an interview, as a means of determining their suitability, redundant. But, apart from the function of interviews in helping to determine the choice between one borderline candidate and another, we believe that the influence of a properly conducted interview upon the student himself is important. He will be in effect applying for a grant of a large sum of public money. A positive effort should be made, in an interview, to remind him that he is seeking the privilege of being backed by the community.[2]

Freedom of choice

17. There are, at present, some restrictions in the public awards system which limit the freedom of students to attend the institution they choose. In England and Wales, local education authorities will generally give award-holders enough to enable them to attend the university of their choice, including Scottish universities, but students taking further education courses may not be given awards unless they attend one of the colleges of the award-making authority. In Scotland, the Bursaries Regulations allow an education authority to give an award for any university or other institution which the student wishes to attend, but to limit the amount of the grant to what would have been paid if the student had attended a nearby institution where the cost would be less; education authorities normally avail themselves of this clause where the student could have obtained admission to a local university or institution but prefers to go elsewhere.

18. These arrangements reflect different educational traditions. Because for centuries Oxford and Cambridge were the only universities in England and Wales, the idea of going a long way from home to attend a university became well established in these countries at an early date. The growing difficulty in recent years of securing a place at English and Welsh universities has had an important effect in consolidating this practice. In Scotland, on the other hand, the universities were established in or near the country's four principal centres, and on the whole it has been the practice to attend the university serving the region in which one lives. This has advantages in establishing close contact between the universities and the schools which feed them. The number of places available is, proportionate to population, still substantially greater than in England and, until the last year or two, qualified students have had no great difficulty in securing a place at the nearest university. Comparatively few Scottish students have wished to attend Oxford or Cambridge; those who have gone there have generally done so after taking their first degree at a Scottish university. With this background, there is an understandable feeling that a student who wishes to go to any other than the nearest university should meet the additional expense himself.

19. The practice in the field of comparable courses in all three countries is analogous to that of Scottish university education. Colleges have been set up in the areas where they were needed to provide courses for local students, and the general custom has been for students to attend the nearest college providing the course desired. The local authorities have, therefore, often thought it unnecessary to give bigger grants to enable a student to take a similar course at some more distant college.

20. While recognising the reasons for these practices, we think it desirable, in the interest of students as a whole throughout Great Britain, that all those with whom we are concerned should have the same freedom of choice

138

that the university student in England and Wales generally has at present. An additional practical reason for this view is that the difficulty in securing places in the Scottish universities, and in the technical colleges, is likely to become greater in the next few years, which will make it more difficult to judge whether the student seeking an award wishes to go to some distant institution as a matter of choice or because he has not been able to get a place at a local one. But the main reason for our view is that much of the value of higher education lies not only in the instruction the student receives but also in the contacts he makes and the life he leads within the student community outside the lecture room and the laboratory. To get the full benefit, it is important that the student body at a university or other institution of higher education should not be drawn from too narrow a field; it will gain richness from a wider one. We recognise that this ideal is limited to a large extent by the availability of residential accommodation for students, but in principle we believe that the system of public awards should not hinder development in this direction, and we have, therefore, had the student's freedom of choice much in mind in making our recommendations. We do not think it likely that students will lightly move to far distant institutions; those who would benefit more from attending a local institution will still wish to do so.

Grant for full period of course

21. It is important that students should be able to rely upon a grant for the full normal period of the course on which they have embarked. We consider, therefore, that all awards should be given—as most are at present —for the number of years required to complete the course, subject only to satisfactory progress and conduct. Students living in England and Wales sometimes have difficulties through the variations in length of university courses. Most degree courses at English and Welsh universities last for three years. Because of this, some local education authorities have refused, where a student wished to take an honours degree course lasting four years, to give him an award for the full course, on the ground that this would involve one year's grant more than would have been necessary if an equivalent qualification had been sought at another university. Similarly, difficulties have sometimes arisen over "intermediate" stages of courses from which many, but not all, students may have succeeded in obtaining exemption through examinations taken while still at school. Moreover, it should not be made difficult for able students who have specialised mainly upon the arts side at school to transfer to science by means of an intermediate year at the university. There are so many variations in the opportunities open to different students that we believe the only fair arrangement is to give an award for the full period of study required by the university or other institution concerned.

Awards for comparable courses

22. The term "comparable course" used in our terms of reference was not defined. When getting statistics from local authorities, we found it necessary to give some more precise indication of the field to be covered. We therefore asked local education authorities in England and Wales to give information about awards for courses leading to qualifications entitling their holders to graduate status under the Burnham Committee reports. The Ministry of Education's Circular 285 (May, 1955) recommended that students over 18 following such courses should get grants at the appropriate university rate, though the circular also made it clear that the Minister did not wish to preclude authorities from giving grants at these rates for other types of further education courses, where they were satisfied that the standard of the course and the needs of the student justified it. In Scotland, the arrangements are more positive. The Bursaries Regulations require the same rates of grant to be given to all students over 17 taking university and further education courses other than certain elementary courses. For convenience, therefore, we asked education authorities in Scotland to give information about awards for courses at the central institutions. Thus the statistics for non-university courses in the three countries are not exactly comparable.

23. Our terms of reference restrict us to students taking courses comparable with those for first degrees. Our recommendations are designed to apply to them, without any restriction as to age. But we did not consider it part of our remit to draw up a list of such courses. Although we recognise that the expenditure of a student taking an advanced course at a technical college will be much the same, whether or not the course leads to a qualification which carries graduate status for the purposes of the Burnham reports, the awards for some of these students fall outside our terms of reference. We have assumed, therefore, that, if our recommendations are accepted for the main groups of students whose courses are clearly comparable with first degree courses, the Government will decide whether, and in what way, they should apply to other students. Should the Government decide to make distinctions by types or levels of course, we think that the Standing Advisory Committee should be asked to advise on the precise classifications.

Practice in other countries: loans to students

24. We were anxious to study the practice of other countries and in the course of our enquiry we gathered evidence about the methods of helping university students from public funds in a number of countries in Europe and elsewhere, including Australia, France, the Federal German Republic, the United States of America and the U.S.S.R. Though this material was of great interest, for the most part the educational systems differ so widely from our own that few comparisons of direct value for our purpose could be

found. We were, however, struck by the official use of the system of loans to students in, among other countries, Norway and the United States and we felt it right to consider the merits of some such system; but, though we recognise that a loan may occasionally be a reasonable way of meeting a particular difficulty, we have had no hesitation in rejecting loans as an integral part of the national awards system. The principle of using loans as a standard means of financing students has now been abandoned by public authorities in Great Britain, and our evidence disclosed no wish to see it revived. The obligation to repay, no matter how easy the terms, must represent an untimely burden at the outset of a career. We far prefer the system of outright grants, with the safeguards against misuse, contained in our recommendations.

The pattern of our recommendations

25. As our report makes clear, on one of the main issues that we were asked to consider (Chapter 7) we find ourselves unable to agree: for this and other reasons, we do not feel able to make a firm recommendation on another major question (Chapter 11). But within Part Two our proposals interlock and are designed to work as a whole.

The need for legislation

26. Certain of our recommendations will, if adopted, require legislation, though its scope cannot be accurately foreseen until decisions have been taken on some of the major issues. We refer at the relevant places to the matters on which legislation would in our view be necessary or desirable. Similarly the acceptance of certain of our recommendations would require the withdrawal, the re-making or the amendment of some of the Statutory Regulations made under the Education Acts.

Public opinion as expressed to us in evidence

27. Finally, we want to say how strongly we have been struck by the contrast between the community of interest and purpose among our witnesses and the wide diversity of their answers to our carefully drawn-up list of key questions. We naturally supposed that representatives of student bodies would have a different point of view from representatives of local authorities upon certain topics, but it was surprising to find how wide a difference of opinion there was, even within some well-defined groups, about the steps which should be taken to improve the present system of awards. It is because we have not been able, except in one or two minor matters, to detect any consensus of professional or public opinion upon how to solve any of our main problems that, in coming to our own conclusions, we regretfully face

the possibility of disagreement from some of those who have been good enough to spend time and thought in providing us with evidence.

PART FOUR

Chapter 11 Administration of grants

265. Up to this point we have referred to "award-making bodies" without seeking to define what these should be, for the views we have expressed have not depended on the type of body responsible for administration.

266. At present, the responsibility for assisting students is undertaken by no less than 181 local education authorities and two government departments. In England and Wales, the local education authorities make about 16,000 awards annually for university study and about 7,500 major awards for courses at further education establishments, while the Ministry of Education awards about 3,800 state scholarships a year, nearly all of them for study at universities. In Scotland, almost all grants are made by the education authorities, about 2,000 a year for study at universities and about 2,000 for courses at the central institutions and similar establishments. The Scottish Education Department itself makes only about 25 awards a year, mainly for study at English universities.

Past practice of the various award-making bodies

Central awards

267. Although we have recommended in Chapter 4 that state scholarships on the present lines should be discontinued, we do not overlook the invaluable part they have played in England and Wales over a long formative period, during which the opportunity and habit of university attendance were being extended over the widest possible social range. They set standards which were welcomed by the local education authorities, and their administration gave the Government first-hand experience of the problems associated with grants to students. We should be sorry if some such direct contact between the central departments and the actual business of making awards were not retained.

Local awards

268. In evidence, we had criticisms of some of the methods of the local authorities in the making of awards. For England and Wales, the main complaint was that sometimes a student who would be assisted if he lived in one area is denied a grant if he lives in another. The chief criticism from our

Scottish witnesses, on the other hand, was that in exactly comparable cases students living in some parts of Scotland get smaller grants than those living in other parts, while all get less than English award-holders.

Reasons for lack of uniform practice in making awards

269. These discrepancies—which we are satisfied occur nowadays less than they used to—are the inevitable result of the present system. Under it, students admitted to a university or college cannot be certain of receiving the financial assistance they need. The scholarships awarded by the Ministry of Education and the Scottish Education Department are limited in number and the students who do not win them have to look to the local authorities for financial assistance. But the local authorities have virtually complete discretion whether to assist any particular student, and in fact do refuse assistance to a minority, including some who have previously been offered a place at a university or college.

(a) In *England and Wales*, as explained in paragraph 33, while the regulations made by the Minister of Education require the award-making powers of local education authorities to be exercised in accordance with schemes drawn up by the authorities and approved by the Minister, the schemes are so drawn that authorities may decline to make awards in particular cases. The policy of all local education authorities is to make an award only where they themselves are satisfied that the student is fitted to take the course proposed. It is not surprising that the standards and judgment used in the process of selection vary from area to area.

(b) In *Scotland*, the Education (Scotland) Act. 1946, requires the power of education authorities to grant bursaries to be exercised in accordance with regulations made by the Secretary of State, but the regulations do not fetter the education authority's discretion to make or refuse an award in any particular instance. The particular complaints which we have quoted in paragraph 268 as being so characteristic in England have not arisen in Scotland because the Scottish education authorities have been willing to take as the basis for making an award the offer of a place by the university or college to the student; they have not insisted on applying their own separate test of educational ability.

270. The local authorities also have discretion, in varying measure, about such matters as the rates of maintenance and other grants and the rates of parental contribution.

(a) In *England and Wales*, standard rates for term-time maintenance and the scale of parental contributions are determined centrally for state scholarships and are recommended to local education authorities for their university awards. All local education authorities have now adopted these recommendations, but there is still variation in the grants given for vacation maintenance and in some other features.

(b) In *Scotland*, some of the rates of grant and the scale of parental contributions are prescribed in the regulations, but these allow the education authorities latitude in the grants to be given for certain purposes.

271. There remain, as a result, throughout England and Wales and Scotland, varying interpretations of what grants should be given to students. But, the evidence submitted to us showed that the great majority of authorities have exercised their award-making powers wisely and with a proper degree of generosity. Indeed, if it had not been for the great increase in recent years in the number of public awards given by the local authorities to the types of students concerned in our enquiry, full advantage could not have been taken of the planned expansion of the universities and of higher education elsewhere.

272. The system cannot be considered satisfactory, however, so long as it is still possible for the intransigence, either witting or unwitting, of some local authorities to cause as much uneasiness as it still does in the student population, among parents and in the universities. Award-making bodies should not, in our view, continue to have the wide discretion that they have at present.

Higher education: a national rather than a local issue

273. This opinion, in which most of our witnesses concurred, that the measure of assistance any student receives should no longer be allowed to depend largely on local judgment, is related to our view of the place of grants in the national educational system. It has to be recognised that, although the majority of boys and girls who stay at school until the age of 17 or 18 are educated in their home areas, mainly at schools conducted by local authorities, after this there is a major change. Many of those who go on to degree or comparable courses attend a university or other institution which is far away from their home and not under the control of their "home" authority. Most universities and some technical colleges now have only a minority of local students. Thus, his "home" local authority usually ceases at this stage to have any direct responsibility for the education of the student; at the same time the student is beginning to look outwards and to be concerned with his life's work, while the State is becoming more directly interested in him as a recruit to the national pool of educated manpower. After their formal education is completed, many young people take up work away from their home districts. In fact, after the age of 17 or 18, the national interest in the continued education of the student grows as the local interest lessens. In saying this, we do not mean to suggest that the local

interest ceases altogether. The student still has ties with his home and his school, and the local community often still takes a "pastoral" interest in him, at least until he launches on his career. The local authorities, in spite of what has been said, have every reason to be proud of the part they have taken in building up the present systems of higher education. They helped to found the modern universities, and some cities are now in the process of founding others; many, entirely spontaneously, make generous grants to neighbouring universities and participate in their administration. Any measures which weakened these links between the local authorities and the universities would involve real loss. The question to be considered, therefore, is how to preserve these links and retain local concern for the student's welfare, while making such improvements as will remove the present grounds for criticism and acknowledge the "national" element in the awards system.

Recommended future policy

274. We have already recommended that, with certain limited exceptions, the offer of a place in a first degree or comparable course should confer on the student an entitlement to such financial help as he needs. But we do not think it feasible, or even desirable, to cover all possible circumstances by tightly-drawn rules. As indicated in Chapter 3, we consider that it is sometimes right that the award-making body should examine individually the merits of making or continuing an award, while in Chapters 5, 6, 8, 9 and 10 we mention a number of situations in which the award-making body should consider special factors in order that the amount of the grant may be fixed with fairness.

Principles recommended for future legislation

275. Whatever the nature of the bodies dealing with the actual making of awards, it is essential in our view that the policy to be followed by them should be settled nationally. We recommend that any new legislation applying to our field should be based on the conception that awards to university and comparable students are an essential part of the nation's provision for the education of its young peoples. We think that award-making bodies should have a duty, not merely a power, to assist students but, as the relevant sections of the present Acts do not apply only to students following the first degree and comparable courses which are our concern, we do not feel prepared to define the terms in which the duty should be expressed. We believe, however, that it would be unwise to attempt to write detailed obligations, such as a duty to give awards to all those who fulfil certain defined conditions, into an Act of Parliament. We feel certain that the details by which the general policy is given expression should be readily adjustable as circumstances change.

276. We therefore recommend that Parliament should place a general duty on award-making bodies to give awards to all students taking first degree or comparable courses who are judged to be capable of benefiting from such an education, and should make the Minister of Education and the Secretary of State for Scotland responsible for settling the detailed requirements, which should include the determination of:—

(a) principles regarding the making of awards, e.g., the circumstances in which awards should be made automatically and those in which some further consideration should be given by the award-making body (Chapter 3);

(b) the rates of grant for various purposes and for different categories of students, and, as far as possible, the circumstances in which each rate should apply (Chapters 5 and 6);

(c) the rates and method of assessment of parental contributions, if retained, and the circumstances in which the contribution should be waived (Chapter 8);

(d) the treatment of other income of the award-holder (Chapter 9); and

(e) special arrangements for students with dependants (Chapter 10).

Standing Advisory Committee

277. The rules on these matters must, as we have said, be adjustable as circumstances change; the many detailed questions involved cannot be answered once for all time. Under the present system, periodical reviews have taken place of the rates of grant and parental contributions, while guidance on particular points has been given to local authorities from time to time in various ways. In England and Wales, the need for consultation among those concerned has been acknowledged by the appointment of ad hoc working parties to undertake the periodical reviews (para. 73). Undoubtedly, some such consultation should precede any decisions by the Ministers on the matters referred to in paragraph 276 but, in view of their wide scope, we do not believe the method of occasional ad hoc consultation would be good enough. For these reasons we recommend that a Standing Advisory Committee be appointed to consider all details of policy which come under review and to advise the Ministers on the decisions to be taken on them. We do not envisage a huge *omnium gatherum* committee on which the attempt would be made to represent all conceivable interests. We look for a membership of, at the most, a dozen, chosen for their personal qualities and not for whatever district or calling they may represent. The committee should, of course, include members with experience of universities, technical colleges, secondary schools and central and local administration. The same committee should cover Scotland as well as England and Wales, with, if necessary, separate sub-committees for each country for

certain purposes. We recommend that this committee should also have the function of advising the Ministers on problems, arising in the day-to-day administration of the awards system, which they may refer to it. As central policy decisions clearly cannot cover every conceivable circumstance, it is to be expected that among the cases settled by award-making bodies there will be a few which throw up real difficulties. This is why we think it desirable that the Standing Advisory Committee should not only advise on policy but also be available for consultation on these problems of detail, which will sometimes disclose questions on which policy decisions are desirable.

The detailed functions of making awards

Two rejected proposals

278. We now turn to the question of the bodies which should be responsible for the detailed work of actually making the awards, that is, of carrying out the centrally-determined policy. First, we must mention two suggestions we received for forms of organisation quite different from that existing at present. The purpose of both proposals was stated as being to simplify the present system by the drastic method of removing the local authorities from the field and with them the complexities arising from their large number and their varying practices.

(a) *Administration by universities and other institutions.*

One suggestion was that grants to students should be administered by the universities, colleges and other institutions of higher education, as agents of the Government. This does not appeal to us. The universities and institutions are not equipped, even if they were willing to attempt it, to take on all the work connected with grants now done by 181 local authorities in Great Britain. There are, in any case, so many universities and other places of higher education that this change would reduce the number of award-making bodies only by about one-half, and the present differences of treatment between areas might simply be replaced by differences between institutions. Larger questions concerning the autonomy of the universities are also raised by this proposal. We reject the proposal, however, primarily on the grounds that it is less likely to achieve a satisfactory solution than other possible methods.

(b) *Administration by a national grants board.*

The other suggestion was that all grants should be awarded by an ad hoc national grants board, financed by public funds but enjoying a degree of autonomy and having whatever regional or local sub-offices and subcommittees were found necessary. Part of this proposition is met by our proposal that a committee should be appointed to advise on policy questions and on difficulties arising from the exercise of discretionary powers. But we are clear that such a committee should be advisory only and that the main decisions about awards from public funds should be taken by the Ministers who are accountable to Parliament for the spending of the funds voted. As to the detailed work of award-making bodies, we consider that, if it is desirable for this work to be centralised, it would be better for it to be done by the Ministry of Education and the Scottish Education Department, than by an ad hoc body not accountable to Parliament and the public.

With the rejection of these two possibilities, the issue narrows down to the question how much of the work, if any, should be delegated to local organisations.

Local authorities as award-making bodies

279. At present the great majority of grants to students—roughly seven out of every eight—are awarded and administered by the local authorities. A considerable amount of time is devoted to the work by authority members, but an even greater amount of time is given by their officials to the more or less routine tasks of receiving applications, assessing parents' contributions and students' grants, making payments and dealing with enquiries. The number of staff engaged in this work, over the whole country, must be quite large, though it is difficult to compute because most of them are not engaged solely on work connected with grants to students. Probably few of them would be released if the work were transferred elsewhere, so that, if any other body were to be responsible for the executive functions of awarding grants, new staff would have to be assembled for the purpose. The accumulated experience of the local authorities and the existence of their trained staff provide strong reasons why the local authorities should continue to take a part in the grants system.

280. There are advantages in applications for assistance being dealt with by the local authority. An award is normally made at the end of a school career, before the student has passed into his new and wider sphere. If the authority's area is relatively compact, he may be able to call at the office personally for information or advice. Occasionally, in borderline cases, it may be necessary to interview him, and possibly his parents; before deciding whether an award should be made, and this is best done near his home. If a system of parental contributions is retained, a local body will also be in the best position to judge whether the parent's statement of income is accurate and to make any enquiries that are necessary. We recognise, however, that there are contrary considerations. Some education areas are so large that sheer size prevents the authority from having all the advantages of local knowledge. Other authorities, for geographical reasons, find it extremely difficult to secure in local committees and panels the representation

of institutions of higher education which is so important. As to parental contributions, some parents, particularly in the smaller areas where it is widely felt that any personal information one supplies may become known to acquaintances from whom one would prefer to withhold it, object to disclosing their financial affairs to a local body.

281. The chief objection to the local authorities having the whole executive function, however, is the difficulty, which has been referred to several times in this report, of securing equivalent treatment for all students. Uniformity of treatment among 181 award-making bodies could presumably be achieved by complete rigidity of central control; but uniformity alone cannot secure fair treatment for all. As we have already shown, we consider a flexibility of approach essential so that the special factors which affect many students can be taken into account. We think this can be achieved only if discretion is given to the award-making bodies on several important matters; and yet we know that, if things are left as they are, with a large number of award-making bodies, different decisions, would inevitably be taken on precisely similar cases by different bodies. This has been amply proved in Scotland, where the present system consists of a comparatively tightly drawn code with power left to the education authorities to use discretion, for the very reason of enabling them to deal with varying individual circumstances.

282. We can see only one way of meeting this very important disadvantage connected with the local administration of grants. This would be to give the students a right of appeal to the Minister of Education or the Secretary of State for Scotland against any discretionary decision taken by the local authority (that is, on all matters which were not prescribed precisely by the rules made by the Ministers). Appeals might arise on such matters as, for example, the refusal of an authority to make an award; the giving of an allowance to reside away from home or for a vacation course; the assessment of the parental contribution; or the treatment of a student's dependants. After such appeals, the local authority would be obliged to change its decision if the Minister found in favour of the student. It is difficult to judge what number of appeals would be made. Probably at first it would be relatively large, but if the Ministers' rulings were assembled and sent periodically to the local authorities by way of guidance, we believe it would later be reduced to quite insignificant proportions.

283. Various objections might be taken to this solution. It is a cardinal principle of educational administration that broad principles of policy are determined by Act of Parliament or statutory regulations, but that the local authorities are left with freedom to fill in the framework according to their judgment of the needs of the situation. The Local Government Act, 1958, and the Local Government and Miscellaneous Financial Provisions (Scotland) Act, 1958, were designed to reinforce this principle. To impose on local authorities an awards system under which most of their

actions were closely controlled by detailed rules, and the remainder were liable to revision on appeal to a Minister, might well be regarded as completely contrary to this principle. But, if the local authorities are to continue as award-making bodies, it would seem the only means of doing away with one of the most widely criticised features of the present arrangements.

Government departments as award-making bodies

284. We turn now to the principal alternative, which is to relieve the local authorities of some or all of the executive functions, and for the Ministry of Education and the Scottish Education Department to pay all the grants to the students with whom we are concerned. Some of the more obvious advantages can be deduced from earlier paragraphs. The number of award-making bodies would be reduced from 181 to two (or three, if the Welsh Department of the Ministry of Education handled awards in Wales), which would make it simple to achieve both equality of treatment in comparable cases and flexibility of approach, combined with consistency, in special cases. The unavoidably complicated regulations, the system of appeals and Ministerial directions, and the interference with the traditional pattern of local government which, it seems to us, would be necessary if the local authorities continued to be award-making bodies, would all be avoided. Another important, but perhaps less obvious, advantage of centralisation is that work processes could be streamlined and much greater use made of mechanisation. The central departments would admittedly need a substantial increase of their staff, but it should be possible to do the work with fewer staff than the total number employed on it by the local authorities and central departments at present. It would be a great practical advantage for universities and colleges to deal with at most three paying authorities; on the other hand, some of them might prefer the greater inconvenience of dealing with many different award-making bodies, because getting students' fees from many sources might be felt to be a safeguard for their independence. Another advantage of central payment would be to stop the difficulties which arise from disagreements between local authorities as to which of them should accept the financial responsibility for awarding a grant to a particular student. Again, a common form of application for assistance would be used, thus removing a well-founded grievance on the part of headmasters of schools which draw pupils from several local authority areas. There would also be a common form of intimation of award, which would ensure that proper notification was made both of the amount of any contribution expected from the parents and of the amount included in the grant for specific purposes, such as books. The last two improvements could be secured in a system of wholly local administration, but not so simply.

285. The prime objection likely to be raised against handling the awards system wholly centrally is the claim that it would involve an unwelcome amount of bureaucratic remote control; or, put more specifically, that the functions of an award-making body, particularly those which are discretionary, could not be handled so satisfactorily from London, Edinburgh and Cardiff as from a number of local centres. Such difficulties might be overcome if the central departments had some system of local agents, in order to enable them to take account of local and personal circumstances. This could well be done by arranging for the local authorities to carry out certain functions; for example, they might be asked to conduct enquiries and interviews on behalf of the departments. It is, however, difficult to judge how satisfactory a centralised system, with or without local agents, would be. The only guidance can be obtained from the post-war Further Education and Training Scheme, which involved discretionary functions, and from the present state scholarship arrangements, but the handling of all university and comparable awards would not be a strictly equivalent task.

286. If centralised administration were to be adopted for the types of award which fall within our terms of reference, there would remain the awards for the further education courses which fall outside them, and which are at present a local authority responsibility. Many of these, especially for courses entered at the age of 15 or 16, demand a degree of local knowledge and judgment which, in our view, would require that they should remain a matter for the local authorities.

Financial considerations if grants are paid by local authorities

287. At present, the awards made by the two Government departments are financed wholly from the Exchequer, while the local authorities' expenditure on awards is met partly from Exchequer grants and partly from local rates. Originally there was an Exchequer grant specifically in aid of this local expenditure, but in 1959 this was merged in the new general grant to local authorities. We understand that about two-thirds of the total current cost of state and local awards for first degree and comparable courses may be regarded as falling on the Exchequer. No more precise indication can be given as to how the cost is shared, because of the way in which the general grant is assessed. The grant is in aid of a whole range of local services, of which education is the largest. The aggregate amount of the grant for each year is determined by the Government after considering estimates of the relevant expenditure prepared by the local authorities. This aggregate amount is apportioned to individual authorities according to objective factors, such as population and rateable values. Thus, the amount any particular authority receives is not directly related to its expenditure.

288. A number of witnesses gave us their views about the effect of the general grant upon any assessment of the alternatives we are considering.

The point was put to us in two different ways. Some of them said that the aid given through the general grant might be insufficient to enable the local authorities to meet the further responsibilities that would be placed upon them, both by any recommendations we made and by the growing numbers receiving higher education, without an unreasonable increase in the level of local rates. This might be found particularly by authorities with an above-average proportion of students getting higher education, since the apportionment of the general grant to such authorities would take no account of the relatively heavy financial burden falling on them. Others said they feared that, for these reasons, some authorities would try to keep down the expenditure from local rates by restricting the number or the value of awards, and that the students would suffer. It is difficult to judge how real these dangers are. The views expressed sprang from natural doubts arising from the absence of any experience of the new system of general grant, which had only just been introduced when we were taking evidence. But it is important that any such possibility should be averted. It is clear that the expansion of the system of higher education must increase the total cost of making grants to students, and acceptance of our recommendations will increase it still further. If the local authorities are to remain responsible for making awards, the general duty to do so and the close central control we have adumbrated would, we believe, remove the present grounds for uneasiness from students and their parents. But, from the authorities' viewpoint, if the general grant were merely increased by a proportion of the additional cost, the burden they had to bear might still seem a heavy one and they might well say that, as so much local discretion had been removed from them, and as the system of student grants was now conceived as a national one, the whole burden should be borne by the Exchequer.

289. With this thought in mind, we considered two suggested special arrangements for financing local authorities' expenditure. The first suggestion was that a percentage Government grant should be reintroduced in respect of expenditure on awards for higher education, but the arguments adduced did not seem to us to justify such a radical departure from the new general arrangements which came into force only a year ago. The other suggestion was that the cost of local authority awards for higher education should be "pooled". The pooling arrangement, which applies to expenditure on certain types of technical education and teacher training, is designed mainly as a means of spreading equitably, over all local authorities, expenditure on services which are provided by only a limited number of authorities for the benefit of the population generally. The expenditure on students' grants does not meet this criterion. We consider, therefore, that we must dismiss both these suggestions and that, if the local authorities incur expenditure on grants to students in the future, it should continue to be aided by the general grant. If, however, the central departments cease

to give awards, and all are made a local responsibility, we think it essential that the amount included in the general grant in aid of the cost of awards should be at least equivalent to the two-thirds of the present cost which is borne by the Exchequer (paragraph 287), plus two-thirds of any additional cost; we emphasise that this is a minimum and that in our view, having regard to the predominating "national" interest and the removal of so much local discretion, the proportion might well be greater.

Financial considerations if grants are paid by central departments

290. The foregoing financial difficulties would, of course, not arise if all grants were paid in future by the Ministry of Education and the Scottish Education Department. The whole cost would then be met from the Exchequer. As the local authorities would thus be relieved of about £18 millions of expenditure, a reduction of the amount of the general grant would no doubt be appropriate.

The case for some grants being paid centrally and some locally

291. Most of our witnesses naturally assumed that in the future, as in the past, some of the awards would be made by the Ministry of Education and the Scottish Education Department and some by the local authorities. As we have already recorded in paragraph 71, a number of bodies appeared to be anxious not only that this arrangement should be maintained, but that the number of state awards should be increased, so that a larger share of the financial burden of university and comparable education was borne by the Exchequer. We have considered whether it is either practicable or desirable to do this if state scholarships are discontinued. We can see that there would be an advantage, if the local authorities were to be the principal award-making bodies, in the two Government departments continuing to make a proportion of the awards, in order to give them practical experience of the problems which arise. The advantage would be much less if our recommendations, particularly for the appointment of a Standing Advisory Committee, are adopted. But we cannot in any case recommend such a division of responsibilities, because it is impossible to identify any clear group of students, as a representative cross-section of the whole, for whom the departments could be made responsible. Unless the group of students were fully representative, the departments would not get the allround experience which would be the reason for such an arrangement. As a means of dividing the financial burden the division of award-making responsibility seems to us to be quite unnecessary; a proper division of cost can be simply achieved under the new financial system by an adjustment of the total of the general grant.

Conclusions on executive functions

292. While we have made positive recommendations in paragraphs 276 and 277 about the way in which considerations of policy should be determined, we feel less able to reach precise conclusions about how the more detailed functions of actually making awards and paying the grants should be handled. It is essential to find a system under which the new arrangements recommended in earlier chapters would work satisfactorily. We can envisage three possible systems, all of which we think could be made to operate satisfactorily, but none of which is entirely free from disadvantages—

(a) the entire responsibility for awards to the students with whom we are concerned might be assumed by the central education departments; or

(b) the central departments might be the award-making bodies, in the sense that they would make the final decisions about making awards to individuals and would pay the grants, but the local authorities would act as their agents in performing some functions which can best be carried out locally (see paragraph 285); or

(c) all awards might be made and paid by the local authorities, under rules drawn up by the two Ministers, but the local authorities' decisions on any matters not determined by the rules would have to be amended if the Ministers so directed after considering appeals by the students; exceptionally, however, the central departments should make the awards to certain students, such as those whose parents are temporarily serving abroad, who cannot be regarded as the responsibility of any particular local authority.

293. There are many practical considerations affecting the choice between these possible courses. Some of these concern a much wider range of governmental policy than we can be expected to pronounce upon. Before making a decision between the three possibilities, we believe the Government should consult the universities, the local authority associations, and probably other bodies; we think this is important because the views about administration and finance which they expressed in evidence were given without any knowledge of the range of recommendations we would be making. For these reasons, we do not make any more detailed recommendations on the question of the parts which the various bodies should take in operating the system of awards.

Notes

1 The Regulations for Scholarships and Other Benefits, 1945 (S.R. & O. 1945, No. 666, as amended);

The State Scholarships Regulations, 1954 (S.I. 1954, No. 957, as amended);

The Education Authority Bursaries (Scotland) Regulations, 1957 (S.I. 1957, No. 1059, as amended);

The Supplemental Allowances (Scottish Scholars at English Universities) Regulations, 1949 (S.I. 1949, No. 818, as amended); and

The Bursaries (Central Awards) (Scotland) Regulations, 1950 (S.I. 1950, No. 1014, as amended).

2 Candidates attending interviews at a number of widely separated universities may be put to considerable expense. This is not strictly within our terms of reference, but we think arrangements should be devised to relieve families on whom this is an unreasonable burden.

60

Excerpts from
HIGHER EDUCATION

[Robbins Committee]

Source: *Higher Education*, Report of the Robbins Committee, London: HMSO, 1963, pp. 4–10 and 365–7.

AIMS AND PRINCIPLES

13. Our terms of reference instruct us to consider the pattern of full-time higher education in Great Britain. We believe that no such instructions have been given to any committee or commission in the past. There have been Royal Commissions on the affairs of particular universities and committees on various aspects of technical education and the training of teachers. There has never been a comprehensive survey of the field of higher education in the sense in which we have decided to use that term.

14. The reason is obvious. Even today it would be a misnomer to speak of a system of higher education in this country, if by system is meant a consciously co-ordinated organisation. The various institutions—the universities, the technical, commercial and art colleges, the colleges for the education and training of teachers—have grown up separately. Moreover, for the greater part of their history, the universities, which were more or less independent of the state, dominated the landscape. Only in the nineteenth century and, on a perceptible scale, only in the latter part of that century did other institutions begin to arise; and even then, although work for a London external degree was done, and often done very well, in some technical colleges, the emphasis was chiefly on part-time study. Therefore, although it can be argued that national needs demanded a more comprehensive survey at an earlier date, it is easy to see why this did not take place.

15. In recent years, however, important changes have occurred both within higher education and in the nation at large. Within higher education two

sets of changes are especially remarkable. First, the financial position of the universities has changed. Although some universities have still substantial sources of independent income, all depend on large grants from the state to enable them to carry out their present functions. Great pains have been taken to see that this position of financial dependence should not impair their legitimate rights of self-government. But it is only natural that the general direction of their development has come to be regarded as a matter of public interest. Secondly, developments have taken place elsewhere. Much of the work done in certain technical colleges and colleges for the education and training of teachers has risen to university or near university level. The establishment of the Colleges of Advanced Technology and the lengthening of the course in the Training Colleges, combined with rising standards of entry, mean that universities are no longer the sole providers of full-time higher education at degree level.

16. During the same period, outside the field of higher education, there have been changes in the community and its position in the world at large. The extension of educational opportunity in the schools and the widening of the desire for higher education on the part of young people have greatly increased the demand for places. At the same time the growing realisation of this country's economic dependence upon the education of its population has led to much questioning of the adequacy of present arrangements. Unless higher education is speedily reformed, it is argued, there is little hope of this densely populated island maintaining an adequate position in the fiercely competitive world of the future.

17. Thus it has come about that, seventeen years after the passing of the great Education Act of 1944, which inaugurated momentous changes in the organisation of education in the schools, we have been asked to consider whether changes of a like order of magnitude are needed at a higher level.

A system of higher education

18. The fundamental question that we have to answer is whether a system of higher education in the sense in which we have used the word 'system' is desirable. As we have said, it is misleading to speak as if there were already a system in this sense. Higher education has not been planned as a whole or developed within a framework consciously devised to promote harmonious evolution. What system there is has come about as the result of a series of particular initiatives, concerned with particular needs and particular situations, and there is no way of dealing conveniently with all the problems common to higher education as a whole.

157

19. There are many types of social activity where the absence of co-ordinating mechanism other than the framework of the law is not a disadvantage. The absence of a plan for everything is not necessarily an indication of chaos. But higher education is so obviously and rightly of great public concern, and so large a proportion of its finance is provided in one way or another from the public purse, that it is difficult to defend the continued absence of co-ordinating principles and of a general conception of objectives. However well the country may have been served by the largely unco-ordinated activities and initiatives of the past, we are clear that from now on these are not good enough. In what follows therefore we proceed throughout on the assumption that the needs of the present and still more of the future demand that there should be a system.

20. In giving this answer to our fundamental question we must guard against a possible misunderstanding. In recommending that there should be a system and co-ordination we are not demanding that all the activities concerned should be planned and controlled from the centre. We set great value upon the freedom of individuals and institutions in any academic system. But this does not conflict with our view that, where there is common provision, there should be co-ordinating principles; and that individual initiative must not result in mutual frustration. Our point is that the central decisions that have to be made should be coherent and take account of the interests of all sectors of higher education, and that decentralised initiative—and we hope there will always be much of this—should be inspired by common principles.

21. Before proceeding, then, to detailed discussion we think it appropriate to outline our conceptions of the aims of higher education and to state the principles that we believe should inspire its organisation.

The aims of higher education

22. To begin with aims and objectives—what purposes, what general social ends should be served by higher education?

23. The question is not a new one; and the answers have been many and various. But of one thing we may be reasonably certain: no simple formula, no answer in terms of any single end, will suffice. There is no single aim which, if pursued to the exclusion of all others, would not leave out essential elements. Eclecticism in this sphere is not something to be despised: it is imposed by the circumstances of the case. To do justice to the complexity of things, it is necessary to acknowledge a plurality of aims.

24. In our submission there are at least four objectives essential to any properly balanced system.

25. We begin with instruction in skills suitable to play a part in the general division of labour. We put this first, not because we regard it as the most important, but because we think that it is sometimes ignored or undervalued. Confucius said in the Analects that it was not easy to find a man who had studied for three years without aiming at pay. We deceive ourselves if we claim that more than a small fraction of students in institutions of higher education would be where they are if there were no significance for their future careers in what they hear and read; and it is a mistake to suppose that there is anything discreditable in this. Certainly this was not the attitude of the past: the ancient universities of Europe were founded to promote the training of the clergy, doctors and lawyers; and though at times there may have been many who attended for the pursuit of pure knowledge or of pleasure, they must surely have been a minority. And it must be recognised that in our own times, progress—and particularly the maintenance of a competitive position—depends to a much greater extent than ever before on skills demanding special training. A good general education, valuable though it may be, is frequently less than we need to solve many of our most pressing problems.

26. But, secondly, while emphasising that there is no betrayal of values when institutions of higher education teach what will be of some practical use, we must postulate that what is taught should be taught in such a way as to promote the general powers of the mind. The aim should be to produce not mere specialists but rather cultivated men and women. And it is the distinguishing characteristic of a healthy higher education that, even where it is concerned with practical techniques, it imparts them on a plane of generality that makes possible their application to many problems—to find the one in the many, the general characteristic in the collection of particulars. It is this that the world of affairs demands of the world of learning. And it is this, and not conformity with traditional categories, that furnishes the criterion of what institutions of higher education may properly teach.

27. Thirdly, we must name the advancement of learning. There are controversial issues here concerning the balance between teaching and research in the various institutions of higher education and the distribution of research between these institutions and other bodies. We shall deal with these later. But the search for truth is an essential function of institutions of higher education and the process of education is itself most vital when it partakes of the nature of discovery. It would be untrue to suggest that the advancement of knowledge has been or ever will be wholly dependent on universities and other institutions of higher education. But the world, not higher education alone, will suffer if ever they cease to regard it as one of their main functions.

28. Finally there is a function that is more difficult to describe concisely, but that is none the less fundamental: the transmission of a common culture and common standards of citizenship. By this we do not mean the forcing of all individuality into a common mould: that would be the negation of higher education as we conceive it. But we believe that it is a proper function of higher education, as of education in schools, to provide in partnership with the family that background of culture and social habit upon which a healthy society depends. This function, important at all times, is perhaps especially important in an age that has set for itself the ideal of equality of opportunity. It is not merely by providing places for students from all classes that this ideal will be achieved, but also by providing, in the atmosphere of the institutions in which the students live and work, influences that in some measure compensate for any inequalities of home background. These influences are not limited to the student population. Universities and colleges have an important role to play in the general cultural life of the communities in which they are situated.

29. Institutions of higher education vary both in their functions and in the way in which they discharge them. The vocational emphasis will be more apparent in some than in others. The advancement of learning will be more prominent at the postgraduate than at the undergraduate stage. The extent of participation in the life and culture of the community will depend upon local circumstances. Our contention is that, although the extent to which each principle is realised in the various types of institution will vary, yet, ideally, there is room for at least a speck of each in all. The system as a whole must be judged deficient unless it provides adequately for all of them.

Guiding principles

30. We conclude this chapter by indicating in broad outline some of the main principles that we have taken as guides in conducting our enquiries and in framing our recommendations.

Numbers and eligibility

31. Throughout our Report we have assumed as an axiom that courses of higher education should be available for all those who are qualified by ability and attainment to pursue them and who wish to do so. What type of education they should get and in what kind of institution are questions we consider later on; and the criterion by which capacity is to be judged is clearly a question on which there may be a variety of opinions. But on the general principle as we have stated it we hope there will be little dispute.

32. If challenged, however, we would vindicate it on two grounds. First, conceiving education as a means, we do not believe that modern societies can achieve their aims of economic growth and higher cultural standards without making the most of the talents of their citizens. This is obviously necessary if we are to compete with other highly developed countries in an era of rapid technological and social advance. But, even if there were not the spur of international standards, it would still be true that to realise the aspirations of a modern community as regards both wealth and culture a fully educated population is necessary.

33. But beyond that, education ministers intimately to ultimate ends, in developing man's capacity to understand, to contemplate and to create. And it is a characteristic of the aspirations of this age to feel that, where there is capacity to pursue such activities, there that capacity should be fostered. The good society desires equality of opportunity for its citizens to become not merely good producers but also good men and women.

The recognition of individual achievement

34. Secondly we have assumed throughout the principle of equal academic awards for equal performance. We think that in any properly co-ordinated system of higher education the academic grading of individuals should depend upon their academic accomplishment rather than upon the status of the institution in which they have studied. We are well aware that there are limits to the realisation of this principle, and that the status accorded by the world to a degree from an institution of long standing and established reputation may well be higher than the status of a degree earned in an examination of comparable severity in an institution of more recent foundation. This is in the nature of things. But it is no argument for retaining formal differences in terminology that do not reflect real differences in attainment.

The status of institutions

35. We wish to see the removal of any designations or limitations that cause differentiation between institutions that are performing similar functions. Distinctions based on adventitious grounds, whether historical or social, are wholly alien to the spirit that should inform higher education.

36. It must, however, be recognised that within the wide field of higher education there is a need for a variety of institutions whose functions differ. There must, therefore, be distinctions between institutions which, though they are all engaged in higher education, have differing functions and a different emphasis. Our concern is that such distinctions should be genuine, based on the nature of the work done and the organisation appropriate to

it, and that nobody should think that in recognising the existence of such distinctions by function we are implying that one kind of institution is more important and valuable to the nation than another. All are needed to provide appropriate educational opportunities and to supply national needs.

37. Furthermore it must be recognised that within these various categories it is inevitable that some institutions will be more eminent than others. It is in the nature of things that talent should attract talent and that where famous intellectual exploits take place, there should develop some concentration of staff and students especially interested in the subjects concerned. Moreover, such concentrations are not only probable but also desirable. A mutual stimulation of speculation and of scholarly standards is a precondition of much that is most valuable in higher education. It is therefore unavoidable that in this respect there should be some differences in achievement and reputation as between institutions. It is also unavoidable that because of the varying expense of different kinds of education and research different institutions should receive different subventions. What is important is that what differences there are should rest clearly on differences of function on the one hand, and on acknowledged excellence in the discharge of functions on the other. There should be no freezing of institutions into established hierarchies; on the contrary there should be recognition and encouragement of excellence wherever it exists and wherever it appears.

Opportunities for transfer

38. If it is true that certain differences of level and function must be expected to persist among institutions, it is also true that such a structure can only be morally acceptable if there are opportunities for the transfer of a student from one institution to another when this is appropriate to his or her intellectual attainments and educational needs. We attach great importance to this.

Organisation

39. The organisation of higher education must allow for free development of institutions. Existing institutions must be free to experiment without predetermined limitations, except those necessary to safeguard their essential functions; and there must be freedom to experiment with new types of institution if experience shows the desirability of such experiments. Our fundamental postulate of the necessity for system and order is not to be in any way construed as conflicting with this. We ask indeed that there should be co-ordination, some principles of policy commonly accepted, some organisation providing for rational allocation of scarce resources. But we

should hold it to be the very bankruptcy of constitutional invention if such conditions were thought to be incompatible with that scope for individual and institutional initiative that British tradition has always held to be one of the main essentials of intellectual and spiritual health.

The maintenance of standards

40. Finally, we must demand of a system that it produces as much high excellence as possible. It must therefore be so devised that it safeguards standards. We began our discussion of principles by emphasising the claims of numbers. It is only fitting, therefore, that we should close it by emphasising the claims of achievement and quality. The two ends are not incompatible. Equality of opportunity for all need not mean imposing limitations on some. To limit the progress of the best is inevitably to lower the standard of the average. A sound educational system should afford full scope for all types of talent at all levels. In the past our universities have tended to set the tone and the pace for other institutions and it is probable that in the future they will have a similar role to play. We are proud to think that they have proved themselves well capable of comparison over the years with those of other countries in fostering intellectual excellence. We hope that this reputation will be sustained and that, while they broaden the basis of education for first degrees, they will also achieve even higher standards in the education of those who show themselves capable of advancing beyond this stage.

CONCLUSION

828. Our Report began with a statement of guiding principles. It postulated the need for a co-ordinated system of higher education; and it laid down the requirements that the system should provide for those who had the qualifications and the willingness to pursue higher education; that it should ensure equal academic awards for equal performance; that it should eliminate artificial differences of status and recognise hierarchy only in so far as it was based on function and attainment; that it should ensure ease of transfer for students, as well as freedom of development and flexibility of organisation for institutions; and finally, that it should encourage the cultivation of high excellence.

829. It is our sincere hope that the recommendations of this Report will go some considerable way towards satisfying these requirements.

830. The systematic co-ordination of policy to meet national needs should be provided by our recommendations regarding the machinery of government.

The bringing together under one Grants Commission of the universities and the Colleges of Education, together with the Colleges of Advanced Technology and their Scottish counterparts, should ensure uniformity in policy and in the principles of allocation over the entire field of autonomous institutions. The administrative and consultative machinery we have recommended should ensure full co-ordination of this sector, both with the branches of further education that continue to be locally administered and with the schools. The assignment of responsibility for the Grants Commission to a minister responsible also for the Research Councils and other bodies with similar functions should emphasise the essential unity of higher education with the advancement and preservation of knowledge.

831. Calculations of future numbers have been made in the spirit of the requirement that all applicants with the appropriate qualifications should have places. Admittedly we have had to assume criteria of selection that are capable of improvement and educational and social trends that are to some extent a matter of conjecture. But, given appropriate machinery for observing developments as they occur and for modifying plans when this proves necessary, we are convinced that our estimate of the need for about 560,000 places in 1980 provides the right target for the realisation of this aim. We are aware that the magnitude of this need will come as a surprise to many. But we have been conservative in our assumptions and, if we had to guess at the probable direction of error, we think it the more likely that we have set our sights too low.

832. The requirement of equal awards for equal performance is met by a number of recommendations. The award of degrees by the Colleges of Advanced Technology should remove the most glaring of present deficiencies. The provision of degrees in Colleges of Education, together with the creation of the Council for National Academic Awards, should ensure that work done in other institutions is also recognised.

833. Such changes would also help to meet the requirement that artificial differences of status among the institutions should be eliminated. There are differences arising from differences of purpose or achievement that it would be wrong to attempt to remove. But there are others that are alien to our conception of the system of higher education of the future; the elevation of the Colleges of Advanced Technology to the status of technological universities, with the far-reaching changes proposed in the status of the Colleges of Education, should go far to remove the present irrational distinctions. Developments in the academic work and the forms of government of other institutions will make the distinctions between categories less marked, and our various proposals for student transfer will mean they offer no impediment to an individual's progress.

834. In these recommendations about organisation we have endeavoured to keep in mind the critically important requirement of freedom and flexibility. Throughout we have conceived present arrangements to mark no more than a stage of development in an evolving system. We have recommended the eventual promotion of further institutions to university status and emphasised the desirability of experiment. We have stressed the importance of wide representation and decentralised initiative in the internal government of institutions. We have endeavoured to elaborate as an articulate code the principles of academic freedom. The recommendations regarding the machinery of government, especially the preservation of the grants committee principle, are all designed to secure the maximum of freedom and flexibility compatible with orderly progress.

835. The last requirement was the cultivation of high excellence and we have made specific recommendations designed to achieve this aim, notably the proposals for the development of postgraduate studies and for the establishment of Special Institutions for Scientific and Technological Education and Research. But it has also been our aspiration to ensure that all our recommendations are informed by the same spirit. At this stage in the history of British higher education, it is a mistake to regard the claims of quantity and quality as being in conflict. Regard for the former is a safeguard against waste of talent; regard for the latter is a guarantee of the worth and merit of the whole.

836. The achievement of all this will not be easy. Teachers and administrators in the institutions concerned have lived for the last two decades under the stress of an expansion unprecedented in our history. They are now called upon to carry through even more strenuous reorganisation and development. But we are confident that, if they are assured of the necessary resources and public support, they will respond.

837. The public and the Government, for their part, will be required to make a more serious estimate of the comparative value of higher education than ever before. Much of the burden can be carried with ease in a regime of higher productivity. But some of it, at least until higher productivity has been achieved, will require a greater sacrifice of resources and manpower than has hitherto been customary. We hope and believe that such a revaluation of national priorities will be made. Not only is it a probable condition for the maintenance of our material position in the world, but, much more, it is an essential condition for the realisation in the modern age of the ideals of a free and democratic society.

61

SOME CONCLUSIONS

John Carswell

Source: S. Carswell, *Government and the Universities in Britain: Programme and Performance, 1960–1980*, Cambridge: Cambridge University Press, 1985, pp. 159–68.

It is not my intention to describe events after 1978, when my direct experience of university–state relations came to an end, but the existence of a subsequent and cataclysmic period must cast a shadow over any conclusions that can be suggested from what I have said so far.

Looking back at the scene as it was in the 1930s one finds it almost unrecognisable, so many and great have been the changes in the relationship between the universities and the state. But this has not, as might appear at first sight, taken the form of integrating the two more closely. The universities of fifty years ago were very closely integrated with the state as it then was, but in a quite different way; and they formed just as indispensable a part of the framework of national institutions as they do now. The links, however, were personal and social, not bureaucratic or formal. The universities and the machinery of Government in both its political and official aspects formed a kind of continuum, in which only the sketchiest of formality was either expected or required to maintain necessary relationships. This was enormously assisted by the small size of the university world and by its concentration in a comparatively few powerful centres. An obscure and confidential committee was all that was needed to transfer the marginal – but essential – Exchequer subsidy to the institutions in a decorous and impartial way.

Since then universities, though only the greater part of higher education, became a conspicuous feature in the general public landscape. Tens of thousands came to depend on them for a livelihood and hundreds of thousands for their careers or hopes. They became bound up in the public mind with the economic future of the country and with the turbulence of students. Many scholars and scientists found themselves acting on a public stage. The universities became subject not only to speculative comment but to weekly analysis by skilful and articulate commentators, many of whom held university posts themselves. Their staffs become unionised, with all the formality that entails. Gradually the social continuum between the state and the universities which had been the original basis of their financial relationship was replaced by an official system.

Two forces had brought about the expansion to which Robbins gave voice in Britain. One was the need, clearly perceived in the wake of the War, but never wholly satisfied, for graduates – above all for graduates in science and technology. The other was the ineluctable pressure for educational advance from one stage to the next, promoted by the concern (and in some cases the ambition) of parents, teachers and institutions. Both these forces were present in most countries, but in Britain the task of satisfying them was assumed in the years following the War, and by common consent, by the state. This was the unspoken axiom of the Robbins Report.

The formal relationship between the universities and the state which had been inherited from the 1930s was capable of sustaining this expansion so long as the general economy was itself expanding, or was, at any rate, not declining. Indeed the protection it gave to the universities meant that there would be some lag between general stringency and the arrival of pressure on university support. But on the other hand the direct connection between university support and the Exchequer made savings on that account only too attractive as alternatives to savings which might have been much larger but were more difficult to achieve. Once the state had plucked up the courage to reach for the tap it was found to lie remarkably ready to hand.

During the period of expansion the system, large though it was, could be steered by a touch of the tiller here and there – a nudge as it used to be called – and by adding desirable developments in what were thought to be the right places. But no serious thought had ever been given to the possibility that – whether because of shortage of resources or shortage of students – growth might actually have to go into reverse. To have foreseen and provided for such a contingency in, say, 1964 would have seemed not only absurd but in a way morally wrong. Just the same, it is one thing to restrain a growth deemed to be unsound, and quite another actually to demand the excision of established fibre: for the excision had to be done, in the last resort, by the very bodies of which the fibre was a part. The principle of autonomy imposed the act as well as the pains of amputation on the patient himself.

In this situation two schools of thought began to emerge. One said that the state was interfering too much and the UGC had become no more than its agent and catspaw. The other argued that in its policies on higher education the state had drifted rudderless and that more effective leadership by it and by the UGC could have avoided the brutal measures that were ultimately taken. One developed from what I have called the high-church view, the other from the evangelical. When the blow fell in 1981 and recurrent grant was ruthlessly cut, I remember Lord Robbins saying the UGC should

167

simply have passed the percentage on to each university without any attempt to differentiate. But there is no doubt in my own mind that such abdication would have meant the complete collapse of the UGC system, and that selectivity was the only course by which not only its authority but the autonomous identity of each university could have been preserved.

From this point of view the recognisable steps from a continuum to a formal and ultimately adversarial relationship can be seen as inevitable: the formation of the DES and its substitution for the Treasury in relation to the universities; the evanescence of the 'dual Accounting Officer' arrangement; the admittance of parliamentary audit; the assumption of control by the state over fees and over salary settlements; the growth of the UGC secretariat and the bureaucratisation of its procedures;[1] all these were no more than symptoms of the situation under which the state had undertaken the responsibility of meeting the needs identified by the Robbins Report.

But if these movements within the Government machine were inevitable, some important decisions were not, and if they had gone otherwise, the story would have been different.

One of these concerns the historical accident by which the Anderson Committee completed its work on student support which was then built into the fabric in advance of the general survey undertaken by the Robbins Committee. Perhaps if the Robbins Committee had been asked to consider student support as well as the pattern and size of the institutional system, it would have come up with the same answer as the Anderson Committee. But this is far from certain. Lord Robbins was not himself opposed to the concept of student loans. But however that may be, at least parliament and public would have been presented with an integrated picture.[2]

The second, and more serious, of the decisions which could have gone otherwise concerned the local authority area of higher education. On this issue the Robbins Report, with its proposal for an overarching Higher Education Commission, offered an escape. The loss of that opportunity is attributable to institutional power. On the one hand the existing universities wished to see the survival of the UGC they knew, with its mission to them and any that might be promoted to join them. On the other hand the local authorities, the educational interests and the Education Departments were unwilling to yield up to a Commission the institutions that remained within their control. Two competing, uncoordinated and jealous sectors was the unhappy result.

The one time at which this could have been avoided was in the immediate aftermath of the Robbins Report when all was fluid. Time was lacking, and a general election was in the air. But if it had been done, not only would the sorrows of binarism have been avoided but the new Commission would have had far more weight in Whitehall than the UGC as it emerged into the new world trying to look as like its old self as possible.

168

Leadership and policy were thus scattered and dispersed. The Secretary of State and his Department were forbidden by convention and policy from intervention but were under constant pressure to intervene: the UGC covered only part of the field, with a strict tradition of respecting the autonomy of institutions within it; and it took twenty years to produce anything resembling effective coordination of the local institutions themselves, let alone of the two 'sectors'. The arithmetic of the Robbins Report so far as it concerned 'sectors' was from that moment irrelevant, and university numbers became a matter of departmental decision.

The failure at the time of the Robbins Report or very soon afterwards to consider the terms of service for the enormous increase of staff that was planned constitutes another missed opportunity. The essential guarantees of professional freedom and the problem of combining rapid expansion with maintenance of quality and future opportunity for the ablest could then have had authoritative and lasting solutions. As it was, the tradition of tenure was assumed almost without discussion, with many unhappy results for the future.

Finally there were the two mistakes that must be laid at the door of the Robbins Committee itself: the failure to take account of medical education and the overprovision for science, both of which I have discussed earlier. Medical education was important because of its enormous potential cost and its manifest social implications; the initial overprovision for science led not only to undue expenditure but to overcrowding and lack of opportunity in the arts, a decline of standards in some science entries, and an addition to the problem of overseas students which had not been foreseen. If in the early sixties some of the capital that was spent on science buildings had gone to medical buildings and the growth of science been matured first in the schools much expense would have been saved and some loss of confidence avoided. Priority, however, was given to science in higher education.

The tables in Appendix I show how grievously the plan for growth in numbers in science and technology was disappointed, and the main reason why this happened. But the shortfall of 83,000 students of those subjects in 1980 feebly reflects the broader picture. The accumulated deficits of previous years since 1962 have come to about 150,000 newly qualified scientists and technologists, with social, industrial and international consequences of a most far-reaching kind which will be felt for many years to come. If, during the next twenty years, the deficit continues at the rate it reached in 1980 its total since the Robbins Report will come to something like three-quarters of a million. While that is unlikely to happen, the calculation illustrates the scale of the problem; and it should be remembered that it is wholly related to what the Robbins Committee projected. It allows for no addition to the total number of university students or for the increased pace of scientific and technological advance.

The other causes which contributed to the reversals of the late seventies and early eighties were not foreseeable, and no committee, Minister or civil servant could have provided against them. They were two in number. The first was the gathering pace of inflation which eroded and finally destroyed the quinquennial planning horizon and reduced managements at every level to a condition of perpetual crisis and fear of worse to come. This was also the prime reason for the appearance of state intervention in circumstances where no administrative device could prevent an item of expenditure as large as the university vote from being included in the successive jerks and convulsions that afflicted financial policy at the centre.

The other is less easy to define. The Robbins arithmetic engendered the habit of thinking in terms of student numbers as the main determinant of planning for the total system, the distribution between main subject areas, and the allocation to institutions. Finance, whether in the form of recurrent grant or of capital expenditure to create new capacity, came second. Yet in the end it was resources, not students, that were in the gift of the Exchequer.

Pressure for more students at a lower unit cost therefore became the inevitable if unspoken policy of all Secretaries of State, and, as the universities began to lose popularity during the later sixties, this policy gained wider support and universities were placed on the defensive.

That the state should ultimately determine the resources it will devote to higher education seems to me beyond dispute; but I am far from sure that the setting of the fraction of the population which ought to receive higher education is a proper function of central authority; and I am still more doubtful whether such a function is appropriate in respect of particular 'sectors', subject groups or institutions. The aid of the state should certainly be withheld from institutions which either fail to attract students in sufficient numbers, or so stretch their staff and resources that they unacceptably dilute the quality of what they offer. But however that may be, the labour and anxiety put into the setting of student 'targets' do not seem to have been justified by the outcome, as the following figures show.

At the time of the Robbins Committee (1961–2) there were 113,000 students in the universities. For the short term (1967–8) the Report proposed 153,000, and for the long term (1980–1) 346,000. The first of these was more than attained – it turned out to be 200,000, despite the fact that the element for science and technology fell considerably below what the Report had recommended both proportionately and absolutely. In the longer term the Robbins proposal for university numbers was not reached: it turned out to be 290,000, though the total for higher education as a whole was more than made up by the expansion of the polytechnics. In the intervening years the 'target' for universities had been hoisted as high as 375,000 (*Education: A Framework for Expansion*, 1972), and even in 1978 was placed at 310,000 (*Higher Education into the 1990s*).

In the middle of this turbulent sea the UGC was expected to float. It was to safeguard the universities and respond to the needs of Governments, acting as a source of wisdom for both, yet equipped with little formal authority. Its more open admonitions, whether they concerned Russian studies, libraries or mergers of facilities, were addressed to universities and met with resistance – in some cases with defiance. Its more covert protests, which were addressed to Governments and usually concerned sudden reductions in resources or equally sudden alterations in the financial arrangements, were partially successful, but as time passed they were increasingly met by sorrowful regrets either that circumstances which were outside the control of the DES, or that consequences for other sectors of higher education, prevented any positive answer. What had been claimed as the UGC's strengths tended to become its weaknesses. At the centre of its philosophy was the doctrine that it did not run the universities. But if it did not, the outsider kept saying, what does?

It was the reverse of Baldwin's famous epigram on the press: responsibility without power. The Chairman and the Secretary found themselves in the sixties habitually denying their power when they spoke to university audiences, and emphasising the managerial responsibilities of universities; while implying – without actually asserting – to Government and Parliament that persuasion, influence, financial pressure could be exerted on the universities to maintain orderly progress. But in the seventies, and still more in the eighties, the method of dealing with this dilemma altered. It began to be said with increasing emphasis by the UGC that failure to follow its guidance could only place the universities in less sympathetic hands, for in everything that truly mattered about university autonomy the UGC was as deeply committed as the highest-church college in Oxford or Cambridge.

So far I have been concerned in this chapter to dwell on a darker side and attribute reasons for the transition from euphoria to discontent which marked these eighteen years. But in a way that transition only marks a much wider transition in national and even in world affairs. That mood of euphoria broke in the later sixties, and student revolt was the foam on the crest of the wave. There was a better side, in which the universities, the UGC and even the DES can claim a share.

The pledges given by the Government in the wake of the Robbins Report for the period down to 1973–4 were more than fulfilled, with a capital endowment and a maintenance of staffing that in no way fell short of traditional measurements; and the Robbins projection for 1980–1, before which the Government of 1963 had hesitated, was nearly achieved for higher education as a whole, despite the need to reduce the programme of teacher training, which Robbins did not allow for. The full increase of university numbers was not achieved, but it did not fall very far short.

Taking a broad view it cannot be said that in achieving this there was much serious encroachment on university autonomy – the fee question

171

being the main exception. This may seem more difficult to accept, but one should remember the replacement of a social continuum by a bureaucratic system which marks the period. A line came to be drawn between the universities and Government which nobody had felt to be there before – not at any rate since King James II sought to impose his choice of President on the Fellows of Magdalen.

The UGC sustained the notion of continuum for a very long time. Its daily life – or rather the life of the Chairman and in a measure the Secretary and senior officials – was much taken up during the period of which I speak by consultations about university problems which were not financial, and much advice which was independent but in no way binding was the result. The UGC became expert in launching small but strategic initiatives – pump-priming grants for technology, industrial liaison officers, allocations to business studies, four-year, high-calibre engineering courses, special grants for advanced study in the humanities.

And even as the system became more encrusted by bureaucratic barnacles – many of them at the behest of the Public Accounts Committee – it never reached the point at which the Secretary could dream of writing, as his counterpart in democratic France had written on a file seeking travelling expenses for a group of university Rectors to attend a conference abroad:

Non. Ces Messieurs voyagent trop.

I have stressed the failure of the programme to fulfil expectations in science and technology, and the fact that this was primarily due to the shortage of women students in these subjects. But the counterpart to this is the immense success of the programme in advancing the position of women in society. It sounds a feeble expression of this to say that the proportion of women students in the higher education system as a whole (including teacher training, where even in 1962 they constituted a majority) rose over the eighteen years from $31^1/_2$ per cent to over 40 per cent. The total in the last year of the eighteen was nearly three times as large as in the first. In many arts and social science departments women students are now a majority. Nearly half the medical students are women and the quotas on women medical students (in some cases the absolute bans) are a remote memory. At Oxford and Cambridge the main preoccupation became the preservation of a handful of colleges where women who wished to do so could have an establishment to themselves. Altogether, between 1962 and 1980 at least one million women graduated.

The notion that universities are somehow apart from the workaday world (unlike other institutions of higher education) has been nourished by literature and has a foundation in the professional detachment and mutual esteem of university people. Just the same, it is an illusion. Far from being separated from the currents of ordinary life, universities are almost excessively sensitive to them and reflect them in a thousand ways. The university world is competitive for funds, for students and for reputation, as well as for religion and good learning. If these rewards are in prospect there is no need to kick universities into a pattern amid cries for responsiveness and relevance. Subject to certain lags as opinion changes course, a nation will get what it needs from its universities if funds, students and reputation are allowed them.

But it cannot be denied that in the period from 1960 to 1978 planning for higher education inside and outside the institutions – and predominantly outside – suffered from flaws of which perhaps the greatest was hesitation between the well-tried and by then well-loved landscape and the attractions of adventure. Both had their claims in those years, but I heard with a chill a distinguished business man declaring in the face of a long list of bids from universities to develop business studies that since neither Oxford nor Cambridge was among them he for one saw no point in continuing the discussion.

Earlier chapters have pointed out failures and triumphs in the Robbins chapter of the history of the universities. The chapter is now closed, primarily because the celebrated 'Robbins principle' has itself ceased to provide an adequate beacon.[3] The word 'qualified' in the famous formula 'all those who are qualified by ability and attainment' acquired definition only because the Committee took the broad level of admission of 1962 as 'qualified' and then enlarged future numbers to allow for larger age-groups and a developing school system producing more candidates at that level. Thus, although it implied no reduction in standards, it did imply a very large expansion of the institutions. But the institutions, once enlarged, could hardly be expected to contract, even if changes in demography made this theoretically desirable to maintain the standards of 1962. So at the turn of the decade the system was faced with the question –as yet unresolved – of substituting something else for 'qualified by the standards of 1962'.

Throughout the period, and indeed after it had ended, decision on this has been obscured and discussion diverted by the priority given to structural questions, as against those of substance. Much of the debate has been carried on as if structures and methods of finance were the keys to effective teaching and research. It is true that the Robbins Committee set a fashion for this by its own emphasis on structure, but it also saw higher education as a larger unity within which many institutions of different kinds could flourish under the broad tree of autonomy. Later developments, especially the binarist approach enunciated by Crosland, impaired this vision and diverted effort from the real objectives.

The state and the universities are like a discontented couple who cannot live without each other: he rich, busy, self-important, preoccupied with the office; she proud, independent and in her own opinion beautiful. The state–husband will always complain about her extravagance and inconstancy, and the university–wife will endlessly denounce his stinginess, jealousy and philistinism. Her parting words in the endlessly renewed argument will be that she knows he has a mistress – 'and very common she is'. But they would not dream of parting: because of the children.

Notes

1 It has sometimes been suggested that the calibre of the staff of the UGC declined as original Treasury personnel retired and DES staff took their places. I have always felt that the UGC should be allowed to trawl more widely in Whitehall – and the universities – for its vacancies, and several successful experiments were in fact made in this direction. But I do not think (and in practice the Secretary of the UGC was in a position to veto any appointment proposed by the DES) that there was any loss of calibre at senior levels. The notion almost certainly derives from the three-fold expansion of the UGC during the Wolfenden era, which necessarily brought in more officers at lower ranks, to whom much business was devolved which would have been dealt with at senior levels in earlier days.
2 There is an interesting discussion of loan finance in the Robbins Report (paragraphs 641 to 647) which makes it clear that the Committee was divided on the issue. Their conclusion – to go on with the Anderson system for the time being but to consider introducing loans later – meant that any later examinations of the question revealed an enormous initial cost which was unacceptable.
3 It is a frequent error to suppose that the 'Robbins principle' means that all those achieving a specific level of achievement in school examinations should be found a place somewhere in the system if they wish for it. This is not the case, and was never stated to be so. It is irreconcilable with the right of institutions and departments within them to decide their own requirements for admission, in terms of both subjects and attainment. Such decisions must obviously take into account, among other factors, the facilities available at that particular place and the range of quality in the candidates for them.

62

PASTS AND FUTURES

Harold Silver

Source: H. Silver, *A Higher Education: The Council for National Academic Awards and British Higher Education, 1964–89*, London: Falmer Press, 1990, pp. 260–72.

Reconstructing a history involves choosing emphases. In the case of the CNAA, as in others, there are inevitably perceptions, interpretations, silences, that are not shared or are differently understood by other participants and onlookers. Some emphases, however, command a large degree of shared attention and agreement, even if there are differences of judgment about why events and processes took shape, whether they might have been shaped or timed differently, and what roles particular people or structures played or might have played. With those reservations it is clear that the CNAA has not been merely a figure in changing landscapes, it has itself been a major contributor to the changes. It has been, as it was intended to be, centrally concerned with widening access to higher education and maintaining and raising standards — two inseparable elements in its work. It has therefore been involved in extending and reinterpreting the curricula of higher education, and creating and taking advantage of the opportunities presented. It has addressed the difficult balance between exercising its own responsibilities and enabling its related institutions to shoulder theirs — with how many cheers for its record in doing so at different times in its twenty-five years of activity is probably the issue most open to differences of emphasis and interpretation. It has taken a process of peer validation and review pioneered by the NCTA and developed it into an instrument which has been at work for institutions and courses serving a majority of the country's higher education students — an instrument which in the late 1980s has been adapting to new relationships. It has made peer validation and review part of the culture of public sector institutions, even in those institutions no longer subject to formal validation by the CNAA. Against the background outlined in the first two chapters it has — together with its related institutions — established new dimensions and characteristics for the 'higher education' which — in the space of a quarter of a century — the universities have come to share with a range of other institutions. Future historians may further find that it also had significant impacts on the universities themselves.

The broadening of access to higher education has been a constant preoccupation of the CNAA in a number of respects. It has been instrumental particularly in establishing the polytechnics and colleges as an alternative sector of higher education, with the increasing numbers of students that we have seen entering the new higher education institutions and the expanded and new areas of study that they have represented. It has pioneered new areas of study — such as business studies and computer studies — before they have appeared in the universities. It has consistently emphasized the importance of the development of provision for nonstandard and mature students, and has emphasized the need for its institutions to take advantage of the opportunities offered by the CNAA's liberal regulations on mature students. From the very beginning it recognized the traditions of public sector institutions in catering for part-time as well as full-time students. After expressing its interest in 1965 in hearing from 'any colleges which have proposals for part-time degree courses in mind, particularly those arranged for mature students', it described its 'considerable pleasure' the following year in being able 'to approve one part-time course leading to its degree of B.Sc., and two part-time courses leading to its degree of M.Sc.'. There was clearly a need for 'part-time courses specially designed for mature students including teachers'.[1] The CNAA has taken up the challenge to acknowledge 'experiential' or 'prior' learning as a contribution to higher education qualifications, and it has developed a capacity to accredit the in-house education and training activities of industrial, commercial and professional bodies. The Credit Accumulation and Transfer Scheme has been a major breakthrough of the 1980s towards broader opportunities for these and other kinds of potential students. The CNAA has also regularly liaised with other bodies — including the Business and Technician Education Council — to examine the mesh between further and higher education courses of study. As one aspect of this interest one of the projects supported by the CNAA's Development Fund and conducted at the Roehampton Institute of Higher Education in 1986–88 was a study of different models of the relationship between further and higher education through 'access courses', the selection and assessment of access course students, access course curricula and management, and the dissemination of 'good practice'.[2] When the government decided to plan for a national framework for such access courses as a mode of transition to higher education it invited the CNAA to act as 'handling agent' for the initiative on behalf of the polytechnics and colleges, and the universities, in partnership with the CVCP. A statement of principles and an invitation to intending validating agencies to apply for a franchise under the scheme were both published in 1989.[3] The concern of the CNAA and its related institutions to widen access has meant greater diversity of institutions, opportunities, courses, and paths through higher education. This has been a central way in which the CNAA has implemented its Charter, and inextricably related to it have been the processes by which it has sought to establish, maintain and enhance standards.

While 'standards' and 'quality' have been the heart of the CNAA's concerns, neither it nor other organizations which provide or are concerned with higher education have been eager to define or to debate the concepts too closely. The National Advisory Body addressed the question directly in 1984 in a paper on 'Quality', acknowledging that it had hitherto been making judgments about quality but 'it has not defined, nor stated explicitly, what that quality is, or consists of'. This Secretariat paper began to fill the gap by summarizing discussions that had taken place, emphasizing 'role or function', the achievement, or otherwise, of declared objectives and processes' (which is very much the basis on which the accreditation of institutions has taken place in the United States). At the same time it emphasized that quantification and measurement were dangerous proxies for judgments of quality, and that such measures were only a part of quality assessment, which is 'ultimately, at least in large part, subjective'. Christopher Ball, as Chairman of the NAB Board, continued the debate with a paper entitled 'What the hell is quality?', and the Society for Research into Higher Education ran a conference on questions of standards.[4] Within the CNAA, especially in the late 1970s and 1980s, officers and committees wrestled with the definition of standards in relation to the Council's terminologies and procedures regarding validation and review, appraisal and evaluation. Summarizing earlier analysis, David Billing in 1983 underlined that standards had to do with more than the level of performance — they were also concerned with 'the calibre and potential of the students at admission; the quality of the students' learning experience promoted by the institution; the final level of achievement of the course aims as reflected in the assessment of students' performance'. The CNAA was therefore concerned with 'the quality of the educational process and its environment, as well as its products, and it is important to note that any estimate of the quality of the process rests largely on the perceptions and judgments of staff, students, examiners, and employers'.[5] A good deal of the CNAA's interest in questions of standards across the years has therefore focussed both on attempts to clarify criteria and on the needs and experience of grappling with them in operation.[6] The CNAA and others have in various ways tried to detect how the validation and related procedures have in precise terms influenced behaviours which affect the standards of course provision and monitoring. An HMI commentary in 1983 on degree courses in public sector higher education, underlined, for example, that 'the processes by which the CNAA scrutinises course proposals before validation have encouraged staff to formulate more explicitly the means and teaching methods through which a measure of integration in the curriculum is achieved'.[7] It is not so much questions of integration that are important here as the pressures towards definition, explanation, explicitness, in relation to those processes which affect the learning experience and its outcomes — teaching methods, attention to curriculum design, assessment, course review . . . It is this that explains the central interest of the institutions and of CNAA committees and visiting panels over the years in questions of professional development or institutional machineries for dealing with the processes which underlie the concern with standards. In 1979, to take a single example, the subject boards of the Committee for Science and Technology, while reviewing course approvals, had detected 'signs of falling academic health, either through original promise not being fulfilled, or through a failure to maintain previously acceptable levels of provisions and performance', and this had to do with resource levels and a range of other particular problems. The academic health of courses had to be 'a matter of continuing concern to all partners in the complex processes of higher education . . . it is no less important to sustain and develop the quality of demonstrably successful courses'. The Committee was therefore invited to give its attention to the matter 'by considering the indicators of academic health and present problems connected with them'.[8]

These are no more than pointers to the CNAA's necessary and continuing concern not only with implementing procedures intended to safeguard standards, but also with analyzing and understanding the nature of the exercise itself. The range of elements in the CNAA's approach to standards is perhaps best illustrated, however, by Sir Michael Clapham's opening address to the degree congregation in 1976. What, he asked, is quality in higher education? And he answered:

> It is the quality of those who teach and those who plan the courses which are taught. It is the quality of those who are admitted to a course of study, and the quality of those who assess and examine them. It is the quality of the academic environment in which teachers and taught alike move and have their being: that unquantifiable, ideal blend of intellectual freedom and intellectual discipline in which ideas multiply and are cross-fertilised, learning flourishes and sciolism wilts. It is an atmosphere which encourages a broad diversity of interests combined with a profound depth of penetration. To some extent it may be enhanced by the nonacademic pursuits available . . . Least important but never to be disregarded, it is the quality of the physical environment; the resources available, the facilities for using them.

Applying this comprehensive statement to the work of the CNAA, he emphasized that it was only the last item in the list that was amenable to other than subjective judgment: 'it thus becomes the Council's task to organise subjective judgment on a vast scale'. He went on to ask whether and how this should in fact be done, in the CNAA's 'complex system of visitations and discussions, both at course level and college level'.[9] In relation to all of the elements in Sir Michael Clapham's list, in fact, the CNAA has had to concern itself with the purposes and operational details of the environment of institutions and the content of courses, the work of external examiners and changing levels of resources, the balance of curricula and the relationship of academic organization and delivery to the pressures of local and national control.

Whatever reservations individuals may have about specific procedures or decisions (or absence of decisions) of the CNAA, it is commonly agreed that the impact of the CNAA on British, and not only British, higher education has, over the past quarter of a century, been in terms of its sustained concern with the expansion of student access and the enhancement of standards. One or the other or both of these elements feature in response to the question: what you would most want to record about the CNAA from its creation in 1964? Jean Rossiter, for example, as one of the CNAA's earliest officers and concerned with the development of new subject areas in former colleges of technology, emphasized that without the CNAA there could have been no polytechnics, given its influence on resources for institutions and their structures — notably the role of academic boards: 'democratization stems from the CNAA'. Cynthia Iliffe, a long-serving officer of the CNAA, notably as Registrar for Business and Management Studies, describes the 1970s as enormously exciting precisely because the work of the CNAA was worthwhile in 'broadening access and expanding the system of higher education as a whole'. Ann Ridler, concerned over a long period of time with the arts and with policy issues, also emphasized the strengthening of the polytechnics in the early years, the development of course review as a major strength of the system, and the contribution to quality in higher education of the encouragement of courses as 'logical, progressive wholes', and the building of a tradition of 'thinking about why'. Roger Woodbridge, Assistant Registrar for Science, with thirteen years experience of the CNAA, emphasized both the conflicts that had been a thread in the CNAA's history, but also the gradual build-up of public awareness of the CNAA and the public sector, especially of the latter. The CNAA had played a large part in this by setting the standards. Although universities were still seen as 'preferable' in the public eye as places to send one's children the public sector had established itself as credible. Edwin Kerr, Chief Officer for fifteen years, picks out the ability of the CNAA to respond to policy developments and influence the system; the contribution to the expansion of provision in subject areas such as teacher education, art and design and management studies — and therefore to innovatory approaches in those areas and such new or newly developing ones as computer science or the creative and performing arts; the development of the institutions' academic boards; opportunities for mature students, and for independent study; modular courses and credit accumulation; in general the planning and coordination of a sector contributing to increases in scale and variety in higher education. Bill Gutteridge, as a university professor and one of the longest-serving members of the Council, including as Chairman of the Committee for Arts and Social Studies, stresses the operation of the CNAA as an informal network within which university and polytechnic people could meet and 'come to terms with each other', as they did for example in the Political Studies Board with which he was associated. For him the success of the CNAA lies in its having set out on the 'tightrope' of standards and opportunities for higher education, and in walking it successfully — 'better, in fact, than anywhere in the world, to ensure that higher education expanded without lowering quality', to ensure that an honours degree, a II(i) or whatever meant something. Marion North, Director of the Laban Centre for Movement and Dance, reflecting on the difficulty of surmounting the first hurdle in obtaining CNAA approval for a degree course, underlines the CNAA's concern with staffing and resources alongside conceptual questions, and judges that the CNAA was ultimately 'asking the right things'. If a degree was to be the first of its kind 'it had to be good'. George Tolley, first Director of Sheffield Polytechnic, long active in the CNAA, including as Chairman of the Management Board, while severely critical of the CNAA's partnership in validation policy and the operation of the subject boards from the late 1970s, underlines the considerable development of quality in degree courses to which the CNAA contributed. One of its great contributions was the development of peer evaluation, and as the 'guardian of standards' it was instrumental in establishing the credibility of the public sector and its degrees within higher education and with employers. Sir Norman Lindop, former Director of Hatfield Polytechnic, long active in the CNAA, including as Chairman of the Committee for Education, and then Chairman of the Committee of Inquiry on Academic Validation, also sharing some of the criticism of CNAA procedures from the late 1970s, considers that the CNAA 'changed the face of higher education in this country' — which is particularly clear if one looks back at the external degree system and compares it with the 'extraordinary developments' which followed. The process of validation was fundamental, a 'critical mechanism', and he has 'not the least doubt of its overwhelming influence for progress'. It 'materially assisted academic development' in those institutions which would never have achieved the maturity and status that they did without the CNAA. The National Advisory Body, commenting on 'the Lindop Report', underlined — as we have seen — the CNAA's contribution to higher education, and it is worth recalling the terms of the NAB's comments:

There can be no doubting the beneficial effects the CNAA has had over the past twenty years on both the standard and the standing of qualifications from public sector institutions . . . these standards

have been achieved while encouraging and accommodating curriculum innovation, more flexible course structure, development into
new subject areas, wider access for students . . .[10]

Clearly concern with standards and access has to be broken down into the
specifics of policy and operation, and from the mid-1960s we have traced
many of the elements involved in both of these. Analysis and judgment
of the CNAA's role therefore involves consideration of the nature of its
responsiveness, including for example to the opportunities opened up by the
James report on teacher education or the Finniston report on engineering.
'Responsiveness' has also to do with perceptions of the state of development
of institutions, of disciplines, of existing and emergent needs in the professions, industry and commerce. It has to do with opportunities of the kind
associated, for example, with the CNAA's role in developing interest in
design management or credit transfer. The concern with standards has
also had to relate both to the CNAA's own procedures in 'guaranteeing'
them, and to the range of institutional characteristics we have considered.
Included, and of central importance to the CNAA from its creation, has
been its concern with research, with emphasizing its relationship to the
academic health of courses and institutions, with monitoring its development or its failure to develop, in general and in specific areas,[11] with
establishing policies for research, with supporting it when opportunity has
arisen, and with acting as advocate on behalf of public sector institutions in
relation to the research councils and other bodies which support research.
The specifics of standards have also involved the CNAA in continuous
efforts to use its networks to promote subject and curriculum development,
through the mechanism of seminars and workshops, conferences and working parties, as well as through the activities of its officers and committees.
   In its concern with the curriculum and its delivery, the CNAA has had
to confront not only questions of standards within individual course and
programme structures, but also questions of desirable 'balance' and the
relationship of students' experience of courses to their employment intentions or opportunities. 'Balance' in the early years of the CNAA meant the
controversial area of complementary and contrasting studies, or the definition of appropriate objectives for courses of study in the polytechnics and
colleges of higher education. It also meant a continuing interest in the
nature and provision of sandwich courses. The interest in employment outcomes has been a matter not only of relationships with employers and the
labour market, but also close attention to those of institutions and their
courses. There has invariably been an assumption in the CNAA's approach
to validation that employment opportunities should to one degree or
another be a concern of institutions in appraising their course proposals and
their implementation. Subject boards have at different times — particularly
at times of shrinking graduate employment — laid considerable stress on

181

the 'market research' aspect of course proposals. In 1982 the CNAA indicated that the points which boards had found to be 'of particular value' within institutions' critical appraisal of their courses were 'statistics of student cohort admission and progression and career outlets'.[12] In the 1980s the CNAA commissioned and supported work intended to provide data on the career experience of graduates with CNAA awards, both in general and in specific subject areas.[13] The CNAA and its institutions developed over the years an approach to courses of study which sought to bring together the traditions of the 'public sector', with its strong interest in the labour market and employment outcomes, and the wider characteristics of a 'liberal' higher education. A 'liberal vocationalism' was the outcome, one in which the vocational intentions of courses were not narrowly conceived, and in which the generally accepted aims of higher education were not divorced from the world of employment.[14]

In all of these characteristics of the CNAA, as we have seen, a dominant one has been its explicitness, and its encouragement of its related institutions to be equally so. The validation of courses and the review of institutions produced an emphasis on documentation which was often regarded in the polytechnics and colleges — particularly by those responsible for producing it — as laborious or ritualistic. What it accomplished at the same time, however, was a constant concern for explanation, for what was often called the 'rationale' of courses, for the definition of institutional purposes which we have seen emphasized by different institutions at different times. The CNAA's own operations have been highly documented, as a result of the accounts of debate in working parties or committees, working papers by officers and reports widely circulated within and beyond the CNAA. The CNAA's record of published policy statements, guidelines, research-based information, consultative documents, reports and the like is considerable. Most of the CNAA's decisions, intentions, debates, responses, controversies or concerns had their reflection in documents circulated to institutions or other forms of public statement. Subject boards and committees not only received detailed documentation, they also recorded and explained their discussions and decisions in detail. Between institutions and the CNAA an intensive communication often developed — whether seeking or giving explanations, making or discussing proposals — which may or may not have related to courses and parochial concerns, disseminating information, making response and counter-response, expressing anxiety, anger or gratitude. The NCTA established and the CNAA further developed procedures which almost inevitably produced such levels of explicitness. The CNAA and its institutions operated from the 1960s in a context of public accountability — whether to Ministers or the DES, or in the general context of the responsibilities placed upon it by its Charter — which made its processes intensely and deliberately open to scrutiny and debate. The very concept of validation, review or evaluation made this true both of the CNAA and of any institution which came into association with it. It was to a large extent this characteristic of the CNAA and its associated institutions that also made the CNAA internationally visible, not only with regard to its role in Hong Kong, but also in the interest shown by institutions, academics, administrators and governments in other countries in its operation. The CNAA similarly often saw itself in international perspective, as when, for instance, the Working Party on Longer Term Developments in 1982 'received information about the systems employed for the assurance of academic standards in other countries — particularly Australia and the USA'.[15]

In the case of the CNAA, as with all institutions, there are difficulties in interpreting and judging the persistence of characteristics — the same features at different times, the confidence that may be both strength and weakness, the procedure that may be both innovatory and conservative, the virtues of continuity and of discontinuity. There is also the difficulty of angle of vision, and as we have seen in precise cases very different judgments may be made of events as experienced from the Council, from the boards, from the institutions, by officers or members, by college principals or course teams, by the CNAA itself and by other agencies. What was clearly consistent strength for some was for others dirigisme or worse. The work of the boards was for some both the essential mechanism for safeguarding standards and promoting subject development, and for others the main obstacle to necessary change in the operations of the CNAA. The role of the Council in providing the necessary benchmarks for quality and comparability was for some an outdated role almost as soon as it took effect, and from then on could be interpreted as a brake on institutional development. Somewhere in the late 1970s and early 1980s is a point at which critics detect what some see as a loss of confidence, and others a failure to grasp opportunities or understand realities. It is only by placing such judgments of strength or weakness in the historical complexities of the time, in the nature of the competing values and constituencies, in the competing claims for attention and priority, that the judgments can be made without excessive portrayal in black or white.

The principal context and component for the history of the CNAA has been the redefinition of 'higher education'. The new contexts developing at the end of the 1980s did not make it easy to interpret the changing roles of the CNAA, but a configuration of well-established, recently changed and new directions for its activities was rapidly taking shape. By the end of the decade some 90 per cent of students in the polytechnics and colleges sector would be in 'accredited' institutions, and eighty-five or so institutions — mainly smaller or specialist institutions or those with only a small proportion of their work at or above degree level — would remain as 'associated' institutions — all of them in vastly changed circumstances. Even by the end of 1988 the Committees for Art and Design and for the Performing Arts, for example, were reporting that 'only a tiny number of colleges remained in a traditional relationship with CNAA',[16] and these 'traditional relationships' were themselves substantially changing. Following the 1987 White Paper and the 1988 Education Reform Act, the institutions were having to tackle simultaneously the new responsibilities of their corporate status, and the implications of their changed academic status vis-à-vis the CNAA. John Brennan interpreted the new position of the institutions in terms of the continuing but changed external accountability of the polytechnics and colleges, and the relationship between their two new sets of responsibilities:

> The messages of incorporation are of financial responsibility, of efficiency, of contracts and markets, and of competitiveness. The messages of accreditation are of academic responsibility, of collective responsibility for standards, of peer review and the institution's place within the wider academic community.

Between the two sets of messages lay those of quality, to which competition was not necessarily antithetical. Shoddy products might not survive in the market place, but in higher education 'the nature and quality of the product is not easy to assess':

> In an increasingly competitive setting, academic institutions may find themselves needing to present ever better evidence about the quality of their work for intending students, for employers of graduates, for funding bodies.

However institutions were viewed, 'rather than being the source of conflict between the competitive and community models of higher education, quality is part of the essential linkage between them'.[17]

Part of the CNAA's continuing role was clearly to be that of providing the system with such 'evidence', and with the intelligence on which national and institutional judgments and policies might be based. The Council in fact now saw itself as 'a national centre for the collection and dissemination of information about academic standards and developments in higher education',[18] and in addition to its work of validation and re-accreditation it was shaping a programme of seminars, meetings and conferences that would contribute to the promotion of enhanced standards. In 1987–88, for instance, a series of regional seminars on the humanities and employment was held at commercial and industrial venues — Wedgwood, the IBM Research Centre and British Steel. The Committee for Life Sciences sponsored a meeting of external examiners, in association with the British Psychological Society, the Association of Heads of Psychology Departments and Plymouth Polytechnic. The Committee for Health Studies held a series of meeting with representatives of professional and registration bodies, the first being with the College of Radiographers.[19] For the following year the CNAA was planning induction meetings for new members, workshops for newly-appointed external examiners and a series of validation workshops to supplement a successsful series already conducted. It intended organizing an annual programme of workshops and conferences on questions relating to the maintenance and enhancement of quality. It saw the development of the Credit Accumulation and Transfer Scheme as a priority, as more institutions introduced schemes based on CATS, and as increasing interest was being shown from many directions. In 1987–88, for example, the scheme was discussed with some 200 representatives of the universities at seminars at Warwick, York, Strathclyde and Oxford universities.[20] By 1989 the CAT scheme had established procedures 'for the allocation of credit towards CNAA awards for in-company training programmes, and about fifteen employing organizations have received credit in this way'.[21] In changed circumstances the CNAA was to continue its dual concern for access and for standards.

As in previous stages of its history the CNAA was also continuing to explore new subject areas or possibilities of awards that would embody this concern. In 1989, for example, the Chief Executive, Malcolm Frazer, was outlining developments in the area of initial education programmes for new managers, in connection with the Council for Management Education and Development. In association with the Training Agency the CNAA commissioned five pilot programmes for such managers, operating at four English polytechnics and one Scottish college, with the aim of 'meeting the requirements of employers and employees for high-quality education based on workplace skills, abilities and competence, while also incorporating an appropriate level of academic rigour'. The outcome was intended to be a new certificate award and, following a review of the Diploma in Management Studies and the MBA, a new hierarchy of CNAA awards in management education.[22] Joint conferences or seminars with other bodies in such fields as media studies also pointed to the possibility of new departures. In relation to established areas of study what the CNAA planned for a beginning in 1988 was a rolling programme of 'subject and course development reviews', to examine changes in courses and their responsiveness or otherwise to academic and social change. These reviews were intended to consider: the number, variety, aims and structure of courses; data about students (from enrolment to employment); developments and trends in the curriculum; innovations in teaching methods and in methods of assessment; links with industry and the professions; developments and trends in research. Information would be collected and collated and disseminated through publications, workshops and conferences. These subject reviews, including topic-based reviews across subject areas, were to take place at five-yearly intervals.[23] The CNAA's continued commitment to resourcing development projects was for work in four priority areas: quality assurance;

higher education and work; continuing education, and extending opportunities.[24] The configuration of developing activities remained United
Kingdom-wide, with a particularly strengthened development in Scotland. By
1987–88 the adaptation of CATS to the needs of Scotland was the subject
of advanced consultations. A newly-reconstituted Committee for Scotland
was designed to play a 'more positive and proactive role in CNAA's work
in Scotland', and it pressed successfully in 1987 for 'a permanent officer
presence' in Scotland,[25] and such an officer based in Scotland was in fact
appointed in 1989. In 1989 the Council was actively developing a 'Five year
development plan', containing a 'mission statement' embodying the CNAA's
commitment to three principal objectives: 'to guarantee standards; to
enhance standards; to promote innovations and more flexible approaches
to higher education without loss of quality'. It spelled out in some detail how
the CNAA intended from this point to pursue its aims and commitments
in the changed contours of higher education, the polytechnics and colleges,
and the CNAA itself.[26]

'Public sector higher education', and higher education in general, were no
longer what they were in 1964, or even in 1984, and nor was the CNAA.
While its relationships with the institutions had changed, it had retained a
major role as a guarantor of maintained and enhanced standards, and it was
defining and developing activities consonant with that role. 'Standards',
'quality assurance', 'access', 'developing opportunities', 'flexibility' ... the
CNAA, its scale, strategies and structures, its related institutions, 'higher
education', had all changed markedly across the quarter-century and with
particular speed in the 1980s, but the essential vocabulary and purposes had
remained the same.

Notes

1 CN *Annual Report 1987–88*, p. 8.
2 CN (1989) *Development Services Briefing 9. Access Courses in Higher Education:
Dimensions of Quality Assurance. An Overview.*
3 CN and CVCP (1989) *Access Courses to Higher Education. A Framework of
National Agreements for Recognition*; *ibid.*, *Procedures for the Approval of Authorised Validating Agencies and an Invitation to Apply*, 1989.
4 NAB, 'Quality' (report by the Secretariat), 1984; Christopher Ball, (1984) 'What
the hell is quality?' in Dorma Urwin (Ed.) (1985) *Fitness for Purpose: Essays in
Higher Education by Christopher Ball*, Society for Research into Higher Education; Graeme Moodie (Ed.) (1986) *Standards and Criteria in Higher Education*,
Society for Research into Higher Education.
5 David Billing (1983) 'Practice and criteria in validation under the CNAA'
in Clive H. Church (Ed.) *Practice and Perspective in Validation*, Society for
Research into Higher Education, pp. 32–3.
6 See R. A. Barnett (1987) 'The maintenance of quality in the public sector of UK
higher education', *Higher Education*, p. 16.
7 DES (1983) *Degree Courses in the Public Sector of Higher Education: An HMI
Commentary*, HMSO, p. 24.

8 CST (1979) The Academic Health of Courses, 24 October.
9 Sir Michael Clapham, Opening Address, CNAA Degree Congregation, 1976.
10 Rossiter, Iliffe, Ridler, Woodbridge, Kerr, Gutteridge, North, Tolley, Lindop — HS interviews; 'NAB's response to the Lindop report', *NAB Bulletin*, summer 1985, pp. 14–15.
11 For example, Harold Silver (1988) *Education and the Research Process — Forming a New Republic*, CNAA.
12 CN (1982) *Procedures for the Validation of Courses*, 1982.
13 John Brennan and Philip McGeevor (1988) *Graduates at Work: Degree Courses and the Labour Market*, Jessica Kingsley; CN Information Services (1988) *'Outcomes' Paper 1: Social Science Graduates: Degree Results and First Employment Destinations*, and (1989) Papers 2 and 3 on art and design graduates and humanities graduates.
14 Harold Silver and John Brennan (1988) *A Liberal Vocationalism*, Methuen.
15 CN *Annual Report 1982*.
16 CN *Annual Report 1987–88*, p. 15.
17 John Brennan (1989) 'Fewer fears over standards', *Times Higher Education Supplement* 27 January.
18 CN *Annual Report 1987–88*, p. 13.
19 *ibid.*, pp. 16–17 and 20.
20 *ibid.*, p. 19.
21 Malcolm Frazer (1989) 'On-site training', *Times Higher Education Supplement*, 10 March; CN (1989) *Development Services Briefing 15. New Initial Award in Management Education*.
22 *ibid.*
23 CN (1989) Draft Five Year Development Plan, 20 March.
24 *ibid.*
25 CN *Annual Report 1987–88*, pp. 20 and 22; Cmin, 17 December 1987.
26 Draft Five Year Development Plan.

63

THE BUSINESS UNIVERSITY

E. P. Thompson

Source: E. P. Thompson, (ed.) *Warwick University Ltd.*, Harmondsworth: Penguin, 1970, pp. 13–41.

Introduction

The first Chancellor-designate of the new University of Warwick was the first Lord Rootes of Rootes Motors Ltd. After his death in 1964 the first students' hall was officially named after him: Rootes Hall. The second Lord Rootes and the Managing Director of Rootes Motors, Mr Gilbert Hunt, took places on the University's governing Council. Mr Hunt was not an inactive member of this Council. As Chairman of its crucial Building Committee he was able to influence policies and priorities in relation to some millions of pounds of capital expenditure (by far the greater part being public – Treasury – money) – which buildings, in which order, which architects. For three years the Building Committee resisted a series of hard-pressed demands from the students, and also from academic staff, whose objectives were to humanize the starkly utilitarian social environment, to desegregate the informal life of students and staff, and to afford to the students this or that measure of control over their own union building. Finally, on 11 February 1970, one more prevarication by the Building Committee on the issue of student control precipitated an occupation of the Registry.

A good deal was unveiled there, some of which filtered through to the outside world – despite a legal injunction – in the next two or three weeks. This is one of the themes of this book. It turned out, for example, that Mr Gilbert Hunt had not confined his active interest in university affairs to the problems of building and of student social life. He had been so kind as to employ the services of the Legal Adviser of the Rootes Organization, Mr N. P. Catchpole, of an industrial 'security officer' and of a shorthand writer, to report on the political activities of a distinguished visiting American professor (perhaps with a view to criminal or deportation proceedings?) and to send on the reports to the Vice-Chancellor 'for your confidential files'. He had also been sending information to the Vice-Chancellor, at his private address, upon the political activities of at least one other lecturer.[1]

Mr Hunt himself was busy in the next week or two since he was doing some unveiling on his own account – of the new Hillman Avenger. It is – wrote the ecstatic motoring correspondent of the *Sunday Express*, Robert Glenton – 'a car for all ages, suitable to be parked outside a discotheque or the town hall'. More than £400,000 was spent by Rootes on promotion and publicity: a jamboree for sales executives and correspondents in Malta, Avenger girls in black leather gear. The Avenger Grand Luxe could come with options – a Luxury, Pathfinder or Personality pack, or an exclusively styled cigar lighter for the top executive. The hard-spined, streamlined form of business efficiency – greater productivity, cost-analysis, the drive for exports – turned over for a moment in the choppy seas of competitive commerce, and revealed its soft white underbelly – swinging 'classless' hedonism, conspicuous sexual display, and an open celebration of money and of success which would have shocked the nonconformist mill-owners and the ascetic Quaker bankers of the first Industrial Revolution. (For this also – one must insist – this glamour of cash and success, this growing style of highly fee'd lecture tours to the United States, of assent to the glamour of Mediterranean conferences, television fees and industrial consultancies – is one way in which close relations with 'industry' can find expression within a university's walls.) Meanwhile, Chrysler International, the new parent of Rootes, was watching the operation quizzically, anxious about throwing good money after bad. 'Rootes must become really profitable as quickly as possible,' said Mr Hunt. 'One thing is sure,' said Mr Glenton in the *Sunday Express*: 'Rootes have gambled millions, their shirts, socks, grandmother's boa and all their prospects, on its doing so.'

The students had only gambled their academic careers. Even their grand-mothers' ostrich plumes were unlikely to stand up against the Avenger Mark II which (it was more than probable) the Finance and General Purposes Committee of the University's Council would unveil in the wake of the injunction. They appealed to public opinion.

Public opinion came up: but only just. The breakthrough came in two areas. First, in areas where the journalist's profession is still respected, the sweeping character of the injunctions provoked the suspicion that someone had something to hide: the *Guardian* and the *Sunday Times* broke surface with important stories. The editor of *New Society* faced a confrontation at law with the University by publishing the article on 'Warwick: The Business University'. And the editor of the *Birmingham Post* simply put down his head and walked through the legal ambiguities of the injunction day after day.

The second area was that of the socialist press. The *Morning Star* was the first national paper to publish the Montgomery documents, and support came quickly from *Tribune*, the *Socialist Worker*, and the socialist and student underground. Here the lightning and very efficient counter-espionage movement of some of the students, in editing and duplicating a selection of documents and in circulating them – not only at Warwick, but in a number of other universities – was the critical factor. Within two weeks a wave of sympathy movement broke out at a dozen other universities.

The preparation of this book for the press is also a lightning operation. It has been put together swiftly by a group of Warwick students and staff, many of whom have been and continue to be deeply involved in the events described. As we write the outcome of these events is still unclear. We would have liked to have pursued our researches further in this and in that direction. We are well aware that we should have done some of this research long before.

In one sense this analysis concerns a specific situation, and one peculiar to Warwick. For example, the files that revealed the objectionable material were not the general student record files of the Registry but the files held in the Vice-Chancellor's area, to which only a few confidential secretaries had access. The Vice-Chancellor's style of operation, the Tyzack Report, the apparent attempt to limit democratic processes and to ensure the loyalty of administrators and staff, the peculiarly subordinate relationship with 'industry' – and the degree of power exerted by a few industrialists on the University's Council – all these may indicate a situation in Warwick which is, in some ways, unique. And, in this sense, it would be wrong not to see Jack Butterworth, and the house that he built, as a self-contained episode. We try to present this episode as cogently as we can, without going into a hundred and one details of in-fighting and of petty academic conspiracy.

In another sense this analysis points towards a general situation, to the operative modes of power and of money in Britain in 1970, and to the relationship of our institutions of higher education to industrial capitalism. The poetic logic by which Mr Gilbert Hunt, Managing Director of Rootes, was simultaneously Chairman of the Building Committee (whose policies provoked the occupation) and author of political surveillance of academic staff, is too neat. He is only one of a group of industrialists whose influence upon the University's life have been felt in pervasive, if less sensational, ways. Nor can the malaise of Warwick be diagnosed in the single personality of its Vice-Chancellor. His policies of ever closer relationships with 'industry' have been staunchly supported at different times by government, by the University Grants Committee, and by Science and Social Science Research Councils, as well as by the industrialists on his Council. And a good part of these policies has been readily assented to by leading members of his academic staff, whose departments have derived from them substantial benefits.

In this sense the case of Warwick no longer appears as unique. How far it is a paradigm or prototype of other places, how far it points towards tendencies only beginning to reveal themselves elsewhere – this is for our readers to decide and, by their own researches, to find out.

It is sobering to realize that the Mid-Atlantic of the Midlands Motor and Aircraft Industry offers one possible model of a British future. It is a febrile, wasteful, publicity-conscious world, whose prosperity floats upon hire-purchase and the shifting moods of the status-conscious consumer; a brash, amoral, pushful world of expense-account living, lavish salesmanship, cock-tail bars in restored sixteenth-century inglenooks, and of refined managerial techniques and measured day-work; a world of mergers and take-overs, of the unregenerate, uninhibited Mammon of the Sunday business supplements; a world in which more than £3$\frac{1}{2}$ million of excess profits can be pocketed from the taxpayer (in part by double-charging on the same contracts), so that even some of the workers on the shop-floor admire the management for getting away with it for so long.

Presiding over this world are some of the new lords of this country. Just as the great landed aristocracy of the eighteenth century exerted their power by manifold exercise of interest, influence and purchase, so the new lords seem to infiltrate the command-posts of our society, including our educational institutions, not through any transparent democratic process, but quietly, in unnoticed ways. They apparently share with their precursors the same assumption that this is *their* world, to dispose of by ownership and by right of purchase. These are the people who know other people; who govern by telephone; who are unaccountable because it is always their inferiors who make up the accounts; who put things in each others' laps.

It was this world which the students of Warwick found themselves suddenly confronting on the night of 11 February; in the next week, as we struggled to break through to public opinion, we were nose-to-nose not only with Rootes but with directors of Courtaulds, Hawker Siddeley and Barclays Bank. In the conflict it became apparent that what was wrong was not a close relationship with 'industry' but a particular kind of subordinate relationship with industrial capitalism – with an industrial capitalism, more-over, which exerts its influence not only directly in the councils of the University but also within the educational organs of the State, and which, from both directions, is demanding, for its better service, an approved educational product.

But, at the same time, it became apparent that this seemingly neutral word, 'industry', was itself the great illusion. To dispense with industry would be to dispense with the very means of life. Industry is more than managing directors, and industrial consultancies for professorial staff. It is also workers and technicians and the organizations of the labour move-ment. The workers at the Rootes factories in Coventry no more welcomed the attentions of Mr Gilbert Hunt and Mr Catchpole than did the students and staff of the University. It became clear that the conflict which had opened on 11 February could not end with the replacement of this or that officer of the University: its logic demanded the radical restructuring, not only of the University's internal government, but also of the relationship between the University and the people of the West Midlands.

The foundation

When examining the early moves towards establishing the University of Warwick, one is soon struck by the vision and enthusiasm of Coventry City Council. After the Second World War their city was going to be rebuilt, and they wanted to have as much pride in what they created as they had had in the beautiful medieval town that had been destroyed. In most people's minds the Cathedral was the symbol of Coventry's regeneration, but the Council wanted more than a symbol. They wanted the city centre to be the heart of a thriving community, and grouped around the Cathedral there would be a theatre, art gallery, library, technical college and swimming pool. All these buildings would be new, and the Council felt they should be well designed and purpose built. Naturally the feeling was that 'to be complete, the city should have a University'.

So the City saw the University as an essential element in the town. Links would be built both ways. The University could contribute greatly to Coventry's cultural spectrum, with people meeting through shared facilities, and provide a more universal outlook to local problems. Coventry would provide the environment and physical necessities, and would confront academics with some of the more basic facts of life. There was a strong feeling in the early days that the University should be a technical institution. This is, of course, understandable in view of Coventry's strong industrial tradition, but it would have been surprising if the labour movement, which was the prime mover of the idea, had seen the University as an institution dominated by managerial style.

In 1954 the first practical steps were taken towards setting up a University in Coventry. At the instigation of the Lord Mayor an *ad hoc* committee, called the Council for the Establishment of a University in Coventry, was formed. Chaired by Mr W. H. Stokes, who had been for many years a permanent official of the Amalgamated Engineering Union, it differed from the later, more successful groups in that, although the trade unions did not then (or later) take much active interest in the proposed University, they *were* represented. Later on they were completely ignored.

The Council focused its attention on the notion of a Technical University which would serve the industry of the area. Various MPs were approached; Richard Crossman, in particular, gave his support and, in a letter to Stokes in April 1954, suggested that the University should be modelled on the

Massachusetts Institute of Technology. There was considerable opposition in the city from those who believed that expansion of the Technical College would serve just as well, and the two city newspapers took up opposing positions. Others, such as Walter Chinn, the City Education Officer, would not support a University which was an entirely technical institution.

The campaign met with no success. After two years the Council presented its report, reluctantly concluding that 'the establishment of a University of Coventry is not a possibility of the immediate future'. They suggested: 'That this council should remain in being for a further period . . . having strong ties with industry, trade unions and bodies representing the general life of the City', but in fact they did not meet again, though various individuals – such as Dr Henry Rees, a lecturer at the Technical College – continued to work for a local university.

On 28 February 1958 the Chancellor of the Exchequer announced to the House of Commons that the government had decided to spend £60 million over the next four years for new university building, involving both expansion of existing universities and the establishment of new universities. This brought new hope to those who wanted a University in Coventry. Dr Henry Rees persuaded the City Architect and a colleage to prepare a plan and a model for a university building, and in December the City Council decided to press for a University in Coventry. It was at this meeting that the two-hundred-acre site now occupied by the University – valuable agricultural and building land worth more than £250,000 at that time, and a great deal more at current values – was earmarked and the proceeds of a penny rate promised.

The Town Clerk, Charles Barratt, and the Education Officer, Walter Chinn, went to see the Chairman of the University Grants Committee for informal talks. They were told that the UGC would be interested, if more public support for the project could be gathered. Specifically they would require that more than one local authority should become involved, and that a considerable amount of money should be promised by local industry.

The next step was to contact Warwickshire County Council. The two education committees met informally and the County gave the idea a rather frosty reception. There was already one University (Birmingham) in Warwickshire, they said, and they could not see what the County had to gain if the University was in Coventry.

The Lord Mayor then issued a formal invitation to Warwickshire County Council to meet the City Council and others interested, with a view to setting up a Promotion Committee. Early in 1960 they met in the Lord Mayor's parlour, in two groups, because of difficulty in arranging a convenient time at short notice. At the first meeting the Warwickshire Education Officer was putting the same discouraging point of view until Sir Robert Aitken, the Vice-Chancellor of Birmingham University, stepped in. He said how very much he welcomed the idea of a new University in Warwickshire and that Birmingham University would give every support. The Bishop of Coventry finally won over the County when he said, 'Let's call it the University of Warwick.' The City at once made this concession over the name and the County promised to meet the City's endowment and provide an equal area of land adjoining that pledged by the City.

Following these meetings the Lord Mayor invited a small group of fourteen friends who had been campaigning for the University to form the nucleus of a Promotion Committee. On 17 March 1960 a letter was sent out in the name of this group to a number of prominent people in Coventry and Warwickshire, inviting them to join the Promotion Committee. The letter was sent to representatives of all sections of the community, except the trade unions. As a result the Executive Committee of the Promotion Committee, which made the application to the UGC, contained no trade unionists, while a third were industrialists. This was significant later, since six of these industrialists were co-opted on to the Council of the University when it was formed in 1965, and they remain there still. Various trade unionists were approached privately by Dr Rees and gave their support, but they seem to have made no attempt to become involved in the Promotion Committee. The trade unions are represented on the governing body of the Lanchester Polytechnic in Coventry, and they appear to have been more concerned with safeguarding the position of the Lanchester with regard to the University than with the University itself.

The Chairman and Deputy Chairman of the Promotion Committee were Lord Rootes and Sir Arnold Hall. Lord Rootes, a local boy made good, seemed the obvious choice to everyone. He was a man very much associated with Coventry, especially because of his work in the War Emergency Committee. The UGC had made it clear that money for the University would be required from other sources, and Lord Rootes was in a position not only to give money himself but also to raise it through his many contacts in industry and his close connexions with the government. Sir Arnold Hall, the Managing Director of Bristol Siddeley, had been involved from fairly early on through his ties with the Lanchester; he has been the Chairman of the University Council since its inception.

The Promotion Committee prepared and submitted an application to the UGC. A year later, in May 1961, Selwyn Lloyd announced in a written reply in the House of Commons:

> The UGC have advised me that, within the scope of the building programme which I have already announced, four new universities, in addition to those which are already being established at Brighton, Norwich and York, should be established as the best means of providing places for some of the increasing number of students who will be coming forward in the coming years. The Committee have

advised that three of the four should be at Canterbury, Colchester and Coventry.

The UGC set up an Academic Planning Board for the University; chaired by E. T. Williams, an Oxford don, and currently Warden of Rhodes House, Oxford, it consisted of academics from various universities, except for Sir Arnold Hall, who moved over from the Promotion Committee, and two other businessmen involved in university administration. Until 1965, when the University Charter came into effect, this board controlled the academic affairs and the Promotion Committee the financial business of the University.

Part of the terms of reference of the Academic Planning Board was to appoint the Vice-Chancellor, in consultation with the Promotion Committee and the UGC. On 25 October 1962, over a year after the board first met, Lord Rootes reported to the Promotion Committee that the Board were 'in a position to make progress with the nomination of the first Vice-Chancellor', and they wished to consult the committee on their proposal. The Board's nominee, J. B. Butterworth, Bursar of New College, was presented to the committee at a luncheon four days later. His reputation at Oxford was, perhaps, less that of a distinguished academic, than that of a successful academic entrepreneur, with good connexions in the Stock Exchange and the world of business, who had successfully increased his college's revenue by re-investing some of its capital holdings. The usual procedures went through smoothly and Butterworth's appointment was announced to the Press a fortnight later. After this long delay, some of the local people on the Promotion Committee felt rather resentful that the committee had been given only one choice.

The Vice-Chancellor's appointment was announced at the same time as plans for a full Graduate School of Business Management, 'the first in Britain', and he was pleased to give it his blessing. For a lawyer, teacher and administrator, Butterworth proved to be remarkably attentive to British industry's view of higher education. Addressing the Old Coventrians' Club a year after his appointment, he suggested 'some kind of joint council' where the University would receive 'the criticism, help and advice of industry and commerce' (*Coventry Evening Telegraph*, 9 December 1963). The Vice-Chancellor reiterated his hopes for 'particularly close association' with business in the following month, when Lord Rootes was made Chancellor, and Sir Arnold Hall Pro-Chancellor. It was now clear that 'some kind of joint council' was to be built into the University itself, and that industry was to be represented by large corporate capital. On 21 January 1964 the *Coventry Evening Telegraph* titled its story 'Industrialists to Head University of Warwick'.

The collaboration of men like Rootes and Hall had already brought more tangible benefits than the mere wisdom of the boardroom. Launching the

University appeal for £4 million from the Institute of Directors building in Belgrave Square, Rootes announced that he already had £1,150,000 through personal contacts: 'What is more I have a few more friends left' (*Coventry Evening Telegraph*, 9 April 1964). The UGC had insisted on strong local support for a University in Coventry, but the enthusiasm at the Institute presumably justified launching the appeal there rather than in Warwickshire. Six months later some of that enthusiasm led the Institute of Directors to establish a professorship of Business Administration, with the understanding that they would be represented on the appointment board.

Meanwhile other interests had responded to the University's self-declared role of partner with industry. Unilever's grant (given to all the new universities) in 1961 was followed by Courtauld's £75,000. The Registrar acknowledged it with the hope that the research to be done 'would be of particular interest to the firm' (*Coventry Evening Telegraph*, 17 February 1964). Pressed Steel Fisher earmarked their gift for a Chair of Industrial Relations. A grant of £40,000 from the Volkswagen Foundation, ICI Fellowships and Dunlop Scholarships followed. Butterworth suggested in his first Annual Report that 'No one would wish a University founded in Warwickshire to develop into something like a liberal arts college'. If such a danger had ever existed, surely it was long past?

In that report of 1965 the Vice-Chancellor also referred to the 'local ethos' which favoured a school strong in science and engineering. Part of that ethos centred on the Lanchester, a highly respected college of technology in Coventry, which some City Councillors had believed would become a university in its own right. In the early stages of planning the University, the Lanchester's governors had expressed their interest in a fusion of the two schools, and finally in 1964 the University Promotion Committee replied favourably. The City Education Committee entered negotiations, the substance of which it did not discuss in public. In private, the University set terms: complete absorption of the College, and acceptance of only those Lanchester staff and students that it wished to take. The opinion of the College governors was that there should be no vetting of staff or students, and democratic representation on governing bodies of the University. A sub-committee met with Butterworth and two other representatives, and by March 1965 a fairly detailed plan of union was announced. It was approved by the City, although fears were expressed that the UGC and the Minister might have doubts.

In August the fears were realized: the Department of Education and Science rejected the plans as being likely to prejudice lower-level studies, and tie up too much of the limited money available for universities. But the Minister's letter came before the City delegation had put their case to him: there was 'surprise and anger' in Coventry. Nothing came of an appeal to the Department by the City, as the Chairman of the Education Committee,

Councillor Locksley, predicted. Time had been of the essence, he explained, and although the City's representation had been before the UGC by April, they had discovered in June that the Vice-Chancellor of the University had not yet presented the University's submission: 'So we lost two valuable months. I was aggrieved about this because I felt that apart from the urgency we should have been doing this together' (*Coventry Evening Telegraph*, 23 September 1965). Other councillors were unwilling to blame the University, but without doubt many citizens of Coventry had questions in their minds. After many attempts and disappointments, they had brought a University to Coventry. And now they wondered what influence they were going to have in its development.

Development was going on at a great pace. Or was it? Many months of tact and enthusiasm had gone into cultivating the British corporate élite, but buildings and governing structure were dealt with in a rather more hurried fashion. Because of the year's delay in appointing a Vice-Chancellor, and further delays in establishing a University planning office, as late as the winter of 1963 there were virtually no plans in progress. Even the location of the site was not finally decided. Yet eight professors had been promised accommodation within nine months, and the first students were due to arrive a year after that; consultation, planning and construction of permanent university buildings usually takes five years or so. The solution was a small, completely self-contained block of buildings to serve as interim accommodation for the University while plans could be drawn up for the main site. At this time the best guess was that the publication of the Robbins Report would result in massive, immediate expansion, and the main site was planned with this in mind. Only at the end of 1963 was it decided that the 1966 bulge of students would be absorbed largely by the older universities. Credit squeezes and cuts in grants played havoc with the plans. Warwick is left with a sprawling, fragmented campus, a fitting expression of the lack of early planning.

A consistent feature in this planning was the insistence of the Vice-Chancellor that all plans should be geared to his megalithic notions of a University of twenty thousand or even twenty-five thousand students. Hence, even in its initial stages, plans had to be in line with setting down a megalithic infrastructure. The large area was set out with a divider and a ruler: Administration nearly one mile from the library and teaching buildings, student residences and social building segregated again, like the service stations on a detour from the motorway. Short-term, interim amenities were discouraged in the name of the plan, and the first generations of students were to be sacrificed in the cause of expansion and high rate of growth. But no documentary evidence has ever been adduced to show that this growth-rate and this twenty-thousand target had ever been given government or UGC approval, or that they ever existed as anything more than an ambition of the Vice-Chancellor and of his close Council advisers.

Much as the development plan should have determined the physical structure of the University, the statutes were intended to define the powers and responsibilities of all its members. Their adoption was also a rushed affair, but with less excuse. The first knowledge Warwick academic staff in general had of the statutes was from the draft posted to them three days before they were asked to give their approval. They did so, perhaps without sufficiently reflecting on the possible implications of section 5 (5), giving the Vice-Chancellor power to exclude any student without explanation or right of appeal, or the dangers in a co-opting clause (15 (1) (D)), which could enable a powerful and united group of men, once appointed, to perpetuate their power indefinitely and hence mould the University (see p. 28). But two days is a short time to consider a constitution, and in any case the way in which the statutes were used was to prove almost more important than their content.

Equally important was the membership of the Council that took power in March 1965. The Promotion Committee and Academic Planning Board disappeared, but many of their most important figures did not. The new Lord Rootes, Sir Arnold Hall, Gilbert Hunt, Lord Iliffe, Sir Stanley Harley, Sir William Lyons and R. J. Kerr-Muir all became members of Council. It is important to note not only who *did* transfer from the Promotion Committee to the Council, but who did *not*. Some of the original Committee were politely given places on the University's Court – an almost powerless body which meets only once a year. The only layman who was not an industrialist who moved on to Council was the Bishop of Coventry: among those who were not co-opted to Council were Sister A. G. Grace, Dr G. S. Atkinson (Principal of Rugby Technical College), Miss J. D. Browne (Principal of the City of Coventry College of Education), the Congregationalist Minister the Rev. D. H. Dale, the Catholic Canon R. Walsh, Dr H. Rees (one of the most active of the original promoters), Mr H. Walker (the Headmaster of King Henry the Eighth School), and a number of civic officials, aldermen and others. These people may all have been too busy and too much committed to other duties to serve on Council, nor were they necessarily the best people to represent the local community on that body; but the self-perpetuating character of an oligarchy of industrialists was at this stage brought several steps closer. There were also six *ex officio* members of local authorities and six (now eight) members of Senate. But the evolution of the University was to be most affected by the ethos of the very powerful men from industry; men who were prepared to work closely with a Vice-Chancellor who was willing to work closely with them. And the ultimate effect came to be the creation, not of a democratic academic community, but a 'well-managed operation', assisting the business corporation and emulating some of its more dubious methods.

Nor did the University show much interest in working with the City which had done so much to bring it into being. Relations were, in fact, often strained. Hostility was first aroused in the city over an alleged deal done over the heads of the City Council which threatened to destroy the beauty of the main road past the University (see p. 143).

Later on the University snubbed the City Council over proposals to share sports and library facilities. The City were thinking of building a large sports stadium and centre near the University to serve all the educational institutions in the city as well as other independent athletic groups. The University, in the person of Pro-Vice-Chancellor Harrison, told the Council that it had not got any money for such projects. On being offered a share in return for the land to build the centre on (land originally a gift from the City), the University said that, only if an equivalent proportion of new land was given, could they release land for such a project. Meanwhile the University was planning a sports centre of its own. At the present time the University is planning to spend a large sum on a swimming pool, whilst Coventry has one of the finest in the country.

As we have seen, Coventry City Council was crucial in preparing and bringing the case for a University in Coventry to the UGC in 1959. Their initiative was in keeping with the whole concept of city planning and organization which the Labour Party had used during its thirty years' control of the council. It is ironic that their ideal of community involvement and democratic government should have been ignored in what was, during this period, their favoured child.

It is appropriate to end with the words of Alderman G. E. Hodgkinson, Lord Mayor of Coventry in 1944–5, one of the chief architects of the rebuilding and replanning of Coventry when the City emerged from the ruins of the war, and a member of the University Court:

> The members of a Labour-controlled City Council who applied their enthusiasms for the 'University Idea' gave it practical and moral support in the formation days. Amongst other things, it wanted a University of original design in accordance with native thrustfulness, a physical academic link between the Lanchester Polytechnic, a close association between 'town and gown', open-door facilities in library services and playing fields, and coordinated shopping and banking arrangements on the campus to avoid unnecessary conflict in planning effective liaison in these matters. The town and gown concept appears to have been overlaid, swamped or forgotten by the dominating business interests. Those who pay the piper least are playing most of the tune. Industry, banking and commerce are at the 'commanding heights' of the University, doing their utmost to keep town and gown apart. Student, academic, democratic and community interests are relegated to the level of second-class citizenship.
>
> (unpublished letter to the Guardian, part published in the Morning Star, 2 March 1970)

The power of the Council

It has been shown that the Vice-Chancellor, soon after his appointment, proposed 'some kind of joint council' between industry and the University (p. 23). In the event such a joint council proved to be unnecessary, since it was provided by the direct representation of industrialists on the University's governing Council itself. The presence of a majority of lay members upon a university's Council is not, of course, unusual. What is unusual is the mode of their appointment, under section 15 (1) (D) of the statutes of the University of Warwick:

> Such other persons, not being members of the academic staff or salaried officers of the University, and not exceeding ten in all, as may be co-opted by the Council.

In older provincial universities at least a proportion of the lay members of Council are appointed by the University's Court – a very large, inactive body, representative of a wide spread of civic interests and organizations. For example the University of Birmingham, which is not notorious for its advanced democratic constitution, has no co-opted members on its Council: its lay membership is made up of the Lord Mayor of Birmingham, five persons appointed by the City Council, and sixteen members appointed by the Court.

But at Warwick the majority of lay members, if they acted together, could be virtually self-perpetuating. The two most powerful officers – the Pro-Chancellor (Sir Arnold Hall) and the Treasurer (R. J. Kerr-Muir) – remain on Council so long as they continue to hold office. The 'co-opted' members serve for a three-year term (section 15 (2) (F)), but may then, if they wish, be 'co-opted' for further terms. Where new members are co-opted (as Messrs Mead, Tuke and Young have been), it is generally understood that their names 'emerge' after consultation between the Vice-Chancellor and the Pro-Chancellor. Since the term of service of local authority nominees may be limited to three years (all the Labour members were dropped after the Conservatives won control of Coventry City Council), the 'co-opted' members are likely to be entrenched in the Council's most powerful committees; and indeed we find two recently 'co-opted' members – Tuke and Mead – together with Kerr-Muir and Butterworth, controlling the crucial seven-man Finance and General Purposes Committee. While all co-opted members are not regular attenders at Council, they have been present in force at crucial meetings where contested issues have arisen and even a few of them, acting together with the Vice-Chancellor and officers and one or two academics, can be expected to dominate decisions.[2]

'Industry' has therefore been able to influence the University, at the level of its planning, financing and development, at a relatively low cost in terms of promotion and donations. Some of the aims of a 'private university' have been achieved within the shell of public money and public legitimation. It is true that the University's Foundation Fund Appeal met with a generous response, exceeding £2½ million, in the main in substantial covenants from industry. It is possible, however, to exaggerate the extent of open-handed charity which was involved on the part of some of the benefactors. The Foundation Fund Appeal brochure noted that:

> In terms of the Income Tax Act 1952, gifts of money for research related to, or for technical education of a kind specially requisite for persons employed in, the business of the donor (or for research related to the class of trade to which the business of the donor belongs) may be treated as an expense of the business for Income Tax and Profits Tax purposes. . . . Further details may be obtained from the Vice-Chancellor.

(This meant that, with tax at 7s 9d in the £, a gift of £100,000 could be met, under a ten-year covenant, at £6,125 p.a.; a gift of £5,000 at £306 p.a.)

It is not therefore surprising that when Ralph Harris, Director of the Institute of Economic Affairs Ltd, wrote to Jack Butterworth (4 December 1968) soliciting his support for the movement headed by Professor Max Beloff, Sir Sydney Caine, Professor H. S. Ferns and others for an 'independent university', he should express his support:

> I have always been attracted by the idea of an independent university and believe that if properly organized it might acquire the considerable funds needed from industry and private support. As a Vice-Chancellor of a state university, I think it might be better if I were not to sign your document. On the other hand, I wanted to let you know of my interest in your proposal.

'Academic excellence', the letter continued, may best be preserved 'in an institution which is totally independent.'

We will examine later how far business interests may have actually influenced academic excellence or general policy at Warwick. The point to note here is that this kind of 'independence' is a mirage. The independence desired is from the State (and its democratic or bureaucratic controls) on the one hand, from the pressures of staff and of students on the other. This independence would only be the other side of the coin of a subordinate dependence upon 'industry'.

The world of industry

On the Council of the University of Warwick we find the following:

Pro-Chancellor	Sir Arnold Hall Chairman and Managing Director, Hawker Siddeley Group Ltd Director, Phoenix Assurance Co. Ltd Director, Lloyds Bank Ltd[3]
Treasurer	R. J. Kerr-Muir Director, Courtaulds Ltd
Council Members	Gilbert Hunt Managing Director, Rootes Motors Ltd Director, Reed Paper Group
	A. F. Tuke Director, Barclays Bank Ltd Vice-Chairman, Barclays D.C.O.
	Sir Richard Young Chairman, Alfred Herbert Ltd Director, Rugby Portland Cement Ltd
	Lord Rootes Chairman, Rootes Motors Ltd
	Sir William Lyons Chairman, Jaguar Cars Ltd Deputy Chairman, British Leyland Motor Holdings Ltd
	Lord Iliffe Chairman, Coventry Newspapers Ltd Vice-Chairman, Birmingham Post and Mail Ltd
	Sir Stanley Harley Chairman, Coventry Gauge and Tool Ltd Director of fifteen other companies President, Coventry Conservative Association
	J. R. Mead Accountant: director of forty-two small companies
	The Right Reverend the Bishop of Coventry

It is this concentration of business interests at the top of the power structure at Warwick which is unusual, rather than the involvement of industry in financing scientific and economic research. A closer look at some of the key figures involved on Council sheds considerable light on the world of industry and the nature of Warwick's involvement in it.

Sir Arnold Hall

Sir Arnold Hall is an engineer of exceptional brilliance. Born in 1915, he obtained a First with distinction in engineering at Cambridge. After doing research there and at the Royal Aircraft Establishment, Farnborough, including work with Sir Frank Whittle on the first jet engine, he became a Professor at Imperial College at the age of thirty. Six years later he was made head of the Royal Aircraft Establishment, where he headed the investigation into the Comet crashes. At thirty-nine he was knighted; the following year, 1955, he joined the Hawker Siddeley Group as a director. His career there culminated in his appointment as Managing Director in 1963, to which the chairmanship was added in 1967. He has sat on innumerable governmental and semi-governmental committees on the aerospace industry, is a member of the Athenaeum, and a Fellow of the Royal Society.

But over this distinguished career, in which Sir Arnold has moved easily between government, industry and academic life, there hangs one question mark. His entry in *Who's Who*, while describing in great detail the rest of his career, omits the fact that from 1958 to 1963 he was Vice-Chairman and Managing Director of Bristol Siddeley Engines Ltd.

On 22 March 1967 the Minister of Technology announced in the House of Commons that Bristol Siddeley 'had repaid to the Ministry a sum of £3,960,000, and that the effect of the repayment had been to reduce the profits made by the firm on sales at fixed prices totalling approximately £16^1/$_2$ million' (*Second Special Report of the Committee of Public Accounts* (hereafter CPA/2), HC 571 1966–7, para. 1). An inquiry (the Wilson Committee) was set up to investigate the whole matter, and in addition the Committee of Public Accounts made an independent investigation of the narrower question of the negotiation of the original contracts, which involved engine overhauls carried out by Bristol Siddeley for the government.

Following these two inquiries a third was set up, by the Committee of Public Accounts, to look into certain apparent discrepancies between the evidence given by the company's representatives to the CPA and the findings of the broader inquiry by the Wilson Committee.

To quote this third inquiry:

> The evidence paints a picture of negligence and irresponsibility in the conduct of the Company's financial administration which your committee found hard to credit in a Company of this standing, even after making the utmost allowances for the many and great difficulties the Company was facing at a critical juncture in its affairs. This applies particularly to the important role played by Mr Davidson, as the Director responsible for the Company's contracts with the Ministry, and to the manner in which the Executive

Committee exercised its collective responsibility for financial administration.

(Third Special Report of the Committee for Public Accounts
(hereafter CPA/3), HC 192 1967–8, para. 21)

That the profits realized on these contracts were exorbitant was agreed by all concerned. Typical figures for selected engines in 1959–60 and 1960–61 were:

	% profit on cost	
	1959–60	*1960–61*
Olympus	51.8	80.3
Viper	44.8	135.2
Sapphire 7	50.7	124.9

(*Wilson Committee Report*, HC 129 1967–8, paras. 80–81.)

The Wilson Committee found that these rates of profit 'were being achieved as a result of false and misleading representations on the part of the Company's estimating and negotiating committee' (para. 83).

The crucial point at issue throughout the two CPA inquiries was whether this state of affairs was known to the Board of Directors. Mr Davidson and Sir Reginald Verdon-Smith (Chairman of BSE at the time) insisted that the Board was not aware of this. Yet it emerges from the Wilson Committee's report that the Executive Committee of the company was well aware of the facts, having considered two reports on the engine overhauls contract, one in June and September 1960, and the other in September 1961.

The Chairman of the Executive Committee at the time was the Managing Director of Bristol Siddeley, Sir Arnold Hall. An Executive Committee minute of June 1960 read:

> Engine Repair Financial Report: Sir Arnold Hall has written to Mr Davidson on a number of minor points which were currently being looked into. It was noted that Orenda profitability was low and that this stemmed from the close surveillance on this contract exercised by the customer from London [in fact a Canadian Government contract]. It was noted also that Viper overhauls were less profitable than might have been expected. . . .
>
> (quoted in CPA/3, para. 184)

At that time Viper overhauls were running at a profit rate of 44.8 per cent.

Despite the fact that the crucial point at issue was whether the Board had knowledge of what was going on at the time, Sir Arnold Hall was never called to submit evidence to either of the inquiries conducted by the Committee of Public Accounts. When Verdon-Smith suggested

... it may be your wish, if you want to explore this point in depth, that you should, perhaps, ask the Managing Director of Bristol Siddeley at that time to answer this question,

(CPA/2, para. 428)

he was rebuked by the Committee's chairman.

As the Wilson Committee report put it:

The facts to which we have referred leave no room for doubt that the Executive Directors of BSE planned in their budgets, from the earliest years of the Company's existence, to obtain huge profits from the Department's overhauls; that they were soon made aware that the achievements were even better than those which they had sought; and that they approved of the trend of events.

(para. 82)

One further point on Sir Arnold Hall. Three documents were found among the Vice-Chancellor's files which were put out by the Economic League. Two were sent to the Vice-Chancellor by Hall. The League is an employers' organization with two main aims: first, to foster the 'free enterprise spirit' by propaganda, verbal and written (twenty-two million leaflets in 1968); secondly, to oppose 'all subversive forces – in whatever their origin and inspiration – that seek to undermine the security of Britain in general and British industry in particular'. In 1968 the League spent £266,000 on such activities. One hundred and fifty-four firms, including British Leyland, Guest Keen & Nettlefold, Tate & Lyle and Barclays Bank, gave donations totalling £61,000.

Two of the documents sent to Butterworth were issues of the League's *Two-Minute News Review* on the activities of the Radical Student Alliance and the Revolutionary Socialist Student Federation. The other, headed 'Confidential', was part of a survey by 'a team of expert investigators' conducted on behalf of the League on 'the growth of extreme left-wing activity among students'. It consists in the main of case-studies: the general impression is that rank-and-file revolutionary students tend to come from broken homes, have personality problems, are dirty and unkempt, take drugs, suffer from acne, are easily 'led', etc. The investigators do, however, allow that some become revolutionaries because of 'a genuine belief that the university "system" is archaic, inflexible, repressive and out of date', and many of their conclusions are considered in tone.

As for Sir Arnold Hall's company, Hawker Siddeley, it was in 1969 the eighteenth largest in the country in terms of assets (£250 million) and fifth largest in terms of employment (98,000). It is heavily involved in defence work.

Gilbert Hunt and Rootes

The Rootes family has, of course, been associated with the University from its very beginning. Gilbert Hunt, who became Managing Director of Rootes in 1967, first got to know Lord Rootes through involvement in the University Foundation Committee's activities. He is of interest here largely as an example of the style of the modern manager, and managerialism is a major product of Warwick's involvement with industry (see sections from the Tyzack Report, pp. 136–43).

Gilbert Hunt was born in 1915. Educated at Malvern College, he then joined the Hawker Siddeley Group, working his way up until he became Director and General Manager of their subsidiary, High Duty Alloys. In 1960 he was appointed Managing Director of Massey-Ferguson (UK) Ltd; finally in 1967 he became Managing Director of Rootes, soon after Chrysler acquired a major interest in the company. At the time Rootes was having its worst year ever: it reported a loss of nearly £11 million. The appointment of Gilbert Hunt to replace the second Lord Rootes, along with massive injections of funds from Chrysler and the British government, was intended to bring about the necessary spectacular recovery. In 1968 Rootes made £1.4 million profits, but in 1969 they were back in the red again. It is clear that unless the Avenger is a huge success, the company will be once more on the brink of disaster.

But what of Gilbert Hunt? Newspaper cuttings throw some interesting light on the sort of man he is:

> A soft-spoken, grey-haired fifty-two-year-old, Hunt is a firm disciple of North American business methods. . . . Apart from the Rolls-Royce Phantom V, Buick and Triumph 2000 he keeps in his stable, Hunt knows little about cars. But when it comes to questions of productivity and business methods, he is in his element.
>
> (*Financial Times* Diary, 22 March 1967)

> 'When you take over a job like this you have to be tough immediately. It's no good waiting five years to be tough – you'll never do it. The hatchet gets blunt. . . . People in British industry are not numerate enough. It is not sufficient to have a good idea. It must be quantified to make absolutely certain that it is viable. Everything must be worked out in mathematical terms'.
>
> (*Sunday Times* Business News, 1 October 1967)

> 'I rebuilt Rootes around an eight-man élite. . . . This is in effect the policy-making instrument of the company, and answerable only to the Board.' Hunt has also instilled a new pride and confidence in Rootes employees. 'There are no secrets between the top management – my key people. I involve them because I believe it is the

vitality, the brain power and the judgement of these key men working with me which is going to make or break the company'.

(*Daily Express*, 4 March 1968)

It is hardly surprising that such a man should be an enthusiastic supporter of greater 'efficiency' in the University, as proposed by the Tyzack
Report. Nor is it surprising that Mr Hunt once spoke heatedly, in Council,
against students who had been demonstrating outside a Rootes factory, and
asked if they could be disciplined and their local education authority be
notified. He also suggested that he might find difficulty in defending Rootes'
contribution to the University against adverse comments by his fellow directors. (It is proper to add that the Chairman of Council, Sir Arnold Hall,
firmly resisted the implications of both suggestions.)

Rootes gave £2,000 to the Industrial Trust last year. This organization
is much more secretive than the Economic League, but similar in purpose.
In an article in the *Observer* (19 October 1969) Paul Ferris described how
he had phoned several firms who had donated money to the Industrial Trust
in order to find out what the Trust did. No one would tell him. Then Lord
Chandos (of Associated Electrical Industries, and a member of Warwick's
Promotion Committee) phoned Mr Ferris and told him that its work
was 'non-political, and in the field of industrial harmony'. When Ferris
wondered whether they kept an eye on 'troublemakers', and said he was
not really clear about their activities, Lord Chandos replied, 'You're not
meant to be clear.'

A. F. Tuke and Barclays Bank

As the Vice-Chancellor's files say:

> I regard the association between Barclays Bank and the University
> of Warwick as especially close. Not only are we Bankers to the
> University and the only Bank represented on the site, but we have
> endowed a Chair, the Chairman of our Local Board serves on the
> Finance Committee, and our Chairman and the Vice-Chancellor
> are friends of long standing who, during their time, have been jointly
> involved in the problems of University finance, i.e. the University
> of Oxford. I cannot think, therefore, that any university could have
> a claim on the Bank's favourable consideration of a need stronger
> than that of the University of Warwick.

The 'Chairman of our Local Board' is Mr A. F. Tuke, member of Council
at Warwick. The Vice-Chancellor used to be Bursar of New College,
Oxford, and member of the Hebdomadal Council. And the 'Chair' with
which Barclays endowed the University? This was the Chair in Management

Information Systems in the Centre of Industrial and Business Studies. The *Coventry Evening Telegraph* of 12 October 1967 reported:

Mr W. G. Bryan, a Vice-Chairman of Barclays Bank, said:

'We are very enthusiastic about this joint venture, which we feel will be to our mutual advantage, and will also benefit banking and the business world generally. . . .

'At present, most of the research in the area of management information services is being carried out in the United States. Now similar facilities will be available in Britain, and we look forward to the opportunity of keeping in close touch with the professor appointed to the chair.' The creation of the new chair is warmly welcomed by the University's Vice-Chancellor, Mr J. B. Butterworth, who said it would strengthen still further the close association with industry and commerce. . . .

'The particular points we would like to see developed are all focused on the problem of putting a value as far as possible on the information provided, on the selection of priorities in the presentation of information to management, the methods of presentation, the economics of computerizing the information processes, and so on.

'Efficiently conducted research in this field, allied to the work on operational research, would be of importance nationally, both in encouraging the use of computers where firms are slow to recognize their value, and in discouraging uneconomic use of computers in those firms where computers are in fashion.'

It will be the sixth chair to be created at the University in the field of social studies as a result of support from industry, commerce, trusts and foundations.

The University's close relation with industry and commerce 'spring from the conviction that a new university has a unique opportunity to experiment and in the case of Warwick to make a significant contribution in the field of industrial and business studies'.

The University emphasizes that it is also aware of the fact that the abler undergraduates have often shown a reluctance to enter commerce and industry.

'It is incumbent upon universities, therefore, as the prime producers of high-level manpower over the whole range of industrial development, to develop courses and subjects which will equip its graduates for problems they will subsequently face in industry and commerce', it is stated.

Barclays' concern for benefiting 'the business world generally' is also evident from their £4,750 donation to the Economic League last year.

Mr A. F. Tuke, in addition to being a Director of Barclays Bank, is also Vice-Chairman of Barclays D.C.O. This bank is a considerable force in the finance world of southern Africa. Two other businesses with interests in southern Africa are represented on the Council. British Leyland, whose Vice-Chairman, Sir William Lyons, is on the Council at Warwick, has been rapidly expanding its manufacturing facilities in South Africa, and Hawker Siddeley have recently formed a South African subsidiary.

One prime social function of a university is to inquire freely and to criticize freely. And the more managed, the more planned, the more 'efficient' the rest of society grows, the more important this function becomes. In pursuing this task in as sensitive an area as Africa, some staff and students might prefer their university not to embrace too closely industries and businesses that have large stakes in the racialist police state of South Africa.

One of the pervasive myths of the mid-twentieth century is that with the replacement of the old-style entrepreneur and tycoon by the property-less manager, there has come about a qualitative change to 'managerial' capitalism. The new manager is seen as running the system 'in the national interest' rather than in the interests of the propertied class. Professor Carl Kaysen, a distinguished American economist, has gone so far as to describe the giant corporation as 'soulful'. The economic and political system as a whole is described as 'pluralist', that is, one in which different interest groups form around different issues, with no clear-cut social divisions.

Where does the University fit into this picture? Professor Clark Kerr, who ran the Berkeley campus of the University of California where many have located the origins of the student movement, answered this question in his book *The Uses of the University*. The University provides skilled manpower and facilities for basic research. And it produces the culture and ideology of the pluralist system.

Thus, Warwick as the Massachusetts Institute of Technology of the Midlands, and Butterworth as a latter-day Clark Kerr.

But the world of industry is emphatically *not* a world of a neutral technocracy working for the benefit of all. It is a world indifferent to the equities of government contracting, a world where excess profits can be milked from the ordinary people, a world of efficiency and quantification in the interests of profit, of connivance at racialist exploitation in southern Africa, of spying on workers and teachers.

In this alternative view, what is our picture of the economic system, and of the way the University fits into it?

In modern capitalism most important industries, and especially those predominant in the Midlands, are dominated by a handful of giant firms. Despite this, it is a competitive world; the competition is not of the static type found in outdated economics textbooks, but dynamic; for, above all, capitalism is an economic system with an inbuilt drive for growth, for accumulation. In an economy based on private property, growth means the accumulation of privately owned assets. This process requires profits, just as it always has done. And the drive for profits in a world dominated by a small number of firms is above all a drive for control.

It is only natural that this drive for control should extend to the University. There is no area in life which is not penetrated by the needs of the giant firm. The University offers skilled manpower and research facilities. It also offers them largely at the expense of the general public: Warwick has had six times as much government money as private. The extension of corporate power over the University need not yield an immediate return for the investment of time and money; the modern giant firm takes a long-term view of its activities.

Notes

1 See page 110. It must be stressed that we have at Warwick no means of establishing the extent of this political surveillance of students and of staff, since the file in which most of this came to light was in the Vice-Chancellor's area of the Registry; and, early in the occupation, other files were removed from this area. Circumstances suggest that the most obnoxious file may have been left behind by an oversight.

2 It is not suggested that all the co-opted members necessarily act together as a bloc with the Pro-Chancellor and Vice-Chancellor.

3 At least thirteen of the thirty-one directors of Lloyds Bank are governors, pro-chancellors, etc. of universities and colleges; the thirteen hold seventeen such posts.

64

TOWARDS AN INDEPENDENT UNIVERSITY

H. S. Ferns

Source: H. S. Ferns, *Towards an Independent University*, London: Institute of Economic Affairs, 1970, 27 pp.

A. The case

There are four principal reasons why an independent university should be established now.

1. Independence

The first reason is moral and social. For nearly three-quarters of a century more and more people of all classes and occupations have become more and more dependent in one way or another upon the state and have accordingly come under its control. It is now becoming increasingly obvious that this dependence and control are doing the community more harm than good, and that the moral and social energy of the people is diminishing through undue and prolonged entanglements in the web of government. The time has come to demonstrate on a large scale and in a sophisticated sphere of human endeavour and necessity that people on their own can meet a community need with no assistance from the state and entirely without state controls other than those designed to preserve the common law rights of individuals. To this end it is here proposed that an independent university be established for the provision of general higher education, the advancement of knowledge and the inculcation of habits of mental and moral discipline.

Such an act of initiative and free co-operation among individuals will energise the community as a whole and serve to kindle the enthusiasm and focus the hope of all who are unwilling to believe that the fate of Britain is to become a stagnant society observing rather than shaping the fate of mankind.

211

2. *Unsatisfied demand*

The second reason is immediate and concrete: to meet an unsatisfied demand for higher education. Assuming that all young people with two A-levels are qualified to undertake university work, the proportion of those who secured places in universities was approximately 65 per cent in 1966. This is no measure of the unsatisfied demand in many areas of study. For example, in 1967 3,667 students applied to read for a combined honours degree in arts in a university known to me. The university established a quota of 85 for entry and admitted 103. Assuming that all the 3,667 had applied to five other universities and all five admitted as many as this university, only one in six was able to enter. Nearly similar stories can be told of the social sciences and a large number of the natural sciences. The only sector in which demand is being approximately satisfied is to be found in some branches of technology.

The reasons for this volume of demand can be recapitulated briefly. More and more young people and their parents recognise that career prospects are becoming increasingly linked with the possession of degrees. There is an element of fashion and purposeless imitation in this attitude, but behind the trend is the increasingly evident need of industry, commerce, the arts, the sciences, administration and public life for men and women who have been trained to find their way into the vast complexity of accumulating knowledge and technique and to use them in the process of living. A degree is simply a sign which enables the work organisations of society to recognise quickly that a young person has undergone training and that there is a reasonable chance that, having been so educated, he or she will be able to contribute something positive to the activity of the organisation. Since the inception of universities in the 12th century, entrants have been predominantly interested in careers. The organisations employing them have taken them because in the university they acquired knowledge of religion or law or science or literature or technology. The acquisition of a humane understanding and a cultivated sensibility is, and always has been, a side-effect of university education, as it is of all disciplined mental effort. To consider humane understanding and the cultivation of sensibility as the main purpose of university education with a view to denying its vocational and practical value in civilised living is a perverse aspect of decadence, and is based on a false view of human experience and of the consequence of educative effort.

Britain has been a comparative late-comer in recognising that the function of universities is much broader than the creation of gentlemen and the supply of educated people to the traditional professions, to the higher public services and to pure scientific research. The British community is, too, a late developer in recognising in industrial and commercial activity, teaching and the public service the need for large numbers of people who are educated to use knowledge in their work and have the self-confidence and judgement which comes from knowing what they are doing. The notion 'theirs not to reason why, theirs but to do as they are told' is no longer an adequate foundation for any organisation. Hence the change in the demand both for higher education and for graduates; and the demand is bound to grow and cannot be arrested unless Britain wishes to drop out of modern life.

But can this demand for higher education be met? The universities are not meeting the demand. There exists what Mr Anthony Crosland, a former Minister of Education, has described as the public sector of higher education: the teachers' training colleges, the polytechnics, the colleges of commerce and technology and colleges of further education, all of which are equipped to provide degrees through the external examinations of the University of London or of the National Council of Academic Awards. But these agencies are insufficient. A recent report suggests that about 11 per cent of those who qualified for university but who did not get places went on to degree work outside universities. Besides being unable to meet demand, these specialised institutions are too heavily oriented towards training for one profession, such as elementary school teaching, to serve completely as institutions of higher education. Having a non-university status they imply something less than university education, and are therefore not considered as desirable as universities in career terms. Whether there is any substance in this attitude is beside the point. The attitude exists, and the attempt on the part of the public authorities to maintain a status barrier in higher education is a real impairment of its effectiveness.

Britain is not alone as a community which cannot satisfy the demand for higher education. In the United States, Canada and Japan, where universities have achieved extremely high growth rates, the demand is still unsatisfied. The State of New York is now planning a state university to take more students than there are at present in all the universities of Great Britain, and this on the top of private institutions like Columbia University with 20,000 students, Cornell with 30,000 and New York University with 41,000. In Britain, on the other hand, the growth rate, rapid as it is in comparison with growth before 1950, is very slow. This is attributable to a number of influences, but principally to two: adherence to traditional conceptions of universities as *élite* institutions for the education of a very small proportion of the population, and dependence on the state as the main source of finance.

The determination to maintain the highest standards of instruction and achievement through all parts of all the universities has meant that they must necessarily remain small with high costs of production. These high costs have been borne, up to about 95 per cent, by the state. At the same time the state has extended its expenditure in a variety of other directions.

Naturally there has been competition for scarce resources, because even in Britain there are limits to the extent to which the government can levy taxes. *The interposition of the University Grants Committee and the state between the universities and their customers has created a situation in which the universities cannot meet demand and tap directly the resources for satisfying it.* In order to get resources they have to compete with other tax-financed activities like the armed forces, the health services, the welfare programmes, the investment in public services, and so on. They have not put themselves in the position of competing for resources with the motor-car manufacturers, the breweries, the electronics industry, and so on.

There is absolutely no evidence that the British people will not spend more on higher education or that the state is obliged to finance universities because the people will not do it for themselves. Nor is there any evidence that young people from the lower income groups cannot find places in a free and independent university system. There are real psychological, moral and political limits to what the state can provide, and these limits are narrower than those that determine what people will provide for themselves in the presence of a felt need like that for food, prestige and opportunities for children. In spite of this the universities have preferred the position of pensioners of the state to that of free enterprises, with the natural result that they cannot respond directly to community demand. They are afraid to stimulate that demand and they do not know how to organise themselves to reap the rewards of so doing.

The vast majority of men and women in university life are no different from those in other walks of life in the motives that move them. They are as interested in money, prestige, promotion, opportunities and security as any other group of people. They compete for resources as much as business men, and when resources are scarce they are as fierce and as conservative as any other breed. If their considerable intelligence and energy were spent directly in satisfying the demand for higher education and in inventing ways of selling their products to an ever-widening body of consumers, they would serve society much more effectively than they do at present by fierce struggles to influence the government through the University Grants Committee to give them a larger share of the limited resources of the state. University vice-chancellors and the University Grants Committee believe they are interested in education because they fight for a place at the public feeding-trough on behalf of their own institutions. In effect their concern with higher education is directed to the preservation of the *status quo* in higher education. Consumer demand is a very secondary consideration, and this is bound to be so under the present method of financing the universities. More than one Vice-Chancellor has gone on strike over the preservation of the staff/student ratio in just the same way as shipwrights have done in the interest of the sanctity of a traditional job rendered obsolete by technological change and community need.

3. Response to the market

To the plain undeniable truth that the demand for higher education is not being met there can be added a third reason for starting an independent university: the need for different and better methods and purposes for higher education. As agencies of achieving intellectual excellence and providing the atmosphere for the discovery of knowledge on the furthest frontiers of many fields of inquiry, the British universities have compared favourably with the best of the great nations of the world. They can be given very high marks for the advancement of knowledge and the cultivation of sensibility. In the pursuit of these achievements they have taken small numbers of well-grounded young people of high ability and subjected them to rigorous courses which have come to be known as honours work. As discovery on the frontiers of knowledge has become more and more specialised, the universities have increasingly specialised their courses, and have exported specialisation to the schools, so that now young people are increasingly obliged to define their intellectual interests and to make major decisions very important in their future careers as early as 14 or 15 years of age, and often just at the moment when their minds are beginning to open out and delight in the broad variety of knowledge and experience. What was once a means of laying the foundation for brilliant achievement is now turning into its opposite and becoming an agency of intellectual narrowness and, worse, of boredom and disgust with learning.

For the very ablest young people premature specialisation is not harmful, because they tend to educate themselves broadly through their high level of awareness of the universe and of their capacity to analyse it. But for the vastly larger number of young people of good average intellectual ability, high specialisation narrows their intellect, and renders them useful to society and reconciled to themselves only if they find the slots in the adult world where their specialised techniques are of value. Much, if not all, honours degree work is designed on the assumption that every undergraduate participating is being fitted to work on the frontier of knowledge, and that, for those who do not, the experience of being so educated develops habits of mind which enable them to cope with the world and themselves. There is something in this argument, but not as much as is widely assumed. In practice a high percentage of the growing body of undergraduates go into business life, administration, the creative arts and elementary and secondary teaching not broadly and humanely educated but acquainted only with the jargon and techniques of narrow specialisms. They are masters of the higher illiteracy, able to live with themselves and serve society only because three years of intellectual effort, even in specialised fields irrelevant to their real life, is better than no intellectual cultivation at all.

The honours system in higher education is an indispensable feature but it should not be the universal pattern of higher education. Higher education which aims at breadth of knowledge and awareness and the development of skill and sensitivity useful and necessary in the average, daily life of the world is not incompatible with intellectual excellence and the stretching of the mental and imaginative powers of young people. Broad education with utilitarian objectives need not be a soft option. Indeed, high specialisation is often a soft option representing an escape from the need to face the world and society and to contend with the confusions of human experience.

There is a place in the system of higher education for undergraduate programmes which aim at general education in the humanities and the sciences *together* and which have practical objectives such as the development of skill in the use of language, the use of electronic aids to thinking such as computers, and the capacity to understand and appreciate works of the imagination. The traditional honours programmes aim at producing discoverers of new knowledge. New programmes with a general education in view will produce *users* of new knowledge: not gentlemanly consumers of culture but people who in their daily lives as business men, administrators and teachers buy, interpret and apply new knowledge. As users their creative part in society consists in organising, transmitting and making available to the whole community what the pure scientists, the inspired artists and original technologists have produced. The notion that there is something second rate and derivative in this role in society is nonsense. Many of Britain's difficulties stem from the poor quality and inadequate education of the administrators, organisers and transmitters of knowledge who are not equal to bringing to bear in the practical context of life the achievements of the *élite* of pure science and the arts. In general what is missing in Britain is *general* higher education because there is a serious failure, first, to recognise the importance of having large numbers so educated and, secondly, to recognise the inherent difficulty of such education.

There is a place in Britain for at least one university which is prepared to say what its students need to study in order to prepare themselves for a creative and responsible place in the modern world: to be governed in designing its programmes by the demands of society and not by the demands of discovery on the frontiers of knowledge. Without attempting to be specific in this matter it is possible to identify the areas in which teaching is required. First, there is education in the use of languages as a means of communication and not merely as a means of studying literature: the ways in which language is used in modern means of communication and the development of skill and precision in its use. Second, there is the development of understanding and appreciation of the imaginative works in literature, the fine arts, architecture and music. Third, the teaching of numerical methods so that quantitative relationships can be understood and computers deployed. Fourth, there is the need to understand the methods and principles of the natural sciences and technology so that the student can grasp sympathetically what scientists and technologists are doing and how they are doing it. Finally, there is the need to understand what the social scientists are doing and the relationship of the social sciences to the life of society.

A big programme? Yes. Most academics will dismiss such a programme as impossible – one that can at best be superficial and almost inevitably misleading. In order to see how this can be done we must turn from the academics to the journalists to see how they transmit the complicated and difficult to the uninformed or partially informed. A high level of understanding joined with a will to study methods of communication can solve this problem. The solution is more challenging than 85 per cent of the problems with which contemporary academics wrestle. And that problem is critical for our culture, our social efficiency, for the creative inter-change of ideas and for the cultivation of sensibility.

4. Variety

There flows from the foregoing a fourth reason for establishing an independent university: the need to preserve and strengthen variety in English education. One of the great but unappreciated strengths of English education as a whole is the variety and individuality which it manages to cultivate, largely through the independence of its schools and its teachers and the absence of centralised systems of curricula design and control. The growth of state financing and control in all branches of education has not yet destroyed that variety but it can do so. We have only to look at what is happening to the universities to grasp the dangers.

The universities are now being engulfed in the long and general trend in British society which entrenches the past, slows down innovation and destroys individual initiative and responsibility; the growth of bureaucratic state control; the impairment of the state as leader and the development of the state as housekeeper and administrator; the universalising of the committee system so that everyone can refer everything to everyone else. Very few people in the British community have ever seriously doubted that an important foundation of the excellence of the universities is their independence; nor do many today. They have been very little the subject of the 'class struggle' arguments which have provided the ideological energy for transferring business enterprise to state ownership or control. None the less they are being taken over by the state. Men like Sir Eric Ashby can produce an abundance of argument[1] to prove that the universities as pensioners of the state are really free and independent. What he cannot deny, however, is the existence of control through financial provision, and that this control through the University Grants Committee, to which is now added the direct participation of the Department of Education and Science, has been the means of making a series of damaging mistakes the cumulative effects of which make it impossible for the universities to respond to the demand for higher education and almost impossible for them to change the direction of their efforts.

Let us be specific about the fundamental mistakes and the consequences now emerging. The University Grants Committee is responsible for the policy of building cottage universities – expensive to build, expensive to operate and ill-designed to concentrate talent and variety of endeavour which are indispensable to high academic achievement. Having created a high-cost system almost totally dependent on the state, the University Grants Committee and the Department of Education and Science are now faced with a crisis. How can the costs be met? The Department of Education decrees sharply differential fees for foreign students. The University Grants Committee decides to expand the arts and the social sciences because they are for the time being low-cost faculties, and to expand them in the new cottage universities. What the effects of these decisions may be on the character and balance of the universities are now very much secondary to the over-riding economic necessities generated by the original errors of the University Grants Committee. An important further consequence is the fear that the pressure to meet the demand for the education of undergraduates and the need to do so in low-cost faculties will have a prejudicial effect upon postgraduate work particularly in the older institutions of international repute. Given the mistakes of the past it is now quite possible that limited resources will be spread so thinly that Britain may cease to possess university institutions of world class.

The decision-makers in the University Grants Committee, the Department of Education and Science and the Treasury are not insensitive men, but they are making purblind decisions because they are part of an elephantine system of centralised control. This foolishness is bound to grow, and is bound to engulf more and more university activity in the cobwebs of committee decisions primarily concerned with the system itself and only secondarily with the problem of education and of research.

The role of an independent university will be to do something different in higher education in terms both of the education provided and of organisation and response to community requirements. If an independent university is able to demonstrate that it can achieve an effective response from the community, it will show the existing universities the way back to independence and, perhaps, encourage some of them to see that they need not rely too heavily on the state for money and can hence have moral and practical claims to independent decision-making.

The case for the independence of universities hardly requires emphasis. There is one aspect of it, however, which has not been sufficiently considered. In the absence of an independent responsibility for its own existence, how can we tell whether a university is any good or not? The real test is whether or not students want to enter it and how much they and their parents are willing to sacrifice in the effort to do so. At the moment some universities are probably better than other universities, but there is no means of knowing. No university has an incentive to attract students and no successful university has the opportunity of building on its successes. If every university had to stand on its own feet, there would be no need for the Auditor General to crawl around the premises seeing how the money is being spent while assuring everyone that he is not interested in policy. The only reasons for interesting oneself in the spending of money are policy and purpose. If every university were independent and obliged to live by the judgement of the community expressed in terms of the use made of its service, there would be no need for the prolonged, complicated, bitter and wholly unnecessary quarrel over the division of scarce resources. The energy spent on debate and intrigue and developing the right connections would be spent on meeting the public demand.

B. Ways and means

How can a private university be started? How can one be maintained? How can it be made to grow?

1. The potential market

Only if there is a sufficiently strong-felt demand can such a university flourish. From the students' point of view any university in the state system is a low-cost university, and an independent university financed by charging the full cost of its services is bound to be a high-cost university. Other things being equal, nearly all students who can gain admission to the state-supported system will continue to prefer the existing universities. This leaves to the private university all the students who cannot find places, i.e. between 30 and 45 per cent of those who get two A levels, a group of some 25,000 or more. To these potential customers of a private university there must be added an undetermined number of predominantly young people who have not got two A levels for one reason or another, but whom aptitude tests reveal are equal to university work. There are another undetermined number of foreign students for whom the fees in existing universities are not so far out of line with those a private university will be obliged to charge. In the category of foreign students there are also the growing number of North American students wishing and being encouraged by their universities to spend one year in universities abroad. Finally, there are a further undetermined number, inevitably very small at first, who may prefer the programme of a private university to that of existing universities and are prepared to pay for this preference. Only careful market research can determine with some measure of certainty the size of this potential student body and its disposition and capacity to finance its own education.

An additional element of some importance is the existence of approximately 200,000 parents in Britain who are willing and able to pay for their children's education in fee-paying schools. Whether this body can be persuaded to add to their expenditure on education by financing three years at a university[2] or to give priority to university rather than primary or secondary education is another matter which requires careful investigation by market research.

2. Cost – and payment

The cost of attending a private university will be of the order of £1,500 a year for fees and moderate maintenance. It will be at once argued that no students – or very few – can spend £4,500 for a university education. How do we know? Since the Second World War, no one has even attempted to provide education on this basis. Let us assume that no student whose parents earn £1,500 or less can or will provide anything to finance the university education of a son or a daughter. Suppose, however, a hire-purchase system is worked out to permit payment over 10 years and this hire-purchase system is based on a non-profit revolving fund charging interest only sufficient to cover bad debts, rising price levels and to act as an incentive to repayment. Total cost to a student would be of the order of £5,500. It is known that university education increases earning capacity[3] and that this increase is larger for students from low-income groups. Suppose over a working life of 40 years a student improved his earning capacity by an average of only £500 a year or £20,000 in all £20,000 on an outlay of £5,500 is not a bad return on money. In most cases the return will be much larger than the minimum here supposed.

In order further to assist student finances a private university must so organise its service work-force that part-time employment at commercial rates is open to students. The highly motivated student will welcome such opportunities, and the presence of the student honourably working to finance his education is something needed to create the serious sense of purpose which should underlie all higher education. Britain is no longer a master and servant society, and the sooner these dead stereotypes are banished from universities the better. Student employment opportunities will serve a moral as well as a financial purpose.

The financial obstacles to developing a private university are largely illusory, provided that the university can offer programmes of study of a kind which will induce large numbers to invest comparatively large sums in the education provided. These provisos are critical for two reasons. Only large numbers will enable the institution to achieve economies of scale and only high fees will enable the university to grow to maturity and maintain its independence. Both these reasons require expansion.

3. *Large numbers of students*

At present in British universities the academic members of the university divide their time unevenly among three activities: teaching (usually in small groups), research and learning, and administration and policy-making concerning their own affairs. A small number additionally engage in consultative work or public service outside their university. The pattern varies with individuals both on account of taste, talent or age, but that is how the total time of academics is spent. One result of this pattern of activities is a staff/ student ratio which is high compared with universities on the continent of Europe and elsewhere in the English-speaking world. Inasmuch as salaries are a considerable component of university costs, unit costs in British universities are high. It is, of course, argued that British universities do in three years what other universities do in four or five years. There is something in this argument, but less than is generally supposed. The work in British sixth forms lasts at least two years, and British first degrees are achieved no younger on average than first degrees elsewhere.

Teaching on the one hand and research and learning on the other are indispensably linked together. One certainly cannot teach in a university without at the same time learning and researching, and it can be argued that research without teaching is undesirable and in some areas impossible. There is really no way round the problem of the university man doing two jobs: teaching and research. On the other hand, university administration and politics consume the time of academics. Many advances have been made in making university administration a specialised, professional activity, but none the less academics, and particularly the more highly paid, still spend much time in administration, and for a minority it is a prestige occupation which is preferred to teaching and learning. Outside consultation and public service work is valuable to a university and must be encouraged provided the university is not converted into a salary-paying machine for people working elsewhere.

This pattern of academic work needs to be borne in mind in considering a 'unit cost-reducing' form of organisation. The teaching-learning combination cannot be altered, but it can be rearranged. If teaching activity can be intensified and professionalised, individual teachers can handle more students. Intensification can be achieved by so arranging activities that the teaching effort is not mixed up with the research and learning effort. In existing universities the academic staff are doing neither one nor the other to full effect because their activities are confused in time. Academic experience points to the fact that most learning and research is accomplished during vacations and during leave of absence, and it is then that real intellectual refreshment is achieved. Teaching depletes energy and intellectual resources, and the attempt to mix research and teaching weakens both activities. Too often academics just do not learn to teach, and succeed in confusing the students and wasting their time.

If a new university recognised that teaching is the main activity at one period of time and learning and research at another, and if staff are chosen *and trained* to teach, there will be a large increase in productivity. The staff/student ratio is at the root of high unit costs, but it does not follow that a low staff/student ratio means neglect of students or exploitation of staff. On the contrary, a private university must seek staff with two known capacities: intellectual capacity and capacity to teach or capacity to learn to teach. Accordingly, individual staff members of a private university will have to be paid considerably more than the staff of existing universities, and they will have to be given at least one year in six of paid leave for intellectual refreshment and the uninterrupted pursuit of intellectual inquiry.

In return for more pay and guaranteed and long periods of free time, the staff member will be asked to have his energies and abilities as a teacher deployed in such a way that large numbers can be handled. Enrolment in each year in a viable private university will have to be at least 3,500. Mass education – the horror of it! Not at all. Modern media of communication will enable a small number of brilliant teachers to reach more students more often than any do at present. At some time those teachers with a capacity for (and training in) face-to-face instruction in small groups will be able to handle more students and stimulate more response if they teach 25 hours a week during terms.

Hand in hand there must be developed a new conception of academic liberty – not necessarily the best or the only conception of academic liberty, but one required for university independence. The idea of a university post as a freehold until 65 to 67 to be followed by a life pension must be abandoned. In its place we must develop the conception of university teaching as a skilled profession with a commitment to the policies of the institution which in turn are determined by the relationship of the institution with the surrounding society. Put briefly, it will be necessary to develop in the university a business conception of duty in place of the aristocratic and rentier conception of duty. In a private university the teacher's liberty will consist in being able to take it or leave it and having the economic means to do so; but not in the liberty to impose his conception of his duty on the organisation. There are many virtues in existing conceptions of academic liberty, but there are many drawbacks too. There is a place and a need for an alternative concept to meet the requirements of university teachers willing to settle for something more than security and the entrenchment of their own interests at the expense of institutional mobility and capacity for quick response to social need and the generation of new knowledge.

4. High fees

The need for high university fees is obvious, but we must define what 'high' means and explain the reason for high fees. Fees will inevitably be high compared with those of existing universities because the full cost of operation of a private university must come from the sale of its services – both of teaching and research. The contribution of fees to the cost of existing universities is of the order of 5–10 per cent. Fees paying full cost will necessarily be high by comparison, but they must also be high in relation to unit costs in order to provide the capital for growth both in numbers of students and in the variety and quality of services rendered. Good orchestras, good art galleries, good theatres and good research institutions are indispensable to a good university. They can only be justified and paid for if their cost is widely spread. If large-scale operation is achieved the gap between high fees and low unit costs can be narrowed, but without the investment made possible by high fees value for money cannot be achieved.

5. Four steps

To establish an independent university, four steps must be taken.

(i) The market

The first essential step is to determine whether there exists in Britain and the world at large a market for the services such a university can provide, i.e. for broadly-based general education aimed at the development of the skill and understanding required to make a positive contribution to an advanced society. If the market is not there or is not big enough, the project cannot be launched.

(ii) The charter

If the answer to the first question is positive, the sponsors of the independent university must secure a charter from the Privy Council. Nothing in the laws of the United Kingdom requires it, but the nature and structure of British society do. Many employers, particularly those organised as professions, will recognise and many can legally recognise only the degrees of a chartered institution. Although the true charter of any university is the quality of its staff and students, an independent university must have the official endorsement which a charter implies. To this end the sponsors must be men and women of good repute as academics and as citizens, and the programmes of teaching and learning proposed must command the approval of people of understanding and good will.

(iii) The capital

The next step will be to secure the capital necessary for land, buildings and an educational hire-purchase revolving fund. About £5 million will be needed. A private university need not refuse outright gifts, but its financial policies should be so designed that its capital costs and depreciation, as well as running costs, are supported from revenue derived from fees and research contracts. To start it will require something that clearly resembles gifts, but in principle there is no reason why the foundation funds should not be repayable over, say, 50 years, should not bear interest and should not be secured on land and buildings. To suppose otherwise is to pander to the false notion that education is a special kind of activity dependent on charitable impulses or state subsidies. This is particularly not true of higher education. One of the basic emotional factors in higher education is a realisation on the part of the students and their parents that what they are undertaking is significant and important for themselves and society and that the effort made to carry out a programme of education has both its costs and its rewards. No matter what the rewards may be, the costs are inevitable, and it cannot but be socially healthy for people to make their choices with some measurable conception of what they are doing.

(iv) Programme of study

If the initial capital can be raised or is reasonably in prospect, the fourth step is to plan in detail the programmes of study. All decisions on buildings, staffing and admissions policy will depend upon the chosen programmes of teaching. This will be the most difficult step to take, for the good reason that it is a step into the unknown. If the programmes are simply borrowing from and/or simplifications of existing university courses, the institution will fail. The plain truth is that a new independent university will have to turn out better-educated people from students who the existing universities have turned down or failed to attract. This can be done by using programmes capable of heightening intellectual interest and intensifying motivation and by using teaching methods which combine intellectual stimulation with the careful development of skill. To achieve such ends both research and imagination of a high order and a new kind will be required. The people to do this need not be numerous but they must be brilliant, inventive and bold: who know what they are doing and who love what they know.

There is no formula for an instant university. An independent university in the British context will necessarily be a very specialised institution in relation to the kind of students it attracts and the kind of education it provides. It can and must become soon after its full establishment a mature university in its provision for a high level of honours work in a limited number of faculties and studies and graduate work in them. No university, if it intends to be good, can rely only on high-quality staff. It must attract some high-quality students who want from the start to do specialised work. That such students are necessarily limited in number (as is true in existing universities) will be recognised as a desideratum in the proposed university, and high-cost programmes will be provided when the quality of the student justifies the cost.

In designing its programmes an independent university must fix goals. Its minimum goals in education must be a degree which means its holder can read English, and write it accurately and felicitously, and use English as a means of communicating with large numbers and as a means of communicating complex information. Existing universities assume students have this capacity, but the assumption is not always true when students enter the universities nor when they leave them. It must aim at developing this power in a foreign language. For English people foreign languages are no longer a matter of taste and inclination. They are a necessity for everyone aspiring to play any directive or creative role in society. They can be taught to all except a small minority of the 'language blind'. And all must be taught the elementary techniques of data processing and data analysis by computers.

Some young people come to universities with some of these skills developed, but the specialisation imposed on schools by the honours system in universities ensures that none have all of them. In an independent university existing skill will be honed finer and new skill developed so that the student has a basic armoury of weapons for survival in international, technological society.

On the basis of these skills the humanities and the sciences can be taught together. The assumption on which the minimum goals rest is simply what experience and common sense suggest: that a person who speaks French is more likely to understand Pascal or Sartre or the politics of the Fifth Republic than one who does not; that a person who can design an elementary computer programme and recognise a significant correlation is more likely to learn some economics or understand an engineering problem than one who cannot; and that one who can read a book and write exact English is more likely to be able to appreciate John Donne or Iris Murdoch or write a report than one who cannot.

The maximum goals of the programme must be to ensure that the graduate is capable of finding his way into any body of knowledge: not to do what the specialist does but to understand what he does, and its relevance to society; to have some feeling for the inter-relationship of the sciences and of the arts.

6. *Admissions*

To achieve these goals the programme must be designed in sequence so that the students move from skill to broad experience to study in depth. Such a programme should aim at making all graduates capable of doing useful work in responsible jobs, and ensuring that at least half are intellectually as able as the first- and second-class honours graduates of existing universities.

Such a programme requires a carefully designed admissions policy. There is no need to assume that existing A-level examinations constitute the sole test of capacity to undertake university education. On the other hand a university which demands from students high fees must be prepared to discover as accurately as possible whether applicants are able to undertake the work required. Selection procedures will necessarily have to be more carefully designed than those of existing universities, and better calculated to discover potential for education than capacity for undergoing written examinations.

C. Conclusion

There seems to be an accumulating body of evidence that British society is not performing as well as its past history and its present opportunities would suggest it can perform. Whether there is any significance or truth in this evidence is difficult to say, but the impression of *malaise* is there and affects attitudes and confidence. Our socio-economic and political organisation seems to have become over-elaborate and constipated. The larger purpose of this proposal to establish an independent university is to see whether there is some way out of our situation by the decentralisation of decision-making and by the creation of centres of individual and institutional decision-making which involve the individual and/or the institution responding directly to the general environment rather than indirectly under the guidance of agencies that seem to understand even less about the problems of response than the individual or the institution itself. If all knowledge is limited and uncertain, and all human beings and agencies make mistakes in their life-strategy, the question is simply what arrangement will minimise the mistakes and maximise correct solutions. In the present circumstances an arrangement that encourages individuals and institutions to plan their own strategies seems on balance to have a prospect of more success than centralised, over-all planning. And such an arrangement does impart excitement to life, which is not an unconsidered trifle.

Assuming that this larger purpose of establishing an independent university is valid in the present circumstances of British society, the problem is to find a practical means for its realisation. It must be recognised that the goal of an independent centre of excellence in teaching and learning can be achieved only in stages; that it can come into being only by doing what existing universities either cannot do or do not wish to do; that what it does must be done on a large scale in order to command the resources necessary to extend the scope and character of its work; that it will produce quality only by learning how to work with quantity; and that, finally, it will be no easy task to achieve the standards of the best teachers and students in existing British universities.

Notes

1 E.g. his Birkbeck College Foundation Oration, reported in *The Times*, 20 January, 1968.
2 Methods of pre-payment of fees by life assurance (with assistance of income-tax rebates) and 'post-payment' by species of hire purchase have been developed in recent years and might be further expanded if the demand for financial assistance with university fees increased.
3 The subject has been studied by, *inter alia*, Professor G. S. Becker, *Human Capital: A Theoretical and Empirical Analysis with Special Reference to Education*, National Bureau of Economic Research and Columbia University Press, New York, 1965; Professor Mark Blaug, 'The Rate of Return on Investment in Education in Great Britain', *Manchester School*, September 1965, and 'Approaches to Educational Planning', *Economic Journal*, June 1967.

65

FUNDING IN HIGHER EDUCATION AND ECONOMIC GROWTH IN FRANCE AND THE UNITED KINGDOM, 1921–2003*

Vincent Carpentier

Source: *Higher Education Management and Policy* 18(3) (2006): 1–22.

The UK 2004 Higher Education Act generated important debates about the relationships between higher education (HE), economic growth and social progress. The range of positions expressed in relation to the increase of annual tuition fees raises crucial questions about the public and private funding of higher education and its individual and social economic benefits. Such controversies have a strong resonance in France where discussion about HE underfunding has already emerged. This article seeks to inform these current debates by combining economic and historical perspectives within a quantitative approach. The analysis of new historical series on funding and development of UK universities since the 1920s and the comparison with similar data for France has put into evidence a long-term link between HE funding and economic fluctuations. In both countries, the expansion in university resources was not linear and may be related to the impact of long economic cycles on public funding. Moreover, in the UK case, private funding periodically increased in order to replace diminishing public funding, rather than taking the form of additional resources. In consequence, private funds did not provide an overall rise in the universities' income. The considerable fluctuations of funding, combined with a more consistent growth of enrolment, led to a recurrent mismatch between resources for and access to higher education. This can explain the wide fluctuations of resources per student over the period and the current underfunding situation. Such historical trends question whether, in the future, increased fees will be a substitute for public spending. Or will variable fees be combined with even greater increases in public funding as part of a national project to support HE students from all social backgrounds and to boost expenditure per student?

Introduction

The close Parliamentary vote on the UK 2004 Higher Educ
firmed the contentiousness of the issues addressed in the Wh
Future of Higher Education (DfES, 2003). The main con.
on the implications of the introduction of variable annual studen ᴄᴄ
fees of up to GBP 3 000 in England. Following the Dearing Report's recommendations (1997), the government considered higher fees as necessary
additional resources to resolve underfunding in a context of competition
from international universities. Access to higher education will not be compromised, the government argues, because upfront fees are to be abolished
and financial support is to be offered to students from poor backgrounds
(Barr, 2003a). But opponents have drawn attention to the deterrent effect
of the rising levels of debt for students upon graduation (Callender, 2003)
and a potential increase of inequality between higher education institutions
(Ainley, 2005; Brown, 2005). Similar concerns were directed towards the
Conservatives' counter proposition to replace fees with higher interest rates
for students' loans (Carpentier, 2004a).

Although there is a consensus on the need to reform higher education,
different views are expressed about the extent and the nature of changes to
be implemented. Most controversies focus on alternative ways of financing
higher education and on the orientation its development and democratisation should take. Key issues concern the relative contributions of private
and public finance, the possible effects in terms of attendance and equity and
the benefits for the society as a whole. The range of positions expressed in
relation to top up fees raises crucial questions about the public and private
funding of higher education and its individual and social economic benefits
(Barr, 2003a; Dearden et al., 2005).

Such issues are not specific to the UK but have become a worldwide
concern (OECD, 2004). For example, the UK debate has a strong resonance
in France where discussion about HE underfunding has already emerged.
Demichel acknowledged that free of charge higher education "is taken for
granted in France" and is part of a culture that will be difficult to change
(2000, p. 14). However, a recent study on education and economic growth
has shown that some universities have already introduced extra fees for
specific services related to sport, photocopying and registration (Aghion
and Cohen, 2004, p. 75). A recent parliamentary report stated that the
question of fees cannot be ignored indefinitely while insisting that no reform
could succeed without a consensus. The report added that, in contrast to
Anglo-Saxon countries where higher education is more generally perceived
as an investment, higher fees could only be introduced in France with the
assurance that this will not harm democratisation (Herbillon, 2004). As in
the UK, support for higher fees is seen as an opportunity to address the
underfunding issue and compete in the knowledge economy. This was stressed

ɪɪ a report to the French Ministry of Economy which strongly advocated a debate about the principle of free HE (Camdessus, 2004). Supporters of higher fees also raise the equity issue: the current system, which combines funding based on low fees and high taxes with a restricted participation by social class, would lead to a "perverse system of redistribution from the least rich to the wealthiest" (Belloc, 2003). Proposed measures vary from sharing the cost of higher education between the state and students (Plassard and Bergès, 1998; Gary-Bobo and Trannoy, 2005) to a deregulation of HE (Lorenzi and Payan, 2003). These controversies are fairly recent and one can expect that such propositions will generate questions on the potential of higher fees to promote equity and on the long-term impact of such a move on participation and the economy.

This article draws on findings from an ESRC-funded research which sought to inform these current debates by examining the long-term links between HE funding and economic fluctuations (Carpentier, 2004b). The aim was to construct and analyse historical series on funding and development of UK universities since the 1920s in order to explore continuities and contrasts with previous HE controversies. Although the article is mainly about the UK, it also intends, by comparing similar historical statistics concerning the funding and development of French universities, to identify similarities and differences between the two countries.

The article is divided into four parts. The first part presents the methodology. The second provides an overview of the main transformations of higher education in France and the UK since the 1920s charting the fluctuations of funding and access. The third part concentrates on the UK and draws on historical perspectives distinguishing different regimes of higher education with specific articulations of funding and access policies. Finally, some conclusions are drawn.

A multidisciplinary approach to HE finance

This article combines economic and historical perspectives within a quantitative approach in order to locate some of the socio-economic driving forces behind the expansion of higher education.

Economic theory and HE policy

Both before and during the debates surrounding the White Paper, there have been fruitful attempts to assess the links between funding and access in higher education and the economy (Barr, 1993; Williams, 1992) and to provide an answer to the fundamental question of "how to pay for mass, high quality higher education" (Barr, 2003b). Following the path of human capital theory (Schultz, 1961; Becker, 1962), many researchers sought to evaluate and arbitrate between public and private funding of HE and its private and social returns (wages and externalities) (Blundell *et al.*, 2000; Mace, 2001; Chevaillier and Eicher, 2002; Wolf, 2002; Barr, 2003a; Johnstone, 2004).

This article seeks to contribute to these debates by examining the links between the funding and development of higher education and socio-economic changes through the theory of systemic regulation. This theory attempts to interpret transformations of the economic system in terms of developing connections with spheres (like education) that are influenced, but not fully determined, by economic dimensions (Fontvieille, 1990; Michel, 1999). The theory suggests that, as education may not only represent a cost for the economy, but also furnish a main determinant of its growth, the development of the educational system may be interpreted, in part, as the outcome of regulation processes between public expenditure on education and long economic cycles. Previous work has shown that the fluctuations of public expenditure on education in the UK since 1833 were connected to 50-year Kondratiev economic cycles (Carpentier, 2003). Similar findings were observed in France (Fontvieille, 1990; Carry, 1999).

Moreover, the fluctuations were reversed to economic cycles before 1945 and then synchronised in both countries. Before 1945, the rapid growth of public funding on education during periods of economic downturn may be explained in terms of an attempt to revive the economy. On the contrary, after 1945, the growth of public educational resources accelerated during the period of post-war prosperity, only to go into decline following the economic crisis of 1973. The 1945 transition to procyclical public educational expenditure may represent the recognition of education as a driving force in the economic system rather than simply a means of correction. In this context, the post-1973 reforms would characterise different options in the search for a new regulation process in order to pursue educational development in a context marked by slowing down of public funding. Such a framework strongly echoes the current debates on higher education.

The article proposes to focus on the specific role of higher education in such a process and seeks to investigate potential relationships between economic fluctuations and the level and structure of funding of universities. HE policy is examined in relation to its wider socio-economic environment (Campbell *et al.*, 2003).The concept of regime of higher education is proposed as an illustration of the interactions between the internal (quantitative and qualitative developments of HE) and external contexts (social change and economic fluctuations) that affect the evolution of higher education. Historically, the successive regimes of higher education would therefore characterise the degree of adequacy between funding and access policies as illustrated by the long-term fluctuations of funding per student.

Towards a socio-economic history of education

This theoretical framework interrogates economic and social interfaces with higher education that were, and still are, major issues for policy making. As Aldrich noted, "the historical perspective indicates the complexity of the relationship between education and economic performance" (1996, p. 109). The historical dimension is therefore crucial in order to reveal the long-term factors that could explain the current relationship between higher education and economic systems. There is a mutual interest in combining economic and historical analysis to understand current educational policies. On the one hand, history can supplement the economic analysis which tends to elude the influence of cultural and socio-political factors on education. On the other hand, some historians of education have recently pleaded for more recognition of the economic dimension in order to interpret past educational policies (Richardson, 1999, p. 132; Goodman and Martin, 2004; Sanderson, 2005).

The approach developed here can be defined as a socio-economic history of education following Simon's idea that "the fundamental educational issues have remained the same through the years – who should be educated, how, to what level or different levels of the service of what social or industrial needs? – So the conditioning social and economic factors continue to operate" (1989, p. 79). The aim of this article is to complement previous histories of higher education (Briggs, 1969; Sanderson, 1972; Anderson 1992) with a particular focus on economic issues through a quantitative evaluation of the impact of past reforms on universities' funding and enrolment.

A quantitative history of funding and development of UK universities (1921–2003)

Following previous quantitative research on higher education (Halsey and Webb, 2000), this study seeks to furnish data about the nature and level of financial resources for higher education, and about the extent to which higher education, in turn, affects the nature and level of resources. The methodology of quantitative history based on the principles of national accounting is used in order to collect and process long-term data (Marczewski, 1961).

The dataset that was produced gathers historical series on funding and development of universities from the early 1920s and is the result of research into primary and secondary governmental and institutional sources; it is now part of the UK Data Archive (Carpentier, 2004c). Funding indicators include the level of the income of universities and its distribution according to its origins (public/fees/endowment/research), the level of expenditure and its distribution by economic categories (wages/consumption/investment). Non-financial data include the number of students and its distribution according to gender, country of origin and other enrolment's characteristics (full or part time and undergraduate or postgraduate), the number of awards and diplomas, the number and structure of staff.

These historical series refer to pre-1992 universities and include all institutions delivering degrees afterwards. It has been difficult to obtain historical data on expenditure relating to advanced courses in colleges of further education. It was also impossible to distinguish between resources devoted to advanced and non-advanced courses within the same establishment. Prior to 1992, therefore, data are supplied only for universities. From 1994, data relating to advanced courses in polytechnics and further education are included.

In addition, the article proposes a comparative perspective dimension which is usually less common for higher education than primary and secondary levels (Crook and McCulloch, 2002). A comparison with the French perspective is helpful in determining the uniqueness or otherwise of the UK development. Previous research highlighted specific developments of HE in France and England in relation to their respective economic policies following the oil crisis of the early 1970s while underlining the possibility of a future convergence (Deer and de Meulemeester, 2004; de Meulemeester, 2003). French data originate from Carry's (1999) quantitative work on education funding until 1996 and have been updated with governmental data (DEP, 1984–2003). Data on enrolment are based on the *Annuaire Statistique de la France* (DSG, 1920–1945; INSEE, 1946–2003). Population data are based on Vallin and Meslé's (2001) work.

The primary aim of this multidisciplinary examination is to investigate the mechanisms that regulated the articulation between the funding and development of higher education and its relationship with the socio-economic system, seeking to resituate the complexity of the current situation.

An overview of the growth of the HE system: 1921–2003

Since the early 1920s, UK and French higher education have experienced tremendous transformations. Among them, significant changes in the level and structure of universities' funding and enrolment may explain the current underfunding situation.

The rise of funding and enrolment but the instability of expenditure per student

The first result shows a dramatic increase in funding for UK and French universities. The Geary-Khamis dollar expresses purchasing power parity, eliminating differences in price level between countries (Maddison, 2000). UK and French expenditure at 1990 prices in 2003 are respectively 150 and

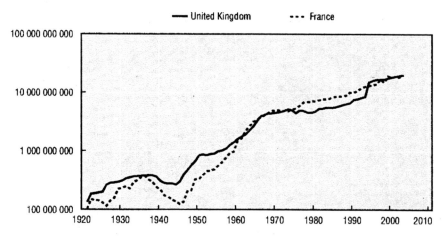

Figure 1 Expenditures of universities (1990 Geary Khamis $), 1921–2003.
Source: Carpentier (2004c).

190 times greater than in the 1920s. Over the period the share of GDP dedicated to the funding of universities rose from 0.06% to 1.4%. The equivalent figures for France are respectively 0.06% and 1.22%.

However, while expenditure increased, the number of students grew 40-fold in both countries.

More significantly, the number of students in UK universities as a share of the 18–30 age group rose from 1.3% to 25% between 1955 and 2002. In France the ratio rose from 2.1% to 23% (Carpentier, 2004b). This rate is lower than the 43% figure traditionally associated with participation in the United Kingdom and related to the government's 50% target for 2010. These figures are for the Initial Entry Rate for higher education which sums the percentages of the age group who enter higher and further education colleges for the first time in each year of age between 18 and 30 (Ramsden, 2003).

Over the whole period massive increases in enrolment were reflected in massive increases in funding. Nevertheless, there were considerable variations within this overall rise. For example, in 2003, expenditure per student in the United Kingdom was more than 3.5 times its level in 1921 (4.5 times in France). In 2003, however, expenditure per student was less than a half of the level of 1973. It is worth noting that falling expenditure per student, which was one of the central issues of the White Paper, began in 1990, before the re-designation of the polytechnics.

British and French expenditure per student were similar both at the beginning and at the end of the period. Much wider fluctuations, however, occurred in the United Kingdom. The following part examines the origins and consequences of these fluctuations by comparing and contrasting the historical evolution of funding and attendance.

234

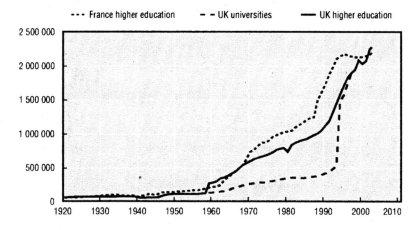

Figure 2 Number of students, 1921–2003.
Source: Carpentier (2004c).

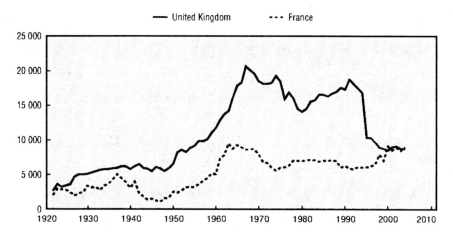

Figure 3 University expenditure per student (1990 Geary Khamis $), 1921–2003.
Source: Carpentier (2004c).

Long economic cycles, university income and access

UK university expenditure conforms to the connections between resources and long economic cycles observed in other levels of education (Carpentier, 2003). The long-term expansion in resources devoted to higher education was not linear and may be related to Kondratiev cycles (Figure 4). Four Kondratiev cycles of approximately 50 years have been identified, each showing expansion and depression phases (1790–1820/1820–1848; 1848–1870/ 1870–1897; 1897–1913/1913–1945; 1945–1973/1973–?) (Loucã and Reinjders, 1999).

235

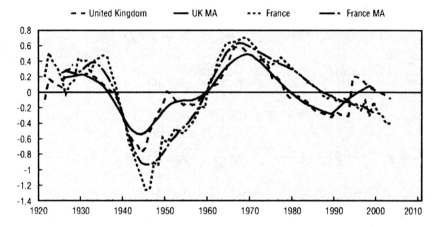

Figure 4 University expenditure, 1990 Geary-Khamis \$, 1921–2003 (2nd order deviation from the regression curve and nine-year moving averages (MA), $R^2 = 0.96$ and 0.93).

Source: Carpentier (2004c).

The increase of expenditure during the 1920s was brought to a halt by the aftermath of the 1929 crisis. The period of prosperity following 1945 led to a dramatic rise of expenditure, although this was halted in 1967 as a consequence of a decrease in capital expenditure that had been driven by the expansion of civic universities and the establishment of new universities. The real funding downfall followed the oil crisis of 1973 and continued until the current period, although a revival of expenditure occurred in the early 1990s with the integration of polytechnics.

A similar pattern may be observed in France where fluctuations also corresponded to Kondratiev cycles. However, France and the United Kingdom experienced different evolutions with respect to the structure of HE funding. There have been some profound organisational transformations in French higher education since the late 1960s resulting in a move away from the old *faculté* and towards the emergence of a *université* identity (Mignot-Gérard, 2003; Musselin, 2004). The 1968 Faure Act initiated this process by structuring the universities around the principles of autonomy, participation in decision making and multidisciplinarity (Minot, 1984). This process met with some resistance but was continued by the 1984 Savary Act which also broadened the funding of higher education mainly from regional government but also from new private resources. In addition to the traditional private contributions like the *taxe d'apprentissage* (paid directly by firms to universities in exchange of a tax remit) and fees, universities are allowed to generate extra income from donations, contracted services, patents and publications. A 1986 White Paper which sought to raise the level of fees was rejected after intense strikes, while in 1988, a four year contract

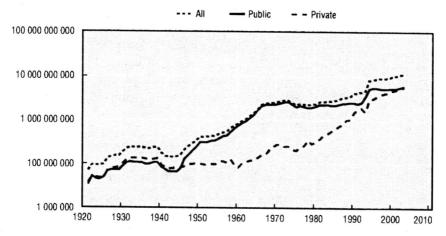

Figure 5 Income of UK universities (GBP 1990), 1921–2003.
Source: Carpentier (2004c).

between universities and the ministry was established in order to move towards a tighter control of funding.

While such reforms represent turning points and a return to the autonomy that universities had lost at the turn of the 18th century (Charle, 1995, p. 17), the income structure of French universities did not change radically over the period. The rise of the share of private resources from 5% in 1960 to 13% today indicates potential developments rather than the transformation of a system which is still essentially publicly funded. In contrast, the relative contributions of public and private resources are key elements in the evolution of the income of UK universities.

Figure 5 shows that public funding was the driving force of university income until the 1980s. Variations in public resources generated the Kondratiev-related fluctuations in HE funding observed above. Public funding nourished the post-war growth of HE income and put a brake on it after 1973 in the context of spending cuts. The revival of income growth did not take place until the early 1980s with a rise in private funding. However, such an increase did not fully compensate for the reduction in public funds and so only partially restored the overall growth in income.

Figure 6 shows that such movements led to substantial changes in the repartition between public and private income of universities. Between 1921 and 1945 public and private resources contributed in broadly equal amounts to the income of universities. Thereafter the share of public funding rapidly increased and reached 90% in 1973. It then fell, so that by the beginning of the 21st century the 50/50 distribution had been restored.

Research was also a major part of the transformation of the income structure of UK universities. The share of university specific funding dedicated

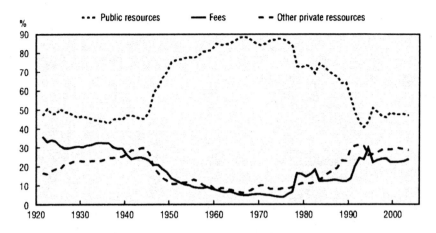

Figure 6 Income structure of universities, United Kingdom, 1921–2003.
Source: Carpentier (2004c).

to research increased from 5% in 1957 to 15% in 2002. The share of public funding of research increased from 50% to 65% from 1957 to 1973 and then started declining to reach 57% in 2002 (Carpentier, 2004c).

The effect of public funding on the income structure of educational institutions was crucial in the development of enrolment in primary education in the late 19th century and in secondary education during the first half of the 20th century (Carpentier, 2003). Such mechanisms became increasingly important in higher education where access policies were still affected by a mixture of public and private funds. In France, where the level of fees remains low over the period, the expansion of enrolment in higher education was mainly driven by policies dedicated to increase participation at the upper secondary level.

Between 1921 and 1974 the share of university income originating from fees decreased from 36% to 4% and rose thereafter to reach 23% in 2002 (Figure 6). Such changes may have influenced enrolment's extent and characteristics, especially as tuition fees are one of the main factors affecting access. Economic cycles and public resources had an impact on the structure and levels of funding of universities and on the replacement of fees by public funding. This leads to the crucial question: Does access drive funding or funding drive access, or both? Increased enrolment was accompanied by a decrease of fees from 1945 to 1973 (Figure 6), especially after 1958 and the implementation of tuition fees subsidies. The post-1973 era led to the partial withdrawal of subsidies in a context of the control of public funding. The number of new students slowed down during the 1980s to grow again during the 1990s. The impact of the increase of fees on access depends on the crucial role of financial aid to poorer students.

238

Fluctuations of public expenditure may be associated not only with the number of students but also with a change of their characteristics. The proportion of postgraduates rose from 6% to 23% from 1947 to 1973 and remained stable afterwards. The share of full time students rose from 69% to 90% over the same period and has subsequently dropped to 58% nowadays.

The share of foreign students was quite consistent over the period, driven by the access from students from the Empire and Commonwealth and other overseas students. However, economic fluctuations also provoked changes in policy towards non-European Union students who became subject to full cost fees from 1981. This was encouraged in order to provide extra resources for universities in the context of cuts in public funding since the 1970s.

In contrast, the share of women students was not affected by economic fluctuations (Figure 7). While things are not clear during the inter war years (a possible decrease of women students after the 1930s crisis demands more research), the increasing participation of women in higher education after the end of the Second World War was not jeopardised by the economic difficulties of the 1970s. This confirms Dyhouse's findings that the proportion of women in higher education increased during the 1960s and even more dramatically during the 1970s for various reasons like the drop in early marriages, the new universities of the 1960s, the end of quotas and more career opportunities for women graduate (2005). Therefore, alongside economic explanations, feminisation should be considered as a major factor of the historical expansion of HE enrolment and funding in both countries.

As a whole, all those indicators suggest that the elite system provided many resources compared to the limited number of students, prior to the

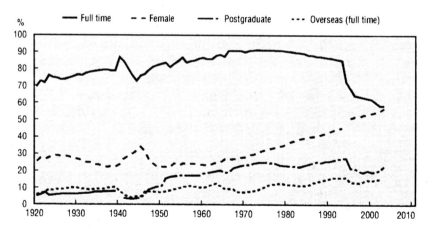

Figure 7 Characteristics of students, United Kingdom, 1921–2003.
Source: Carpentier (2004c).

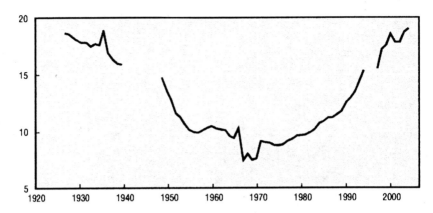

Figure 8 Number of students per full time academic staff, United Kingdom, 1926–2003.
Source: Carpentier (2004c).

mass system that developed in the 1960s in a context of growing funding. The increase of enrolment was maintained in the 1970s in a context of diminishing resources. In this context, access might have been developed to the detriment of quality. Figure 8 shows that the student/full-time staff ratio decreased until the early 1970s and increased thereafter. This increase may also be the consequence of the casualisation of staff.

These developments suggest that diminishing funding per student led to a change of characteristics of students and more differentiation. Similar results were observed in France where many researchers insisted on the difference between expansion and democratisation of higher education (Verger, 1984, p. 404; Deer, 2005).

The historical lens seems to show connections between the level and the structure of universities' income and the number and characteristics of the student population. It is then interesting to examine the historical articulation between funding and access policies that could explain the long-term evolution of quantitative and qualitative developments of higher education.

Regimes of HE: the historical articulation between funding and access policies

The following focuses on the UK experience and provides a long-term description of the evolutions of expenditure per student by revealing different historical sequences of articulations between the funding and access policies.

Figures 3 and 9 clearly show different upward and downward phases of expenditure per student, suggesting the alternations of different regimes of higher education. The notion of a regime of higher education seeks to

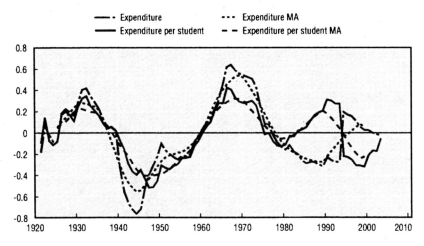

Figure 9 University expenditure GBP 1990, United Kingdom, 1921–2003 (Second-order deviation from the regression curve and nine-year moving averages (MA)), $R^2 = 0.953$ and 0.78.
Source: Carpentier (2004c).

characterise the articulations between the internal development of universities (funding, access, staff, quality) and their external socio-environments (economic fluctuations and social changes). The following seeks to identify these regimes and to examine the factors behind the transition from one to another in order to place the current situation in perspective.

1921–1932, rise of spending per student: more resources for a limited enrolment

The creation of the University Grants Committee in 1919 symbolised the growing involvement of the state (Shinn, 1980; Shattock, 1994) in a context where public expenditure increased from 5% to 10% of GDP. Education's share of all public expenditure grew from 6% to 10%. However, the share of public expenditure on education devoted towards higher education remains stable at around 2%. The structure of university income did not change as increasing private and public resources equally drove the rise in funding. University expenditure was multiplied by 3.5. Enrolment was growing at a slower pace than funding, which explains the doubling of expenditure per student over the period.

1933–1944, decrease of spending per student: the stagnation

The Great Depression led to the decrease of non-military public expenditure as a share of GDP. Such movement particularly targeted public expenditure on education which stagnated from 1932 and decreased during the war (Carpentier, 2003). The slower growth of university funding was the result of a brake upon both public and private resources (Figure 5).

Both expenditure and enrolment stagnated and decreased during the war. It is worth noting that reductions in the former preceded the latter. The stagnation of expenditure combined with a moderate growth of enrolment explains the decrease of expenditure per student.

1945–1972, the Robbins era or the golden age

The golden era of British universities is traditionally associated with the Robbins Report (1963) that Lowe considers as the first attempt to co-ordinate the development of a system of HE in modern Britain (2000, p. 83). Nevertheless, the rise of enrolment started earlier. Enrolment rose threefold until 1967 and its share of the 18–30-year-old age group rose from 2% to 6% (Figure 2). One important aspect of this period was that increases in funding preceded the growth of enrolment. This was part of a context where public expenditure on education's share of GDP rose from 2% to 6%. Higher education's share of public expenditure on education increased from 3% to 12%. While public involvement became orientated to all universities (Salter and Tapper, 1994), the share of university income from public funding grew from 50% to 90%. Increases in funding were greater than the growth of enrolment, thus explaining the considerable rise in expenditure per student. Increased public funding promoted enlarged access, by the removal or reduction of fees, and sustained a qualitative development as shown by the decrease in the numbers of students per staff. Students of 1973, as compared with their counterparts in the 1950s, were increasingly female (from 22% to 30%), studying on a full-time basis (from 72% to 90%) and participating at postgraduate level (from 6% to 24%) (Carpentier, 2004c).

Quantitative and qualitative indicators suggest that this phase was really the golden age for higher education when funding improved access without harming quality.

1973 to 1980, between cuts in spending and democratisation

The 1973 oil crisis opened a new era which marked a decline in public funding of the educational system (Carpentier, 2003). For universities, reductions began in 1967 in a context of declining capital expenditure on new universities which indicated the end of the Robbins era. The major slowdown, however, took place in the aftermath of the 1973 economic crisis. Reductions in public funding were not compensated for by increased private resources (Figure 5). Therefore, the overall level of university income dropped.

The conjunction of high enrolment and a reduction in overall resources led to a 25% decrease of expenditure per student from 1967 to 1980. This period demonstrates a mismatch between funding and access policies that is also observed in France where funding per student dropped by 20%.

1980–1990, the illusory expansion of funding per student

The moderate increase of funding per student during this period was caused by a slowdown in the growth in student numbers combined with a modest increase in funding. The number of new students was stable while the number of students from abroad increased. Full-cost fees for overseas students were introduced in 1980 as one of the first pieces of evidence of the Thatcher approach to higher education. Reductions in public funding, coupled with a rise from private sources (fees and private research) produced a dramatic shift in the public/private income structure (from 86%/14% to 56%/44%).

Access grew slowly and reductions in staffing led to a rise in the student/staff ratio (Figure 8). Staff wages as a share of expenditure fell from 55% to 48% (Carpentier, 2001). The increasing expenditure per student was not the result of higher enrolment connected to even greater rise of funding like it was the case during the Robbins era but was on the contrary the combination of a slower growth of access and a policy of public austerity for which the rise of private funding did not fully compensate.

1990s, the growing disconnection between funding and access

A decline in public funding coupled with an increase in private resources produced a modest rise of total income but the explosion of enrolment led to a dramatic setback in spending per student. The important result is that the downward trend took place as early as 1990 when subsidies were replaced by loans and before the 1992 act. The polytechnics, whose expenditure per student was lower than pre-1992 universities, deepened the lack of resources per student of the HE system as a whole but did not provoke it. Moreover public grant constitutes 35% of income of traditional universities against 55% for new universities (Webber, 2003). As a result, trends towards more private funding slowed down in 1993 before rising again in 1995. Thus integration into the university sector increased polytechnics' reliance on private income.

1999–?, the stabilisation

In 1999, a brake was applied to the decrease of expenditure per student which began in the 1980s. This new regime of growth is based upon an increase of both public and private resources (the increase of public funding was combined with the increase of fees in 1998 and the rise of private funding for research). Increasing income contrasts with the previous period but does not compensate for the rapid growth of student numbers. The expenditure per student is then stabilised. The White Paper proposed to increase the level of income of universities and to change the structure of funding.

There are still uncertainties about how these reforms will affect the relationship between participation and resources in higher education. The new fee regime may produce changes not only in the level and structure of funding but also in the number and characteristics of students. The trajectories of these indicators will determine whether the 2004 HE act will be viewed as a transition towards a new regime of higher education involving a balanced between funding and access policies or as an instrument to control public funding by returning to a past elitist regime of higher education.

Conclusion

The historical perspective provides evidence on some recurrent mechanisms of articulation between funding and access in HE that can illustrate the successive and interrelated changes that led to the current situation:

•   The long-term expansion of universities' resources in the United Kingdom and France was not linear and a consistent link was found with 50-year Kondratiev economic cycles. Post-war growth, ended by the oil crisis of 1973, corresponded with acceleration and, later, a slowdown of funding.

•   Economic cycles provoked not only changes in the level of expenditure of UK universities but also dramatic shifts in their income structure. Public funding was the driving force for university income until the mid 1970s. Private funding (including fees) periodically increased in order to replace diminishing public funding, rather than taking the form of additional resources. In consequence, private funds hardly provided an overall rise in the income of universities.

•   The considerable fluctuations of structure and levels of funding, combined with a more consistent growth of enrolment, led to a recurrent mismatch between resources for and access to higher education, explaining the wide fluctuations of expenditure per student in the United Kingdom over the period and the current underfunding issue.

The passage from one regime of higher education to another can be connected with economic fluctuations, social changes and demography articulated around crucial turning points and different temporalities (1945, the beginning of massive public funding; 1960s, the expansion of enrolment; 1970s, the control of public expenditure; 1980s, the beginning of private expenditure expansion).

The combinations of those factors led to a reversal of the link between funding and access policies in the early 1980s. Figure 9 shows that the fluctuations of resources and resources per student diverge around that time suggesting that:

- Until 1980, access and funding fluctuate in the same direction, the latter driving the former. The UK experience shows that fees can harm access and highlights the crucial role of financial aid to students as a variable of correction.
- After 1980, changes in the level and structure of universities' income are still linked with economic cycles' impact on public expenditure while access fluctuations progressively become less dependent on economic movements. The rise of participation, which was originally driven by the support of public resources, increasingly responds to political, social and cultural factors. As a result, the students' characteristics and their mode and level of enrolment tend to become variables of adjustment to fluctuations in funding.

With respect to policymaking, such historical trends question whether, in the future, increased fees will be a substitute for public spending. Or will higher fees be combined with even greater increases in public funding as part of a national project to support HE students from all social backgrounds and to boost expenditure per student?

This article did not deal with another important issue raised by the 2004 HE Act which relates to the potential effects of the introduction of the variable fees upon higher education institutions. Supporters of the Act have considered the introduction of variable fees as an opportunity to increase diversity and promote efficiency in English higher education, while its opponents see it as a potential source of tension and inequality between institutions. Current data highlight significant discrepancies between the patterns of development and funding of UK universities (or groups of universities). Research also shows that the expansion of higher education combines with growing differences in students' profiles between institutions (Reay *et al.*, 2005). Those discrepancies also exist in France where there is a strong hierarchy within universities and between universities, *Grandes écoles* and *Instituts universitaires de technologie* (Bourdieu and Passeron, 1964; Bourdieu, 1989). A recent study investigated the different strategies that individual universities may develop in order to adapt to the new environment brought by the reform (Temple, Shattock and Farnham, 2005). Such prospective research could be complemented by a historical and quantitative investigation into how past reforms of funding and access impacted on the different kind of institutions that shaped the HE system over the last century.

Note

* This article is a substantially developed version of a paper published as "Cycles longs et financement universitaire: une perspective historique sur les réformes actuelles au Royaume-Uni", *Économies et Sociétés*, Cahier de l'ISMEA, Hors Série, n° 40 (2005), pp. 1607–1634.

References

Aghion, P. and E. Cohen (2004), *Éducation et croissance: rapport pour le Conseil d'analyse économique*, La Documentation française, Paris.

Ainley, P. (2005), *For Free Universities*, Inaugural Lecture, University of Greenwich, 19 January.

Aldrich, R. (1996), *Education for the Nation*, Cassell, London.

Anderson, R. D. (1992), *Universities and Elites in Britain Since 1800*, Macmillan, Basingtoke.

Barr, N. (1993), "Alternative Funding Resources for Higher Education", *Economic Journal*, Vol. 103, pp. 718–728.

Barr, N. (2003a), *Financing Higher Education: Comparing the Options*, LSE Working Paper Series, June.

Barr, N. (2003b), "Financing Higher Education: Lessons from the UK Debate", *The Political Quarterly*, Vol. 74, No. 3, pp. 371–381.

Becker, G. S. (1962), "Investment in Human Capital: A Theoretical Analysis", *The Journal of Political Economy*, Vol. 7, No. 5, pp. 9–49.

Belloc, B. (2003), "Incentives and Accountability Instruments of Change", *Higher Education Management and Policy*, Vol. 15, No. 1, pp. 23–40.

Blundell, R., L. Dearden, A. Goodman and H. Reed (2000), "The Returns to Higher Education in Britain: Evidence from a British Cohort", *Economic Journal*, Vol. 110, pp. F82–F99.

Bourdieu, P. and J. C. Passeron (1964), *Les héritiers, les étudiants et la culture*, Éditions de Minuit, Paris.

Bourdieu, P. (1989), *Noblesse d'État: Grandes écoles et esprit de corps*, Éditions de Minuit, Paris.

Briggs, A. (1969), "Development of Higher Education in the United Kingdom: Nineteenth and Twentieth Centuries", in: NIBLET, W. R. (ed.), *Higher Education: Demand and Response*, Routledge, London, pp. 95–116.

Brown, R. (2004), "The Future Structure of the Sector: What Price Diversity?", *Perspectives*, Vol. 8, No. 4, pp. 93–99.

Callender, C. (2003), "Student Debt: The Impact on Participation in Higher Education", *Universities UK Seminar on Student Debt*, 5 February, London.

Camdessus, M. (2004), *Le sursaut: vers une nouvelle croissance pour la France: rapport pour le ministère de l'Économie, des Finances et de l'Industrie*, La Documentation française, Paris.

Campbell, C., V. Carpentier and G. Whitty (2003), "Educational Financing and Improvement: Conceptual Issues and Policy Debates in the UK", *Revue Suisse des Sciences de l'Éducation*, Vol. 3, pp. 455–477.

Carpentier, V. (2001), *Système éducatif et performances économiques au Royaume-Uni: XIXe et XXe siècles*, L'Harmattan, Paris, 2001.

Carpentier, V. (2003), "Public Expenditure on Education and Economic Growth in the UK, 1833–2000", *History of Education*, Vol. 32, No. 1, pp. 1–15.

Carpentier, V. (2004a), "An Elitist's Manifesto", *Times Higher Education Supplement*, 17 September.

Carpentier, V. (2004b), "Higher Education and the UK Socio-Economic System", ESRC Research Report, RES-000-22-0296.

Carpentier, V. (2004c), *Historical Statistics on the Funding and Development of the UK University System*, 1920–2002, UK Data Archive, *www.data-archive.ac.uk*.

Carry, A. (1999), "Le compte satellite rétrospectif de l'éducation en France 1820–1996", *Économies et Sociétés*, Série AF, Histoire quantitative de l'économie française, Vol. 25, pp. 1–281.

Charle, C. (1995), *La République des Universitaires 1870–1940*, Éditions du Seuil, Paris.

Chevaillier, T. and J. C. Eicher (2002), "Rethinking the Financing of Post Compulsory Education", *Higher Education in Europe*, Vol. 27, No. 1–2, pp. 69–88.

Crook, D. and G. McCulloch (2002), "Comparative Approaches to the History of Education", *History of Education*, Vol. 31, No. 5, pp. 397–401.

Dearden, L., E. Fitzimons, A. Goodman and G. Kaplan (2005), *Higher Education Funding Policy: Who Wins and Who Loses?*, IFS Commentaries.

Dearing, R. (1997), *The National Committee of Inquiry into Higher Education: Higher Education in the Learning Society*, H.M.S.O.

Deer, C. and J. L. De Meulemeester (2004), "The Political Economy of Educational Reform in France and Britain: 1980–2000", *Compare*, Vol. 34, No. 1, pp. 33–51.

Deer, C. (2005), "Higher Education Access and Expansion: the French Experience", *Higher Education Quarterly*, Vol. 59, No. 3, pp. 230–241.

De Meulemeester, J. L. (2003), "Convergence of Higher Education Systems in Europe: the English and French Examples", *European Educational Research Journal*, Vol. 4, No. 2, pp. 628–647.

Demichel, F. (2000), "Governance in Higher Education: the Viewpoint of France", *Higher Education Management*, Vol. 12, No. 2, pp. 7–15.

DEP (1984–2003), *Repères et références statistiques sur les enseignements, la formation et la recherche*, Direction de l'évaluation et de la prospective, ministère de l'Éducation, Paris.

DfES (2003), *The Future of Higher Education*, White Paper, Department for Education and Skills, January.

DSG (1920–1945), *Annuaire statistique de la France*, Direction de la Statistique Générale, Paris.

Dyhouse, C. (2005), "Women in Universities: An Historical Perspective", ESRC Research Report (RES-000-22-0139).

Fontvieille, L. (1990), "Education, Growth and Long Cycles", in: Tortella, G. (ed.) *Education and Economic Development since the Industrial Revolution*, Generalitat, Valencia, pp. 317–335.

Gary-Bobo, R. and A. Trannoy (2005), "Faut-il augmenter les droits d'inscriptions", *Revue Française d'économie*, 19(3), pp. 189–237.

Goodman, J. and J. Martin (2004), "Editorial: History of Education-Defining a Field", *History of Education*, Vol. 33, No. 1, pp. 1–10.

Halsey, A. H. and J. Webb (2000), *Twentieth Century: British Social Trends*, Macmillan Press Ltd, London.

Herbillon, M. (2004), *Rapport d'information déposé par la délégation de l'Assemblée Nationale pour l'Union européenne sur l'enseignement supérieur en Europe*, Assemblée Nationale No. 1927, 17 November.

INSEE (1946–2003), *Annuaire statistique de la France*, Institut National de la Statistique et des Études Économiques, Paris.

Johnstone, B. (2004), "The Economics and Politics of Cost Sharing in Higher Education: Comparative Perspectives", *Economics of Education Review*, Vol. 23, No. 4, pp. 403–410.

Kaiser, F. (2001), *Higher Education in France: Country Report*, CHEPS Higher Education Monitor, Enschede.

Lorenzi, J. and J. J. Payan (2003), *L'Université maltraitée*, Plon, Paris.

Louca, F. and J. Reijnders (1999), *The Foundations of Long Wave Theory*, Edward Elgar Publishing, Cheltenham.

Lowe, R. (2002), "Higher Education", in: Aldrich, R. (ed.) *A Century of Education*, RoutledgeFalmer, London, pp. 75–92.

Mace, J. (2001), "Top-Up Fees: Theoretical and Policy Issues", *Higher Education Review*, Vol. 34, No. 1, pp. 3–19.

Maddison, A. (2000), *The World Economy: A Millennial Perspective*, OECD, Paris.

Marczewski, J. (1961), "Histoire quantitative, buts et méthodes", *Cahiers de l'Institut de Sciences Économiques Appliquées*, Série A.F., Vol. 115, No. 1, pp. 3–54.

Michel, S. (1999), *Éducation et croissance économique en longue période*, L'Harmattan, Paris.

Mignot-Gerard, S. (2003), "Who are the Actors in the Government of French Universities? The Paradoxal Victory of Deliberative Leadership", *Higher Education*, Vol. 45 (1), pp. 71–89.

Minot, J. (1984), *Les universités: après la loi sur l'enseignement supérieur du 26 janvier 1984*, Berger-Levrault, Paris.

Musselin, C. (2004), *The Long March of French Universities*, RoutledgeFarmer, London.

OECD (2004), *On the Edge: Securing a Sustainable Future for Higher Education – Report of the Project on Financial Management and Governance of Higher Education*, Organisation for Economic Co-Operation and Development, Paris.

Plassard, J. M. and F. Berges (1998), *Financement de l'enseignement supérieur et redistribution*, Rapport pour la Direction de la Programmation et du Développement, Éducation Nationale, Paris.

Ramsden, B. (2003), *Review of the Initial Entry Rate into Higher Education*, National Statistics Quality Review Series, Department for Education and Skills.

Reay, D., M. David and S. Ball (2005), *Degrees of Choice: Class, Race, Gender and Higher Education*, Trentham Books, Stoke-on-Trent.

Richardson, W. (1999), "Historians and Educationists: The History of Education as a Field of Study in Post-War England Part II: 1972–96", *History of Education*, Vol. 28, No. 2, pp. 109–141.

Robbins, L. (1963), *Higher Education, Report and Appendices*, H.M.S.O., London.

Salter, B. and T. Tapper (1994), *The State and Higher Education*, Woburn Press, London.

Sanderson, M. (1972), *The Universities and British Industry 1850–1970*, Routledge and Kegan Paul, London.

Sanderson, M. (2005), *The History of Education and Economic History*, ESRC Seminar Series: Social Change in the History of Education, University of Exeter, 4 March.

Schultz, T. W. (1961), "Investment in Human Capital", *The American Economic Review*, Vol. 51, No. 1, pp. 1–17.

Shattock, M. (1994), *The UGC and the Management of British Universities*, Society for Research into Higher Education, Guildford.

Shinn, C. H. (1980), "The Beginnings of the University Grants Committee", *History of Education*, Vol. 9, No. 3, pp. 233–243.

Simon, B. (1989), "The History of Education", in: Gordon, P. and R. Szreter (eds.) *History of Education: the Making of a Discipline*, Economica, Paris, pp. 55–72.

Temple, P., J. Farrant and M. Shattock (2005), *New Variable Fee Arrangements: Baseline Institutional Case Studies for the Independent Commission*, Research Report for Department for Education and Skills, London.

Vallin, J. and F. Mesle (2001), *Tables de mortalité françaises pour les XIXe et XXe siècles et projections pour le XXIe siècle*, INED, Paris.

Verger, J. (1984), *Histoires des universités en France*, Bibliothèque Historique Privat, Toulouse.

Webber, G. (2003), "Funding in UK Universities: Living at the Edge", *Perspectives*, Vol. 7, No. 4, pp. 93–97.

Williams, G. (1992), *Changing Patterns of Finance in Higher Education*, The Society for Research into Higher Education and Open University Press, London.

Wolf, A. (2002), *Does Education Matter? Myths about Education and Economic Growth*, Penguin Books, London.

66

PROFESSIONALIZATION AND HIGHER EDUCATION IN GERMANY

Charles E. McClelland

Source: K. H. Jarausch (ed.) *The Transformation of Higher Learning, 1860–1930*, Stuttgart: Klett-Cotta, 1981, pp. 306–20.

What was the relationship between the professionalization of occupations and higher education in Germany between 1860 and 1930? Although the question artificially delimits our inquiry, the abiding centrality of higher education to professionalization in Germany cannot be disputed. This centrality in all advanced societies is assumed even by otherwise antagonistic analyses.[1] Furthermore, it was, if anything, greater in Germany, where the higher educational system had largely evolved to its classic form before high industrialism, was a state monopoly, and was in a position to control the demands of many occupational groups for professional legitimation.[2]

These preliminary remarks about the peculiarity of professionalization and higher education in Germany suggest an interactive triangle. The professions themselves (including their representative organizations) and the institutions of higher education were joined by the German states in pushing or retarding professionalization. The state was not only the ultimate arbiter of higher educational policy through its ministries and budgetary grants by offices and parliaments, its "state officials" in chairs and other professorial or educational offices, its examination commissions for aspirant professionals, its post-educational certification system and its decision-making powers concerning many individual careers. It was also a tone-giving abstraction, model, and dispenser of ideas of prestige.

The professions

In 1860, relatively few occupations were professionalized. Such general indicators of professionalization as highly specialized formal education,

codes and traditions of occupational behavior, special privileges and obligations, and organization of members of the same occupational group were
characteristic of only a few professions.[3] What set the professions off from
other trades was the general connection of their formal training with universities, the special mysteries of their knowledge, the high degree of elaboration
of their codes of behavior, privileges, and obligations, the autonomy of their
practice, and a large amount of respect for their organizations.

The most important professions in the German states in 1860 were the
traditional callings of clergyman, physician, graduate in law, and academic
professor. All clergymen and professors as well as a large proportion of the
legal graduates practiced their professions as officials of the church or state.
Partly for this reason, private professional organizations were weak or non-
existent, particularly on the national level. Official disapproval of agitation
for German national unification had throughout the early 19th century discouraged universal German professional organizations. Those that did exist
were often undifferentiated, such as the *Verband deutscher Naturforscher
und Ärzte* (League of German Natural Scientists and Physicians), which had
been founded in the 1840s to promote science.

Membership in a fully recognized profession was thus tied very strongly
to higher education and to the subsequent legally defined initiation into the
practical experience represented by the equivalent of years of poorly paid
internship. For this reason, "new" professions (e.g., engineer, schoolteacher,
private architect, or economist) tended to form vocal, activist organizations
that could lobby effectively for recognition of their status and, typically, the
upgrading of educational paths into their occupation.[4] The model for a
professional career had already been loosely set by the "old" professions.

The connection of the prestige of a learned profession with the officially
prescribed initial steps in a career (culminating in higher education, state
examinations and apprenticeship) indicates that association with public
authority (the churches or the state) rather than with the "professional"
organizations tended in 1860 to establish the identity of a profession. If
closeness to such authority lent prestige, distance from it had the opposite
effect.

The vaunted academic freedom of the universities and of professionals
in many areas of expertise to choose between state and private service were
all mere privileges granted by the state. German sociologists from Tönnies
(postively) to Dahrendorf (critically)[5] have pointed to the exceptional degree
to which German values in modern times have differed from "Western"
ones in emphasizing *Gemeinschaft* over *Gesellschaft* (public virtues over
private virtues), and the priority of demands by the state over those of the
individual or organizations of individuals. In this climate, professional
organizations have frequently had to battle harder than their counterparts
in other countries against the charge of serving only their "private" interests. They have had to emphasize their cooperation with the state and its

educational system, to align themselves with the state's rhetoric and imagery concerning their professions, and to press their demands in a very gingerly fashion.

The complex position of law graduates in the professional hierarchy may serve to illustrate this point. German law graduates could choose to enter one of two branches of the legal profession: the administrative and judicial divisions of the state or private practice. Despite the fact that such private attorneys *(Rechtsanwälte)* were officers of the court, they had always been held in lesser esteem than law graduates in the judiciary and civil service. But after a lowering of barriers to private practice, culminating in the national *Reichsanwaltsordnung* of 1878, private attorneys, no longer strongly tied to the state and the court system, ironically began complaining about a decline in their status. Though required to be as well-qualified as any judge, they did not have the prestige or, in most cases, the earnings of their colleagues on the bench. The number of attorneys increased both absolutely and in relationship to the population after 1878; the reform also appears to have led to a reduction of the attorneys' real average income. By turning private legal practice into a more genuinely "free" profession, the German states increased the prestige gap between the state lawyers (higher civil servants and judges) and attorneys at law. Despite the later organization of attorneys on a national scale and discussion of ways to raise the honor and incomes of private lawyers, the gap within the legal profession persisted until after 1930.[6]

The persistence of high prestige attached to the traditional university-oriented professions, especially those that involved direct civil service status, caused the evolution of the professions in Germany to follow a somewhat different path than in other countries. Sociological theory of professions that departs from relatively free British or American conditions cannot apply to professions in a highly bureaucratized and authoritarian society.

Both the "old" and "new" professions were organized into autonomous, private associations after 1860. Early attempts dating back to the 1840s and even before had mostly foundered on the rock of state opposition, particularly against national organizations. But by about 1860, the new current of nationalism in Germany and a more liberal attitude by many states led to more successful organizational attempts. German attorneys organized nationally in the *Deutscher Anwaltsverein* in 1870; physicians, in the *Deutscher Ärztevereinsbund* in 1873. Typically such organizations took the form of an alliance among already existing local groups; they then attempted to set up local chapters where none existed. Other members of the "old" professions were less quick to organize nationally, partly because they were not "free" practitioners like attorneys and physicians, but rather officials. The *Deutscher Juristentag,* or legal convention, did organize in 1860 and included some civil servants, such as judges, state's attorneys and professors, but it was cautious not to lobby for *Standesinteressen,* that is, the legal profession's self-interests: instead, it devoted much of its attention initially to reform and codification of German law. Even the private professional organizations claimed that an interest in the scientific and benevolent side of their occupations was the major reason for their foundation, and meetings of professional societies in the first decades after 1860 did indeed spend a great deal of time discussing non-material issues.

The remaining "old" professions were even slower and usually organized only in the face of some perceived threat. Protestant pastors founded the *Verband deutscher evangelischer Pfarrervereine* in 1892, following the lead of a local organization in Hessen that was prompted to act by a government decree ordering pastors not to get mixed up in anti-semitic agitation. University professors did not create an organization until 1907, largely spurred by their perception of unwarranted government interference in academic self-government. Once founded on high-sounding principles, however, most of the national associations of the "old" professions gradually spent more and more time on so-called *Standesfragen* or questions of material and status self-interest.[7]

"New" professionals followed a somewhat similar pattern. Relatively independent ones (engineers, dentists, and apothecaries) organized as early as the 1850s, whereas those employed by the state (e.g., schoolteachers, surveyors) delayed until much later. In the case of both "old" and "new" professional organizations, the tendency was not to press for the dissolving of ties with the state, but only for their rearrangement. Physicians and attorneys, for example, felt uncomfortable with the relative deregulation of practice by the legislation of the liberal phase of the North German Confederation and early *Reich.* The medical organizations constantly called on the state to suppress *Kurpfuscherei* (unlicensed health-care) and lobbied for legislative aid in their long guerilla war against Bismarck's health-insurance funds. Attorneys sought to raise their status by seeking government-granted honorary titles. Gymnasium teachers by the end of the 19th century clamored for officially proclaimed equality with the minor judiciary. Engineers fought unsuccessfully to have the state protect the title *Ingenieur* from use by mere mechanics and tinkerers. In all these cases and many others, one can perceive a thread of yearning for a nearness to public authority outside the ranks of the professions.

Some "new" professions with highly bureaucratized career patterns found it necessary to organize and agitate for greater state recognition of their professional status. Teaching groups in particular protested about their increasingly difficult economic position and their lack of professional autonomy. Non-tenured teachers in universities and other tertiary educational institutions, e.g., *Privatdozenten* and many *ausserordentliche Professoren,* organized a league of "non-full professors" (*Nichtordinarienbund*), and high school teachers did the same. A characteristic feature of public organizations in the German *Reich* after about 1880 was an increased pursuit of economic self-interest, sometimes quite blatantly. An example of the trend may be drawn from the history of the *Verein deutscher Ingenieure*. The VDI was founded in 1857 as a league of Germans in technology, industry, and applied science. For many decades it attempted to fuse the interests of engineers, laymen interested in technological developments and industrialists. While it rallied around a high vision of the social utility of *Technik*, many members began splitting off from it in the 1880s to join new, more vigorous interest-oriented groups.[8]

The organization even of such "old" professions as medicine and law indicates comparable difficulties in establishing universal norms of professional conduct and, additionally, an uphill battle to wrest control of professional standards from the state. Before 1873, the German medical profession was organized locally. Most states had some kind of *ärztliche Standesvertretung* (for example, "chambers" of physicians), but by no means all. The *Deutscher Ärztetag* might better be called a "convention" than an "association" of medical practitioners, but it often sought to influence government medical policy and to achieve a role for the local medical "chambers" in such matters as licensing, professional discipline, and titles. In 1882 the *Ärztetag* met in Nürnberg and called for a national physicians' law, parallel to similar legislation for German lawyers four years before. Such legislation was meant to unify professional conduct and rights and, very clearly, set up local medical organizations where they did not exist and grant all such organizations sweeping rights over the profession. Their demands suggest the relative organizational weakness of the German medical profession previously and the correspondingly large role of the state organs of medical affairs.[9]

Despite slow beginnings, by 1930, virtually every professional group had organized and indeed overorganized. The characteristic feature of this later wave of organization was, however, its heterogeneity. Among all the professions, old as well as new, it proved impossible to achieve a national unanimity and corresponding singleness of representation. Traditions of localism long outlived the unification of Germany into a single state in 1871. Despite the political unity of Germany, admission to and regulation of the medical profession, the bar and bench, the clergy, and university teaching were still matters for the states, not the *Reich*, to administer. By the eve of the First World War, virtually all professional organizations, both old and new, were clamoring in one way or another for more state intervention to protect their status and incomes. These demands only increased in number and volume in the unsettled era between the world war and the collapse of the Weimar Republic. Thus to understand the professions and their organizations, we must also understand their relationship to the state.

The state and the professions

The new princely *Polizeistaat* of the late 17th and 18th centuries assumed, along with greater tasks of war and taxation, an increasing amount of responsibility for the "public welfare." At the same time, the professions were held in fairly low esteem by both the public and the princely bureaucracies.

At the beginning of the 18th century, for example, the king of Prussia decreed that lawyers in his realm should wear knee-length black robes. He did this not to heighten their dignity, but merely to make them identifiable in the street, so that the people could "see the scoundrels coming."[10] At about the same time, an official of Hanover referred to physicians as "exterminating angels" whose main tasks were to hurry along the death of their patients and bury them methodically.[11]

By the end of the 18th century, however, many states had begun to take measures to improve the quality of the professions and to bureaucratize them. As universities were reformed and granted much greater freedom of instruction, examinations became more and more necessary to insure that graduate candidates for professions had not overly abused their freedom from standard courses. Official boards were appointed by the government to administer state examinations. Medical, legal and clerical careers began, by the early 19th century, with a post-university examination and often an extended period of on-the-job training. Thus the state took away with one hand a part of the new academic freedom it granted to students with the other.

Because studying for a profession was expensive and the unpaid period of post-examination training financially burdensome, the state's requirements in effect discouraged all but a few poor people from the professions. Government pressure helped keep the size of the student body and the old professions relatively stable until about 1870.

The German states achieved this stability by discouraging the formation of independent professional organizations and upholding regulation by government or quasi-government agencies such as the *Ärztekammer* or local physicians' chambers. Not only were competence and professional standards determined by the states through examinations and official supervision of professional conduct; but even the political and religious opinions of the professionals were carefully scrutinized. Since most members of the old "free professions" were in one way or another public employees of the state, they were easily intimidated.

The new professions emerging in the 19th century enjoyed comparatively more freedom from government interference, at least initially. The state authorities tended at first to look upon the new professions as mere trades. Even the education, certification and supervision of the new professions differed radically from the old: schools for engineers or schoolteachers were little more than drill grounds and barracks for their immature charges. They were allowed far less chance to develop independent minds and develop self-esteem than university students.

Between 1850 and 1930, however, the German states and the *Reich* itself went through several distinct phases in attitudes toward the professions, both old and new. A period of liberalism in the 1870s produced greater independence for some of the older professions, notably medicine with the *Gewerbeordnung* of 1869 and law with the *Reichsanwaltsordnung* of 1878. From the 1880s until the First World War, however, the German states resumed their supervisory role, though without quite the crushing authoritarianism of the early 19th century. Private professional organizations, for example, were now tolerated and even heeded occasionally by government policymakers.

The Weimar Republic, by tendency both liberal and weak, was unable or unwilling to intervene very effectively in matters impinging on the security of the professions.

This bare sketch of the relationship between the German states and professions may lead us into the arena in which both interacted most strongly, namely in that of education. It was here, through the virtual state monopoly of higher education, that the German professions were most profoundly affected by state power. Yet the institutions of higher education themselves had a considerable amount of autonomy, and professors were able to exert influence on both state policy and the professions as such. It is the peculiar relationship among state, education and professions to which we now turn.

Higher education and the professions

Between 1860 and 1930 the higher educational system raised the standards for all learned professions, most dramatically for the new professions. It legitimated the professions through a rising amount of study of increasingly complex information over a longer and more arduous course. Working in the opposite direction, however, it had no way to choke off the rising stream of would-be professionals through the system.

The traditional monopoly of the universities over preparation for the recognized and limited professions in 1860 gave way to broader inclusion of non-university higher education by 1930, as in the case of the bestowal of degree-granting rights on the technical colleges. But the universities retained in many ways a model character throughout the period. Efforts both to upgrade the status of non-university tertiary institutions of education in the direction of university-level *Wissenschaft* and the effort to introduce into the universities study programs regarded by many professors as suspiciously "practical" testify to the continuing residual prestige of the traditional university model.

The expansion and diversification of higher education therefore took the form of founding new specialized professional schools instead of incorporating new pedagogical functions into existing universities (or even technical schools). Despite some degree of openness to added pedagogical functions in the 18th century, the universities of the early 19th century rejected the inclusion of "practical" training *(Ausbildung)* and accepted instead a mission of providing almost exclusively "theoretical" training, preceded more and more necessarily by the classical secondary education in the gymnasium. Government educational officials themselves accepted the distinction between this ethically and spiritually superior *Bildung* even as they perceived the need for "practical" higher education. The result was the foundation of technical, agricultural, etc. schools, which were often placed under the control of such government bureaus as that of commerce.

With the passage of time, these schools evolved into more clearly tertiary institutions, with student bodies of a median age comparable to university students, a more complex curriculum with the growing introduction of theoretical courses and rising qualifications for the teaching staff. But the pattern of separate institutional creations for new tertiary educational needs was set firmly enough by the 1860s that the universities were never seriously considered as seats for these new departments of applied learning. Such efforts as were made to integrate technological training into the university curriculum were notable for their rarity, and even they encountered discouragingly stiff resistance from the universities themselves.[12]

This continued division between universities and other tertiary educational institutions set parameters for professional self-consciousness among graduates of both types. In the thinking of one important group "after a synthesis [of the two types of education] had failed, disputes over rank, social claims and questions of titles became merely an expression of the independent rise of the engineers, a part of the confrontation between realism and idealism, technology and educational humanism entrenched in traditions."[13]

The culture of *Wissenschaft*, the maintenance and transmission of which the university professors more and more consciously invoked in the late 19th century, was paradoxically being undermined to some degree within the universities themselves. Many contemporaries complained about *Brotstudenten,* who were allegedly intent on acquiring only the minimum of knowledge to pass on into one of the learned professions as rapidly as possible. *Brotstudenten* threatened the professoriate, for the faculties could not very well defend their case against admitting the claims of the emerging *new* professions unless they could maintain in the training of the *old* professions a high level of Humboldt's "purposeless" scholarly and scientific study for its own sake. To use Jamous and Peloille's terms, they sought to introduce a higher degree of "indeterminate" professional knowledge. A good example of this effort may be found in the training and examining of law students.

The guarantee of *Lehrfreiheit* and *Lernfreiheit* (freedom of teaching and learning) in German universities theoretically left the student free to "mold" *(bilden)* his own spirit through his own choice of lectures, readings, and possibly original research. This idiosyncratic confrontation between the student and knowledge was supposed to produce a more flexible, broad and active mind, one ultimately capable of grasping the principles of any subject rather than one limited to a corpus of passively acquired expertise. For professionalization, this kind of education had serious contributions to make: the student could internalize the responsibility and autonomy of professional practice before entering the profession. The student's socialization was in theory more effective for being self-acquired rather than imposed as a "code" from without.

Professions also required minimum common standards of expertise, however, and these were in practice imposed on the aspiring student by his consciousness of the state examinations awaiting him after the university. The lawyer, clergyman and physician had to trim his university courses to the expected pattern of state examinations. It was well-known to students through rumor and, in some cases, government prescription which professors' courses were "musts" for the successful passage of state examinations. Furthermore, many senior professors were actually members of the state examination commissions, a fact which made their lectures even more compelling.

Despite their reluctance to include new "practical" disciplines, universities were not wholly averse to the acceptance of new "scientific" ones, as Peter Lundgreen has pointed out. Specialization within traditional disciplines ultimately caused the creation of new chairs, seminars and institutes. These in turn sometimes legitimized the claims of practitioners of these new disciplines that they constituted a new profession, or at least a distinct subdivision of a profession. The multiplication of chairs and institutes in chemistry after 1860, for example, was followed by a rising demand for recognition of the graduate chemist. By the mid-1880s, with the increasing importance of the German chemical industry, demands were raised to introduce special state examinations for "academically trained" chemists so as to distinguish this emerging *profession* from the mere *trade* of chemist practiced by people without sufficient academic education.[14] The *Verein Deutscher Chemiker* (German Chemists' Association), led by many chemistry professors, not only began demanding a state examination for chemists in 1896 but came to view chemical education as something best rounded off with an academic doctorate. More professorships and higher standards of instruction constituted other demands by German chemists concerning education.[15]

Still, such recognition of new professional disciplines by the creation of universities' chairs often stumbled over the determined resistance of conservative professors. As late as 1919, for example, the field of sociology was denounced as inappropriate for university study by the historian Georg von Below.[16] New disciplines and specialties such as psychology, psychiatry, public hygiene, social work, pedagogical science and many more struggled with mixed success to find a place in the traditional higher educational system.

In the end, efforts by professors themselves to resist "chartering" new professional specialties could only slow down but not prevent their expansion. Even under the German Empire, but most definitely under the Weimar Republic, such attempts served only to delay the implementation of new chairs and institutes, or to force the establishment of higher educational programs for new disciplines into non-university channels.

A good example of this tendency may be drawn from one of the least successful new professions, public elementary schoolteaching. Dissatisfaction with status, working conditions, and salary was a chronic story in this occupation, but by the end of the 19th century schoolteachers had decided that demanding university education as a career qualification would help alleviate all problems. Finally, after World War I, reforms in this direction were begun, but not completed. Instead of sending future elementary schoolteachers to a university just as gymnasium teachers always had been, the old teacher-training institutes were upgraded here and there into "pedagogical academies" the status of which was not really equal to that of universities or technical colleges. The teachers' failure to achieve full academic study damaged their ability to improve their social prestige and incomes right down to the end of our period.[17] By contrast, teachers in higher schools (Oberlehrer) were able to increase their status through harder examinations, more semesters of attendance at the universities and more successful lobbying by their organizations. By 1909 they had won their long battle for nominal equivalence in rank with judges and for higher salaries.[18]

The rapid and disproportionate expansion of enrollments in tertiary institutions of all types, marked enough between 1860 and 1900, and stunning thereafter, indicated a potential weakening of professorial control over recruitment into the professions. By general agreement among contemporaries, the rapid expansion involved mostly careerists grasping for professions attainable only by university or other tertiary training. The universities had to admit all qualified secondary school graduates as one part of the Humboldtian heritage, and the professoriate had few effective weapons with which to winnow out unfit or poor students.[19] With the exception of medicine, there were no examinations before students left and controls through seminar or laboratory work could only function if the students submitted to such exercises. Even physical attendance at lectures was uncontrollable in most disciplines, as Gustav Schmoller, a professor of law and economics, complained in 1886.[20] Yet professorial annoyance with class cutting did not lead anybody to suggest obligatory class attendance, for that was held to be a serious breach of academic freedom. Furthermore, greater restrictions on the student body might have reduced the increased lecture-fee income of the professoriate. Thus the faculty members had to choose means of influencing the professional training of students other than external coercion.

The most obvious of these means lay in the example of the professors themselves. The wide acceptance among the professoriate of the idea of *Wissenschaft* as a goal orientation meant that German professors were hired and promoted largely on the basis of their scholarly and scientific productivity. Professors of medicine, law and the natural sciences, for example, contributed to the advance of those disciplines in the broader society with discoveries or, in the case of law, advice to governments on the framing of legislation. Theologians and humanists in the universities set the parameters of discussion and research in their fields, with direct effects on the activities of pastors, teachers and publicists. Likewise, professors in the technical colleges made direct contributions to German engineering.

For this reason, the role model of the professor as an examplar of his profession had an important, if unmeasurable, impact on students. In the culture of *Wissenschaft,* the student ideally learned method, not merely the results such method had produced. To be sure, in the increasingly overcrowded German higher educational institutions, not all students could or would avail themselves of the opportunity to learn method in the relatively intimate and demanding arena of the seminar or laboratory course. But for those who did, great opportunities were available for trying their own hand at applying the most advanced methods; and the result, when successful, should have been a heightened degree of professional self-confidence on the part of the students. Did those students whose studies were carried out in close proximity to the professoriate therefore experience different career patterns in their later professions, when compared to the *Brotstudenten,* who did the minimum to gain access to the professions? Clearly in some professions, such as academic teaching, the difference was crucial, whereas in other fields, such as law, it may have been far less significant.

A more concrete influence of the professoriate upon the professional preparation of German students operated through the post-educational institution of examination boards for the professions. Their composition and the nature of the test differed in detail from one profession to another and from one German state to another. They were by law and custom *state* examining boards, so that the states determined in principle who would be appointed to them. The corpus of required professional knowledge was determined in general by government regulations. The boards usually contained a certain number of civil servants whose expertise lay in the area to be examined. For example, officials of the established state churches would sit on examining boards for clergymen; those from the medical departments, on medical examining boards; those from the judiciary or general administrative departments, on boards to examine graduates in the law; and so on. But the professoriate could influence both the composition of the boards and the content of the examinations. On the one hand professors were informally consulted by the government about appointment to boards and regulations concerning examination content, and on the other hand they were actually appointed to the boards themselves.

The formal composition of the boards could range from 100% civil servants, as in the case of the Prussian state examination commissions for lawyers and civil servants down to 1864, to 100% professors, as was traditionally the case for candidates for teaching positions in the universities. The professoriate agitated, sometimes successfully, for greater formal representation of professors on those boards having few or no such examiners. In the case of the legal examining boards, they argued that testing by civil servants alone led to an exaggerated emphasis on practical knowledge to the detriment of theoretical knowledge obtained through higher education in the law. Since the legal examining boards were among the most frequently and vehemently attacked by the German professoriate (and often enough by the legal voluntary organizations such as the *Deutscher Juristentag*), it may be illustrative to dwell on their history at some length.

Certain German states already had by the 1870s examining boards for judges, civil servants *(Verwaltungsbeamte)* and attorneys that were entirely composed of university professors. Württemberg was widely regarded as possessing one of the best of these, and the relative seriousness of the study of law at the University of Tübingen was believed to derive from the professorial nature of the examining commission.[21] Prussia, however, while amending its laws in 1864 and 1869 to provide for a university professor on the legal examining boards, assigned a preponderant influence to the members of the state judiciary and thus to such "practical" expertise as knowledge of how to draft a brief correctly. Law professors complained from the 1870s through the 1920s about the results. These included lax attention to formal university study of the law, reliance by students on private coaches *(Einpauker)* to prepare them for examinations, and a well-deserved public skepticism about the stringency of law examinations and, consequently, the qualifications of those who passed them.[22] Even professors were divided over the question of creating boards solely from professors or from a mixture of professors and civil servants. The German Jurists' Association resolved on a combination of both, thereby criticizing the Prussian practice of overrepresenting non-university legal experts.[23] By the 1920s, the pressure from university professors and the voluntary associations to which they belonged had resulted in somewhat greater influence by professors on North German examining boards, but not enough to satisfy the professoriate. In the eyes of some professors, the inauguration of a codified civil law *(Bürgerliches Gesetzbuch)* for all Germany in 1900 as the basis for most university teaching had merely encouraged students to think in ever more "practical" terms about the law and to overlook the indeterminate side of legal knowledge connected to a broader culture:

The university should bring before the soul of the student the world of law as a product of culture in a systematic context; it should present law as conditioned by political, economic, ethical, and religious factors; it should show the student—always in a systematic context—how the norms of law dispose themselves around this cultural life and under the standard of justice, and how individual questions fit into the system of law.[24]

The ongoing thrust and parry of "practical" against "theoretical" orientations in legal examinations involved the certification of not just one but several professions departing from legal examinations. The civil service had its own second examination for its young members after a stated period of service, whereas the bar did not. Thus for the sake of the social standing of the German bar, if for no other reason, an examination system that would certify the kind of values mentioned above had more meaning than an easy, publicly-despised one. And German law professors were able to impress this view on the bar, at least until it began to split in the 1920s: "The elite of the profession consisted of highly competent lawyers steeped in an idealistic conception of their profession and, strange perhaps in as mundane an occupation as the law [sic], in ideals of *Bildung,* of literary culture, and a refined personality."[25] It is perhaps significant that the Weimar Republic brought a heightened consciousness of the division between the traditional court lawyers and the rapidly increasing corporate lawyers. Diminished economic security for many practitioners prompted calls for a *numerus clausus* to limit the number of lawyers—and more demands for heightened professorial powers on the examining boards.

In contrast, the medical faculties in our period had considerably more control over admission to their profession. Not only did they participate more in post-university examining boards, but they insisted on examinations given to aspiring medical students in the middle of their studies. The problem with German medical education therefore does not appear to have lain so much with quality, but with quantity. Most foreign observers gave German medical training high marks and urged emulation by their own countries.[26] But the German medical professional organizations, to which most medical professors belonged, raised their voices ever more loudly after the 1880s against the production of too many M.D.s by the universities.[27]

In at least one case, certification by professors alone could raise complaints that too little attention was being paid to practical knowledge. Graduate economists, whose numbers grew dramatically after World War I, confronted this problem:

The study of economics in the postwar era has developed into a subject for the masses that culminates in the doctoral examination, especially that of the *Dr. rer. pol.* . . . On the one hand, a purely scientific examination was devalued; on the other hand, a purely theoretical training in no way sufficed for a practical profession. Professors of economics and economists in the public positions and the private sector took exception to all this.[28]

Such an admission by professors themselves that academic credentials alone (in this case, the doctorate) are inadequate preparation for the professions indicates that professors preferred to influence state examining bodies, not abolish them in favor of a less controllable system of university certification alone.

In addition, the professors had at their disposal the obvious professionalizing tool of curricular determination. The freedom of teaching for the professor was far less circumscribed than the freedom of learning for the profession-bound student. The *venia docendi* of most German professors gave them the right to offer courses on subjects of their choosing. Nevertheless, professors (particularly those with chairs) were obliged by their office to lay out systematically the basic knowledge in their field in the course of "public" lectures. Since the chairholders giving these lectures tended to be the leading professional authorities in their institutions, their course content had a heavy impact on the professionalization of students. Given the diversity of the entire German system of higher education, there was no uniform professionalization. Moreover at least those students who availed themselves of the chance, could also take the "private" and specialized courses offered by *Privatdozenten* and *ausserordentliche Professoren* in particular. Along with a constantly growing number of smaller advanced classes such as seminars and "exercises" *(Übungen)*, these provided in theory a wider field for the development of professional autonomy. But their number and the quantity of their student clientele did not grow as fast as the general student population, particularly after 1900. Thus it must be concluded that large numbers of students made little use of them and clung instead to the straight and narrow path of professional preparation in the main-line courses. For such students the curriculum thus meant exposure to the *Ordinarien*, whose prestige was also reflected by their highly visible role in the professional organizations of Germany.

Professorial participation in such organizations closes the circle of professional definitions through higher education. Although statistics are difficult to find in secondary literature, a few figures are indicative. In an old profession such as law, legal professors were disproportionately represented in the governing levels of the *Deutscher Juristentag*. Founded chiefly by practitioners, this national organization had by 1900 eight professors out of 20 jurists sitting on the governing board. Of 36 presidents of the organization between 1860 and 1931, no less than 28 were university professors.[29]

Even in the relatively new professions, academic teachers appear to have taken a strong role in voicing the concerns of professional organizations about educational matters. The German Chemists' Society, to name but one example, turned to professors of chemistry for leadership in tightening up recruitment and curriculum in higher education.[30] It is a relative rarity in the annals of professional organizations before 1930 to read pronouncements that professional higher education was "too academic" as members of the League of German Architects (including Taut and Gropius) complained in the 1920s. But even in a case such as this, those who sought fundamental educational reform for private architects were operating from a base in the *Bauhaus* and were themselves teachers.[31]

Although conclusions about the relationship of professionalization and higher education in Germany between 1860 and 1930 must remain very tentative at this stage of research, a few generalizations emerge for further testing. First, the professions themselves grew vigorously in this period, as did their representative organizations. These organizations possessed less unity, singleness of purpose and autonomy than comparable ones in Britain or the United States. In the course of time, many of them evolved away from preoccupation with the scientific or scholarly basis of their profession and increasingly became lobbies for special interests. As such, they were not *vocally* concerned about higher education (although some concern was always shown). The professional organizations appear to have been generally satisfied with higher educational preparation, with two major exceptions. These were a demand for longer periods of higher education or tighter examination procedures and, after World War I, the call for a *numerus clausus* restriction on admission to higher education as a means of throttling "overcrowding" in the professions. The "new" professions demanded higher education or equal recognition of their special kind of training with that provided by universities, and they were somewhat less concerned about *numerus clausus;* but the tendency remained comparable.

The professional organizations did not need to concern themselves very much with changing higher education because the state guided both the standards of training and the certification of the trained. Despite occasional charges of corruption or at least laxity in this system, most practitioners appear to have accepted the state's monopolistic role. They asked only that examining boards and curricula become themselves more professionalized.

For reasons somewhat exogenous to the professions, the German professoriate had itself adopted a modern professional ethic by the 1870s and led the assault on poor educational preparation for the professions. This was true first in the universities, later in the technical colleges, which emerged as true professional schools toward the end of the 19th century. Since professors came to play a stronger and wider role in the state certification process *and* played a vital role in professional organizations, they were in a position to dominate or at least lead discussion of educational reform. As both state officials and highly respected members of professional organizations, professors were in an excellent position to mediate between the two. Down to 1918, at least, they used this influence to improve professional education and lure greater funding from the states, while also doing little to stem the flood tide of enrollments and qualified professionals pouring through the universities and technical colleges. The result in the 1920s was a well-trained but vastly under-employed professional force that one critic called ominously in 1932 *Doktoren ohne Brot.*[32]

Notes

1 See Talcott Parsons, "Professions," *International Encyclopedia of the Social Sciences* (New York, 1968), 536–46; and H. Jamous and B. Peloille, "Professions or Self-Perpetuating Systems? Changes in the French University-Hospital System," in J. A. Jackson (ed.), *Professions and Professionalization* (Cambridge, 1970), 109–152. For a sample of German conceptions of professions (which differ markedly from Anglo-American ones), see J. F. Volrad Deneke, *Klassifizierung der Freien Berufe* (Cologne and Berlin, 1969) 13–30; Hans Kairat, *"Professions" oder "Freie Berufe"* (Berlin, 1969), 12–38; Helmut C. H. Gatzen, "Beruf bei Martin Luther und in der industriellen Gesellschaft" (Dissertation Münster, 1964); also Arthur Salz, "Zur Geschichte der Berufsidee," *Archiv für Sozialwissenschaften und Sozialpolitik,* 37 (1913), 380–423.

2 To illustrate this point, one might compare the repeated invocations of *Wissenschaft* (science or, more broadly, a theoretically grounded expertise) as the highest goal of education by German professors with the constant attention to "customer service" among American professors at the end of the 19th century. See Burton J. Bledstein, *The Culture of Professionalism: The Middle Class and the Development of Higher Education in America* (New York, 1976), esp. Chapter 8.

3 It might be mentioned that some of these characteristics had at one time been found in the artisan occupations organized into guilds, which were continuing their long decline in German states in 1860.

4 G. Hortleder, *Das Gesellschaftsbild des Ingenieurs* (Frankfurt, 1970), 18–20; Hans Schimank, *Der Ingenieur* (Cologne, 1961), 39–41.

5 Ferdinand Tönnies, *Gemeinschaft und Gesellschaft* (Leipzig, 1887); Ralf Dahrendorf, *Society and Democracy in Germany* (Garden City, N.Y., 1967).

6 Fritz Ostler, *Der deutsche Rechtsanwalt, 1871–1971* (Essen, 1971), 207–9.

7 For a superficial survey of the German professional organizations down to 1906, see W. Kulemann, *Die Berufsvereine,* 6 vols. (Jena, 1908), esp. vol. 1.

8 Hortleder, 44–9.

9 Anon., "Die korporative Organisation der Ärzte," *Schmollers Jahrbuch,* 6 (1882), 1363–4.

10 Adolf Weissler, *Geschichte der Rechtsanwaltschaft* (Leipzig, 1905), 310–16.

11 J. G. von Meiern, cited in Götz von Selle, *Die Georg-August-Universität zu Göttingen, 1737–1937* (Göttingen, 1937), 27.

12 For an example of one such effort see Karl-Heinz Manegold, *Universität, Technische Hochschule und Industrie. Ein Beitrag zur Emanzipation der Technik im 19. Jahrhundert unter besonderer Berücksichtigung der Bestrebungen Felix Kleins* (Berlin, 1970), esp. Chapter 3.

13 Manegold, 80.

14 See H. Ortloff, "Über die Gewerbefreiheit der Chemiker und die Bezahlung ihrer Konsultationen," *Schmollers Jahrbuch,* 9 (1885), 969–71.

15 B. L. P. Rassow, *Geschichte des Vereins deutscher Chemiker* (Leipzig, 1912), 74–7.

16 Georg von Below, "Soziologie als Lehrfach. Kritischer Beitrag zur Hochschulreform," *Schmollers Jahrbuch*, 43 (1919), 1271–1322.

17 For a full picture of elementary schoolteachers, especially their educational background, see Rainer Bölling, *Volksschullehrer und Politik. Der deutsche Lehrerverein 1918–1933* (Wiesbaden, 1978); Manfred Heinemann (ed.), *Der Lehrer und seine Organisation* (Stuttgart, 1977); and Helmuth Kittel, *Die Entstehung der Pädagogischen Hochschulen, 1926–1932* (Berlin, 1957), a less critical account than Bölling's.

18 Hartmut Titze, "Die soziale und geistige Umbildung des preußischen Oberlehrerstandes von 1870 bis 1914," *Zeitschrift für Pädagogik*, Beiheft 14 (1977), 107–28.

19 For a rather interesting comparison of the German and American systems, with much praise for American hardness toward poorly qualified students, see Heinrich Waentig, "Die amerikanischen Law schools und die Reform des Rechtsunterrichts in Preußen," *Schmollers Jahrbuch*, 26 (1902), 1439–68.

20 Gustav Schmoller, Review of Georges Blondel, *De l'enseignement de droit dans les universites allemandes* (Paris, 1885), in *Schmollers Jahrbuch*, 10 (1886), 613.

21 See von Kräwel, "Die einheitliche Regelung unserer ersten juristischen Staatsprüfung," *Schmollers Jahrbuch*, 9 (1885), 512. Other states having a completely professorial examining board by this time included Bavaria, Saxony, and Hesse. Although attorneys were "liberated" from many regulations in 1878, they still had to qualify in the same way as aspirants for judgeships.

22 For a detailed discussion of the situation in the 1870s, see Otto Gierke, "Die juristische Studienordnung," *Schmollers Jahrbuch*, 1 (1877); 1–32; for the 1920s, Ernst Heymann, "Die juristische Studienreform," *Schmollers Jahrbuch*, 46 (1922), 109–161.

23 Von Kräwel, "Die einheitliche Regelung," 516.

24 Heymann, "Juristische Studienreform," 117.

25 Dietrich Rüschemeyer, *Lawyers and Their Society* (Cambridge, MA., 1973), 178.

26 A classic example is found in Abraham Flexner, *Medical Education: A Comparative Study* (New York, 1925).

27 Not only were professors prominent in the League of German Medical Associations *(Deutscher Ärztevereinsbund)*, which was to be expected; they also joined the purely interest-oriented *Leipziger Verein (Hartmann-Bund)* in large numbers. Well over half of German medical professors belonged to it by 1910, according to Bernhard Puppe, *Die Bestrebungen der deutschen Ärzte zu gemeinsamer Wahrnehmung ihrer wirtschaftlichen Interessen* (Wiesbaden, 1911), 21.

28 W. F. Bruck, "Zur Reform des Bildungswesens der Juristen und Volkswirte," *Schmollers Jahrbuch*, 52 (1928), 458.

29 Deutscher Juristentag, *Verhandlungen des 25. Deutschen Juristentages* (Tübingen, 1900), III, xiii; Ernst von Caemmerer *et al.* (eds.), *Hundert Jahre deutsches Rechtsleben*, 2 vols. (Karlsruhe, 1960), 2, 45 ff.

30 Rassow, *Verein deutscher Chemiker*, 74 ff.

31 Bernhard Gaber, *Die Entwicklung des Berufsstandes der freischwebenden Architekten dargestellt an der Geschichte des Bundes Deutscher Architekten BDA* (Essen, 1966), 124–8.

32 Friedrich Maetzel, "Doktoren ohne Brot," *Die Tat*, 23 (1931–2), 1004–11.

67

NATIONAL SOCIALISM AND THE GERMAN UNIVERSITIES

Notker Hammerstein

Source: *History of Universities* XVIII(I) (2003): 170–88.

The historian's job, in large part, is to present past events in a sober, object-ive, and methodologically sound way. With regard to the history of the Third Reich, of course, much remains highly charged, and with good reason. Even today, the eruption of barbarism in twentieth-century civilized Europe remains difficult to grasp. Nevertheless, scholars have made some progress in investigating our recent past. But even as we are increasingly well-informed about the period, new efforts are still necessary—even more so as regards the history of the German universities during the Third Reich, which for a long time eluded any rigorous investigation. No doubt there reigned the assumption that it was best to dispose of uncomfortable mem-ories and let matters rest quietly. Indeed, an article on the role of geography as a discipline during the Third Reich dates critical reflection only to the 1980s and 1990s, when the collective silence was finally broken.[1] Or, as the intro-duction to that same volume put it: 'The traditional view of the relationship between science, technology and National Socialism was radically ques-tioned ... The former construction of contrast between "bad", distorted science and "good", true science, being highly ideological itself, gave way to a rational, neutral "Science is what scientists do"'.[2] Not only have uni-versities, industrial laboratories, and students been pressed into research in order to achieve better and more differentiated analyses, but publications in the history of science and universities have proliferated—as the biblio-graphies of the ASTA of the Mannheim University make clear.[3]

All this is undoubtedly true: our knowledge, especially about the sciences, have greatly expanded and gained in depth and scope. Monographs on various disciplines and their practitioners during the Third Reich—once a rare exception—have multiplied. These new studies have led to equally new insights, at the same time refining and affirming those admittedly few, but

267

reliable, works on the history of universities during the Third Reich already written. Thus, the basic outline of how the Nazi policy for scholarly research —if ever there was such a thing—developed is pretty clear. The same is true of the policies of the universities and research institutes during the Third Reich.[4] This paper aims to provide a brief outline of this relationship.

The question that first comes to mind is: why did this examination of Third Reich universities and scholarship begin so late? Apart from an understandable reluctance to uncover past sins, there exists another—and to my mind more crucial—reason. The professors who remained in office, or who where reinstated after 1945, were convinced that the German universities had remained 'in essence healthy' ('*innerlich intakt*'). Such a judgement was reiterated by Hermann Heimpel—to quote only this distinguished professor—during a 1956 debate in which the German universities were accused of being shackled by tradition and infiltrated by Nazis: 'The German university is healthy to the core' he vehemently responded.[5]

And yet another line of defence has also been mobilized. The last vice-chancellor of the University of Freiburg during the Nazi period—the mathematician Wilhelm Süss—insisted that he had accepted academic offices 'in the hope of leading the university through the difficult times with its internal integrity intact'.[6] And, indeed, he was seemingly able to do so. Not only did he manage to replace the hard-line Nazi who led the lecturers' association (*Dozentenbund*), but he enabled a persecuted colleague with Jewish relations (*jüdisch-versippt*, as it was called) to survive.[7] This second position may be summed up as follows: many decent Germans remained in their positions in order to prevent something worse. That, at least, is how they saw it. The fact that this also allowed the Nazi state and the Nazi system to continue to function—and this applied from as early as 1933— seemingly did not occur to them.[8] Such may be characterized as one of the 'dilemmas of . . . upright men', to paraphrase Heilbron's characterization of Max Planck. Even Planck, the international famous 'spokesman for German Science' believed 'with many others . . . that Hitler would have to moderate Nazi policies in order to stay in office. This is a capital point in judging the behaviour of Planck and men like him. They hoped that what they deemed to be a valuable contribution of National Socialism—the call to national cultural renewal, unity, and glory—would subsist, and they expected that the excesses would fade away'.[9] Of course, such a 'justification' could hold true only for the first few years. Yet even as time went on, there remained the problem of being a scientist of German nationality, of being a German not wanting to leave his mother country. Heilbron shows just how difficult the choices were that these men faced: 'There are those who think that Planck could and should have done more'. Even Einstein and Max von Laue criticized him for not being more *obdurate*. 'But whereas Einstein was a free spirit, who had little attachment to Germany and felt no responsibility for the institutions that supported him there, and Laue was not so highly placed as to suppose that he could influence the course of events, Planck had both responsibility and position, and a rule for exercising them. He decided that it would be more fruitful to stay and salvage rather than to run and gesture. And he had his fruit in the nuanced independence of the Academy and the Kaiser-Wilhelm-Gesellschaft during the tenure of office'.[10] This has already raised questions that would have been incomprehensible to most contemporaries. After all—and it is important to remind ourselves of this—the Nazi state was not based on rule of law. It was a barbarous dictatorship that did not shy away from annihilating those who opposed it, even supposed opponents, not to mention entire ethnic groups.[11] Middle-class people [bürgerliche Menschen] were often intimidated. It required a great deal of courage to oppose this system as well as the broad spirit of the times.[12] There is an anecdote told about a young man's conversation with the ferocious Nazi adversary, Ernst Robert Curtius. When the young man said that he, for one, couldn't take the National Socialists seriously, the famous Romanist answered: 'You have to take a government seriously when it maintains concentration camps'.[13]

But let us return to the notion of 'preventing something worse'. In our context, this means looking at the development of the scholarly disciplines themselves. Did the eruption of National Socialism mean that the academic disciplines were instrumentalized and ideologized? Were research and teaching paralyzed? Were the only successful disciplines those that served the Nazis' belligerent intentions? Did universities and academic disciplines become nazified?

To start with the last question first. Astonishingly, the Nazis had no genuine programme for the universities; indeed, they had no fundamental position at all on academic matters. The Nazi 'world view' was too crude and too sketchy to permit any clear directives for universities and scholarship to be extrapolated from them.[14] The profound irrationalism, the value placed on instinct and force, the cult of youth, and the anti-intellectualism of Nazism did not dovetail well with the ethos of the universities. Hitler's deep mistrust of anything even remotely academic, his low opinion of scholarly achievements, and his own superficial education meant that he himself issued no directives that his followers could have used as guidelines. He despised intellectuals, fearing their rationality and authority. Moreover, they prevented physical training, military drill, blind activism, and a blind cult of the *Führer* from being accepted as the real—and the highest—goals of education. Intellect weakens the instinct, Hitler once said, and his opinion of academics was that 'unfortunately, we need them; otherwise—I don't know—they could be exterminated or something one day'.[15]

This left Hitler's companions and henchmen rather puzzled with regards to what was to be done with the universities. Self-proclaimed interpreters therefore, at least in the early years, attempted to impose their views on what constituted National Socialist scholarship. These included the early vice-chancellors Martin Heidegger, Ernst Kriegk, and Alfred Baeumler. All were in agreement on this matter: 'We must seek a new harmony; we must endeavour to regain the lost totality and, in addition, to elevate and strengthen the stunted and neglected sides of life'. Among other nonsense, it was claimed that under all circumstances scholarship depends 'upon nationality: its bearer is the heightened, selectively bred folk personality', in the words of Kriegk.[16]

Thus, in fact, there existed no such thing as National Socialist scholarship that could have taken its place alongside, or that would have replaced, the older academic disciplines. What was praised as Nazi scholarship, and what would be established in the universities, was a rather shabby thing. It included military science—it was never clear what exactly this meant—and the study of races or racial theory. To be sure, the consequences of this 'scholarship' were more than disastrous. To start with, it constituted a part of eugenics or racial hygiene, generally studied in Europe and America at the time, which insisted that humans and peoples are biologically determined.[17] After the rediscovery of Mendel, Darwin's work was further continued with the result that at the end of the nineteenth century, a number of anthropological and biological notions intended to address social and medical problems were brewed up together. The Nazis developed their own policy based on this brew, which led to the death of countless people. They also made these ideas, which elsewhere in Europe were regarded only to a limited extent as theoretically viable, into the fundamental doctrine governing knowledge of the world and of people. As early as 1934 Hans Schemm, the first Bavarian Culture Minister under the Nazis, had defined National Socialism as 'politically applied biology'.[18]

Apart from these two indeterminate, yet ultimately deadly disciplines, only *Volkskunde*, prehistory, and early history were valued and encouraged by the Nazis. The aim was 'to promote the study of the prehistory of the spirit', to cite the introduction to the theology of 'primordial conditions' that was popular in the 1920s and later expanded. It was hoped that the exploration of a primordial culture would result in the 'rebirth of the Nordic race and the liberation of humanity for the curse of civilization'.[19] The 'blood bond' of spiritual qualities—of what is characteristic of our type, of what is in our blood, the racial aspect of our nature'—was to provide the universal key to understanding. Customs, the old Germanic ways, the attitudes of German peasants were to be not only studied, but imitated in order to realize the new type of person and state.[20] Animating these scholars—who were highly esteemed and supported by Heinrich Himmler,[21] among others—was the ambition to demonstrate that a direct connection existed between Germanic history and the present, and to play down the significance of the classical influences of antiquity and Christianity.

Serious attempts were made to interpret the 'medieval myth of the German *Kaiser* . . . in Wotanistic terms' and to set it free from its 'Jewish and classical roots'. A Germanic community ethos, which offered a contrast with the corrupt, western, individual ethos of the metropolis was discovered. A 'massive simplification in the way we live', as Eugen Diederrichs had demanded as early as the 1920s, was promoted. Emotionally-laden youth organizations, an idealization of the simple, rural peasant life, and a new feeling of community entered into a fateful symbiosis. In practice, this could go so far as genocide, the notion of a chosen people, and the ideology of a greater German *Reich* extending far beyond Eastern and Central Europe.

Distinctly irrational goals were pursued by thoroughly rational arguments and methods provided by academia and technology. A typical representative of this disastrous mixture of conviction and knowledge, often the result of a superficial education, was Heinrich Himmler. His image of the Germanic peoples, his vision of the SS as an intellectual élite, his belief in a doctrine that held that the world had been created from cosmic ice (and claimed divine ancestry for the Germanic peoples),[22] and his utter imperviousness to rational argument are good illustrations. A telling example is his response to the suspicion, expressed in 1940, that Frederick the Great had been a homosexual: 'And even if a dozen so-called proofs were put before me, I would push them aside and declare that they had been retrospectively put together because my feeling tells me that a man who seized Prussia's place in the sun cannot have had propensities such as those possessed by these homosexual weaklings.'[23] The full danger of a confused world-view, combined with determined activism and a will to prevail, becomes apparent here.

These academic and pseudo-academic disciplines that aligned with the regime make it difficult for us to draw appropriate conclusions about the relationship between universities and National Socialism. Their contemporary wrong-headedness, even with professorial support, actually leads us away from the real question. If we look at the general run of academic disciplines, we see little evidence of ideologically compromised research efforts. In mathematics, chemistry, physics (leaving aside the unsuccessful side of this subject, the 'Deutsche Physik'), medicine, and the humanities, research continued to be successful and to achieve the usual standards. In many respects, it even stood up to international comparison. Most professors valued this highly. Even in the *Reichswissenschaftsministerium*, the Nazi Ministry for Education and Science, the German scholarly tradition was described as objective and conforming to scholarly ethos, in other words, as *wissenschaftlich*. Its point was to serve the subject, not political interests or prescriptions. Since the days of the Wilhelmine empire, when German scholarship led the international field in many disciplines, German professors had deliberately viewed themselves as unpolitical (although this attitude naturally also had political ramifications). They did not, however, reflect on this more closely. They believed, like Planck—to paraphrase Heilbron again —'that science stands above politics. Its international ideal . . . was both an earnest and an example of its transcendence; and just here the western powers acted politically, the Germans scientifically'.[24] It was simply accepted that scholarship was not bound by temporal limits; it was neutral, objective, and, up to a certain point, international.[25]

Of course, ever since the nineteenth century this last point must be viewed in the context of an unresolved conflict. Universities and scholarship were increasingly seen as contributing to a nation's status. They served national self-assurance, and actually opposed the older, international, *res publica litteraria*.[26] After World War I tension increased markedly when Germany was subject to an international boycott, even though it was not fully enforced. It had been decided at the London conference of the inner allied Academies of Sciences to exclude Germans from all international meetings for at least twenty years. Hence, the recovery of Germany's leading position was an important scholarly, as well as national, goal.[27] One could point out many important scientists, and quote many a line. Let it suffice to mention again Max Planck, who voiced his opinion at the Berliner Akademie der Wissenschaften on Leibniz-Day 1919: 'For science is one of the last assets remaining after the ravages of war ... And it is these ideal goods we will need most if we hope to rebuild our country ... Never was it more important to cultivate intellectual assets than in this world of growing intellectual impoverishment'.[28] We should remember just how cataclysmic the end of the war was perceived—politically, mentally and intellectually—by most professors. The enormous unexpected defeat of the once seemingly strong Reich, while accepted for the time being, nonetheless called for an extraordinary amount of explanation from the once state-pampered professors. The Versailles Treaty, however, quickly put an end to any moderate and reasonable approach. This resulted in a deep, and often complete, rejection of the new state, this 'parliamentary republic' of Weimar. 'The world as I knew it has been destroyed', concluded in 1923 Ulrich von Wilamowitz-Moellendorf, thus voicing the sentiments of many.

In the eyes of many professors, the political orientation toward majorities, and the party's efforts to control these majorities, contrasted sharply with the seemingly reasonable and fact-based rule of bureaucrats' over the realm of science during the time of the Kaiser. This last remained both the ideal and the yardstick, having already guaranteed the world-wide recognition of German scholarship and science. 'We have come a long way from there', stated '*Vernunftrepublikaner*' Friedrich Meinecke in 1926. 'Public life is dominated by a cacophony of voices shouting about their particular interests, pressuring even larger political parties. We feel free of such pressure and thus should not shy away from using our factual knowledge and good reason to voice the necessities of the nation'.[29] To his mind, the German professor was an embodiment of objectivity, open-mindedness, and impartiality rather than a being driven by considerations of party allegiance, majorities, and political considerations and prepared to compromise: the overriding axiom seemed to be that a professor had to be proficient in his field of study and remain above the petty squabbles of politics.

Such a perception allowed many professors after 1945 to assume that, in Heimpel's words, German scholarship in general had remained intact. This appears to be confirmed if we look at the transition from dictatorship to the post-war period which took place in 1945. Roughly one third of German lecturers had been judged 'incriminated', and thus forced to leave and undergo denazification, while more than two thirds were found 'not guilty'. Denazification went according to the rule book. Membership in the NSDAP —a prerequisite for almost every new professor from 1938 on—or in one of the affiliated organizations like NSKK, VDA, NSDoz. Bund might be deemed critical, even if the person was hardly a loyal supporter of the regime and tried simply to demonstrate loyalty to the *Volksgemeinschaft*. Hence, the relatively large number of people incriminated. Certainly there existed the zealous Hitler-devotees, yet their numbers dwindled the longer the war dragged on, and few outstanding minds could be found among them. Some of them even managed to slip through the loopholes of denazification; on the whole, however, everyone tried to make sure that the cleansing-process was as complete as possible. And this denazification policy was implemented not only by the occupying powers; from the start, the Germans themselves were heavily involved, particularly in the universities, where the process of sifting-out was strict. Those who were implicated were resented for having sinned against the universities and the scholarly ideal.[30] All this suggests that contemporary appeals to classicism, neo-humanism, and idealism were taken seriously; that a process of self-cleansing was underway; and that an attempt was being made to return to the good old German tradition again.

Thus, from the contemporary point of view, the assessment quoted at the beginning of this paper is quite understandable. Ericksen states that it was an inherent difficulty in the German post-war universities, where the denazificated professors lectured, to believe that serious cleansing was really necessary. Nor is it contradicted by the fact that many of those who were dismissed were able to return to their jobs after 1951. A serious shortage of a new generation of scholars, and the need to deal with a large number of students (including many veterans of the war), meant that, in retrospect at least, Nazi sins had to be forgotten and the (apparently) cleansed had to be brought back into office. And there were only a few—like Wilhelm Ebel in Göttingen—who had the impudence to claim to have defended academic values against others who were the real Nazis.[31] But that is another topic, and I can do no more than refer to it here. Generally, one can say that this process of denazification 'assisted in the German transition to a post-Nazi, democratic tradition. In particular, it stigmatized and essentially criminalized National Socialist beliefs, so that post-war advocacy of the Naziideology never proved a viable and/or attractive option within German academia'.[32] Thus the question arises anew: to what extent is it true to say that the German universities remained intact in the face of National Socialism? In a short review of these twelve years, I should like to approach this question from a different angle.

To start with, I shall cite two statistics of some interest. In 1937, 45 per cent of the professors and lecturers with the status of civil servants were newly appointed. Thus, in the first four years of the Nazi regime, more than one third of the teaching body had been changed.[33] Various reasons can account for this statistic, including age, expulsion, and forced retirement. Could the new appointees continue to work within the old scholarly traditions? Or were they infected by the new spirit?

Another statistic, only partially relevant here, is no less interesting. Also in 1937, 10,000 out of 18,9000 school-leavers with the *Abitur* examination which qualified them to enter university, opted to enter the military instead.[34] The reason for this choice was not the prevalence of a militaristic attitude, but the fact that an academic career was unattractive, encumbered as it was with a number of unpopular obligations such as participation in lecturers' camps and training courses, and attitude checks. The career of an academic, previously held in high regard, had suffered permanent damage. This quickly resulted in a shortage of new academics/scientists—a problem that was as much lamented as it remained unsolved. Universities were only partly able to fulfil their duty in recruiting and educating future scientists.[35]

In the universities the so-called seizure of power on 30 January 1933 seemingly produced no remarkable events. It was certainly not generally rejected. During the Weimar Republic, many professors had kept their distance from the state. To reiterate: looking back with longing to the position and respect they had enjoyed during the *Kaiserreich*, they argued that universities should be unpolitical, by which they really meant that they should not have to show any commitment to a democratic state. The autocratic *Kaiserreich*, the ideal of the nation, and concentration exclusively on the subject were regarded as obligatory models. Humiliation by the Treaty of Versailles, the international scholarly boycott, squabbling between the political parties, real poverty, and the cash shortages of the Weimar years made the *Kaiserreich* shine even brighter in retrospect. Thus even in 1933, most university lecturers were in favour of a strong state and strong political leadership figure. They were not National Socialists; during the first years of the Third Reich only 1.8 per cent were party members. Most Nazi supporters at the universities were to be found among the students,[36] and only a few among careerist lecturers. But as the promises and the national slogans of the Nazis seemed to reflect their own views and many of their wishes—even if they were too loud and too proletarian for the tastes of most professors—there seemed little reason to oppose the brown revolution. Hence, there was no resistance. In individual cases there was distance, rejection, and contempt, but only in a few cases did this become political.[37]

A similar dynamics applied to the announcement and consequences of the so-called Law to Re-establish the Career Civil Service, passed on 7 April 1933.[38] Its intention was the exact opposite of what its name suggests: it led to the most flagrant injustices imaginable; its targets were all alleged opponents, but especially scholars of Jewish origin. Within a comparatively short time, one third of the lecturers at some universities, such as Berlin and Frankfurt-on-Main, had been dismissed, driven away, or humiliated. At other universities, the numbers were lower. On the whole, however, the expulsion of Jewish academics meant a large haemorrhaging of scholarly competence, and it profoundly damaged the reputation of the German universities, at least in retrospect. At the time, only few objected to this barbarous act, and even among those who were affected, some saw this as an exaggerated, but understandable, reaction by the new state imbued with national pride. Their reasoning was not that it made openings for younger people, who could now move up; it simply expressed the general anti-Semitism that had a history in the universities and that was prevalent even among scholars.[39] There were exceptions, of course, but these were rare. As Oskar Perron, a mathematician from Munich, writes: 'The Nazis took their reforms seriously, and set about destroying the universities from the first day. I had been invited to give a lecture at the University of Göttingen, an important centre for mathematics, in the summer of 1933. The professors were already packing their bags, and the student rabble dominated the field. And then I experienced the most painful disappointment of my life. Something that I had believed was quite impossible, happened. A number of prominent scientists, and not only the opportunists who saw a chance to get rid of the competition, now toed the Hitler line and did not shrink from speaking of good Aryan and bad foreign or alien (*artfremd*) maths and physics, thus turning their German fatherland into a laughing stock in the eyes of the whole world'.[40]

Freiburg's vice-chancellor Josef Bauer, a doctor of divinity, noted in his diary after the first National Socialist conference of vice-chancellors: 'Closing the doors against Jews did not cause any principled attitude. Much was said about the dignity of academe, yet little was seen of this... The feeling of helplessness was ominously present, it would have taken the Göttinger Sieben to come up with a dignified stand. This crucial hour saw us pitifully small'.[41]

Scholars, then, behaved no differently from the rest of society. No matter that they had previously claimed to be intellectual and moral leaders whose only yardsticks derived from the subjects themselves. In this context it is certainly correct to say—as a prominent intellectual who as a young man had himself erred put it in retrospect—that the universities had thus violated their 'innermost law for living'. They had thereby 'cancelled the institution's solidarity with its ostracized and persecuted members', argued Franz Wieacker. This, he went on, caused 'even deeper damage... than the external devastation wreaked by National Socialist university policy'.[42]

The perverse, atavistic burning of the books on May 1933 went off relatively peacefully, accompanied at most by some head-shaking. This was intended to be an independent contribution by the German student body to the National Socialist cultural revolution. In Göttingen, for example, 'renewal' and 're-awakening' were the slogans. The 'purifying flames' into which the most diverse books were flung testified to an intellectual regression. Led by a dualistic world view—they knew what was right and what was wrong—students as well as professors behaved as if this anti-intellectual action marked a new intellectual departure, and created a new, *völkisch* reality within the *völkisch* experience of community. They determinedly turned away from 'democracy, liberalism, individualism and humanism'.[43]

Universities as institutions or corporations had to adjust, as it were, to the new world view. Not autonomy and corporate self-administration, but authoritarianism along the lines of the *Führer* state was prescribed. The vice-chancellor as *Führer*, the deans as the *Führer* of their various faculties, were to impose authority and to guarantee their colleagues' loyalty.[44] The fact that older ideas and ways of behaving frequently undermined the new decrees made it possible to assume that an inner free space, freedom of research, and sometimes even freedom of teaching were still possible at many universities. The universities by no means explicitly endorsed the principles of order and the notions that the National Socialists considered desirable. Not even a majority of the universities did. Many high-ranking Party members, in turn, took umbrage at the fact that this academic distance was maintained, and deemed it as something that needed to be fundamentally changed. For the time being, however, other more pressing tasks prevented this from happening.

The universities, understandably enough, regarded Nazi activism, the way in which the representatives of the new world view pandered to the masses, their anti-intellectualism and even primitiveness as disturbing, even as a number of ideal links with this world view continued to be possible.

The National Socialist party often complained about the lack of acceptance and support by the universities. Thus the 'university' of Alfred Rosenberg, the ideological pope but outsider in party political terms, was intended to make good this defect. It was to give a boost to those disciplines 'which, with their fossilized traditions at the universities, are not moving forward ideologically'. The opposition between Nazism and scholarship was to be eliminated by action. 'What is important is for university professors gradually to learn; it is not enough for individual faculty members to wear the party badge, even if they are sincere Nazis. The task is to develop existing tendencies under the intellectual leadership of the *Führer* of the *Reich*, and to organize a common academic endeavour which follows a clear ideological line'.[45]

Even such a prominent NS event as the conference at Göttingen organised by Reichsdozentenbundführer Walter Schultze in the summer of 1940 (it was intended as the start of a new academy for university teachers) ultimately failed to comply with the ideas of vigilant Nazi-ideologists who quite plausibly hinted at opportunism as the main reason for the attendance even of those professors who sympathized with their ideals. Even convinced National Socialists did not live up to the standards of a man like Alfred Baeumler, who reported on 18 November 1940: 'Every one of the men Schulze is so eager to mention—Heyse, Weinhandel, Höfler, Wetzel—is of course known in academe not as a prominent National-socialist—why should they be?—but rather as an ambitious colleague aiming to gain more profile for his subject through the party legitimization. Nothing is to be gained by Schultze's attempt at handling academic policy in such a slapdash manner'.[46]

The astonishing thing about such pronouncements, which could easily be multiplied, is that the Nazis were aware that the universities were following a course of which they disapproved but they put off tackling the problem. Nor was this simply a coincidence. Many high-ranking Party members shared the *Führer's* low opinion of academia. At most, they accepted that an individual genius who brought about an unexpected insight or breakthrough served the cause of progress, and was of some significance. In their view, however, continuing study, the tedious and uninteresting pursuit and investigation of problems, was unimportant. Even the intention, openly acknowledged from 1936, of being prepared for a possible war—the declaration of the Four Year Plan—changed nothing in this respect. The fact that the First World War had in many respects been a technical war had taught neither the Nazis nor the military to take the appropriate precautions in order to hold their own in such a fight. Instead, they preached military virtues, tactical supremacy, and military spirit, whatever that might mean. Scientific and technical research, by contrast, tended to be neglected as useful but less valuable. This made far more difficult the job of those functionaries responsible for education and research within the state and party apparatus of the Third Reich—from May 1934 in the *Reichswissenschaftsministerium*, the Ministry for Education and Science among others functions.[47] They recognized early on the main problem, namely that the rising generation of scholars and scientists had become massively depleted. This problem, much discussed throughout the Third Reich', was never resolved.

Naturally, the universities and technical universities were ordered to do what they could to support the Four-Year Plan. Many ordinary research projects that had long been underway could be continued under the pretext that they were important to the war effort. But even before the war, it had become clear that in many fields the Western powers, and in particular the United States, had established a clear lead. Hefty criticism of the funding of research did not, of course, change the basic attitude of the military and of the country's leaders. When this deficit became obvious during the war,

Albert Speer, the Armaments Minister appointed after Todt's ominous death, received far-reaching powers from Herman Göring to combat it.[48] But by this time it was already too late. Plans and new measures had no effect, and even Heinrich Himmler, who increasingly tried to get involved in Third Reich research policy, was unsuccessful.

The war itself brought about many changes for the universities. Students and professors were conscripted. Women (who had so far been excluded from tertiary education) were increasingly able to study. The necessities of war distracted the Nazis from pressing the universities into their service more successfully. After Nazi rule was seemingly consolidated around 1937, the universities received more freedom to pursue their activities. In many cases they were proud of this new autonomy which, of course, only lasted so long as the universities, professors, and students demonstrated their loyalty to the state. Under such conditions, the universities often volunteered their services for the successful development of important disciplines, which were intended not only to benefit the war and the people as a whole, but also to raise the university's reputation and standing among universities and scholars.

The war also dulled the senses. Becoming accustomed to death, pain, and cruelty, researchers could forget the demands of the scholarly ethos and the conditions under which research should be possible. Himmler's SS was the first to make possible criminal experiments on human beings, thereby revealing a contempt for human life unparalleled in the twentieth century.[49] To point out that in general these experiments were not the work of prominent researchers and that only a minority was involved does not make them any less dreadful.

In 1941–42 it became clear to many that Germany had over-exerted itself and that it was nearing the end of its productive power. Once again, people began to place their hopes in miracle weapons, inventions, and unthought of solutions, and this gave ingenious scholars the opportunity to expand and secure their activities. Thus in recent studies younger historians have argued that 'considerable numbers of scientists mobilized themselves for the war effort'. Thus, the corrupted or abused scientists now became participants, who 'growing from within science itself' had a role in the construction of national socialist politics'.[50] Endowments for research were expanded and many scholars in the humanities could quietly continue their research in their own quiet niches, provided that the Nazis thought them useful. This was why most scholars endeavoured to keep this privilege: exemption from active service and permission to be left undisturbed to work in one's field of choice (or even sanctioned and patronized) might prove seductive not only in a dictatorial-state conducting a murderous war, but for any ambitious and dedicated scholar. Only individual mistakes and crimes—for example in medical research—can be adjudged criminal behaviour. Taking advantage of given circumstances—while certainly questionable ethically—remains a fundamental human weakness. This is precisely the dilemma faced in any commonwealth where law, human rights, humanity, and tolerance count for nothing.

The fact remains that as the war went on, successful and ground-breaking research was carried out in many institutions in universities, institutes of science and technology, the Kaiser-Wilhelm-Gesellschaft, and industrial laboratories. This research has been considered an important contribution to the modernization of German science and philosophy. One might generally agree with such an assessment for chemistry, mathematics, synthetic materials, aeronautical research, metallography, physics, geography, and even medicine. Even in the humanities a 'Kriegseinsatz der Geisteswissenschaften' had been organized, which saw nearly every professor as an actor—in many cases for the sole purpose of obtaining printing-paper for their theses.[51]

To be sure, modernity in these fields offered a stark contrast to the official glorification of peasant life, the ancient Germanic tribes, and the simple country life.[52] This was, and still is, an insoluble problem with respect to the Third Reich. A pre-industrial party and a military obsessed with privileges based on status are incompatible with a modern scientific sector and plans for technical education. Thus, after initial attempts were made to bring the universities into line with party policy, they were marginalized, especially when they offered little resistance to the new and unreasonable demands and inhuman laws, and the illegal treatment of their own members.[53] This deceptive illusion of having-been-left-in-peace led those professors and scholars who were not found personally culpable but whose actions were nonetheless tainted to embrace the idea after 1945 that they had served their cause; that they had not allowed themselves to be corrupted; and that, ultimately, they had maintained their integrity. All understandable, but hardly correct.

Nevertheless, one should not neglect to point out that most of these men did volunteer to rebuild a German state. Re-education as well as the memory of the universal ideals that had developed during the classic neo-humanist and idealist periods—above all, the will to live in a well ordered prosperous Rechtsstaat—served as a guarantee for the successful start of the Bundesrepublik. Ericksen describes the dichotomy or dialectical process of these events: 'Support of, participation in, and responsibility for the crimes of Nazi Germany spread pervasively throughout the professions and the German populace. It was naive of German professors to think they had not been part of the problem, even if it was a natural self defense to deny culpability. Despite their participation in the 'Political University' of the Third Reich, however, academics turned toward democracy and participated in the democratization of German universities in the postwar world'.[54]

References

1. Mechthild Rössler, *Geography an Area Planning under National Socialism*, in Margit Szöllösi-Janze (ed.), *Science in the Third Reich* (Oxford and New York, 2001), 59–78, at 73.
2. Robert N. Proctor, *Racial Hygiene. Medicine under the Nazis* (Cambridge, Mass., 1988), 9.
3. *Hochschulen 1933–1945* (Bibliographie), Schriftenreihe des ASTA Mannheim, vol. 4 (Mannheim, 1998); *Hochschulen 1933–1945. Nachtrag zur Bibliographie sowie Übersichten über Rehabilitationen und Gedenken nach 1945*. Schriftenreihe, vol. 6 (Mannheim, 1999).
4. Hellmut Seier, 'Universität und Hochschulpolitik im nationalsozialistischen Staat', in Klaus Malettke (ed.), *Der Nationalsozialismus an der Macht* (Göttingen, 1984), 143–265; Idem, 'Die nationalsozialistische Wissenschaftspolitik und das Problem der Hochschulmodernisierung', in *Nationalsozialismus und Hochschule. Projektberichte zur Geschichte der Carolo-Wilhelmina* (Braunschweig, 1994), 55–68; Peter Lundgreen (ed.), *Wissenschaft im Dritten Reich* (Frankfurt am Main, 1985); Herbert Mehrtens, 'Wissenschaftspolitik im NS-Staat—Struktur und regionalgeschichtliche Aspekte', in Wolfram Fischer *et al.* (eds.), *Exodus von Wissenschaften aus Berlin. Fragestellungen—Ergebnisse—Desiderate— Entwicklungen vor und nach 1933* (Berlin and New York, 1994), 245–266; Monika Renneberg and Mark Walker (eds.), *Science, Technology and National Socialism* (Cambridge, 1994).
5. 'Die deutsche Hochschule in ihrem Kern ist gesund'. Hermann Heimpel, *Probleme und Problematik der Hochschulreform* (Göttingen, 1956), 7.
6. Quoted from Universitätsarchiv—Freiburg im Brsg. Personalakte Wilhelm Süss.
7. Notker Hammerstein, *Die Deutsche Forschungsgemeinschaft in der Weimarer Republik und im Dritten Reich. Wissenschaftspolitik in Republik und Diktatur* (Munich, 1999), 460ff.
8. Herbert Mehrtens, 'Verantwortungslose Reinheit. Thesen zur politischen und moralischen Struktur mathematischer Wissenschaften am Beispiel des NS-Staats', in Georg Füllgraff and Annegret Walter (eds.), *Wissenschaft in der Verantwortung* (Frankfurt am Main and New York, 1990), 37–54.
9. John L. Heilbron, *The Dilemmas of an Upright Man. Max Planck as Spokesman for German Science* (London, 1986), 149–50.
10. Ibid., 200f.
11. Martin Broszat, *Der Staat Hitlers* (Munich, 1973).
12. Cf. Notker Hammerstein (ed.), *Deutsche Bildung? Briefwechsel zweier Schulmänner* (Frankfurt am Main, 1988).
13. Frank Rutger Hausmann, '*Vom Strudel der Ereignisse verschlungen*', *Deutsche Romanistik im 'Dritten Reich* (Frankfurt am Main, 2000), 97.
14. Notker Hammerstein, *Die Johann Wolfgang Goe the-Universität Frankfurt am Main. Von der Stiftungsuniversität zur staatlichen Hochschule, 1940–1950* (Neuwied and Frankfurt am Main, 1989).
15. Joachim C. Fest, *Das Gesicht des Dritten Reiches. Profile einer totalitären Herrschaft* (Munich, 1988), 351.
16. Hammerstein, *Johann Wolfgang Goethe-Universität*, 386.

17. Peter Weingart, Jürgen Kroll, and Kurt Bayertz, *Rasse, Blut und Gene. Geschichte der Eugenik und Rassenhygiene in Deutschland* (Frankfurt am Main, 1988); Mark B. Adams (ed.), *The Wellborne Science. Eugenics in Germany, France, Brazil and Russia* (New York and Oxford, 1990).

18. Gerhard Grommer, 'Bezüge der NS-Lebenskunde zur Ökologie', in Christoph Meinel and Peter Voswinkel (eds.), *Medizin, Naturwissenschaft, Technik und Nationalsozialismus. Kontinuitäten und Diskontinuitäten* (Stuttgart, 1994), 144.

19. Helge Gerndt (ed.), *Volkskunde und Nationalsozialismus* (Munich, 1987).

20. Klaus von See, *Barbar—Germane—Arier. Die Suche nach der deutschen Identität* (Heidelberg, 1994).

21. Michael K. Kater, *Das 'Ahenerbe' der SS 1935–1945. Ein Beitrag zur Kulturpolitik des Dritten Reichs* (Stuttgart, 1974).

22. Brigitte Nagel, *Die Welteislehre. Ihre Geschichte und ihre Rolle im 'Dritten Reich'* (Stuttgart, 1991).

23. Kater, *Das 'Ahenerbe' der SS*, 96.

24. Heilbron, *The Dilemmas of an Upright Man*, 103f.

25. Hammerstein, *Die Deutsche Forschungsgemeinschaft in der Weimarer Republik*.

26. Thomas Nipperdey, *Deutsche Geschichte 1866–1918, II. Arbeitswelt und Bürgergeist* (Munich, 1990).

27. Brigitte Schroeder-Gudehus, *Deutsche Wissenschaft und internationale Zusammenarbeit 1914–1928* (Genf, 1966).

28. *Sitzungsberichte der Preußischen Akademie der Wissenschaften zu Berlin* (1919), 548.

29. Hammerstein, *Die Johann Wolfgang Goethe-Universität Frankfurt am Main*, 28 f.

30. Ibid.

31. Robert P. Ericksen, 'Denazification at Göttingen. Negotiating the Transition from a National Socialist to a Democratic University' (Paper read at the colloquium of the International Commission for the History of Universities, Oslo 2000).

32. Ibid.

33. Bundesarchiv Potsdam (now BA, Berlin-Lichterfelde), REM 666.

34. Karl-Heinz Ludwig, *Technik und Ingenieure im Dritten Reich* (Düsseldorf, 1974), 275ff.

35. See note 7.

36. See Michael Grüttner, *Studenten im Dritten Reich* (Paderborn, 1995).

37. Hausmann, 'Vom Strudel der Ereignisse verschlungen'.

38. Hans Mommsen, *Beamtentum im Dritten Reich* (Stuttgart, 1966).

39. Notker Hammerstein, *Antisemitismus in deutschen Universitäten 1871–1933* (Frankfurt am Main and New York, 1995).

40. Freddy Litten, 'Oskar Perron. Ein Beispiel für Zivilcourage im Dritten Reich', *Mitteilungen der Deutschen Mathematiker-Vereinigung*, 3 (1994), 27.

41. Eduard Seidler, 'Die akademische Elite und der neue Staat', *Acta Historica Leopoldina*, 22 (Halle/Saale, 1995), 17.

42. Franz Wieacker, in *250 Jahre Georgia Augusta—Göttinger Universitätsreden 84* (Göttingen, 1988), 39.

43. Albrecht Schöne, *Göttinger Bücherverbrennung 1939* (Göttingen, 1983); Grüttner, *Studenten im Dritten Reich*, 76f.

44. Hellmut Seier, 'Der Rektor als Führer', in *Vierteljahreshefte f. Zeitgeschichte*, 12 (1964), 105ff; Notker Hammerstein, 'Humboldt im Dritten Reich', in Rainer C. Schwinges (ed.), *Humboldt International* (Basle, 2001), 469–484.

45. Reinhard Bollmus, 'Zum Projekt einer nationalsozialistischen Alternativ-Universität: Alfred Rosenbergs "Hohe Schule"', in Manfred Heinemann, *Erziehung und Schulung im Dritten Reich, 2, Hochschule, Erwachsenenbildung* (Stuttgart, 1980), 128.

46. Bundes-Archiv Potsdam (now BA Lichterfelde), NS 8, 240.

47. See Hammerstein, *Die Deutsche Forschungsgemeinschaft in der Weimarer Republik*.

48. Joachim Fest, *Speer. Eine Biographie* (Berlin, 1999).

49. Benno Müller-Hill, *Tödliche Wissenschaft. Die Aussonderung von Juden, Zigeunern und Geisteskranken 1933–1945* (Reinbek bei Hamburg, 1984); *Medizin im Nationalsozialismus* (Munich, 1988); Jürgen Pfeifer (ed.), *Menschenverachtung und Opportunismus. Zur Medizin im Dritten Reich* (Tübingen, 1992).

50. Szöllösi-Janze (ed.), *Science in the Third Reich*, 11.

51. Frank Rutger Hausmann, *'Deutsche Geisteswissenschaft' im Zweiten Weltkrieg. Die 'Aktion Ritterbusch' (1940–1945)* (Dresden, 1998), 37.

52. Ludwig, *Technik und Ingenieure im Dritten Reich*, 300ff; Doris Kaufmann (ed.), *Geschichte der Kaiser-Wilhelm-Gesellschaft im Nationalsozialismus. Bestandsaufnahme und Perspektiven der Forschung* (2 vols, Göttingen, 2000).

53. Dieter Langewiesche, 'Die Universität Tübingen in der Zeit des Nationalsozialismus. Formen der Selbstgleichschaltung und Selbstbehauptung', *Geschichte und Gesellschaft*, 23 (1997), 638.

54. Ericksen, 'Denazification at Göttingen'.

68

THE COMMISSION ON GERMAN UNIVERSITIES

Lord Lindsay of Birker

Source: *Universities Quarterly* IV (1949–50): 82–8.

In the spring of 1948 the British Military Government in Germany appointed a Commission to report on the future of German universities in a democratic state. It was meant to be something like a Royal Commission in this country. It could concern itself of course only with the universities in the British Zone. It consisted of Germans with the exception of two foreigners—one Swiss, Professor von Salis, Professor of Modern History in the famous Technical University of Zurich, and one from this country, myself. There were four professors—from Hamburg and Gottingen, the Technical University of Aachen, and the Head of the Teachers Training Institute at Kiel. The Chairman was the respected head of the German Co-operative Wholesale Society. There was a trade unionist, two clerics, the Dean of the Cathedral at Cologne, and an Evangelical Bishop from Dusseldorf, and one woman, an officer in the educational administration of Nieder-Sachsen. We started with the inevitable questionnaire sent to all universities and technical universities, in fact all the "Hochschule", in the British Zone, and to representatives of German opinion. We interviewed witnesses, mostly from England and America, and had many meetings and much informal discussion, and sent our report to Military Government in October. When we began we were all at sixes and sevens, but our report was unanimous. The unanimity was genuine. We did really agree.

It is most instructive for one like myself, long accustomed to consider the problems of British universities, to be brought into this kind of contact with German universities. The approach was so different. We in this country, I at least, have the vaguest ideas of how "the mission" of the universities should be defined. I know something of the difficulties facing the existing ones, and I have my ideas of the things which have to be done in society which only the universities can do. But with that empirical attitude I am ordinarily content, unless something makes it impossible.

How different the German approach! The German universities of the present day still reflect the "idea of a university" formulated by von Humboldt in the beginning of the nineteenth century—a clear and unifying idea which can be stated without difficulty. In the nineteenth century, at least in the early part of it, German universities, re-created by these new principles, were the leaders of German thought and the admiration of the learned world. Now, the former glory had, it was agreed, largely departed. The German universities, instead of leading Germany, had put up practically no resistance to Hitler. They were distrusted by a large section of the community; their isolation from it is widely complained of. They are still admirable centres of research, but they provide their students with no philosophy of life. They complain, as we complain, of the departmentalism, the *Zersplitterung*, of their studies. Except for a select few, their students are predominantly concerned with vocational studies. Something has gone wrong.

We had to make up our minds at the outset whether the Humboldtian idea of a university was completely out of date or whether it could be reinterpreted in the light of contemporary modern conditions. We all agreed that only in the second way could the German universities be preserved, and that our task was to preserve the great qualities of the best in German universities and yet, if possible, point the way for the remedying of their defects.

The idea of a German university

The idea of a university as the Germans conceive it is easily stated. It is a society of teachers and scholars united in the pursuit of "the truth". The method of this pursuit is a close unity of research and teaching, "*Forschung und Lehre*". The essential condition of this pursuit of the truth is freedom, *Lehrfreiheit* and *Lernfreiheit*. The teacher is to be free to follow the wind of the argument wherever it leads him, and the scholar—remarkable demand in our eyes—is to be free to choose his teacher or teachers and under him to devote himself to what branch of learning and take what examination he pleases. The German word *Die Wahrheit*, which I have translated "the truth", is, especially in these days of logical positivism, really untranslatable and even Germans admit that the conception as they use it depends on a philosophy now outdated. The "seamless robe" of the truth has long been torn in pieces by technology.

How the fine flower of German universities grows from this conception is not hard to see. It implies the professor with the self-chosen band of scholars, each learning and also taking his part in research. Its methods are the seminar and the colloquium, its only mark of distinction the doctorate. It implies, of course, a very high standard in professor and more especially in students. If we ask "Who is capable of really rising to the opportunities of this system?", the answer is a very small proportion indeed of those who wish to come to a university. What happens to the rest? They ordinarily take no university degree and compete for civil service examinations of one kind and another, which in Germany are far more technical and professional than they are with us.

It would not be hard to make the German universities self-perpetuating research institutes and nothing else. It would then be necessary to find other institutions to train the young who were not going to be professors, but needed education from 18 or 19 to 22 or 23 if they were to play the part in society of which they are capable. To abandon the German universities to be mere research institutes seemed a council of despair. The Commission therefore addressed itself to the consideration of the isolation of the universities from the rest of the community. It began with a significant change in the statement of the function of the university. Its aim, they stated, is the pursuit of truth through research and teaching *in the service of man*. Truth is no longer to be regarded, is the implication, as a self-sufficient independent end. The worth of its pursuit is qualified by those significant five last words.

The service of the community

The universities then are to serve the community, of course in their own significant way, of the validity of which they are to be judge. Their service to the community consists in the pursuit of truth and truth is not necessarily what the community or its representatives wish the universities to teach. Therefore the universities' teaching must be free and yet they must somehow in their constitution be in touch with the community. This dilemma was formerly met in a fashion in the German universities by the carefully defined powers of the Minister of Education, and, in Prussian universities, of "the Curatorium". The Commission feared that these arrangements might not in these days safeguard the freedom of universities as they had in the past, and in any case did not think they provided for the proper relations between the universities and the community.

The Commission propose something not unlike the constitution of the new English universities, a *Hochschulbeirat*—like the Court—a large number of representatives of all bodies concerned with educational questions, trade unions included, and then a *Hochschulrat*—or Council—a small body of not more than ten with a whole-time Principal, the chosen members being elected in equal numbers from the Court, the Senate and the Culturminister. There had been something like this in the Universities of Bremen and of Cologne, but on the whole these are revolutionary proposals. The German universities have been governed by their Senates, indeed one might almost say by their Faculties, and their reaction to these proposals for the introduction of a lay element is often to say that the result will be the government of the expert by the ignorant.

The fragmentation of studies the Commission propose to cure by the institution of what they call a *studium generale*—a general course incumbent on all students. Several German universities, notably Tubingen, Heidelberg and Gottingen, have already made experiments of this kind and it is interesting to notice how unanimously the German technical universities are pressing for the setting up or the enlargement of a "philosophic" faculty. The German reaction against over-specialisation is, I think, stronger than ours. They have perhaps suffered more.

The Commission propose, in dealing with the Senate and Faculties, to break down the monopoly of the professors by insisting on the representation of lecturers on Faculty and Senate, and to create a new kind of professor whose main job shall be teaching. The position of the lecturers at present is acknowledged by everyone to be unsatisfactory. Their only hope of a career is to become a professor, their only hope of becoming a professor is by their distinction in research. I was reminded as I listened to their complaints of the position of the assistant in Scottish universities fifty or sixty years ago. As we have found out, a regular establishment of lecturers and a career for the senior lecturer are the only cure for this evil. The Commission propose something on those lines—to put the emphasis of the university's function more on teaching, *Lehre und Forschung* rather than *Forschung und Lehre*.

The technical revolution

To go over all the proposals of the Commission would take too long. I hope readers will get the report and study it. But I may be allowed to conclude with some general reflections. The history of the German universities in the last hundred and fifty years is full of instruction to those who are considering the "crisis of the university." They began under such happy auspices, inspired by a unifying and illuminating idea. The truth their professors and scholars sought was a unified body of knowledge. To be a student of one of their great teachers was as well a training for public life and government, for membership of the learned professions and for the advancement of learning itself. Their professors and students formed a small and learned aristocracy in days when aristocracies of one kind or another were taken for granted and their leadership accepted.

Then came what I shall call the technical revolution. That meant that whereas in earlier times the great mass of productive work was performed by customary and hereditary skills, now, more and more, efficient production depends upon the extent to which scientific research inspires and directs industrial production. That means an enormous demand for technical specialists, who must, many of them, have university or similar training. The old balance of studies is completely upset. Whether we follow the German model and distinguish between technical universities and universities proper confined to the basic subjects, or muddle them, all together in the English manner, does not really matter. The university output will consist increasingly of technical specialists who have not been trained to be citizens. Hitler met the difficulty by proposing that the universities should train a select governing class whose orders the technicians trained elsewhere would unhesitatingly obey. Some such distinction between institutions meant for technical experts and institutions for administrators exists, I am told, in Russia. A democratic community cannot submit to that specialization of its ruling class. All its citizens ought to have some sort of skill and be, therefore, specialists; but equally all ought to have an understanding of the purposes and common life of the community and be educated as citizens. They need not necessarily go to university institutions of the same kind, but all university institutions will somehow have to fulfil both these purposes and we can no longer pretend that by being given the training needed for technical purposes a student is also educated. We are beginning nowadays to recognise that education in science and in the humanities must go together. The Germans seem to me, as I have said, to have already taken this dilemma more seriously than we have. Their experiments are not the product of the Commission, they were already being started when the Commission was appointed. They are well worth studying. Of particular interest I thought were the proposals to set up or develop "philosophical" or sociological faculties in the great German technical institutions.

But to consider the place of universities in a *democratic* community raises another problem in whose solution we in this country are undoubtedly ahead of Germany, far though we still have to go. There is nothing in Germany to equal our adult education movement.

Universities and the industrial revolution

Consider again the effects of the industrial revolution. In a successful industrial nation the spirit of scientific research is to take the place of customary and hereditary skills. But that is to take the place of craftsmanship in the old sense. Can the spirit of scientific research, the eagerness to ask whether what is being done cannot be done better or whether what has been thought cannot be thought better—can that spirit take over the sense of quality which craftsmanship gave? Ideally, I believe it can. But how thoroughly do we suppose this spirit of scientific research can permeate a community, or how thoroughly are we determined that it shall permeate a community? For there are two answers to this question—the one oligarchic, the second democractic. The oligarchic solution is to train a minority of highly skilled technical specialists directing a majority of unskilled machine-minders who have lost the sense of quality formerly given by craftsmanship and have been given nothing to replace it. That is virtually a slaveholding aristocracy or oligarchy. The democratic solution would be to ensure that the spirit of scientific enquiry, as I have defined it, permeates in some degree or other the whole community, and to provide educational institutions to bring this about. These institutions to my mind will have to be of different kinds. We have already in this country accepted the view that secondary schools should be of different kinds and, whatever our practice may be, we preach that each of those kinds of school should have a distinctive quality of its own without being graded as higher or lower. I think that if we are to become a democratic community pervaded by the spirit of scientific research, we shall have to have an equal, if not a greater, variety of institutions at the university stage.

These may seem to English readers far-fetched conclusions. Nothing like them will be found in the report of the German Commission. They have been borne in on me by considering several things—(a) the great difference which the widespread advance of adult education, both vocational and non-vocational, has made to the universities of this country. University professors in Germany tend to regard themselves as an élite, set apart from the rest of the community. Adult education has largely cured our universities of that. (b) The German distinction between universities proper and technical universities. The complaint of isolation from the community does not apply to the Technische Hochschule. They may have defects but they are eager to deal with them. They believe in extra-mural education and have active plans for its development. There is, I know, considerable difference of opinion among scientists in this country about the soundness of this distinction. I was much impressed by it. The Technische Hochschule of Zurich is quite distinct from the University of Zurich but as distinguished. If we here regarded our university institutions as having different but equally important functions, we might consider the different functions which the community needs universities to fulfil, without quarrelling about prestige.

Thirdly, it is impossible to consider the contrast between the best things in German universities, which are very good indeed, and their defects, without seeing the danger of attending too much and too exclusively to the high standard *one is accustomed to*. That tends to mean high standard in a narrowing circle. Undoubtedly some of the defects from which the German universities are suffering come from their exclusive consideration of high standards in research and neglect of other standards such as high standards of teaching, of usefulness to the community in other matters than learning, and so on. I may perhaps sum this up by saying that if I had to choose between the American university system with its great variety and its frequent lapses from any standard, and the German with its exclusive occupation with a high standard in research, I should choose the former.

69

Excerpt from
THE UNIVERSITY REFORM
OF TSAR ALEXANDER I,
1802–1835

James T. Flynn

Source: J. T. Flynn, *The University Reform of Tsar Alexander I, 1802–1835*, Washington, DC: Catholic University of America Press, 1988, pp. 1–25.

THE ISSUES

In May 1802, not much more than a year after the murder of his father elevated him to the throne of Russia, Tsar Alexander I paid a visit to Dorpat and took part in a ceremony that marked the formal opening of a new university. Both the assembled local nobles, who founded and financed the new institution, and the newly recruited professors, who disagreed sharply with the nobles on most matters touching university policy, expected the tsar to make clear his support for their position. In his address of welcome, the professors' spokesman promised that he and his colleagues would take "special concern for the poor."[1] In reply, Alexander seemed to go out of his way to signal support for the professors' desire to open the university to all academically qualified candidates, without regard to social class. His reply delighted the professors and horrified most nobles. Delighted or horrified, both professors and nobles before long had reason to doubt whether the tsar meant what he seemed to say. Confusion and doubt about his intentions may have been sown deliberately by Alexander in order to confuse and disorganize those who would oppose his plans. By design or not, confusion and doubt came to the new institution at Dorpat as to many, perhaps most, reforms attempted in Alexander's time. The many reforms attempted not only had in common the doubt and confusion they often occasioned; they also had common origins in the reformers' expectations and experience, and also in aspects that seem not to have occurred to the reformers.

1. The question of reform

The reign of Alexander was clearly the reign of a reformer. The times, the era of the French Revolution and Napoleon, and Russia's situation, poised between Catherine the Great's accomplishments and Paul I's attempts to reverse them, made some sort of far-reaching change all but inevitable. Moreover, the young tsar clearly thought of himself as a reformer and meant to carry out that role. Yet the end of Alexander's reign was marked by confusion and doubt so strong that some advocates of reform were near despair. Part of the reason was the reforms' failure to achieve their stated goals. That failure only partly explained the doubt and confusion, however, for in some ways some reforms achieved their goals but nonetheless were regarded as failures. The personal characteristics of the tsar played a role, but the question of reform in the Russia of Alexander I was confusing not only because the tsar was enigmatic, or possibly himself confused, but also because the situation was complex and every problem multifaceted. Russia faced many challenges that crowded together, requiring that something, often something quite far-reaching, be done, and done quickly, to change or to fortify basic political and economic institutions. The challenges came in the sharply threatening form of military peril as well as in the benign form of aspirations to make significant improvement in economic development, health, and welfare. Additional complexity stemmed from the reformers' need to choose among many competing concepts of reform that often were mutually contradictory if equally plausible and well recommended. Not surprisingly, the reformers often found it difficult to decide which model to follow, and they tried to combine more than one approach in meeting one need or another. Most important, the reform plans were not undertaken as desperate emergency measures to ward off danger. They were taken up in a spirit of optimism, as the paths to a better future, established on the certainties of science and reason and marked with the highest human values, whether of secular-minded humanism or otherworldly pietism. Naturally, therefore, many looked forward with confidence to the development of reform. Failure in these circumstances was so unexpected that it seemed especially disappointing.

In some areas success was achieved, if at a very high price. The Russian army was entirely transformed. In tactics, organization, training, and equipment the army came to match the best of the relatively small professional armies that had been fundamental to successful modernization, particularly in central Europe. In recruitment and relation to civil society, the army kept its Petrine ways, traditional by this time. But in the strikingly high percentage of the population directly engaged in the military, the Russian army more than matched the new mass armies of the era of the French Revolution and Napoleon. These changes proved not temporary responses to wartime emergencies, but became permanent transformations. During the reign of Alexander I an army whose strength was not quite 400,000 troops became a peacetime standing army of a good deal more than a million.

In some other areas Alexandrine reforms clearly failed. Serfdom was a basic feature, perhaps the basic feature, that sharply distinguished Russia from the progressive Europe whose successes the reformers wanted to emulate. Alexander's government, in particular the group of personal friends and advisers who formed his "Secret Committee," had no difficulty in agreeing that serfdom was an economic and political anachronism that retarded economic growth and social development, and that it was a moral outrage as well, inescapably producing both misery and disorder. There was no lack of ideas for reform. The so-called Free Farmers Act in February 1803 launched a program intended to try capitalism as an answer to serfdom by encouraging those peasants who could, as individuals or even as communal organizations, to purchase their lands and freedom, showing the way that the pursuit of self-interest would promote the common good by undermining serfdom. Other solutions were tried, at least in part as pilot programs for the whole empire. In the Baltic province of Livland in 1804 serfs were granted hereditary rights to the land, but not personal freedom. In neighboring Estland in 1811 serfs were granted personal freedom without rights to the land. Either procedure seemed to many to promise to undermine serfdom, though neither did. The military colonies program, begun in 1810 and pushed vigorously after 1816, approached the problem from the opposite end. No longer relying on the motivation of self-interest, the government would transform peasant lives by the use of state power and military discipline. There was a better way of life for rural Russia, and the government knew what that way was, if it could but find the way to motivate people to pursue it. These and other programs and policies showed that there were many possible solutions to the problems of serfdom, though all proved deficient in practice.[2]

The reform that produced the foundation of the Russian university system had its origins, then, in a time of wide-ranging change. Dwarfed by comparison with the scope and vast numbers involved in the changes in the military, and seldom meeting problems as intractable as those rooted in serfdom, the university reform shared with other aspects of the reform effort the sort of goals Alexander formulated, and the variety in sources and resources available to meet them. In general terms, two quite different concepts of the path to reform coexisted, that of enlightened absolutism and that of constitutionalism. At Alexander's accession, Russia already had long experience in attempting to choose between them. An important part of that experience was the frustration inherent in the paradox that Russia's reformers repeatedly found it necessary to turn to state power, if not arbitrary despotism, in order to achieve constitutional gains.[3] Paul I, and Peter III at mid-eighteenth century, made especially noteworthy attempts to follow the example of the great Peter, using state power to make Russia more efficient and more just. Both had reigns cut short by assassination. Their use of state power seemed to many merely arbitrary, capricious abuse that justified the most extreme forms of resistance to what otherwise had to be regarded as legally constituted authority. This circumstance gave Alexander significant advantages in the early months and years of his reign. Since his grandmother, Catherine the Great, had removed him from his father's house and care, he was not associated with Paul's reputation for cruel caprice. For many, the end of Paul's caprice was the definition of reform. The news of Paul's murder, at which "people cried with joy and embraced one another as on Easter Sunday," therefore made it possible for Alexander to appear the reformer without making hard choices but by merely repealing some of Paul's more obnoxious edicts.[4]

It was not long, however, before Alexander had to begin making choices. Some of those choices seemed to indicate that he appreciated the need not only to avoid gross excesses in the abuse of power but to develop institutions that could restrain such abuse by promoting constitutional growth on something like the British model. There were men, often with high-level experience in Catherine's government, who well understood enlightened reform in such terms. Alexander appeared to encourage them by founding a "permanent council" in which some of them could provide legal advice to the tsar, and by establishing a "commission on the composition of the law" to plan revision of the legal system. He asked A. P. Vorontsov, whose appreciation of British political and legal practice was well known, to draw up a model constitution, the "Charter of the Russian People." Expressing concern for the Senate's "traditional" rights, Alexander also asked it to draw up a constitutional proposal for itself. In the manifesto issued at his accession, moreover, Alexander promised to rule in the spirit of his grandmother Catherine, a promise that naturally called up visions in the minds of gentry of the constitutional guarantees of gentry rights of person and property made in the charter of 1785. Such steps might have developed institutions and practices to promote something comparable to the constitutional government of the British model. They would foster the growth of liberty by protecting the interests and rights of at least some segments of society. Preserving a balance between the central government and other institutions and groups, such steps meant developing constitutional government in the sense of limiting the power of the central government by requiring it to govern through, or at least with the consent of, institutions devoted to maintaining the rights of established groups. In Russia that clearly meant, in the first place, respecting the rights and interests of the higher nobility, with attention too for the Orthodox Church and the provincial gentry. Many therefore regarded such steps, not as hopeful reforms, but as fundamentally unsound. The stable excellence of a British constitution was not the only outcome of such policies. Montesquieuian balance could promote a reactionary defense of vested interests against the common good, as witnessed in the *Parlements* of pre-revolutionary France, blocking all responsible reform until they too were swept away in the great 1789 revolution. Alexander, in any event, was no amiable, or lazy, Louis XVI, knuckling under to the selfish defenders of private interests, and therefore he did not seriously countenance for long any of these constitutional steps. By late 1804 all these attempts at reform had been abandoned or crushed, most spectacularly when the tsar angrily rejected the Senate's attempt to exercise its "right" to protest new laws that enfringed upon established gentry rights.[5]

It would say too much, nonetheless, to argue that Alexander had thus revealed himself as despotic or hypocritical. There was something ambiguous in both theory and practice to pursuing liberty, justice, or even simple efficiency by granting to established groups or institutions the right to promote their own interests as the common good. Enlightened absolutism was the way out of that particular dilemma, using the power of the state to remove obstacles to liberty, justice, or efficiency, including the obstacles formed by the traditional rights of established groups and bodies, such as the nobility and clergy. Enlightened absolutism had its own dilemma, demonstrated poignantly in the career of the ruler who was perhaps the most serious and principled of those called enlightened absolutists. Joseph II found it necessary to organize an efficient secret police, whose arbitrary exercise of power was itself a denial of liberty, to combat those citizens of the Habsburg realms who seemed ready to use their newly gained freedoms from traditional constraints to pursue their own goals, which often were in fact at odds with those set by the reforming monarchy. A way out of this dilemma seemed offered by the notions of *Rechtsstaat*. The reforming state formulated goals in terms of an order of society both just and efficient, knowable by science and reason, and thus attacked the order of society founded on tradition, or indeed on any concept of reason inconsistent with the mechanistic assumptions of the *philosophe*. The *Rechtsstaat* was enlightened absolutist in its use of the state's power to pursue those goals, but it also committed itself to the law it formulated, guarantee that the arbitrary exercise of state power would not undermine liberty and justice. Alexander was open to this notion, which lay behind much of the institutional and legal reform, including the educational, undertaken in the early years of his reign.[6]

The enlightened *Rechtsstaat* clearly stood in need of men able and willing to formulate and implement programs to achieve its goals. Not surprisingly, every state in enlightened Europe during the age of Enlightenment made some effort to develop an educational system that could provide such men for its services. Reform in higher education became indeed both means and end, required in order to pursue reform goals and so necessary that it was pursued as one of the essential reforms. Three among these efforts proved particularly important in the development of university reform in Alexander's Russia: the development of German universities, especially Göttingen; the struggle between secular reformers and clerical, especially

Jesuits, for a new school system in Poland; and the academic reforms of the Habsburg Empire, as introduced into Russia under Catherine the Great.

Göttingen's great success made it uncommonly influential. Though relatively new, founded in 1734 in a small and not very important town, Göttingen soon made its mark. It fostered university autonomy rooted not so much in the traditional defense of the rights and liberties of established institutions and classes as in the results achieved by a faculty that worked in academic freedom for both teachers and learners, and whose scholarship contributed to the community the constant development of knowledge. These results, moreover, bore fruit in the utilitarian sense of providing the best training for men who would carry forward the *Rechtsstaat*'s programs. Such a combination of virtues made the model of Göttingen all but irresistible, particularly as they were brought into the Russian reformers' discussions by M. N. Murav'ev, who was personally close to Alexander and to academic leaders at Göttingen. Jesuits and the Polish National Education Commission sharply disagreed about many important issues, but both worked hard to develop schools whose graduates could compare well with Europe's best in both up-to-date competence in their fields and in motivation to use their gifts for the good of the wider community. Moreover, in the details of organization and curriculum, both came closer to agreement than either seemed likely to admit. Adam Czartoryski, who was especially close to Alexander personally, was both well informed on the achievements of educational reformers in Poland and intent on fostering their further development.[7]

Murav'ev was particularly important becase his influence tended to encourage some choices while precluding others. He, and Czartoryski as well, took very seriously the development of the university in fostering reform. In many ways this was a minority view in the late eighteenth century. Enrollment in most universities in western Europe was declining sharply. Some centuries-old institutions closed forever. Many enlightened critics sought to help mankind achieve liberation from the dead hand of the past by encouraging the development of new institutional forms for education. Many argued that the university was among the decaying institutions rooted in the past that should be replaced with more rationally conceived ways of providing education for a new, progressive, era. As often as not, such critics were quite right to argue that many universities had become centers of pedantry, not of learning, whose academic autonomy was most useful for faculty nepotism, securing jobs for friends and relatives, not for the defense of professional values. Göttingen, and Halle and some others, were exceptional not only in their academic excellence but also in making the traditional university an institution to foster reform rather than an obstacle in the way of enlightenment.[8]

The institutional and intellectual legacy of Catherine the Great's work in educational reform matched the importance of Göttingen's example.

The school system Catherine founded in 1782 was based on the "decreed Enlightenment" characteristic of Catholic Europe, though it was first worked out and made successful in Protestant Prussia. The "Allgemeine Schulordnung" of Johann Felbiger was first successfully applied in Prussian Silesia, then throughout the domains of Frederick the Great, then throughout the Habsburg Empire. The fundamentals of the system were the development of a series of textbooks for all the basic subjects, from reading, writing, arithmetic, and basic religious and moral doctrine through advanced, gymnasium and/or *realschule*, courses in mathematics, sciences, languages, and social studies as well as in religion and morality. Training programs for teachers in the most efficient methods of getting the contents of this series of texts into the heads of pupils stressed oral drill and memorization. Up-to-date command of the essentials of a modern, useful education, thus, could be efficiently delivered to ever-wider segments of the population. Obviously wildly different in tone and temper from the Göttingen notion of what education was about, this system had achieved noteworthy success in the villages of the Habsburg Empire, even as Göttingen-minded reformers attained some success in reform of the empire's universities. Catherine, ever impressed with success, brought to Russia one of the officials who had played a major role in developing the system in the Habsburg lands with Slavic populations: Teodor Jankovic de Mirievo.[9]

Mirievo joined the School Commission (*Komissiia ob uchrezhdenii uchilishch*) Catherine founded in 1782 to plan and supervise the development of a new system. In a decade of work, the commission introduced into Russia the essentials of the Felbiger system. At the village level its quite uniform basic curriculum aimed at providing general literacy and numeracy, together with indoctrination in religious and social values likely to foster loyalty and cooperation. Graduates of the village school were prepared for advancement to the middle school (*malaia* in the designation adopted in Russia) to be opened in each county seat, which prepared its graduates for the "main" secondary school to be located in each provincial capital. The teachers' college that the commission opened in St. Petersburg provided training in the curriculum and methods of the system.

Mirievo, and the commission, tried to do more than duplicate the Austrian model. In the Habsburg lands, the secondary school in each province (called the "Normal School") was the top of a three-step ladder, designed primarily to train teachers for the lower schools and people equipped with enough of the basics of a general liberal arts education to make useful candidates for the lower echelons of the public services or of private enterprises. Such people were not eligible for admission to universities, to prepare for careers in the senior levels of the public services or the church. Mirievo proposed that the main secondary school do just that, becoming in effect (and as it turned out often in name as well) the gymnasium, the secondary school that trained students for university admission. The top of the ladder in Russia, then, would be a network of universities that Mirievo proposed would join Russia's only existing university at Moscow. Most striking, in the context of the authoritarian sort of enlightened school system Mirievo helped to build, was his proposal that the projected universities should have Göttingen's academic freedom, the "right of free teaching." Moreover, he argued that, unlike the system in the Habsburg lands, the system should make no class or "age" distinctions.[10]

Mirievo also put forward proposals for the universities from former colleagues in Austria who wanted law taught, not as professional training in the faculty of Russian law, but in the philosophy faculty, as a system of logic derived from fundamental first principles. To provide genuine learning, then, as distinct from mere utilitarian vocational training for bureaucrats, Mirievo thought law students in Russian universities should study German law rather than Russian, for German law could provide not only good "examples" but also the distance to encourage objectivity, and thus reliance on reason rather than on tradition as the standard for law. Göttingen, and many other universities, in central and eastern Europe had fostered reforms that did both, providing vocational training at a high professional level for bureaucrats in *Staatswissenschaft*, without surrendering either philosophic studies of the enlightened empiricist and/or idealist sort or, for that matter, the values of the old classics curriculum, especially Latin philology.

Many members, including P. A. Zavadovskii, one of Catherine's favorites whom she appointed chairman of the commission, argued against these recommendations from Mirievo, since they required distinctions and priorities that did not need to be made and overlooked some points that did need stressing, such as the need to develop a curriculum that used the Russian language as the most efficient means to promote the "spread of learning" in Russia. Remarkably few objections, however, were raised against the notion that not only should the system provide the rudiments of literacy for all, but that the village school should form the foundation stage, open to all, in a single system that extended up through the university. One of the commission's projects endorsed the view of the renowned Lomonosov that the only requirement for admission to a university in Russia should be adequate academic preparation. The commission explicitly defended the rights of peasants to higher education, quoting Lomonosov that "everyone may become a student no matter what his rank or age." While none could doubt that in Russia as elsewhere the goals of this enlightened reform were practical, even utilitarian, their moral dimension was underscored by the commission's declaration that the Russian nobility no more risked "degradation" in attending schools in common with other classes than "when they hear the word of God together with the unfree in the churches."[11]

In some ways, the commission's proposals and plans were not new or original. Catherine had received many plans for an empire-wide educational system offering a basic general education to all, including a very detailed one that she solicited from Diderot in 1777. Indeed, she had published one herself a decade earlier. A curriculum that stressed general education, rather than vocational training, had been the rule rather than the exception in all Russia's modern schools since the great reformer, Peter I, founded them at the beginning of the century. Nonetheless, in 1782 an empire-wide system still did not exist and, though most schools offered general education, or liberal arts and sciences at the gymnasium or at other more advanced schools, most were also professional schools, sponsored by one or another agency to train for itself recruits who were chosen from one or another social class. Despite the emphasis on general education, or liberal arts, most curricula in Russian schools had developed as "professional" education, offered as training for one or another vocation or profession, normally to members of the social class for which that vocation or profession constituted the usual way of life. Indeed, that education came to form an important part of the definition of that class.[12]

The commission that Mirievo chaired developed able staff members, such as N. I. Fuss, who was well versed in the plans and proposals and seriously interested in realizing them in practice. Not surprisingly, much remained only plan or proposal. No new universities, for example, were founded. Nonetheless, a good deal was achieved in practice. The commission founded a teachers' college in St. Petersburg that recruited sons of Orthodox clergy to train as teachers in the new system. In the early 1780s there existed in Russia not many more than 50 state-supported schools, enrolling fewer than 5,000 students. At the end of Catherine's reign, Russia had at least 550 such schools, enrolling 62,000 pupils. It was especially important that the new secondary schools had been placed in towns that previously had no school at all. In sum, at the turn of the century, educational reformers in Russia had to deal not with a *tabula rasa* but with the beginnings of an enlightened system already in place.[13]

2. Planning a new system

Tsar Paul, as in much else, attempted to undo his mother's work in education. During his brief reign the number of schools and students declined. Perhaps the main consequence of his effort was the stimulation of a sense of urgency, underscoring for many the importance of further reform in education. Many were convinced of the importance of the work and were confident that Alexander would provide the necessary leadership. Friedrich LaHarpe, one of the tutors provided for Alexander by his grandmother Catherine, left Russia when Paul became tsar, returning to his native Switzerland with a French army. In August 1801 he gladly accepted Alexander's invitation to return to Russia to assist his former pupil in the great work of reform. At the same time, Alexander asked another former tutor, Murav'ev, to begin a study for the reform of Moscow University. A minor official, V. N. Karazin, in March 1801 wrote a long letter to Alexander, praising what he presumed was the new tsar's intention to undertake reform. Alexander responded by asking Karazin to draw up some proposals for reform in education. He responded to a suggestion made by P. A. Stroganov by calling together a small group of friends, the so-called Secret Committee, to begin discussion of what needed to be done. In the first months of his reign, then, Alexander found it easy to gather advisors on educational affairs, as on other matters too, who had confidence in him and in the prospects for reform.[14]

In December 1801 the Secret Committee took up the question of education. The committee began its discussion with a detailed proposal from LaHarpe. LaHarpe's draft argued that Russia badly needed an empire-wide educational system, since progress was possible only in societies whose citizenry was literate. He called for the foundation of a ministry of education to supervise the work of a network of universities, which would train the teachers needed to staff a complete school system down to the primary grades. Russia, said LaHarpe, had (or soon could have) three universities, at Moscow, Dorpat, and Vilna. He proposed three more, at St. Petersburg, Kazan, and Kiev. The universities, under the supervision of the ministry, would be the top of the educational ladder, reaching down to the local level, providing control and supervision as well as trained teachers for all the schools in their areas. To facilitate control, LaHarpe suggested that the universities, not any police agency, have censorship authority in all parts of the empire. The Secret Committee all but ignored LaHarpe's plan, in part because the members did not share Alexander's personal esteem for LaHarpe, but also because his proposal was so unexceptional. It closely resembled Mirievo's plans, and many others too, and expressed no better than many others the goals and principles and general ideas on organization and curriculum shared by nearly all in enlightened Europe who agreed that state authority was needed to foster progress in education. Since that was a diverse, as well as large, circle, LaHarpe's proposal did not advance the discussion very far.[15]

The Secret Committee's own discussion advanced the argument not much further. Novosiltsev agreed to write up a proposal to flesh out LaHarpe's rather general statement. Stroganov said that, important though the details would be, it was especially important to understand the main goals. Russia needed especially, not "particular reforms" providing better vocational or professional training at one thing or another, but general education for the masses. The masses needed to have the general education that would permit them to become members of society, capable of exercising the full rights of citizenship. On the other hand, Stroganov thought it obvious that Russia needed better professional training as well. He drew upon his knowledge of French practice, which he had studied extensively, attempting to sketch a system that could meet both needs, providing enlightenment through general education for all while also providing specialized curricula for special vocational needs. A bit hazy on detail, Stroganov nonetheless was clear on insisting that a clear distinction needed to be made between education aimed at general enlightenment and education aimed at professional training. Czartoryski agreed that it was important to make that distinction, and suggested that therefore the schools run by the army, to cite one obvious example, should offer technical training in their specialties and not be a concern of the ministry of public education. Alexander thought it difficult, if not impossible, to draw that line in Russia. Army schools, such as the cadet corps, had to offer general education along with professional training, since the students were unlikely to acquire the necessary general education elsewhere, while the schools that provided basic general education also had to offer vocational training in order to be useful to their localities. Stroganov seemed at various times to see the wisdom of both points of view.[16]

Vague and meandering though it was, the Secret Committee's discussion outlined a general plan that closely resembled that of LaHarpe, or of Mirievo, or of others. They projected a ministry of education to supervise a system of universities that supervised schools organized in a ladder down to the villages of the whole empire. The schools would operate on a classless, or all-class, basis, providing enlightenment for all by offering general education leading up to a liberal arts curriculum and at the same time the development of improved vocational and professional training. The committee spent little time or energy in providing details. The drafting of detailed plans was left to others, who could take up the work upon the foundation of the ministries. An *ukaz* of 8 September 1802 founded the ministries, including the ministry of education. Novosil'tsev contributed the draft, but the law on the ministry expressed the general ideas agreed upon by the whole committee. The Ministry of Public Education (*Ministerstvo narodnogo prosveshcheniia*) would provide "enlightenment" (*prosveshcheniia*) to the whole "people" (*narod*). The minister's full title was "Minister of public education, of the training of youth and the spread of learning," a title expressing well, if in a general way, the overlapping goals of the new ministry.[17]

Alexander at once introduced a note of confusion by naming Zavadovskii to the office of minister. Zavadovskii had few of the qualities of character or intellect that distinguished many of his colleagues who had served the government of Catherine II, such as A. P. Vorontsov. A "favorite" who served Catherine as chairman of the School Commission, Zavadovskii had shown little interest in pushing forward the reforms proposed. LaHarpe and others complained that Zavadovskii was not a suitable choice, for he was not likely to prove zealous in moving in the direction the reformers had in mind. Alexander saw no difficulty in the appointment, telling LaHarpe that it was no more than a gesture to mollify conservative opinion, while his colleagues in the ministry saw to it that Zavadovskii did not "block the good we are trying to do."[18]

Chief among those colleagues was Murav'ev, who was appointed assistant minister on 8 September. On the same day a new agency was founded, the Commission on Schools (*Kommissiia uchilishch*) to serve as the ministry's planning board. Murav'ev was joined on the commission by Czartoryski of the Secret Committee and his friend Count Potocki, one of the ablest of those engaged in the struggle for reform in Poland before the last partition; General Klinger, the director of the First Cadet Corps; and three members of Catherine's old commission, including Fuss. A newcomer, V. N. Karazin, was named chairman. This commission's chief assigned task was to "found universities where they do not yet exist." The universities were to supervise all schools in their areas. The commission was also to work out the details for the schools' "dependence" on the universities and the relationship to the ministry of all the institutions placed under it, including the Academy of Sciences, the Russian Academy, all schools (with the insignificant exception of those under the direct patronage of the dowager empress), all presses, public libraries, laboratories, museums, and all other institutions for the "spread of learning" and, finally, the organization of censorship, now the responsibility of the ministry of education.[19]

This commission had a short career, in good measure because much of its work was well advanced, if not already accomplished in principle. The noble assemblies of the Baltic provinces in early 1802 sent the tsar their plan for a new university in Dorpat. Alexander approved the plan, but changed it almost completely from what the noble planners had in mind. Far from dominated by the nobles, the plans were turned about by the tsar, to provide academic freedom for a self-governing faculty, which was to cooperate with the central government's ministry in providing the education soon to be required of all candidates for places in the state services, regardless of the candidate's social class. In May 1802 Alexander, on a visit to Dorpat, again made clear his support for the faculty's idea of enlightened reform. In September, when the commission began its work, the Dorpat faculty's leader, Parrot, hastened to St. Petersburg to contribute his proposals. Zavadovskii, "bringing up a new objection every day, indeed every hour," did all he could to delay the work, but when Parrot complained to the tsar, Alexander at once issued orders to implement Parrot's plan. The commission began its work, then, with a detailed draft for a university statute worked out and approved by the tsar.[20]

The contributions of Murav'ev reenforced both the general idea and many of the details of the Parrot drafts for Dorpat. In March 1802 the Secret Committee asked Murav'ev to chair a committee (Potocki, Fuss, and Karazin were the members) to study Moscow University, comparing it to the "best foreign examples" in order to propose reforms for the Russian university. Murav'ev, for whom the best foreign example was without question Göttingen, collected testimony from well-known Göttingen professors. All stressed the importance of academic freedom, made possible by the institutional autonomy of the university, and devotion to the development of the higher learning. Nearly all denounced the evil influence of directives from without, especially from the government or church, and also the danger of offering training and professional education rather than leading the student into the self-development nourished by liberal, humane, studies. Professor Brandes argued that a university must not be an institution for training or "upbringing" but a "scholarly corporation" devoted to higher learning. Moreover, it could not maintain "schoolboy discipline," for in the university the student "learns to walk by himself." August Ludwig Schlözer, who knew Russia well at first hand, warned particularly against the evils of state control, which, he said, stifled scholarship and thus defeated the true purpose of the university.

Christopher Meiners, a well-known historian of higher education, amplified Schlözer's points. He recommended, indeed, that universities be located away from the capital and that the government official in charge of the university not reside in the university town—all measures in hopes of minimizing government influence on the internal workings of the university. Meiners was especially insistent that the university devote itself to higher learning in the liberal arts, avoiding professional, applied training as much as possible, for he was convinced that in the long run humane studies produced better men, men whose values made them also the better specialists. He wanted particularly to avoid training in law, theology, and medicine, but urged that these faculties stress their history and philosophy. Even in medicine, the student should get as much pure theory as possible, avoiding applied training. Meiners was convinced that the wisdom of his views had been demonstrated in the Habsburg lands, concluding that the failure of much of the reform in higher education on the Göttingen model resulted from tight government and church control in a program that tried to use learning as the path to developing efficiency in state services.[21]

No member of the Murav'ev committee questioned Meiners' assertion that university reform in Austria failed because it was a Roman Catholic state, and succeeded elsewhere in Protestant states. Nor did any wonder whether failure in some measure was inevitable for a reform that tried to combine the absolutist's interest in training efficient and loyal civil servants with self-directed academic freedom, and tried to use the autonomous university itself as the agency to manage a system of lower schools that offered a curriculum prescribed by the central government and stressed drill and memorization in its teaching methods. Murav'ev shared the views of his Göttingen friends and declared that academic freedom was "necessary not only for the development of education . . . but also for raising popular morals." At Murav'ev's request, Moscow University loaned one of its senior professors to the committee. Professor Bause, a Saxon with a doctorate from Leipzig, had long preached that Russians were too ready to borrow from the West and should now concentrate on development of native values, specifically a university curriculum that used the students' native language, Russian, as the medium of instruction. This, naturally enough, was a welcome proposal. The Murav'ev committee then contributed plans that stressed the patriotic, as well as the practical, goal of developing instruction in Russian at the same time that it recommended the corporate autonomy of Göttingen as the best model for university organization.[22]

Parrot and Murav'ev supplied the materials that the Commission on Schools took up at its first meeting in September 1802. The chairman, Karazin, was not present. He had Alexander's consent to locate one of the new universities in Kharkov, his home town, and had already left to begin the preparations there. Murav'ev and Mirievo were not appointed to the commission but took part in all its meetings. The group parceled out the work: Klinger to work out the details of the proposals for the lower schools, Parrot for Dorpat, Czartoryski for Vilna, and Fuss for the other universities. Mirievo argued for a university in Kiev, but after the meeting of 4 October gave up, agreeing to a university in Kharkov instead, together with Moscow, St. Petersburg, Dorpat, Vilna, and Kazan. In late October Karazin returned to St. Petersburg and presented a plan for the university in Kharkov completely different from the Göttingen model, since "everything in Russia should be new and self-developed." His plan was ignored. The commission met for the last time on 22 October, discussing Murav'ev's materials on Moscow University.[23]

The personnel of the commission were also members of the ministry's governing board, titled the Main School Administration, which summed up the commission's work in the first major piece of legislation of the educational reform, the "Preliminary regulation for public education," issued on 24 January 1803.[24] The regulation announced that "Public education in the Russian Empire is a special state department, entrusted to the minister of that department and under his direction managed by the Main School Administration." In order to provide "for the moral formation of the citizenry, corresponding to the duties and needs of each class, four kinds of schools are established, namely (1) village [prikhodskiia], (2) county [uezd], (3) provincial or gymnasia [gubernskiia ili gimnazii], and (4) universities." Though this definition seemed to call for a class-differentiated system, in detail the system described called for a ladder system, each school leading to the one above, open equally to all classes, and stressing general education at the village level leading to liberal arts at the gymnasium and university levels. The village school stressed reading, writing, arithmetic, and a course based on the text that Catherine the Great's commission provided for the purpose of moral formation, The Duties of Man and Citizen. The two-year county school pursued the same goals, introducing the rudiments of history, geography, philosophy, political economy, and natural history. The four-year gymnasium course took all these subjects further, adding modern and classic languages, and taking mathematics through trigonometry. The schools were to follow not only this prescribed curriculum, but even prescribed hours, students spending thirty hours a week in class in a six-day week (half-days on Wednesdays and Saturdays), teachers responsible for twenty class hours each week. The village school was under the direction of an inspector from the county school, who held the ninth rank in the Table of Ranks, only one step from achieving heriditary nobility in the system that Peter the Great created to supplement if not to replace nobility of birth with aristocracy of talent and achievement. The village school inspector, therefore, was meant to be a figure of importance, as was the inspector for county schools provided by the provincial gymnasium, who held the seventh rank and was empowered to "require" the assistance of the local marshal of nobility.

3. The university statutes

This systematic embodiment of the "decreed enlightenment" in education led the student up the educational ladder to the university, which was in its curriculum and organization modeled after the quite different sort of enlightenment provided by Göttingen. The regulation divided the empire into six educational districts (*okrugi*), in which all schools were under the control of the six "universities founded for the teaching of sciences at the highest level; besides those already in existence at Moscow, Vilna, and Dorpat, others are founded in the St. Petersburg, Kazan, and Kharkov districts. . . ." Each university's administration was to be headed by a rector elected by and from among the professors in their "general university meeting." Professors too were to be elected by the faculty and, like the rector, "confirmed" by the ministry. Professors received the seventh rank, rectors the fifth, in the Table of Ranks. The university was required to supervise the work of all lower schools in its district, providing at least one on-site inspection for each school each year, and reporting annually to the ministry's Main School Administration. The Main School Administration was made up of the "curator" (*popechitel'*) of each district and others named by the tsar. The curator was responsible for the good order of all schools in his district and was required to visit his university at least once every two years. Put another way, he was to live in the capital and thus, if the expectations of the Göttingen advisors worked out, would not unduly influence the ordinary process of the university's work and life.[25]

The enlightened absolutist's goal of increased efficiency was stated in section 24. "Five years from the opening of the schools in his district," it read, "no one will be admitted to civil service which requires legal or other knowledge who has not completed study in a state or private school." The next section empowered the universities to grant degrees, the first, *Kandidat*, requiring successful completion of a three-year course and bringing with it the twelfth rank, i.e., "officer" status. The autonomy of the university was furthered by the provision that each university have its own court for its own members, from which appeals could go only to the Senate. The universities were organized into faculties, each to elect its own dean. The four deans and the rector made up the administrative board to manage the university. This autonomous university was required to maintain a "teachers or pedagogical institute" to prepare students for teaching the required curriculum prescribed for the lower schools. These students would be state-supported and upon graduation would be required to serve at least six years in teaching.

On the same day, 24 January 1803, a law "on the establishment of academic districts" listed the provinces to make up each district and appointed the six curators: Murav'ev for Moscow, Czartoryski for Vilna, Klinger for Dorpat, Novosiltsev for St. Petersburg, Potocki for Kharkov, and Manteuffel for Kazan.[26] This law promised separate "statutes" for each of the universities. The Main School Adminstration held an organization meeting that very day. It agreed that Parrot should provide the statute for Dorpat, Czartoryski that for Vilna, and a "general" statute worked out for the others. In March they issued a proposed budget for the universities, agreeing that each should have twenty-eight professors (at 2,000 rubles each), and forty state student stipends (at 200 rubles each), the same figures as Parrot's plan for Dorpat the previous December. Czartoryski submitted a preliminary "akt" for Vilna in mid-April and a final statute that became law on 18 May 1803. Parrot's statute for Dorpat was issued in September. The draft statute for Moscow was ready in May 1803.[27] It was not promulgated, however, until November 1804. Stroganov ascribed the delay to Zavadovskii's sloth, though something more significant may have been at issue. In August 1803 Zavadovskii revised Parrot's draft statute for Dorpat, making it read that the university accept students from "every free class" rather than "every class." The Main School Administration protested that this revision produced "unacceptable conclusions." They argued to Alexander that "abuses which might arise from unlimited acceptance into the university of persons of all classes are prevented by the very rules written into the statute," since before acceptance the student must "present information about his legal status." The Main School Administration's statement was a good deal less clear than Zavadovskii's revision, for it did not indicate what use the university was to make of information about the students' legal status. Nonetheless, Alexander favored their explanation, and Zavadovskii was overridden.[28]

Despite the occasional ambiguity, the university statues were in most matters both similar and clear enough on the main goals. All called for universities organized into four faculties and a pedagogical institute. All provided for university autonomy and academic freedom; rectors and deans to be elected from and by the professors and the faculties to set their own standards in teaching, examinations, and all other aspects of the life of each university, as well as forming the censorship authority for each district. All called upon the faculties to teach their subjects at the highest levels, while at the same time extending knowledge through their research and writing. All incorporated the Preliminary Regulation, calling upon the universities to manage the schools of their districts. All made similar statements on goals. Czartoryski's "akt" of 19 April 1803 said that Vilna University served "for the formation of useful citizens, for all classes and all types of state service." The Vilna statute (18 May) declared that the university taught "the sciences useful for the citizen of every class in the various types of state service." Parrot's statute for Dorpat (12 September 1803) said that the university was founded for the "common good" and ". . . therefore accepts as students people from every class of native Russians and foreigners. . . ." The Moscow statute (5 November 1804), and the nearly identical ones for Kazan and Kharkov issued on the same day, defined the university as "the highest learned organization, founded for the dissemination of learning. In it youth prepare for entrance into the various branches of state service. . . . Among the sciences taught in the university are those necessary for all who wish to be useful to themselves and to the Fatherland, no matter what role in life or which service they choose."[29]

The Moscow statute added to the Preliminary Regulation's description of the *kandidat* degree, for those who completed the three-year course, a provision for an *attestat* for students who did not successfully complete the course but who "have had the courses for all the necessary knowledge and wish to leave the university. . . ." The *attestat* would show the time spent in study, the courses taken, the recommendation of the professors in those courses, and a statement of conduct signed by the officers of the university. The *attestat* carried with it no right to any level in the Table of Ranks, but it was clearly aimed at providing admission to the services for those who had made some progress in the new system. It was, then, a concession to practicality, for it was obvious that the new system could not soon meet the manpower needs of the services with candidates who had completed the *kandidat*. There were other concessions too. The village school was the base of the new system. Thus, every village, or two, depending on population, "should have" a village school that took in "every class of children, without discrimination by sex or age." The school year in the village was to run "from the end of field work, continuing until the beginning of field work in the next year." The Moscow statute did not repeat the Dorpat statute on accepting students from "any rank or class," but the description of the village school and its place in the ladder system made clear enough the intent to open the system to all classes. However, the village school was not funded by the central government. The universities and other schools were, but it was impractical to attempt funding village schools throughout the empire. In the hope, perhaps, of stimulating local support to make good this lack, the village schools were allowed to teach agriculture, in addition to the required general education subjects. Similar considerations led to other concessions, such as accepting proposals from merchant guilds to add optional courses in "commercial sciences" to the required courses in gymnasia.[30]

Notes

1 Friedrich Bienemann, *Der Dorpater Professor Georg Friedrich Parrot und Kaiser Alexander I* (Reval, 1902), 115–116. This address is reprinted also in E. V. Petukhov, *Imperatorskii Iurevskii, byvshii Derptskii, Universitet 1802–1865* (Iurev, 1902), 112–113 and in N. K. Shil'der, *Imperator Aleksandr I, ego zhizn' i tsarstvovanie,* 4 v. (SPB, 1904–05), II, 32–36.

2 Allen McConnell, "Alexander I's Hundred Days: The Politics of a Paternalist Reformer," *Slavic Review,* 28 (1969), 373–393, and the same writer's *Tsar Alexander I: Paternalistic Reformer* (New York, 1970), 1–44, 138–147, are excellent introductions to the question of reform in the early years of the reign and to serfdom and the military colonies. For legal and institutional reform, see Marc Raeff, *Comprendre l'ancien régime russe* (Paris, 1982), 124–132. For the army, see John L. H. Keep, "The Russian Army's Response to the French Revolution," *Jahrbücher für Geschichte Osteuropas,* 28 (1980), 500–523. Nothing comparable exists for the problem of serfdom. Among the better brief discussions are Jerome Blum, *Lord and Peasant in Russia* (Princeton, 1961), 539–545; George Yaney, *The Systematization of Russian Government: Social Evolution in the Domestic Administration of Imperial Russia 1711–1905* (Urbana, 1973), 162–164.

3 This point is particularly well made in David L. Ransel, *The Politics of Catherinian Russia: The Panin Party* (New Haven, 1975), 269–289, and its terms learnedly discussed in Marc Raeff, *The Well-Ordered Police State: Social and Institutional Change through Law in the Germanies and Russia 1600–1800* (New Haven, 1983), 195–250. See also Raeff's "The Domestic Policies of Peter III and His Overthrow," *American Historical Review,* 75 (1970), 1289–1310. V. O. Kliuchevskii, *Kurs Russkoi Istorii* in *Sochineniia* (8 v., Moscow, 1958), V, 186–193 remains a useful summary analysis of Paul's reign as one of principled reform, rather than merely despotic arbitrariness.

4 Quotation: *Karamzin's Memoir on Ancient and Modern Russia,* Richard Pipes, ed. and trans. (New York, 1966), 136. There was, of course, much in Peter III and especially Paul I that was obnoxious, cruel, capricious, and despotic. In that, at least, they were like the ruler whose tradition they meant to carry on: Peter the Great.

5 O. A. Narkiewicz, "Alexander I and the Senate Reform," *SEER,* XLVII (1969), 115–136, thoroughly presents the issues, concluding that it is "doubtful" in any case that the Senate reforms ever could have led to "genuinely democratic reforms." Karamzin protested on another occasion, citing Montesquieu to point out that "It is bad when a servant obtains mastery over a weak lord, but a prudent lord respects his choice servants, and considers their honor his own. The rights of the well-born are not something apart from monarchical authority— they are its principal and indispensable instrumentality by means of which the body politic is kept in motion." Pipes, *Karamzin's Memoir,* 200.

6 For good discussions, sensitive to the ambiguities in both these ideas on constitution and Alexander's approach to them, see Marc Raeff, *Michael Speransky, Statesman of Imperial Russia* (The Hague, 1957), 29–46; Patricia K. Grimsted, *The Foreign Ministers of Alexander I* (Berkeley, 1969), 49–55. Reflecting their importance for the whole history of Imperial Russia, these questions have become the focus of an extensive literature in both the West and the Soviet Union. A lucid and learned discussion of the questions and the literature is in David Christian, "The Political Views of the Unofficial Committee in 1801: Some New Evidence," *Canadian-American Slavic Studies,* v. 12 (1978), 247–258.

7 On the appeal of Göttingen's example, see Klingenstein, "Despotismus und Wissenschaft," *Wiener Beiträge zur Geschichte der Neuzeit*, Bd 3 (1976), 127–155. On the Jesuits and the National School Commission, see Stanislaw Litak, "Das Schulwesen der Jesuiten in Polen: Entwicklung und Verfall," *Wiener Beiträge zur Geschichte der Neuzeit*, Bd 5 (1978), 124–137.

8 R. Steven Turner, "University Reformers and Professorial Scholarship in Germany 1760–1806," *The University in Society*, L. Stone, ed. (2 v., Princeton, 1974), II, 495–531, provides a judicious introduction to the problem of university reform in eighteenth-century Germany.

9 Max J. Okenfuss, "Education and Empire: School Reform in Enlightened Russia," *Jahrbücher für Geschichte Osteuropas*, Bd 27 (1979), 41–68, and Isabel de Madariaga, "The Foundation of the Russian Educational System by Catherine II," *SEER*, v. 57 (1979), 369–395, are superior, well-informed discussions that make entirely obsolete such earlier treatments as Nicholas Hans, *History of Russian Educational Policy 1701–1917* (London, 1931) and W. H. E. Johnson, *Russia's Educational Heritage* (Pittsburgh, 1950).

10 George M. O'Brien, "Maria Theresa's attempt to Educate an Empire," *Paedagogica Historica*, v. 10 (1970), 542–565, provides a useful introduction to the system's development in the Habsburg lands. The changes from the Austrian system that Mirievo introduced in Russia had echoes in the programs and practices of the Polish National Education Commission, of the Jesuit network, and of French reformers both before and after 1789. None, however, seem to have directly influenced Mirievo, who came to propose changes from the Austrian system through his own experience in applying the Felbiger system to the Slavic-speaking, Orthodox villages of the Habsburg empire. For details on Mirievo's work in Russia, see Peter Polz, "Theodor Jankovic und die Schulreform in Russland," in *Die Aufklärung in Ost- und Südosteuropa*, Erna Lesky, others, eds. (Koln, 1972), 119–174. See also J. L. Black, *Citizens for the Fatherland: Education, Educators, and Pedagogical Ideas in Eighteenth Century Russia* (Boulder, 1979), 130–151. On Mirievo's work under Maria Theresa, see Philip J. Adler, "Habsburg School Reform Among the Orthodox Minorities, 1770–1780," *Slavic Review*, v. 33 (1974), 23–45.

11 M. I. Sukhomlinov, *Izsledovaniia i stat'i po russkoi literature i prosveshcheniiu*, 2 v. (SPB, 1889), I, 56. S. V. Rozhdestvenskii, "Universitetskii vopros v tsarstvovanie imp. Ekaterina IIoi i sistema narodnago prosveshcheniia po Ustavam 1804 goda," *Vestnik Evropy*, 1907 (No. 7), 29.

12 The best discussion of the "class-professional" character of the schools remains S. V. Rozhdestvenskii, *Ocherki po istorii sistem narodnago prosveshcheniia v Rossii v XVIII–XIX vekakh*, I (SPB, 1912), 264–281. The combination of general and liberal with technical and vocational education is well described at its beginnings by Max J. Okenfuss in "The Jesuit Origins of Petrine Education," *The Eighteenth Century in Russia*, John Garrard, ed. (Oxford, 1973), 106–130, and "Technical Training in Russia under Peter the Great," *History of Education Quarterly*, 13 (1973), 325–345. Undoubtedly the best analysis of the role of class-professional education in defining, and tightening, class lines in eighteenth-century Russia is Gregory L. Freeze, *The Russian Levites: Parish Clergy in the Eighteenth Century* (Cambridge, 1977), 78–106.

13 M. T. Beliavskii, "Shkola i sistema obrazovaniia v Rossii v kontse XVIII stoletiia," *Vestnik Moskovskogo Universiteta*, 1959 (No. 2), 105–120, concludes that Catherine's reforms were more successful than previously realized. See, e.g., P. Miliukov, *Ocherki po istorii russkoi kul'tury*, II (4th ed., SPB, 1905), 327, which gives for the year 1796 a total of 316 schools with 17,341 students. For

these Miliukov figures, see also Hans, *Russian Educational Policy*, 32; Johnson, *Russia's Educational Heritage*, 60, 263.

14 Arthur Boehlingk, *Friedrich Caesar LaHarpe*, 2 v. (Bern, 1925), II, 40–41; Sukhomlinov, *Izsledovaniia*, II, 116–117; Nikolai Mikhailovich, *Graf Pavel Aleksandrovich Stroganov*, 3 v. (SPB, 1903), II, 5–7, 26–29 (hereafter cited as Stroganov); Shil'der, *Aleksandr*, II, 32–36.

15 The notes kept by Stroganov are the main source for the committee's work. For the committee's discussion of LeHarpe's plan, see Stroganov, II, 144–148.

16 *Stroganov*, II, 26–29, 40–44, 208–212, 225–226. The members of the Secret Committee, N. N. Novosiltsev, V. P. Kochubei, Adam Czartoryski, and P. A. Stroganov, had in common not only personal friendship with Alexander, but relative youth (Novosiltsev was the eldest, born in 1761) and yet considerable experience in government. E. E. Roach, "The Origins of Alexander I's Unofficial Committee," *The Russian Review*, v. 28 (1969), 315–326.

17 *Polnoe sobranie zakonov rossiiskoi imperii*, 243–248 (No. 20406).

18 Nikolai Mikhailovich, *Imperator Aleksandr I* (Petrograd, 1914), 363 (Alexander to LaHarpe, 7 July 1803).

19 *Sbornik postanovlenii po ministerstvu narodnago prosveshcheniia*, 15 v. (SPB, 1875–1902), I, 4–5.

20 Parrot's work in St. Petersburg is carefully described in E. E. Martinson, *Istoriia osnovaniia tartuskogo (b. Derptskogo—iurevskogo) universiteta* (Leningrad, 1954), 53–61. His plan, issued as an "akt" by the ministry, 12 December 1802, is in *Sbornik postanovlenii*, I, 6–12, Bienemann, *Parrot*, 164, prints his complaint to Alexander about Zavadovskii's stalling.

21 Rozhdestvenskii, *Istoricheskii obzor*, 56–57; Sukhomlinov, *Izsledovaniia*, I, 42–56. Schlözer spent much time in Russia; his first visit was in 1771, and he taught Russian history at Göttingen from 1772. Edward Winter, ed., *August Ludwig v. Schlözer und Russland* (Berlin, 1961), 1–41.

22 Murav'ev quoted in Rozhdestvenskii, *Istoricheskii obzor*, 39. On Bause, see *Biograficheskii slovar professorov i prepodavatelei Imperatorskago Moskovskago universiteta*, 2 v. (Moscow, 1855), I, 68–85.

23 The record of the Commission's meetings, printed in S. F. Platonov, ed., *Opisanie del arkhiva Ministerstva nardonago prosveshcheniia* (Petrograd, 1917), 88–90, suggests that the members planned further discussion on Moscow University and offers no hint that they realized that the 22 October meeting would be the last. Members continued to submit materials for the commission's files as late as July 1804. The proposals made by Fuss and Mirievo are printed in Rozhdestvenskii, *Materialy*, 380–395. Sukhomlinov, *Izsledovaniia*, I, 56–58, discusses the various plans, stressing the features and language that appeared in the final legislation in 1803–1804. The best discussion of the commission is Rozhdestvenskii, "Universitetskii vopros," *VE*, 33–37.

24 *Sbornik postanovlenii*, I, 13–21. Many summaries are available, including Rozhdestvenskii, *Istoricheskii obzor*, 50–51; Hans, *Educational Policy*, 37–38. Perhaps the best is in M. F. Shabaeva, ed., *Ocherki istorii shkoly i pedagogicheskoi mysli narodov SSSR: XVIII v.—pervaia polovina XIX v.* (Moscow, 1973), 198–199.

25 Alexander named to the first Main School Administration all the members of the School Commission. For all personnel of the Main School Administration for Alexander's reign, see Sukhomlinov, *Izsledovaniia*, I, 490–491. Catherine's old School Commission continued to function until March 1803, carrying out a number of tasks at Zavadovskii's direction and preparing reports on the lower schools. Professor Beliavskii has found that the reports contained much

misinformation. S. V. Rozhdestvenskii, "Komissia ob uchrezhdenii narodnykh uchilishch 1783–1803 g. i ministerstvo narodnago prosveshcheniia," *ZhMNP*, 1906 (May), 17–18; Beliavskii, "Shkola i sistema," *VMU*, 1959 (No. 2), III.

26 *Sbornik postanovlenii*, I, 21–22. Manteuffel was the leader of the noble opposition to Parrot at Dorpat and had been elected "president" of the university by the noble assembly. Alexander abolished the office of university "president" as "unnecessary." Manteuffel knew nothing whatever about Kazan and was soon replaced as Kazan curator. It seems likely that he was appointed simply to keep him busy in St. Petersburg while Parrot and the faculty completed the organization of the new university at Dorpat.

27 Tsentral'nyi gosudarstvennyi istoricheskii arkhiv (Leningrad), fond 733, opis' 28, delo 23, listy 1–11. Hereafter TsGIAL.

28 S. V. Rozhdestvenskii, "Soslovnyi vopros v russkikh universitetakh v pervoi chertverti xix veka," *ZhMNP*, 1907 (May), 84–85; Rozhdestvenskii, "Universitetskii vopros," *VE*, 41. For Stroganov's comment on Zavadovskii, see Stroganov to Novosiltsev, 28 October 1804, in A. N. Pypin, *Die Geistigen Bewegungen in der ersten Hälfte des XIX Jahrhunderts*, B. Minzes, trans. (Berlin, 1894), 143.

29 The statutes are printed in *Sbornik postanovlenii*, I, 39–46 (Vilna), 139–199 (Dorpat), 295–331 (Moscow, Kharkov, and Kazan). The reasons that St. Petersburg's statute was not forthcoming are discussed in chapter II. Most differences among the other five statutes proved inconsequential. The exception was the different treatment of theology. At Dorpat the theology faculty was a Lutheran seminary. At Vilna the theology faculty was a Catholic seminary. At the others no provision was made for a theology faculty. Courses in Orthodoxy were listed for the faculty of moral-political science, but no effort to offer these courses was made for many years.

30 Rozhdestvenskii, "Universitetskii vopros," *VE*, 446; Rozhdestvenskii, *Istoricheskii obzor*, 51–52. Franklin A. Walker, "Popular Response to Public Education in the Reign of Alexander I (1801–1825)," *History of Education Quarterly* (Winter, 1984), 527–543, based on the periodical press, particularly *Moskovskiia vedomosti* and *Severnaia pochta*, finds much evidence of favorable local response to the government's plans, including donations from many individuals and noble, merchant, and clergy groups interested in founding and assisting village schools in their communities.

70

THE AMERICAN STATE
UNIVERSITY TODAY

Alexander Kinghorn

Source: *Universities Quarterly* X (1955–6): 69–79.

Numerous commentators on higher education in America, especially those who set their standards with reference to British universities, have professed to doubt whether the American State University may be properly styled a 'university' at all. From these we hear of 'factory methods', 'low standards', the curse of fraternities, degrees awarded wholesale, often in the most curious fields of knowledge, useless and picayune research on the part of the faculty, and so on *ad infinitum*.

Of course it is all true enough, up to a point, and the average American professor would readily admit the widespread existence of these phenomena, but the State university can only be properly appreciated against its own background, and it is misleading to judge it with one eye on the British university, which is not its counterpart and fulfils an entirely different function. The State university is owned by the taxpayers of the State which it serves, and is administered by a legislature acting through a Board of Trustees which is responsible for its policy. The members of this Board are as a rule appointed by the Governor of the State and are usually men of wealth, prestige and political power. Authority is, in the final analysis, out of the hands of university officials, who have little or no say in the setting of entrance qualifications; these are generally nominal and inevitably elastic. When a President or Chancellor is appointed, his office is inclined to be 'political' in the baser sense of the word, and those who hold such offices continue to do so only so long as they are prepared to act as executives for the policy-makers who control the purse-strings. Individual heads of departments are not usually subjected to much interference as far as the arrangement of curricula and the employment of staff are concerned, but beyond this they have little power. Their salaries are paid by the State, and everyone connected with the actual running of the university, from the President to the campus labourer, is a State employee.

The theory of the State university is based upon an interpretation of the word 'democracy' which, in connexion with American education, has come to mean that schooling to the highest level available is every man's right. Educators have set themselves to provide opportunities for every person to train themselves to the limits of their capacity, and university teachers, though they believe whole-heartedly in the ideal of higher education for all, realise now that the wholesale application of such a theory does not go far towards solving the practical problems brought about through unlimited college entry. Many of them in fact, are now prepared to admit, however unwillingly, that this costly experiment has turned out to be a failure. European critics of the U.S. system are apt to forget that it is an experimental measure, and also that the ideals of the traditional academic scholars are implicit within it. Their claim that the B.A. degree has been debased in America ignores the fact that the ancient aristocratic traditions have not been considered important by the experimenters who set up the American B.A. and put it within the reach of the average man. The notion of an intellectual élite is quite foreign, in a literal sense, to the American, and he would exhibit violent hostility towards any attempt on the part of educators to make university degrees exclusive. At the same time, paradoxically enough, he is perfectly willing to accept a ruling class made up of high-powered industrialists, since they are 'practical' men who seem to him to be directly responsible for raising his standard of living to its present high level. As far as he is concerned, education ought to be a training for life in modern America, and every citizen should be educated as a matter of course.

Since a stress on the social skills—the taking of one's place in American society as a 'normal' citizen—makes itself felt from the primary level onwards, the old-fashioned 'three Rs' have, to a great extent, been routed, and there is not much attempt on the part of the public-school teacher to impart a European-style grounding to his charges. Those who would try to gear their instruction to the college admission level find, in many instances, that it is an impossibility. A great deal of time is spent on non-academic activities which, one might be justified in thinking, should be reserved for out-of-school hours, and parental opposition to 'cramming' is usually strong enough to discourage the most conscientious pedagogue. One parent complained to the principal of a large school in Texas that her eleven-year-old son was being overworked—he had been made to learn forty spellings by way of preparation, one of these being the excessively difficult word 'arithmetic'! The offending teacher was politely warned off. Very little homework is set in the public schools, even in the highest classes. In addition, these schools have of late fallen into the hands of a group who consider 'teaching methods' to be of greater importance than a teacher's academic knowledge of his subject. The champions of method have succeeded in establishing certain technical requirements for student-teachers which take no account whatsoever of their professional capabilities. A young man may thus instruct high-school pupils in the pre-college class in, say, history or mathematics provided that his certificate in education displays twelve or eighteen 'hours' of method, even though he himself has passed only an elementary college course in these subjects.

The end result of all this is that students enter their State university with a very poor academic background, but a very strong 'social' sense and a thorough orientation in American middle-class society, in which dancing, mingling without embarrassment with members of the opposite sex, mechanical skills such as driving cars, team sports (especially football) and an inordinate respect for wealth all loom large. The education that they have undergone up to this time has been of one sort; once in college, they are asked to accept another sort altogether, in which the traditional curriculum plays a large part, and since their most impressionable years have been spent in a Forest of Arden, it is perhaps not surprising that they try to prolong them for as long as possible beyond the allotted span.

Thus we find two opposing forces at work on the student—the life of ease and merriment which he has brought with him to college, represented by a welter of social activities, fraternities, sororities, sports and group organizations of all kinds, and, alongside it, the life of study which he is by training ill-equipped to undertake, with all its pitfalls, examinations to pass, standards to maintain, mental discipline to achieve and, something quite new to him, a threat of failure if he does not satisfy his teachers. Between the two the freshman student is often at a loss, and apt to flounder in a morass not by any means of his own making. It is true that by European standards those of the undergraduate schools in an American State university are to be considered low, but they are none the less demanding enough as far as the average American high-school product is concerned.

Unfortunately, the deficient preparation of the incoming students forces most professors and lecturers to spend a disproportionate amount of time on elementary instruction[1] (on a level corresponding to that of the fourth form in an English grammar school), and much of their teaching, even on more advanced levels, is directed towards changing the attitudes inculcated by the high-school. It is, however, surprising how rapidly these years of lost time are made up, and although the first few weeks in his new environment are inclined to harrow him with fear and wonder, the brighter freshman generally realizes quickly enough that he must somehow adapt himself to it. To preserve his reputation in the group, if for no other reason, he must settle down to independent study.

Yet there is, as may be imagined, a colossal wastage. It is safe to say that of the average annual intake into any given State university during the post-war period, less than half proceeded beyond the second year of the four-year degree curriculum. This number includes the many who regarded the university simply as a social stamping-ground and ignored their studies, those who failed the examinations, gave up in despair or were compulsorily removed, and the few who could find no value in what such an institution had to offer them. It may be argued that it is better for everyone to have the opportunity to see what the inside of a university looks like, on the grounds that it will make for a more enlightened citizenry, but in practice it is social pressure which forces about half the nation's eighteen-year-olds into college, and not any desire on their part either to assert their 'rights' or to work for a degree. Such motivation, or the lack of it, is to be roundly condemned. although it may, like conscription, help to relieve the congestion on the American labour market. A recent article comparing the British and American educational systems stated that the majority of American children 'graduate' from high school at 18, that half of all 18-year-olds enter college, and that about half of these eventually receive a Bachelor's degree. To the uninitiated, this horde of graduates might be thought to indicate a national level of academic training second to none in the world, and certainly far above that of England, where 70 per cent of children leave school at the age of fifteen and only about 5 per cent are admitted to a university. But when the visitor from abroad perceives, on closer inspection, that the standard of instruction and examination varies from university to university, from college to college, from department to department, and even from class to class within one department (ranging from excellent to completely inadequate), he is inclined to mistrust a system which overcomes the problem of handling excessively large numbers of freshmen students by the indiscriminate appointment of part-time instructors, and teaching assistants of low qualifications. The unfortunate freshman may be unlucky in his teachers and thus often gets very little indeed from his elementary courses.

The student's reactions to this is, considering his previous training, normal enough. The bare minimum of study, usually something less than he is told to do, and the reliance upon the formula that a united front of apathy towards book-learning will be sufficient to remove most academic obstacles for himself and his fellows is, sad to relate, the characteristic feature of the average State university student at all undergraduate levels. The method of grading examinations, from A to F, with encouraging and discouraging plusses and minuses, permits the majority to avoid the F grade. A grade of D is easily obtained, and a gentleman's C is standard. Those who are energetic members of a fraternity find that the formidable resources of this clique are at his disposal in the shape of tutors, cribs, and even carefully-organized files of old essays, so that there is little excuse for his dropping below the C level. Such results satisfy the social group, and the stigma, if any, is upon the superior student who defies the cult of mediocrity and sets himself above his fellows by consistently getting A's. Academic competition in college, as in the high-school, is frowned upon, and although there are prizes and awards for almost every other form of activity, from blowing smoke rings to growing the longest beard, there are hardly any for scholastic proficiency.

Since there is no great natural desire on the part of the majority of undergraduates to embark on a career of learning for its own sake, most entrants show preference for a course which will yield some obvious material rewards. Hence the State university has largely become an instrument to advertise the 'vocational' aim of education at the expense of other aims, and it is a fact that most State universities show signs of becoming nothing more than trade schools. The proportion of students training for occupations, such as business, hotel-management, radio and television, domestic science and dietetics, journalism, and the like, is far in excess of those reading languages, literature and philosophy. Funds for purposes of vocational training are, moreover, much more readily forthcoming than are those for the support of arts subjects, and there is no comparison between the equipment of the business school and that of the average Department of English. Departments of classics are mostly very small and have very few students, even on the elementary level. All this may be considered 'anti-intellectual', and indeed it is, but it is perfectly in keeping with the designs of a strongly materialistic society. The students have always been reminded of the value of 'being practical', and have developed a half-baked but nevertheless firm distrust of theory. They can see the point in acquiring a useful skill, but they find it very difficult to justify the acquiring of a philosophy, since, after all, their future employer will judge them on their capacity to do a specific job of work competently, and not on their general cultural background. Even freshman English is called a 'skills' course in composition, and taught as a useful social accomplishment, not as a foundation for 'culture'. Culture as the European understands it is regarded as an ornamental appendage to living, and not as part of living itself. The society which the State university is supposed to represent is predominantly a business society, which can grasp facts more easily than ideas, and in their efforts to become a part of it and aid its continuity, the students conform to its ideals and requirements. Not to be 'skilled' is to be eccentric, and eccentricity of this kind, even though it may go hand-in-hand with an encyclopaedic knowledge of European history, is an object of derision in this society.

It must be remarked that the aims of the educators are not generally in accord with such a definition of the objects of a university training, since the power of the traditional curriculum is, though waning, still great enough to condition much of the university policy. At present the degree programmes fluctuate between arts and vocational courses, and there is a good deal of disagreement among educationalists as to what kind of a man the State university should send out into the world. Although it is generally admitted that every student ought to be exposed to doses of literature and philosophy during his first two years in college, the third and fourth years find very few who are not devoting their energies to a strictly professional curriculum.

In theory, such 'exposure' is supposed to turn out enlightened young men and women, of all-round qualifications, who are knowledgeable in a wide variety of subjects and can take their places as mature voting citizens. In practice the results of the so-called 'liberal arts' curriculum are very different. The majority of students who complete it leave with their vocational qualifications, the assumption that a course signifies knowledge, a distaste for the liberal arts and the woolly-minded theorists who control them, and an even more firmly-rooted conviction that to make money is the only worthwhile thing in life. In short, they are mentally atrophied; far from having been an inspiration, their studies have had the opposite effect, and have deadened their capacity for systematic thought. It is this anti-intellectualism which they take with them, and the disappointing thing about it is not that they have forgotten the substance of their arts courses, but that they dismissed it enthusiastically and are, in spite of it, ready and eager to attach the label 'useless' to all things cultural. Of course, one must realize that few of them really believe sincerely that the Humanities are nothing more than a decoration, but the herd instinct is strong, and the social group must be adhered to, right or wrong. It is therefore not so remarkable that very few American college graduates ever buy non-technical books not strictly connected with their professional interests, either during or after their stay in college. This is a sorry result of such an expensive education, which, far from whetting the appetite of the individual for more knowledge, seems to have the contrary effect upon the bulk of those who undergo it.

Those students who go into graduate work are usually of a higher intellectual calibre than their fellows, and, it is to be hoped, have scholastic convictions, but it is all the same doubtful whether many of them at this stage are really equipped to enter upon serious research. It would be better for them to spend an extra year in acquiring a background which the B.A. course has failed to provide. Yet in one year the American graduate student may produce a thesis and obtain a Master's degree which has little to recommend it save as a training in preparing a formal dissertation, with bibliography and foot-notes. Droves of high-school teachers lured on, not by the bait of knowledge infinite, but by the prospect of a substantial rise in salary pursuivant upon the acquiring of the M.A., descend annually upon the summer school, there to take vacation courses and grind out 'theses' literally by the score in a spirit which is anything but admirable. Every now and then one may encounter an exceptional piece of research, but it cannot be denied that most of these productions are dull, wooden précis which have no business to be called 'research' at all. That they should entitle their authors to dub themselves Masters of Arts is a sorry reflection on the graduate schools which unblushingly promote this kind of hack work.

The same may be said, with reservations, for 50 per cent of Doctoral dissertations. Since the Ph.D. is the maximum and minimum qualification for entry to the academic profession, and carries with it a mystic initiation into what has been referred to as 'the most expensive and least luxurious club in the world',[3] it must, by hook or crook, be obtained as quickly as possible. Comparatively few Ph.D. candidates are full-time research students; most are engaged in elementary teaching in the department from which their doctorate is to come and a good deal of their time is taken up with the correction of freshman essays. The embryonic Ph.D. must somehow make up for the shortcomings of his previous training by feverish cramming, since he is supposed to have a sound general knowledge of the entire field of his subject as well as a specialist knowledge of his research topic. Many State universities have an 'up or out' rule, which threatens the candidate with dismissal if he does not complete his course work and lodge his dissertation within five years.

Under such a programme as this, it may be imagined that many Ph.D.s are entirely lacking in the strong convictions of the sincere scholar. They want to teach in a college, but not to write a dissertation. Since the first is denied them without the second, they resign themselves to several years of what they admit is drudgery, and become Doctors of Philosophy with sighs of relief and a soundly-implanted loathing of 'research' in any shape or form. For the next decade, they may serve their dissertation to learned journals in the shape of articles, and ascend the promotion ladder as university teachers knowing very well that the powers care little whether they teach well or not. The poor teacher is answerable only to his own conscience, but woe betide the Ph.D. of less than seven years' standing who does not publish—he will perish, no matter how fine a teacher he may be.

Many departments keep a 'Departmental Bibliography of Work in Progress' and urge staff members to keep it up to date. Were all the hypothetical articles and books in these files to become fact, our libraries would have to build extensions, but fortunately, perhaps, half of them remain 'in progress'. The condescending attitude towards American scholarship exhibited by British critics of the U.S. is indeed none too harsh on much of the other half, but book for book, there are quite as many first-rate publications in academic subjects put out in America as in Britain or anywhere else. But American experts, per capita, probably create more useless reading for other experts than do their counterparts abroad, since the scholastic positions they hold depend very largely upon their personal bibliographies, and there are many more outlets, in the form of professional and semi-professional journals, for deliberately contrived articles than there are in other countries.

There are, it is true, a few 'enlightened' departments who scorn this spurious scholarship, but these are not found in State universities. Under such a system, the genuine scholar stands in danger of lagging behind in the jockeying for position which attends his first few years as a university teacher, and many men of this type go unrecognized for too long. It is simply not possible for a young Ph.D., however talented, to spend twenty years in thinking out a monumental work and another fifteen in writing it, as is common in European universities. In the U.S. he must conform to the materialistic *mores* and produce. Hence the cult of mediocrity is served once again: promotion is a matter of seniority and the steady production of articles, and the young brilliant man, unless he is very fortunate, must simply wait until he becomes an older brilliant man before he is given the opportunity of teaching even M.A. candidates. It is a general truth that most arts departments pay more deference to the mature hack than to his less experienced, but obviously more brilliant colleague (though the latter's worth is invariably afforded tacit recognition). In consequence of this, the sharp wits of young Ph.D.s are condemned to blunt themselves on freshman and sophomore courses of the most elementary kind, and by the time the latter become senior, they readily acquiesce in the perpetuation of the whole static system. For such acquiescence, they should not be judged too harshly, since for something like fifteen years a tremendous gulf has separated their research from their teaching, and the work which they did for their own Ph.D.s has probably never been put to any direct use in the classroom. In any average English department, something between 50 and 80 per cent of the faculty are engaged in teaching nothing but freshman and sophomore classes, in which only a mere trickle of students have any intention of specializing in the humanities. Critics who rail at the State university in the usual terms of 'factory methods' and 'student apathy' leave unsung the fate of the real sufferers, namely, the students and young instructors whose curiosity is dulled by these causes. Nowhere perhaps is alertness, eagerness to learn, originality of approach or other such qualities less honoured than in these over-grown institutions. Too many examinations are 'objective' by nature (due partly to large classes, partly to sheer lack of imagination), and demand 'yes', 'no', or 'one sentence' answers to question on literature. One sophomore class was asked, with respect to Gulliver's third voyage, 'How high did the flying island fly?' Although the professor in question (a scholar of considerable reputation in research) probably set this question and others like it because he was realistically aware of the need to discipline the student to achieve the crudest kind of comprehension, it indicates something of the deplorable atmosphere which prevails at this level.

The intelligent students who demand more from their State university than they appear to be getting are beginning to raise their voices in complaint. In this they have been joined by a group of liberally-minded scholars, including several university Chancellors, and ex-Presidents. One of them recently called the American colleges 'cultural flophouses', or havens of rest which serve the purpose of keeping the young out of mischief until they reach the age of responsibility. And when the President of a large

State university says, as one did in a speech last December, that a college education frequently ruins what might otherwise have been a good plough-boy, mechanic or artisan, he stands in less danger of being considered 'undemocratic' than he did even two years ago.

From a student committee on curriculum at the University of Texas we have a pamphlet recommending a change in academic policy. The opening paragraphs are worth quoting, since they sum up the current situation in most, if not all, of the State institutions of higher learning in America:

'The university, reflecting the desire of its supporting citizenry for a "useful" rather than a sound education, is in imminent danger of being derelict in its duty to develop well-rounded, responsible personalities of breadth and judgment with a keen sense of civic awareness. The meaning of education has been corrupted into a "trade-school" attitude that makes little attempt to prepare students to make value-judgments, to develop vigorous and independent habits of thought, and thereby enable him to accept, safeguard, and enrich his heritage of freedom by exercising his duties in an intelligent and responsible manner. . . .

'. . . There is an increasing tendency for business, industry, and the professions to recognise that the college graduate of to-day fails to meet their expectations. . . . They see, too, that the substitution of mere job-training for a balanced education fails completely to meet the desparately-felt need for leadership with vision and flexibility.

'. . . The university cannot allow so many of its students and graduates to remain satisfied with "capsule literature, comic-strip art and platitude religion", to continue irresponsibly in the exercise of civic duties in a democratic nation, and to be unable to function properly as industrial and business leaders. . . . Too often the student is not concerned except with what will contribute either to his material welfare and pleasure or to his graduation at the earliest possible date. Apathy towards serious study and a cynicism towards general cultural values seem to be the order of the day. . . . Too frequently his courses are duplicatory, dull, inefficient, and handed to him in capsule form by sometimes incapable, often uninterested, and always underpaid teachers. Little wonder he absorbs so little, is prone to cheat, and has little respect for his instructor!'[4]

Statements like this are a happy sign for the future, and in a country as ready to experiment as America, it is reasonable to assume that drastic changes in the whole practice of State-controlled education, from the elementary schools up to the university level, are due to take place before many more years have passed.

Notes

1 A recent survey taken at the University of Illinois demonstrates the decline in the standards of entrants during the period 1939–54. In 1939, for example, 7 per cent of freshmen failed the placement tests for freshman English and had to take instead a noncredit course in basic rhetoric before registering for the ordinary composition course. In 1947 this number had risen to 14 per cent and by 1954 it was 42 per cent. Allowing for the increased enrolment of the post-war years, these figures would still appear to have some significant relation to the academic standards of Illinois high-schools.

2 J. A. Campbell's 'Chemical Education in England' (*Journal of Chemical Education*, XXXI, No. 11, November 1954), 581–6.

3 Jacques Barzum, *Teacher in America* (Boston, 1945), 196.

4 'Education and the University' (Report of the Committee on Core Curriculum of the Student Assembly at the University of Texas, January 1955).

71

AFFIRMATIVE ACTION

Sheldon Rothblatt

Source: S. Rothblatt, *Education's Abiding Moral Dilemma: Merit and Worth in the Cross-Atlantic Democracies, 1800–2006*, Oxford Studies in Comparative Education, Oxford: Symposium Books, 2007, pp. 277–300.

The setting

Among the many purposes of the California Master Plan for Higher Education was a partitioning of institutions by mission, and hence by funding for missions, in order to provide a principle of merit recognition that would also allow for the strong possibility of upward mobility. Student demand for higher education in the state was to be accommodated within a linked three-tiered system of colleges and universities. Each system would be capable of growth, although Clark Kerr himself did not really want the campuses of the University of California to grow beyond 27,500 undergraduates and postgraduates, hoping that they would never achieve the mammoth size of Midwestern state universities. Once a campus had achieved its maximum allotted size, or seemed in reach of it, a new campus would be built. This may have been a sort of memory under different conditions of his love for small colleges such as the Swarthmore that he had attended, but it could never be achieved within the structure of a research university. The University of California at Santa Cruz, which Kerr hoped would be a 'Swarthmore in the redwoods', was to have that special, more intimate character. He died expressing disappointment that Santa Cruz had not truly developed as a collegiate university.[1]

The Berkeley and Los Angeles (UCLA) campuses have now grown well beyond Kerr's planned limit, the consequence of a decline in income received from state revenues putting on hold any further increase in the numbers of campuses in the UC federation, apart from one still developing, the University of California at Merced in the interior Central Valley of California which has experienced sustained population growth. Undergraduate demand for entry to the University of California campuses, never greater than today, has to be contained largely within the structure of the presently constituted University. One consequence is that the pressure for admission to existing campuses has increased to a point where selection is more problematical than at any other historical moment. It is doubly problematical in light of the history of affirmative action, a phrase without a precise meaning, which is part of its difficulty, but encompassing measures for increasing the numbers of particular minority groups and especially those who on paper lack the academic qualifications to compete against students with better records and stronger family support. The paradox for elite institutions is that the wish to admit more undergraduates with Latino and African-American backgrounds occurs at precisely the historical moment when the academic barriers to entry are greater by being more academically competitive.

The difficulty is common to all elite institutions, but to illustrate the historical changes we can continue discussion of the University of California. Before the 1960s, entrance to the University of California campuses was not nearly so competitive. Despite the mixed quality of California's secondary schools, virtually anyone who met the basic eligibility standards was welcomed, and for most campuses (there were far fewer unitary campuses at the time) this situation remained true for several more decades, with the qualification that as the Scholastic Assessment Test (SAT) was adopted in the 1960s, intimations of the future were present. But at the two large undergraduate campuses of Berkeley and UCLA the future had already arrived. During the 1980s and 1990s a greater output of fine students from California's better high schools enabled these two campuses to benefit from the competition for limited places that rising numbers allowed. The demand for entry has increased to the point where Berkeley and UCLA each received from 26,000 to 38,000 applications for 4000 freshman places.[2] The rejection rate for these two campuses is therefore substantial. However, it must be remembered that some applicants will be redirected to other campuses, and some will decline an offer.

Furthermore, the network of California feeder schools, public and private, was becoming even more highly differentiated into select and non-select high schools. One study reported that in the year 1999, 100 elite schools, to include some public high schools, provided one-fifth of the freshmen admitted to all the campuses of the University of California. By sharp contrast, high schools with low income and minority students sent only one of every 200 students accepted. Regional dominance was also apparent. The better schools were in the San Francisco or Los Angeles suburbs, the poorer ones in the interior valleys or lower-wage counties. The familiar formula held up: private or public suburban secondary education, wealthier catchment areas, regional location and the consistently critical variable of parental education. The formula was similar in Britain.[3] One major exception to trends in California was a state school that did not serve an affluent population and contained a substantial number of ethnic minorities, especially

Latino. School representatives attributed their success to competitive entry, a strong academic curriculum and high expectations[4], a forthrightly elite combination that most American urban secondary schools were unable to employ. (Nothing was said in this source, however, about whether rejected students were then admitted to less competitive public high schools, thus contributing to their academic difficulties.)

Meritocracy had apparently triumphed; and for precisely that reason the goals of affirmative action could not be met unless mechanisms were found to re-establish the principle of worth in a new political environment. Admissions officers throughout the United States, spurred on by campus administrations, started adopting strategies that were to increase the suspicion, long part of the American admissions process, that decisions were being made on non-academic grounds. Before about 1945, legacy preferences at the leading private institutions, combined with outright prejudice even at some public campuses, meant that many outstanding applicants were never accorded even rudimentary attention. Little public fuss was made about such matters. Country-club social exclusion was simply accepted. The existence of numerous alternatives eased if not entirely removed the pain. That was the past. But as affirmative action was a publicly aired issue from the start, with high legal and governmental participation, the press weighed in. The result has been greater media scrutiny and closer questioning, altering the way in which admissions officers can defend themselves.

The historical background to affirmative action

The policies, sentiments and views accrued under the curious phrase 'affirmative action' need to be included in the same category as other efforts to define and reconsider merit-determined entry to higher education. Major academic umbrella associations, such as the Association of American Colleges and Universities in Washington, DC, have made heavy commitments to the principle of 'diversity'. A 2003 issue of the Association's newsletter, *Diversity Digest*, equates diversity with democracy and puts affirmative action very broadly into 'the context of a long, ongoing struggle toward racial equality and full inclusion for all Americans'.[5] Viewed from this perspective, which is common enough and provides a moral justification for efforts to re-institute group quotas in higher education, affirmative action is an extension of the history of civil rights. Consistent with this position is that although the legitimacy of affirmative action appears to rest on its inclusion of all minority ethnic groups, in practice its special target has been the African-American community. Asian-Americans, who are certainly a numerical minority, as are Jews, are nevertheless excluded from consideration because they are high-achievers.[6] Despite the poorer records of Latino pupils and students, experienced analysts of the American melting pot

322

phenomenon such as Nathan Glazer are confident that integration and success will follow in due course.[7] Women, who some 30 years ago were regarded as appropriate subjects for affirmative action recruitment, are now in the majority as undergraduates and heavily represented in the professional schools (as in other rich democracies). Increasing the numbers who are appointed to professorial positions remains a campus objective; but in so far as women faculty are substantially represented in the humanities and social sciences, the educational issue is recruiting more of them to the hard sciences and engineering. This conclusion is familiar to students of the comparative study of universities.

The arguments are no less controversial than intelligence quotients, achievement and aptitude tests, high-stakes examinations and other means of selection. Arguably, the controversies over affirmative action are even more bitter and certainly wider ranging, involving legislatures, courts of law, professional associations, employers and civil service recruitment. Even words chosen to describe the nature of the groups which are to be advanced are contentious. Are we speaking about 'races', a word with a long history, so long that it was once used in England to mean 'nationality'[8], or do we mean 'ethnicity', a word with looser meanings? Trow explains that Americans are more comfortable speaking about ethnic identities than about racial adherence. The nation was formed from innumerable national, religious and ethnic identities, categories that overlap (especially in matters of food, dress and other manifestations of an imported identity) and eventually merge. Affirmative action at one level is an attempt to assimilate African-Americans to a familiar identity, to transform their self-image from one of racial bonding to one that is merely another ethnic group capable of assimilating in traditional fashion. But at another level, by insisting upon particular educational or hiring preferences, affirmative action confirms racial identity and perpetuates a sense of fundamental group differences. This goes against the American tendency to subordinate personal and group identity to a national norm. Since, as Trow points out, higher education in the United States has usually subverted group identities, to include working-class identities, by promoting the values of liberal democracy, affirmative action is a historic counter-thrust that has divided the nation.[9] The American university of the second half of the twentieth century prided itself on not 'reproducing' the prevailing social demarcations. Affirmative action – or some forms of it – therefore represents a fundamental reversal.

'Race' has a more invidious lineage than ethnicity, its biological referent suggesting that it is not a voluntary self-description to be used at will but a firm and fixed genetic condition that individuals cannot jettison. Even in milder form it still implies that one's descent is permanent. Both words are used interchangeably in discussions about affirmative action, but the continuing use of 'race' as an ascribed category keeps alive the notion that the USA has not progressed beyond slavery. 'The practical political rationale' of this, says Wilensky, 'is that racial prejudice and discrimination are so firmly institutionalised in American society that a race-neutral policy accenting equality of opportunity will perpetuate inequality'. In effect, successful white students are made to feel guilty. One minority group is set against another, and 'hideous historical memories' are awakened. And far from being an advantage to society, Wilensky continues, 'Racial-ethnic-religious-linguistic criteria for state allocation of rewards in a society with hundreds of minority groups is subversive of the coalition politics necessary to reduce poverty and inequality and enhance family well-being'.[10]

Affirmative action in the United States arose in the 1960s as part of the spirit of President Lyndon Johnson's 'Great Society' and in the context of extending the rights of citizenship to African-Americans. The terms were first used by Johnson in an executive order of 1956. Any agency in receipt of government contracts was required to pledge that discriminatory hiring practices did not exist. The executive order was preceded by the landmark 1954 Supreme Court decision of *Brown* v. *Board of Education* declaring school segregation to be unconstitutional, and in 1956 the decision was extended to include higher education. Title VI of the Civil Rights Act of 1964 empowered federal bodies to withhold funding from offending colleges or universities. By the 1970s federal representatives were requiring institutions to provide statistical information on affirmative action.[11]

So the first point to note is that apart from the history of grass-roots attempts to correct hiring and other discriminatory practices – such as the boycotts and picketing of local businesses in the 1960s – the authority of the courts and of Washington became the hammers of a Not So Great Society in order to further the declared values of an open and democratic one. A community that had long suffered indignity from injustice and bigotry was now to be welcomed into the nation of which it had been a part for virtually as long as anyone else (except for the Native American population). The emphasis was initially on the removal of barriers and restrictions in fulfilment of the democratic dream of equal treatment. The decision in *Brown* v. *Board of Education* provided the opening for even greater judicial activity as more and more barriers to equal educational access were identified. Lower federal and state courts were brought into the battles and handed down confusing or impractical rulings. The unequal distribution of financial support for school districts resulting in wide disparities in teaching resources became a major legal issue for the entire nation, and state court after state court entered into the fray. The basic judicial principle was whether schools provided an 'adequate' education for all (another way of invoking the federal constitution's equal protection clause), and the definition of adequate proved to be a headache for state legislatures, which had trouble applying the principle to education and to particular aspects of the schools curriculum. Under what circumstances could the teaching of cardiopulmonary resuscitation be determined as adequate? Wyoming's legislature wrestled with that one before replacing the course with instruction on how to balance a checkbook and manage a retirement portfolio.

In 1989 the Supreme Court of Kentucky took the extreme step of ruling that the state's entire education system was in violation of Kentucky's constitution. North Carolina's Supreme Court went the other way and decided that equal educational opportunities in every school district were not after all guaranteed by the constitution of the state if something like a 'sound basic education' was offered. This decision was more in the spirit of the old discredited south and did not appear to conform to the ruling in *Brown* v. *Board of Education*. The basic problem was that while courts of law could rule and then order, they could not legislate for or manage schools. They were not competent to judge the resources available for education, and their rulings were ambiguous or open to further challenge by school boards, teachers, legislatures and ethnic associations.[12]

Furthermore, the courts, as we will notice in the University of Michigan case, continued to issue divided and contested rulings, and judges appeared to be as conflicted about how to distinguish between merit and worth as anyone else. An ongoing case in the California courts in 2006 is as fine an illustration of the dilemmas as can be found. The judge in one of the county courts in the northern part of the state ruled that the state's recently instituted and mandatory school-leaving examination in English and mathematics was unfair because some schools were providing poor quality teaching that hindered their pupils from passing. More than half the seniors who failed the examination could be described as economically disadvantaged. Of nearly 47,000 pupils – 10.7% of the senior graduating class – less than 6,000 were white. African-Americans comprised another 6,000. But close to 30,000 were Hispanic. Cutting across these ethnic categories was the larger problem that well over 20,000 pupils were struggling with English as a second language. The lawsuit against the state in fact was brought by an affected Hispanic pupil represented by a San Francisco law firm.

In a liberal democratic environment, pupils are responsible for any inadequate performance; but under social democratic conditions, the blame shifts to the institutions. The court held the schools, unqualified teachers and inadequate textbooks to blame for poor examination performances. One related question that arose after the ruling was whether failing a school exit examination also meant the loss of a diploma certifying successful completion. In other words, could a diploma still be awarded if all the other criteria had been met? The court thought that a diploma could be issued but should carry a notation as to whether the examination had actually been passed. The press has not mentioned what the likely reaction of potential employers might be. In any case, second-chance America usually offers another try. In the current Californian situation, unsuccessful pupils have recourse to summer classes and free tutoring and can retake the exit examination as many times as necessary. Furthermore, given the open enrolment provisions of the community colleges, high school students can move forward into that segment even without diplomas.

California's senior examination was strongly supported by the governor, business employers and voters. An appeal therefore went immediately forward, bypassing the lower appellate courts to land in the lap of the California State Supreme Court. Within a short period, the Court invalidated the lower court's ruling and reaffirmed the legality of the senior examination. But as in other affirmative action cases to be mentioned, the Supreme Court's decision was split. The vote was 4 to 3, and the case of the failed examination has not been put to rest. It will go forward to yet another court of law called the Court of Appeal. So yet again, as so often in the educational history of the United States, a simple and straightforward solution to the question of academic standards and quality eludes consensus. Standards are necessary, but not if consequences follow from a failure to meet them – in which case either the standards are adjusted to prevent failure, or other institutional solutions are devised to keep the possibility of educational mobility alive. The attorney defending the pupil who (momentarily?) lost issued a statement virtually claiming that the receipt of a diploma was a constitutional right, although he added that the requisite courses had to be passed.

One other puzzle is whether pupils failing the examination were otherwise qualified to graduate, for some appear to be deficient in all respects. Another puzzle requires mention since it so well fits the patterns described in this book. The pupil who brought the lawsuit evidently compiled a close to perfect grade point average at her more or less inner-city school. Her senior class ranking was 12 out of 413, and yet she did not manage to pass an examination covering basic work in two cornerstone subjects.[13] (No mention was made in the press of her actual scores, or whether she had been unsuccessful in both subjects.) If it should be the case that her facility in the use of the English language on the examination was inadequate – which appears to be fairly common – one wonders how she or others with solid academic records managed to achieve high grades in the first place. We have yet another instance of a high school record about which university admissions officers might have qualms.

With its long history of remedial instruction and variable standards, American higher education has more than enough places for educationally low achievers. Besides community colleges, numerous private institutions exist that are not in the brand-name group and are more than willing to welcome substantial numbers of under-represented groups. Non-select institutions are better able to cope with the under-prepared student than are the elite private and public institutions. Many have developed an 'urban' or service mission that makes them highly sympathetic to the social problems existing in cities, and they are accustomed to part-time students, dropping out and lower degree completion rates. Colleges and universities that are mainly commuter institutions are not particularly concerned with the importance of residence as part of elite formation. They are not preparing elites, and they are not feeding their graduates into the leading professional and doctoral-granting schools, although this of course happens.

The problems of recruiting and advancing the fortunes of minority students are more acute for the higher education segments competing for the best students, for their model of academic achievement is not as flexible as in the other kinds of institutions.[14] In the beginning, they were often careless in the services that they provided for minority undergraduates, expecting them to manage on their own – this was true of the large publics – without understanding that as they had never been competitive before, they were unlikely to transform themselves in the course of a short semester. Adequate consideration was not given to whether students admitted from minority groups to undergraduate status were prepared for new experiences; but it needs to be added that pressures to admit under-prepared students were strong enough to defeat any hesitations on academic grounds. The outcomes were often calamitous: high early drop-out rates and the consequent loss of self-esteem. The pressures from the state and from sections of the interested public were for admission rather than for the progress to be made after admission. Possibly the long history of social promotion in American high schools accustomed students to believing that come what may, the institution would protect them. After much tribulation, colleges and universities realised that if their affirmative action policies were to succeed, more counselling, tutoring and financial resources were required. Undergraduates drawn from families that had achieved some measure of middle-class status did better. Although there were concerns that they did not do quite well enough, their difficulties were not nearly of the magnitude experienced by students recruited from the inner-city ghettos or barrios.

The amount of information regarding affirmative action that is available in published form or on the Internet is overwhelming. The following discussion is not intended to review every salient aspect of the issues and controversies but to situate them in the longer-developing history of the dilemmas posed by the two democracies and by their corresponding conceptions of worth and merit.

Affirmative action policies regarding admission

An understandable desire on the part of those who felt that the normal process of corrective historical change was far too slow led to thoughts on how to move disadvantaged groups more quickly into the educational mainstream. As mentioned, to begin with, affirmative action policies utilised descent as a classification; and while descent is still used, categorisation by income has become more evident and is less controversial. It is historical in so far as universities and colleges have long recognised need as a factor in bestowing awards and because low income also includes most of the minorities usually identified by race and ethnicity. Immediate social and economic amelioration, it was said, required affirmative action: government legislation was one means, and institutional policies that increased the chances of admission to higher education were another. Public institutions such as the campuses of the University of California had long used a 'special admissions category' to recruit students with particular talents that had not shown up in standardised testing: athletic abilities, musical excellence, journalistic attributes, leadership qualities. Special admissions had proved to be a useful category over the decades, sometimes as low as only 2% of undergraduate freshman entries and at other times as high as 18%. For a time after the Second World War, given the special circumstances of returning veterans, special admissions comprised almost 40% of first-year entrants at Berkeley and UCLA. After adoption of the Master Plan, which succeeded in raising standards somewhat, use of the special admissions category diminished. But when the question of recruiting more members of minority groups began to be central, it was again resorted to, hovering around 6%.[15] This appeared to be a reasonably simple entering wedge, acceptable in so far as little needed to be said about it, and no one really wanted universities to give up a practice that added flexibility to the admissions process. It was an established principle that some abilities were not exactly testable.

More and more the sentiment was voiced in the press and legislatures that the numbers of minority students in higher education generally or on specific campuses ought to broadly reflect their percentages in the general population. (This strategy in reverse, noted earlier, had once been used to discriminate against Jews, who were said to be 'over-represented' at universities.) Depending upon how society was divided up, this might be clearer in multiethnic California or New York City than in other states and cities where relatively few minorities dwelled, in which case affirmative action advocates would have to use a national rather than a regional context. But at any rate, the word 'broadly' was hardly easy to translate into specific policies. Expressed in the form of percentages, it required a specificity that may not actually have existed. For example, students who qualified as African-American might also be Spanish-speaking and therefore Hispanic, or in a certain limited case, Sephardic-Jewish, whose members were not regarded as minorities despite size. Women, of course, belonged to every single group in the minority or the majority. How should they be counted when meeting broad numerical recruitment goals? Students of mixed ancestry were a taxonomical puzzle, being forced for admissions purposes to declare an unnatural identity, thus encouraging a certain element of hypocrisy. To refuse to declare an identity where a desirable one could be claimed might jeopardise selection. And as in all cases of numerical tabulation, checking off the appropriate box created and perpetuated firmer categories than in the real world.

The easiest path to achieving breadth in admissions was to resort to a tactic that had long been discredited but to call it by other names. The nefarious phrase *numerus clausus* was not used, but more and more one heard about 'racial set-asides', 'guidelines', 'targets' or even outright quotas. The admissions pie could be divided in any number of ways so that less competitive groups did not have to be measured against the high flyers but only against others in a similar category. The sophisticated tinkering with admission categories that went on at the Boalt Hall School of Law at the Berkeley campus amounted to a de facto racial quota according to a careful researcher. Admittance was heavily weighted against Asian and white applicants.[16] The Master Plan had specified the percentages of students in a given high school class that would be eligible for admission to the University of California and the California State University and College system. The University would draw its freshman candidates from the academically top 12.5% of all high school graduates in the state. But that put the graduates of weaker high schools at a disadvantage; and although well ranked in their home institutions, they might not fare so well against statewide competition. But what if the criterion for eligibility was simply inclusion among the top 4% of any high school? Since it was assumed that underrepresented students came from the weaker high schools, might this improve minority representation? These kinds of considerations and experiments went on all over the United States, and there is no reason to believe that they have either ceased or are likely to cease as long as problems central to the determination of merit through education exists. For those with historical memory, anything resembling a quota, no matter how 'affirmative', is a reversal of a long battle won through the adoption of meritocratic entry criteria.

Affirmative action was justified on the grounds of fairness, although it is not at all evident that fairness requires recruitment by invented categories. Another argument was the social democratic position that the educational advancement of minorities was in the best interests of the nation. No one can disagree with an argument so obviously based on the ideal of democratic citizenship. In so far as contemporary democracy requires that citizens possess some element of higher education in order to participate in and receive the benefits of a free society, a high participation rate is certainly a virtue. But does the argument from citizenship suggest that its benefits can only be obtained by initial entrance to an elite university? Or is a modern solution to citizenship the availability of many forms of interlinked higher education as envisioned in the California model?

A more dubious argument was that the admission of minority students who might be under-prepared was necessary because of the need to establish diverse campus learning environments. But the acceptance of the argument for diversity depended upon the kind of diversity meant, for in many respects the American college and university of the last decades of the twentieth century were more diverse when measured by national representation

329

than ever before, or as might be said, 'virtually' diverse. Certainly Asian-American student participation at the University of California had utterly transformed the social composition of the federation. Furthermore, there was not one but many distinct Asian-American heritages, ranging from the old, established families that had emigrated from China and Japan a century or more ago, and then Korea, and the newer families from southeast Asia.

Before affirmative action was adopted as an admissions policy, diversity had other meanings. It usually referred to the availability of many types of intellectual discourse and interests. Universities had evolved into places that valued freedom of thought. Older forms of conformity derived from social and religious dogmatisms were no longer accorded much of a friendly reception, if they were even noticed, and the long reign of the 'gentleman C' was moribund, certainly at the elite campuses, although other institutions, particularly in the American south, retained a reputation as 'party schools'. No one spoke very openly about 'nerds' and 'grinds'.[17] But the new definition of diversity did not refer to this important change, although proponents might speak about the importance of different patterns of upbringing and experience in a world in which global travel was important. How much campus diversity meant where majority and minority students did not exactly mingle but lived in de facto segregated residences, ate at separate tables in the cafeterias and joined clubs and religious associations that were comfortable rather than ethnically diverse was not a question that was always openly asked.

Regarding students not as members of groups but as individuals was a simple principle much respected in the history of liberal democracy and supportive of the meritocratic ethic. But when this argument was advanced, it met the objection that universities and colleges had always made exceptions to merit when it suited their interests. Admissions practices now attacked as reverse discrimination were in fact well established in American university history and, furthermore, still in vogue. Private institutions had long given preferential treatment to the children of their graduates, 'legacy preferences' as they were called. One estimate in 2003 was that the sons and daughters of alumni still comprised some 10% of admits to Harvard, Yale and Princeton, about the same at the University of Virginia (where 91% of the students were white) and at least double that at Notre Dame. But was it possible that despite being the children of alumni, these undergraduates had earned admission by successfully competing? Some doubt was cast on this by a Department of Education study of 1990 that concluded 'that the average Harvard legacy student was "significantly less qualified" than the average non-legacy student in every respect except sports'.[18]

It is necessary to say that few academics or possibly members of the general public had any objection to special efforts for encouraging African-American, and later, other minority students to apply for admission, either through public advertising or by visits from recruiters to urban high schools. Nor were there great objections to new summer bridging programmes to acquaint potential students with aspects of a university culture or to provide remedial instruction to improve chances of admission. There were precedents for all of these, and certainly students from wealthier families had long had access to commercial testing and preparation agencies in the hope that such attention would improve their chances of being selected. Furthermore, public opinion was favourable to any efforts that promoted initiative, hard work and ambition as being well within the accepted ideal of liberal democracy. If potential minority students demonstrated that they had the interest and the discipline to improve their academic attainments, no one could possibly demur if they elected to participate in activities designed to assist them in competing for university entry. Many educators now also realised that expecting low-achieving students to be competitive without a lengthy period of grooming was unrealistic. Preparation for university had to commence much earlier. Cognitive skills could not be developed at the last moment. The problem lay in the schools, and programmes were needed that would reach pupils in less than ideal circumstances to start the long process of pointing them towards higher educational goals.

The opposition to affirmative action

Many were disturbed by the intense conflict, largely unforeseen, between issues of social justice arising from past circumstances and an American belief that discrimination of any kind, negative or *soi-disant* positive, was, in democratic terms, morally wrong. As the definition of an elite university was one in which places were limited, the acceptance of one kind of student meant the rejection of another. The acceptance of more poorly-prepared students simply because they were members of a group defined as 'disadvantaged' or, less invidiously, 'under-represented', meant that outstanding students might not find places in specific colleges and universities and would not receive the award for achievement promised since infancy. And there was sufficient evidence to prove that under-prepared students fell by the wayside unless standards were substantially relaxed. A study by the Law School Admissions Council of some 27,000 students entering 160 American schools of law in 1991 drew sobering, if by now unsurprising conclusions. African-Americans dropped out of the schools at a rate twice that of whites. Passage of the bar examinations was also doubtful, with a failure proportion of six times that of white students after many tries. The problem was especially acute within highly select institutions. A *Wall Street Journal* article of June 25, 2003 noted that about 4000 African-Americans took the Law School Admissions Test each year (a standardised national aptitude test). Of these, despite highly respectable undergraduate grade point averages, only three dozen at most scored as high as the ninety-third percentile, whereas the median scores at some six leading American law schools were at the ninety-eighth percentile.[19] In response to these findings, it was said that African-Americans suffered from a 'stereotype threat' and hence tended to conform to negative perceptions of their abilities. Rather than discard affirmative action, steps were needed to support students admitted under those guidelines.[20]

Legal challenges to affirmative action had commenced early, but the decisions handed down by state and federal courts were contradictory, providing mixed signals as to the legality of quotas, racial set-asides, or guidelines. The question was whether affirmative action policies furthered the cause of racial equality by providing preferences, and it certainly could be said that such a goal had not been envisioned in the original legislation. Therefore the courts were being asked to rule on a wholly new problem for which they had no adequate guidance beyond a history of racial discrimination in the USA. This was no longer overt but might be structural in the sense that ability sorting according to academic competition and high-stakes testing militated against the selection of targeted minorities.

By the beginning of the new millennium the reaction to affirmative action policies had reached a point where the initiative voting process in California (laws originating outside the legislature) resulted in the passage of legislation forbidding the use of policies that resembled quotas. Other states either followed the California pattern or considered it, but such legislation was also a blunt instrument. Universities, as already mentioned, had devised numerous subtle and sophisticated ways to avoid charges of overt reverse discrimination. The second Bush White House announced its opposition to race-based admissions, although, apparently, not to the principle of a 'diverse' student body.[21] By 2003 several leading universities announced that they had reconsidered their affirmative action policies. Princeton and the Massachusetts Institute of Technology, for example, said that they would discard or alter minority-only summer programmes and scholarships. Threats by anti-affirmative action groups to challenge the existing policies through recourse to the Department of Education's Office of Civil Rights may or may not have caused the change.[22] The major political parties were inevitably involved. Although it is always necessary to be cautious in asserting generalisations, by and large the Democrats tended to support various affirmative action initiatives while the Republicans were more reluctant.

Writing in the *Times Higher Education Supplement* for February 14, 2003, Alan Ryan repeated what had often been noted: affirmative action policies also assisted those who already enjoyed the advantages of family, income and associations.[23] Along these lines, some years earlier, Trow, visiting a much-cited book supporting affirmative action co-authored by two former Ivy League presidents[24], noticed a surprising fact overlooked by adoring press reviewers. The numbers of African-American students counted in the book were not only the few 'trophy minority students'; they were also students whose academic records made them competitive with any other group of individuals. How simple it was for rich Ivy League institutions to recruit the top minority high school talent. They had a long and hugely successful history of doing so and a fine supply of cash to provide scholarships. Even the best of the public universities and their professional schools were unable to compete for this stratum of ability. 'Nowhere', said Trow, 'have the authors demonstrated, in their piles of survey data, that a black student who is admitted on his own merits to [state universities and colleges] is significantly disadvantaged in relation to an affirmative-action admit to Princeton or Harvard'. The mind-set of the authors troubled him. 'The notion that you have to go to one of the most selective universities to fulfill your potential, or to become a leader in America, betrays an elitist[25] conception of American life that ignores how widely dispersed power and influence are, how diverse the origins of our institutional leaders are'. The higher education future for African-Americans, as indeed for all Americans, was higher education itself, pure and simple, and to offer marginal advantages for the few who are no more likely to be leaders in American society than any of the others was superfluous.[26]

For the elite institutions, the difficulties were most pronounced in the first decade of affirmative action, and the educational situation improved, as expected, when the children of university-educated, middle- or higher-income minority parents started attending universities and colleges. Writers have commented on the wealth of alternatives available to Ivy League institutions. 'Yale can choose between a legacy, a Latina, and a national-science competition finalist, depending on which hole needs another pigeon, each applicant with two 800s on the SAT'. The freedom to reach deeply into a pool of applicants and still come up with stellar choices is simply not an alternative for the overwhelming numbers of colleges and universities. Possibly out of the several thousand four-year institutions, Pulitzer Prize winner Louis Menand commented, more students were rejected than accepted by only some 200 of them. The rest admitted four-fifths of their applicants.[27]

Even without the assistance of affirmative action policies, minority students with top scores can gain admission to virtually any of the institutions that fall into a category of select. Trow's analysis of admissions at the University of California has revealed another pattern of attainment, even after the abolition of racial preferences by, first, the Regents of the University of California in 1996 (but subsequently reversed by them) and second, by the voters of the state through the passage of Proposition 209 in the year following. Under these changes, minority applicants who did not receive places at the most selective of the University of California campuses (such as Berkeley) 'cascaded' to other campuses in the system, or possibly even to private colleges and universities where preferences remained.[28] Another group was certainly admissible to the many campuses of the California State University and College system, from which they could transfer into the University of California (another indication of how often student transfer is ignored in arguments over admissions). Furthermore, a large percentage of students were not checking off the conventional ethnic identity boxes. They were declining to state or indicating 'other'. How many of these substantial numbers of potential students were of mixed ancestry or resented classifying themselves? The likely answer is that the numbers were sufficient to offset any losses that supporters of affirmative action were declaring to be a major catastrophe resulting from the passage of Proposition 209. Trow accused university presidents, admissions officers and others who were fully committed to affirmative action of disregarding the deep divisions over racial preferences existing within academia and the actual strong dislike of outright discrimination. He called the suppression of such opinion 'consensual coercion'.[29]

An important caveat in all discussions of selection requires reiteration. In calculating the size and composition of any candidate pool, allowance has to be made for self-selection. Accusations that universities have not accepted sufficient numbers of students from selected ethnic groups do not adequately take account of the fact that as in all educational matters involving opportunity, expectations are built up early in childhood. Without them, high school graduates leave education for employment or, as in the case of so many disadvantaged students, they fail to even graduate from secondary school. The result is a pool of university-bound applicants lacking in the diversity that is so much a goal of admissions officers.

The Michigan University case of 2003

The historian might wish to say that the national confusion over the two democracies, over how to measure personal worth and decide when the good of society must take precedence over the good of the individual, was resolved by two landmark decisions taken by the Supreme Court in 2003. But the historian inclined to view the outcome of a bitter fight as ended by the highest court in the land is destined for disappointment. A generous conclusion is that the Court enunciated several important principles reaffirming American conceptions of justice and fairness. A more quizzical position is that the Court reaffirmed only the divisions and ambivalences existing before the Michigan University case was heard. The fact that both sides to the dispute over affirmative action claimed victory after the decision was handed down, those who opposed racial and ethnic set-asides, and those who supported their use, is a perfect indication of the contradictory nature of the Court's findings. Those findings alone capture the underlying and possibly permanent dilemma in the American democratic ideal. But as an important footnote, the historian must also stress that although the decisions were meant to apply broadly to any higher education institution, they were issued in conjunction with lawsuits brought against a state-run university numbered amongst the top 10 research universities in the United States. Presumably those believing that their rejection by a private university or college was illegal could bring lawsuits of their own, yet we need to remember how much more freedom in the admissions process private institutions have always enjoyed.

Two parallel cases made their way up to the Supreme Court, *Gratz* v. *Bollinger* and *Grutter* v. *Bollinger*. (Lee Bollinger was then the President of the University of Michigan and presently holds that position at Columbia University.) The first concerned the use of an add-on points system for particular minority applicants in the undergraduate admissions process simply because they were members of targeted groups. The petitioners were Jennifer Gratz and Patrick Hamacher. The Court ruled 6–3 against this practice as constituting an outright discriminatory quota. The second case was brought by an applicant denied admission to the University of Michigan School of Law in 1996. Discovering that minority students with weaker overall academic records had been admitted while she was rejected, Barbara Grutter, the petitioner, who was white and 43 years of age, argued discrimination on the customary two grounds: violation of the equal protection clause of the Fourteenth Amendment to the United States Constitution and the Civil Rights Act of 1964. The Court found against the petitioner by a split decision of 5-4.

Earlier, lower federal courts had divided on the law school case. On March 27, 2001 the US District Court, Eastern Division of Michigan, concluded that Grutter's rejection by the law school was indeed a constitutional violation. But on May 14, 2002, the US Court of Appeals for the Sixth Circuit, comprising Kentucky, Michigan, Ohio and Tennessee, reversed the decision, supporting the University. The University had maintained that its law school admissions policy, which did not involve the points system used in undergraduate admissions, was necessary to achieve greater 'diversity', or in legal language, affirmative action was a 'compelling interest' for the University, and by logical if unstated extension, for society as a whole, or rather, for the state of Michigan. But as one critic derisively observed, law graduates of the University of Michigan tended to obtain employment outside the state. Only 16% remained in Michigan, as opposed to nearby Wayne State University Law School, almost all of whose graduates stayed.[30] The issue was really not diversity qua diversity, as the unsympathetic Supreme Court Justice Clarence Thomas said (he himself an African-American), for that could be easily achieved by lowering admission standards. Michigan wished to be 'diverse' while retaining its reputation as among the top 10 research universities in the nation.[31] This point was specifically underlined by Supreme Court Justice Sandra O'Connor in her majority opinion which referred to the importance of select institutions in forming future elites.[32] In any case, Thomas's dissent did not affect the final decision. The Court agreed with the University while expressing the hope that in another quarter of a century preferences would no longer be necessary. Affirmative action, depending upon how it was applied and carried out, was legal only as a temporary measure, and the Court noted that the University of Michigan itself promised to work towards development of colour-blind admissions.

Numerous interventions and *amicus curiae* briefs were filed on both sides, deluging the court with opinions and viewpoints derived from the long history of affirmative action extending back to the Bakke case of 1978 when a white student was rejected by one of the University of California medical schools despite a record better than minority admits (*Regents of the University of California* v. *Bakke*). The California Supreme Court ruled that racial quotas were illegal, but the decision was overturned at the federal level and appeared to uphold the use of race in admissions. However, as is often the case, the language of argument and decision was fractured, roundabout, full of points, sub-points and dissents, and hardly absolutely clear-cut in the reading. As normally interpreted in admissions, the Bakke decision appeared to support race as a factor in admissions, especially in the phrasing used by Justice Powell, but race was to be employed only in conjunction with many of the other variables comprising an individual admissions case. The decision enabled university admissions officers to decide just what kind of a 'factor' a particular applicant's ethnicity might be. If the Bakke case had been a clear and unambiguous binding precedent, presumably the University of Michigan law school case would have been unnecessary, the issue having been resolved two and a half decades earlier.

Lawyers for the University of California contributed mightily to the confusion surrounding the Bakke case, basing their argument on quite another issue, possibly uncertain of how the judges would view an admissions policy that featured racial set-asides. At stake, said the University's attorneys, was the institution's autonomy, which gave it the right to set admissions criteria. From the University of Chicago or the University of Cambridge, where Edward Shils also enjoyed an academic appointment, came his droll comment that the 'University of California, having yielded to the pressure of the federal government to introduce quotas, now claimed the privilege of doing so as a prerogative of the autonomy of universities'. For Shils, this topsy-turvy behaviour was proof that universities like California had lost all self-respect.[33]

As only to be expected, arguments circulating for years reappeared in the University of Michigan case. Was racial favouritism necessary to compensate for past injustice, and if so, how far into the past and for which groups: only for African-Americans, Hispanics (but presumably not of immediate European descent), Native-Americans but not the descendants of Japanese-Americans placed in 'relocation' camps during the Second World War, or Jews, the prime target of discriminatory admissions practices in American universities and colleges before about 1946 or 1950?[34] And was the University of Michigan taking it upon itself to compensate for all of the national injustices of the past or just for its own racial exclusionary policies, as the language of its lawyers seemed to suggest and which the University would of course be quick to deny? If a heterogeneous student body was indeed the primary objective of race preference, would a favourable ruling have to be applied to some hundred historically black colleges and professional schools from which so many African-American leaders had come, excluding those institutions from certain federal entitlements? True, founded in periods of rampant bigotry, they were, like women's colleges, institutions to advance educational opportunities otherwise unavailable. Now lawyers disingenuously argued that the black colleges were in fact diverse. They were not. Should they too be required to adopt affirmative action goals?[35]

Opponents were also able to point out that any form of ethnic classification has the effect of encouraging stereotypes. The argument for diversity, for example, as used repeatedly through the 1990s, suggested that one's ethnic or racial background was alone sufficient to enrich a university collegiate environment when so many other kinds of life experiences and modes of thought were the genuine fabricators of a learning environment. Thinking of individuals as members of groups rather than autonomous persons was, from the position of opponents of affirmative action, the liberal individualism of this book, fundamentally contrary to the entire meaning of the American democratic legacy.[36]

To preserve some shred of American liberal individualism, the Court in *Grutter* v. *Bollinger* had asked that the use of ethnic and racial circumstances be narrowly confined to individual circumstances and not imported in the service of quotas, a restatement of one aspect of the Bakke decision that more or less confirmed many of the admissions practices in place. At the same time the Court acknowledged, with clear misgivings, the wider utility of affirmative action, accepting the principle that affirmative action served the interests of universities, and through its graduates, society itself. It is possible to see in this ruling a cowardly validation of the double standards existing in American higher education, a signal to universities to continue using 'camouflage' in the admissions process, 'twenty-five years of hard-to-detect race-driven admissions'.[37] It is also possible to detect in the arguments, the language and the two decisions of the Court, one striking down a quota in all but name, the other providing space for continued use of affirmative action in individual cases, the same confusion about the determination of merit for elite selection existing in the nation at large.[38] The conflict between merit and worth, between liberal and social democracy, remained unresolved even in the hands of the highest and most respected court in the land.

Multiculturalism

The movement to include courses in the university that fall under the designation of 'multiculturalism' is an aspect of the history of affirmative action.

In and of itself, a multicultural course does not particularly represent a departure from principles at work in the American higher education curriculum. Many courses existed that could be said to fall under the rubric, any course in the social sciences or humanities that comprised more than one nation's history, literature, culture, anthropology or sociology. Furthermore, comparison is an excellent method for learning about tribal, ethnic or national differences. Thus far nothing has been said that is objectionable.

The problem, like so many problems in the history of merit and worth, is the context in which a movement or a tendency occurs, which is one reason why multiculturalism became controversial. The other contributing factor was that the proponents of multiculturalism had a political and social agenda that required them to insist that courses in multiculturalism be made mandatory. Again, many institutions had core curricula programmes which required students to take specific courses. Several, like the St John's colleges in Annapolis, Maryland and Santa Fe, New Mexico or Shimer College in Chicago only offered a compulsory curriculum of great books. However, undergraduates who chose to attend such institutions understood at the outset that a core of prescribed courses was the only option; and if they preferred a course of studies that allowed for more choice, the alternative was to attend elsewhere. In the case of multiculturalism, mandatory courses of a special character were required in addition to other specified requirements in a chosen field of study, removing some of the elective choices that were formerly on offer.

It was also the case that multicultural courses furthered an understanding of American history and culture as the story of discrimination against minorities; at least, that was the suspicion of opponents. Whereas such a viewpoint could be obtained in more conventional majors, and doubtless was, the fact that the courses were optional meant that the required messages might not reach a majority of undergraduates and certainly not those in the crowded engineering or science fields where fewer options were ever allowed. What therefore concerned the opponents of multiculturalism was not the existence of such courses as additions to the curriculum, but that pressure for them originated from the same corners that supported affirmative action and that it was likely that they would be taught from a political perspective that opponents would not regard as balanced. There is no simple way to describe the kinds of courses that were offered in colleges and universities throughout the United States, nor the spirit in which they were taught or whether they encouraged freedom of debate on subjects that had become inordinately sensitive.

At Berkeley a peculiar solution was adopted. Multicultural courses were required, but there was no single model for them. Individual members of the faculty were asked to submit proposals for such courses, of which there could be dozens that were accepted, no two alike except for the minimal requirement that at least two different cultures were compared in each course.

Students retained full choice in the kind of course they wished to take in order to satisfy the general requirement; and there is no reason to doubt that they chose according to criteria always available to them: some knowledge of the instructor and the views that were likely to be promulgated, and some understanding of the thrust of the course from the reading materials created for it. One overriding object of the multicultural movement was to form a campus environment supportive of affirmative action policies by explaining with the use of largely social scientific materials why the history of minorities and justice required them. The focus was on groups. Critics of diversity and multiculturalism concluded that these efforts to alter admissions and teaching were often being used as instruments of indoctrination or even intimidation. Those who argued against their use were stigmatised as racist. Similar movements were taking place in schools, as well as in Britain in the culture and media courses well satirised in Laurie Taylor's columns for the *Times Higher Education Supplement*.

One irony is that one of the demands of the student radicals of the 1960s was the elimination of required courses altogether on the grounds that students were mature, knew their own interests and should be free to pursue any subject that pleased or interested them. They also hoped to loosen the assessment system by replacing marks with simple pass or fail grades, thus yielding more time for political or other activities that could be undertaken without fear of penalties. Some movement in this direction did in fact take place, although it is not at all clear that students enrolling in pass or fail courses have used them as easy options. To their credit, they have often performed extremely well in them. At any rate, the introduction of compulsory multicultural courses was at variance with earlier student demands.

Given the interpretive latitude that has always existed in the humanities and the social sciences, it was simple enough for the partisans of multiculturalism to scoff at objections that their teaching was neither objective nor, in Max Weber's famous phrase, 'value free'. French philosophers such as the late Jacques Derrida assured their readers that the truth of any proposition hardly mattered since language, by its very nature, was always ambiguous or misleading. Opponents counter-attacked by accusing multiculturalists of being post-Marxists concealing what was in effect an attack on majority (read 'bourgeois') culture. Debates occurred over the meaning of 'relative knowledge'. Those who argued that some values were superior to others, some research results more plausible and defensible than others, some teaching more inclined to respect opposing views than others, were told that relativism was a historically necessary counterweight to dogmatism more than a commitment to a particular ideology. For if such a commitment was the principal aim of challenging existing beliefs and positions, it too was subject to the rule that all forms of relativism were obedient to relativity. At any rate, relativism was not to be confused with subjectivity.[39] If there were 'culture wars' over how to read and interpret evidence, especially evidence that lent itself to class, ethnic and gender biases, there were also 'science wars' in which even the disinterested disciplines were declared to be as subjective in their findings as any other branch of knowledge. Discarding the principle of objectivity altogether, some academics argued that scholarship was inevitably 'political': every interpretation was of ideological use and ought to be placed at the service of those accepting the necessity to change social values.

Possibly none of these positions was absolutely new. The relativity of truth had long been a subject of intellectual discussion, extending back centuries in fact, or perhaps an eternity, back to medieval theories of motion and Greek discussions of appearance and reality. Urbanologists, economists, social workers and educational reformers had always used research to support interventionist policies. The German 'Higher Criticism' of the Humboldtian university had certainly challenged received opinion. That was its purport. But what was once primarily academic and slowly absorbed if at all into general culture was now an advocate's primary instrument, leading to renewed debates about the truth of all knowledge, in which the followers of continental social science, postmodernism and deconstruction were fully engaged. Jurisprudence itself was affected. Battles occurred between those who held that the original intention of law always governed its application and others who insisted that the interpretation of statutes and constitutions was no more independent of social mood and opinion, or class and ethnic bias, than the reading of a novel or the analysis of a historical document. What, after all, was a 'fact'? Even more, the culture and science battles were aligned with the wider national conflict over the meaning and use of affirmative action precepts.

Well before the end of the twentieth century a counter-movement was in swing to contest the extensions occurring in the original affirmative action concept. The alleged benefits of multiculturalism in creating an open-minded society were both attacked outright and the evidence for them subjected to close methodological inspection. Questions were raised about whether social science 'experts' called to testify in courts of law regarding the value of diversity in education were using highly flawed analytical instruments. As usual, survey data was held to be unreliable. So much depended upon how questions were put. After all, respondents would be expected to be in support of the general goals of a democratic society but not necessarily (unless specifically asked) in accord with the particular means adopted by the proponents of diversity. When existing methods of measuring the value of diversity policies were applied, doubt was thrown on their purported blessings. Advocates were also accused of establishing or helping to establish a new 'politically correct' standard of debate. Views that were not in accord with affirmative action were regarded as impermissible and simply wrong; and those who were thus labelled wondered whether the new threats to academic freedom were not from outside the academy but from within.

The history of academic freedom had always been written as a defence of heterodoxy. The enemies were governments, churches or uninformed public opinion. Academics themselves were depicted as beleaguered but tenacious in defending their right to speak out, not in general it needs to be said, only in relation to their areas of professional competence.[40] Universities prided themselves on possessing a heritage of fearless and independent expression (a conclusion easily challenged on historical grounds), but how true was that plea when some of the policies in support of affirmative action were considered to lie beyond appeal? Some argued that the diversity movement even stigmatised African-American students by implying that special props were needed to steer them through the curriculum, to include disparaging what was referred to as 'white European culture'. The claims for diversity as both an educational tool for improving learning and a fulfilling outcome were thus rejected by scholars of reputation, which did not discourage other scholars of reputation, and especially university administrators, from insisting on the wisdom and justice of their affirmative action approaches.[41]

Notes

1 About a year before his death, Kerr asked me to write a history of the 'failure' of the Santa Cruz campus. I was not able to undertake the project. I also did not regard the campus as unsuccessful, but I understood that a fully collegiate public sector university was Kerr's very special lifelong dream. He wondered whether that dream would have been better achieved had the individual colleges attracted more endowment income, thus becoming more like the Oxford and Cambridge colleges. But as I saw the situation, a collection of Swarthmores could not really be incorporated into a multiversity research university federation.

2 John Douglass, 'A Transatlantic Persuasion: a comparative look at America's path towards access and equity in higher education', in *Understanding Mass Higher Education: comparative perspectives on access*, ed. Ted Tapper & David Palfreyman (London: RoutledgeFalmer, 2005), p. 237.

3 Reporting on the poor performance of Afro-Caribbean boys at school, with only 27% getting as many as five A-C grades at GCSE, *The Economist* noted that poverty rather than ethnicity seemed to be the problem as poor white boys came up even more badly (*The Economist*, March 12, 2005, p. 14).

4 Reported on CASNET for November 19, 2003.

5 The column by Carol Geary Schneider, the president, Volume 7 (2003), p. 1.

6 In the fall semester 2004, 41% of the Berkeley undergraduates were of Asian-American ancestry as against 31% of the white students. This constitutes nothing less than a social revolution in the history of the campus. The percentages for other groups fall off rapidly: Hispanic, 10%, African-American, 4%, Native Americans, 1%. The postgraduate statistics are different. White students were 46% of the student body, Asian-Americans only 17%. International students were 18% (*Cal Facts 2004*).

7 Nathan Glazer, '*Grutter* Accommodates the Intractable', *Academic Questions*, 16 (Summer 2003), p. 17.

8 As in some of the books by the historian George Macaulay Trevelyan (1876–1962).

9 Martin Trow, 'Class, Race, and Higher Education in America', in *Reexamining Democracy*, ed. Gary Marks & Larry Diamond (London: Sage, 1992), pp. 275–293. In the early political history of the United States, the Whig party, fearing that class distinctions would develop within a market economy, stressed the importance of individual merit over class. An 1833 Whig wrote that while distinctions exist, 'we have a right to demand that these distinctions shall be graduated as nearly as possible to the principles of human nature, and the claims of individual merit. Let talent laboriously cultivated, let wealth honestly earned, let virtue sacredly cherished, each have its distinction' Quoted in William J. Reese, *The Origins of the American High School* (New Haven: Yale University Press, 1995), p. 46.

10 Harold L. Wilensky, *Rich Democracies, Political Economy, Public Policy and Performance* (Berkeley and Los Angeles: University of California Press, 2002), pp. 713, 714.

11 Numerous sources exist for this information, but a shorthand version is in Stanley Rothman, Seymour Martin Lipset & Neil Nevitte, 'Does Enrollment Diversity Improve University Education?' *International Journal of Public Opinion Research*, 15 (Spring 2003), pp. 8–26.

12 Peter Schrag, *Final Test, the Battle for Adequacy in America's Schools* (London and New York: The New Press, 2003), pp. 61 et passim, 233 et passim, 241–242, 254.

13 *San Francisco Chronicle* (May 9, 2006), pp. A1 and A10; (May 11, 2006), p. B8; (May 13, 2006), pp. A1 and A7.

14 What follows is based upon my experience as a dean of students in the College of Letters and Science at Berkeley in the 1970s.

15 John Douglass, 'Anatomy of Conflict', in *Color Lines, Affirmative Action, Immigration, and Civil Rights Options for America*, ed. John David Skrentny (Chicago: University of Chicago Press, 2001), p. 124.

16 Daniel J. Guhr, *Access to Higher Education in Germany and California* (Frankfurt am Main: Peter Lang, 2002), pp. 274–287. Guhr reports (p. 274n.) that he encountered difficulty obtaining data from Boalt Hall.

17 A useful typology of American undergraduates appears in Helen Lefkowitz Horowitz, *Campus Life: undergraduate cultures from the end of the eighteenth century to the present* (Chicago: University of Chicago Press, 1988).

18 Reported by the Associated Press for March 5, 2003 and posted on CASNET. Similar information appears in *The Economist* for January 10, 2004, 'Lexington', p. 27.

19 Thomas E. Wood, 'Race, Admissions, and Litigation after Michigan', *Academic Questions*, 16 (Summer 2003), pp. 19, 22n.

20 *Wall Street Journal* (November 5, 2004), p. B3. The Law School Admissions Council's principal researcher, a professor of law at the University of California Los Angeles campus, had actually been involved in designing preferential formulas to aid disadvantaged students.

21 At least Alberto Gonzales, the White House Counsel and now Attorney General, so stated in an address to a Latino affirmative action association, prompting one politician to describe the Administration as 'bipolars'. *New York Times* (June 28, 2003), p. A10.

22 Bryan A. Keogh as reported on CASNET, May 7, 2003.

23 *Times Higher Education Supplement* (February 14, 2003), Opinion, p. 13.

24 William G. Bowen & Derek Bok, *The Shape of the River: the long term consequences of considering race in college and university admissions* (Princeton: Princeton University Press, 1998).

25 An atypical use of the word for him.
26 Martin Trow, 'California after Racial Preferences', in *The Public Interest* (Spring, 1999), pp. 64–85. Trow's paper was first delivered in October 1998.
27 Louis Menand, 'The Thin Envelope', in *The New Yorker* (April 7, 2003), p. 90.
28 Trow, pp. 80–85.
29 Ibid., pp. 24–27, 38.
30 Michael I. Krauss, 'The Underside of *Gutter*', *Academic Questions*, 16 (Summer 2003), p. 33.
31 Ibid.
32 Mentioned by Nicholas Lemann, then dean-elect of the Columbia University Graduate School of Journalism, in a piece for the *New York Times* (June 29, 2003), Ideas and Trends, p. 14.
33 *Universities, Politicians and Bureaucrats: Europe and the United States*, ed. Hans Daalder & Edward Shils (Cambridge: Cambridge University Press, 1982), pp. 472–473, 486n.
34 Alan Ryan ironically describes how Jews could be excluded even without an explicit *numerus clausus*: a football team is needed, or students from South Dakota or Tennessee (where few Jews reside), and then there are legacy admits, etc. *Times Higher Education Supplement* (April 11, 2003), Opinion.
35 Krauss, p. 35n.
36 Numerous documents pertaining to the University of Michigan case, including court transcripts, can be found online as *Grutter* v. *Bollinger*.
37 Abigail Thernstrom, 'Codifying a Double Standard', *Academic Questions*, 16 (Summer 2003), p. 9.
38 The media like to think of the University of Michigan as having 'won' *Grutter* v. *Bollinger*, a dubious supposition at best. The press cannot understand why minority applicants and acceptances are 'down' at Michigan one year after victory. The answer is that one year is hardly a trend, and reporters do not know how to question admissions officers on how they compile and use statistics. So much for methodological sophistication. See, for example, jwisely@detnews.com, reported by CASNET on October 26, 2004.
39 Christopher Herbert, *Victorian Relativity, Radical Thought and Scientific Discovery* (Chicago: University of Chicago Press, 2001), pp. xv, 24, 75, 143.
40 An understanding easily violated by academics who like to think of themselves as unattached public intellectuals rather than the career specialists that they are.
41 *The Economist*, ibid. Also one conclusion of a two-part study by the National Association of Scholars and distributed through CASNET on April 24, 2003.

72

BLACKS IN HIGHER EDUCATION TO 1954

A historical overview

John E. Fleming

Source: Gail E. Thomas (ed.) *Black Students in Higher Education: Conditions and Experiences in the 1970s*, Westport, Conn. and London: Greenwood Press, 1981, pp. 11–17.

Prior to the Civil War, the institution of slavery dictated the Nation's policy toward black Americans and prescribed the norms and social values which specified "appropriate" and "inappropriate" black behavior. For example, the slave code that developed early in the English colonies prescribed the conditions under which blacks worked and lived. Among the restrictive legislation passed to control the slaves was the prohibition against slaves reading and writing. Because this policy was dominant, particularly throughout the South, it was only under the most exceptional circumstances that blacks were able to create learning opportunities. However, some slaves did learn to read and write in clandestine schools and, in some instances, from their masters. These slaves passed on the knowledge they acquired to other slaves.

In large Southern urban areas like Charleston, South Carolina and New Orleans, free blacks attempted to establish their own schools. However, the existence of these schools often depended upon the capriciousness of whites who were generally opposed to educating people of color. Other educational opportunities for blacks existed on a limited basis. For example, some colonization societies provided training opportunities for blacks on the condition that blacks agreed to emigrate to Liberia or Haiti upon completing their education. But most of these organizational efforts included few blacks and had no general impact.

As the Civil War approached, many blacks had reached the conclusion that their best chance for higher education lay in establishing their own educational institutions. At that time (1850–1856) very few (less than

5 percent) blacks out of a population of 4.5 million could read or write. Lincoln University and Wilberforce College were the only two black schools established in the 1850s by blacks in their effort toward self education. The efforts of blacks were later joined by enthusiastic Northern missionaries. Together, these groups were able to promote the first massive effort to educate blacks. The American Missionary Association established Fisk University and Talladega College in 1865. Morehouse College, Shaw and Howard University were other historically black institutions established between 1865 and 1867.

During the Reconstruction Era (1868–1877), interested blacks and their white allies in the South laid the foundation for universal publicly supported education for both black and white Americans. During this time, Northern missionaries, who traveled throughout the South, publicized their belief that emancipated slaves were fully capable of benefiting from higher education. Unlike Northern missionaries who advocated a liberal arts education for the free man, General S. C. Armstrong, founder of Hampton Institute (1868), held and promoted the belief that blacks were less competent than whites, and that blacks should be granted a separate education that was of a lower calibre (Bullock, 1967). Southerners showed increasing acceptance of Armstrong's philosophy. In addition, the political climate of the era in most states was conducive to such a philosophy. Separate development for the races received the support of the federal government when the Supreme Court upheld the doctrine of "separate but equal" some twenty years later in *Plessy* v. *Ferguson* (1896).

The *Plessy* decision became the basis for a plethora of Jim Crow legislation and an increase in violence toward blacks. The "separate but equal" doctrine was even advocated in the federal government by President Woodrow Wilson who permitted increased segregation in governmental offices (Logan, 1970). During the Jim Crow Era, Booker T. Washington, a major advocate of segregation, gained prominence among whites. In his "Atlanta Compromise" speech at the Atlanta Cotton Exposition in 1895, Washington noted that the development of separate institutions for blacks and whites was the road to peace and harmony in the South (Logan, 1970). In addition, Washington urged blacks to cultivate friendly relations with Southern whites and urged whites to help the nonviolent blacks who labored for them. Washington also promoted the belief that blacks should devote themselves to learning agriculture, mechanics, commerce, and domestic services.

Encouraged by the Armstrong and Washington philosophies, Southern whites operated on the assumption that blacks should do no more than obtain an education that would prepare them for lower status positions in society. This assumption became apparent in the varied amounts of educational funds that were allocated to black public educational institutions in comparison to white institutions. For example, in one county in Alabama, secondary school officials paid salaries of $3,940 to black teachers who taught 10,745 black students and $28,108 to white teachers who taught 2,285 students (Logan, 1965).

Black colleges made great strides under very difficult circumstances. Of the 88 historically black four-year colleges which survive today (Turner and Michael 1978), forty private and 17 public institutions were established between 1865 and 1890. These institutions were mainly primary and secondary schools, but gradually they developed normal schools and college programs for the education of black teachers. The teachers were able to substantially reduce the illiteracy rate among blacks throughout the South. Nevertheless, white state and educational officials conveniently reasoned that the lower quality schooling that blacks needed required less expenses than the higher quality education that was necessary for white students. This type of logic was also extended to public higher education when the Second Morrill Act of 1890 was passed to include the establishment of black land-grant colleges where states maintained a public policy of segregated education. The colleges that were developed for blacks were of poor quality with inadequately trained teachers and teaching facilities. Moreover, these institutions were initially non-degree-granting agricultural, mechanical, and industrial schools. None of the 17 black land-grant colleges offered a liberal arts education prior to 1916., although one or two institutions offered a four-year degree program (Holmes, 1934; Bowles and De-Costa, 1971).

After his death in 1915, the influence of Booker T. Washington gradually declined and blacks increasingly demanded a liberal arts education for their children. In addition, blacks realized that "special education", as advanced by Washington, was inadequate to meet their needs as the demand for agriculture decreased and new jobs in manufacturing, trade, and industry appeared. This recognition was especially applicable to blacks who had migrated from rural areas into developing industrial urban centers. The burden of providing blacks with a liberal arts and more relevant education was then assumed by the private black colleges established after the Civil War by Northern missionaries. Although these institutions were also forced initially to provide blacks with elementary and secondary education, by 1928 most of them had eliminated these elementary and secondary departments and were able to concentrate on college level curriculums. By 1930, black educators had persuaded the Southern Association of Colleges and Secondary Schools to include black colleges in its accreditation process; but because of segregation, black colleges could not achieve full membership. In 1933, black educators formed the Association of Colleges and Secondary Schools for Negroes whose purpose was to promote the upgrading and improvement of black colleges.

By 1930 approximately 19,000 students were enrolled in black colleges (Aptheker, 1973). In addition, the rate of illiteracy among blacks had been reduced from 60 percent in 1895 to 25 percent by 1930. In 1939, 119 doctoral degrees had been awarded to blacks by the leading white colleges and universities. Most of these recipients had obtained their undergraduate training from the black colleges. W. E. B. DuBois was one such recipient who had received his college training at Fisk University and had obtained his Ph.D. from Harvard University.

Many blacks took pride in the accomplishments of the private black colleges and in blacks who had successfully advanced in higher education. However, DuBois, along with other civil rights leaders and concerned blacks quickly came to the conclusion that the doctrine of "separate but equal" was a major inhibiting force to the further progress of blacks in higher education. During this time, black colleges were still receiving unequal and discriminatory treatment through state and federal support and technical assistance.

In response to the position of blacks, the National Association for the Advancement of Colored People (NAACP) spearheaded the assault on the doctrine and separate development in the federal courts. In 1935, Donald G. Murray was unsuccessful in his attempt to enter the University of Maryland's segregated school of law. Murray's failure stimulated a class action suit by the NAACP charging the University of Maryland with discrimination and in violation of the 14th Amendment to the Constitution. In 1936, the Court ordered the University of Maryland to admit Murray to its school of law. The Murray decision was followed by four additional NAACP suits which attacked the doctrine of "separate but equal" in higher education: *Missouri ex rel Gaines* v. *Canada* (1938); *Sipuel* v. *Board of Regents* (1948); *Sweatt* v. *Painter* (1950) and *McLaurin* v. *Oklahoma State Board of Regents* (1950).

Based on the Court's ruling in *Murray* and the later four cases, the NAACP had established a successful attack on the doctrine of "separate but equal." The suit in *Gaines* was filed after the University of Missouri School of Law denied Lloyd Gaines (a black graduate of Lincoln University) admission to its Law School. The Supreme Court held that Gaines was entitled to equal protection of the law and that the state of Missouri was obligated to provide him with a legal education substantially equal to that offered whites. The Court's ruling in *Gaines* (1938) established the principle that if states did not provide educational facilities for blacks equivalent to that provided for whites, then blacks had to be admitted to white institutions (Haynes, 1978). *Sipuel* (1948) and *Sweatt* (1950) also involved the refusal of white state law schools to admit blacks to their programs. Sipuel reinforced the precedent established in *Gaines* that blacks had to be admitted to white graduate and professional schools if no black institutions existed. The ruling in Sweatt constituted the first time that the Supreme Court ordered admission of a black student to a white institution on the grounds that the black law school established by the State of Texas (Prairie View) failed to offer blacks equality of educational opportunity (Haynes, 1978). The

McLaurin (1950) case involved a black student who was admitted to the University of Oklahoma's graduate school but who was required to eat and sit apart from his white classmates. The Supreme Court ruled that such discriminatory treatment violated McLaurin's constitutional rights and that McLaurin was entitled to the same treatment within the graduate school as his white classmates.

The Court's posture in *McLaurin, Sweatt,* and the previous cases paved the way for the landmark ruling in *Brown* v. *Board of Education of Topeka* (1954). The Supreme Court consolidated the *Brown* case with four similar cases in the District of Columbia, Delaware, Virginia and South Carolina. In response to *Brown* and these four cases, the Supreme Court unanimously held that the doctrine of "separate but equal" was unconstitutional and violated the Equal Protection Clause of the Fourteenth Amendment. Chief Justice Earl Warren, who delivered the Court's opinion, held that "enforced school segregation imposed an inferior status on the Negro children". Although the ruling in *Brown* was aimed at elementary and secondary education, it had broad consequences and implications for higher education which were articulated almost a decade and a half later in *Adams* v. *Richardson* (1973), when the Supreme Court ruled that states had to dismantle their dual system of higher education for blacks and whites.

References

Adams v. *Richardson.* 480 f.2d 1159 (D.C. Cir. 1973).

Aptheker, H. (1973) The Education of Black People: Ten Critiques, 1906–1960. Amherst: The University of Massachusetts Press.

Bowles, F. and F. H. DeCosta (1971) Between Two Worlds: A Profile of Negro Higher Education. New York: McGraw-Hill.

Bullock, H. A. (1967) A History of Negro Education in the South From 1619 to the Present. New York: Praeger.

Brown v. Board of Education of Topeka 347 U.S. 483 (1954).

Fleming, J. E. (1976) The Lengthening Shadow of Slavery: An Historical Justification for Affirmative Action for Blacks in Higher Education. Washington, D.C.: Howard University Press.

Haynes, III, L. (1978) A Critical Examination of the Adams Case: A Source Book. Washington, D. C.: Institute for Services to Education.

Holmes, D. O. W. (1969) The Evolution of the Negro College. New York: Arno Press and the New York Times.

Logan, R. W. (1965) The Betrayal of the Negro from Rutherford B. Hayes to Woodrow Wilson. New York: Collier Books.

—— (1970) The Negro in the United States. New York: Van Nostrand Reinhold Co.

McLaurin v. Oklahoma State Regents 339 U.S. 637 (1950).

Missouri ex. rel. Gaines v. Canada 305 U.S. 337 (1938).

Murray v. Maryland 182 A 590 (1935): 169 Md 478 (1937).

Plessy v. Ferguson 163 U.S. 537 (1896).

Sipuel v. Board of Regents of University of Oklahoma 322 U.S. 631 (1948).

Sweatt v. Painter 339 U.S. 629 (1950).

Turner, W. H. and J. A. Michael (1978) Traditionally Black Institutions of Higher Education: Their Identification and Selected Characteristics. Washington, D.C.: National Center for Educational Statistics, U.S. DHEW.

73

APARTHEID IN THE SOUTH
AFRICAN UNIVERSITIES

John Rex

Source: *Universities Quarterly* VIII (1953–54): 333–40.

The Afrikaans word 'Apartheid' has, by now, almost qualified for a place in the Oxford Dictionary. Throughout the British Commonwealth politicians are prepared to take a stand for or against what they believe to be a general description of the Malan Government's policy. But it is to be doubted whether many of those who talk about 'apartheid' have a clear idea of what it means. This is to be expected since 'apartheid' is a slogan-word, which conceals rather than reveals the nature of the policy which it is supposed to describe. Literally it means 'separateness' (of the various racial groups). But since 'separateness' has always been the policy of the United Party in South Africa, it is difficult to see why the policy is so strongly associated with the name of Dr. Malan. The United Party bears full responsibility for the Lands Act confining African peasants to reserved areas. It was the United Party which segregated urban Africans by means of the Native Urban Areas Act, and the United Party which introduced the Native Representation Act putting African voters on a separate voter's roll. Finally, even though it is true that a Nationalist Government legalized the Industrial Colour Bar with the Mines and Works Amendment Act, the United Party accepted that Act when it was later returned to office.

Dr. Malan's Government, however, has carried the doctrine of separateness as far as possible towards its logical conclusion, and it is in this process that it has raised new issues of expediency and of morality. Among the most important nationalist measures already passed are:

1. The extension of segregation to the Cape Coloured and Indian communities.
2. Stricter measures to control the influx of Africans into towns.

3. The imposition of segregation in public buildings and transport where none previously existed.
4. The banning of mixed marriages.

In addition to these there are other measures which are in the process of being passed. They include:

1. The removal of the Cape Coloured voters from the common voters' roll.
2. The elimination of already segregated 'blackspots' in the middle of White occupied Urban areas.
3. The abolition of racially mixed Trade Unions.
4. The transfer of Native Education from the Provincial Authorities to the Native Affairs Department.

Thirdly, there are policies, which it is not at present proposed to implement by legislation, but which government propaganda aims to encourage independent bodies to carry out. Among the most important of these policies is the exclusion of black students from 'white universities'. The basic structure of segregation itself raises important moral and political issues, and much might be said of each of the Nationalist policies we have mentioned, but neither of these will be discussed here. The discussion will be confined to those apartheid measures which directly affect university education. They are in any case amongst the most important, because here at least the doctrine of 'apartheid' has to be challenged on moral grounds rather than on grounds of expediency and party advantage, which have loomed large in the discussion of other apartheid measures. The aim of this article is to show the extent to which separateness prevails already in the South African universities and to discuss the issues of principle, of concern to university people everywhere, raised by the Government's attempts to obtain a still greater measure of segregation. Apartheid applied to university education has two main aspects. These are, firstly the attempt to segregate students for residential, social and academic purposes, and secondly the provision of different sorts of education for students of different races.

We must begin with a factual survey of the existing university provision and the extent to which segregation is already imposed. South Africa has eight universities for full-time students, one university which provides only for external students and one college affiliated to but not a corporate member of one of the universities. There are four Afrikaans-speaking universities at Stellenbosch, Pretoria, Bloemfontein and Potchefstroom. None of these admits non-European students. The University of South Africa, having shed its various member colleges, as they each attained university status, now provides only external degrees, but examines and provides bilingual correspondence courses for students, regardless of race.

The four English-speaking universities are the University of the Witwatersrand (at Johannesburg), the University of Capetown, the University of Natal (at Pietermaritzburg and Durban), and Rhodes University (at Grahamstown). The Fort Hare Native College (at Alice in the Eastern Cape Province) is affiliated to Rhodes University. It is in these universities that the degree of segregation is less strict, and it is they who are most concerned about the question of apartheid.

The Universities of the Witwatersrand and Capetown admit non-Europeans to all courses, but in both cases they are required to live in separate hostels. In 1947 there were 182 non-European students at Witwatersrand and 100 at Capetown, representing 4 and 2 per cent of their respective enrolments. The number, though limited by the high cost of university education, is rising.

The University of Natal has three colleges, two for Europeans in Durban and Pietermaritzburg, and one (Sastri College) for non-Europeans. In 1947 Sastri had 340 students, most of whom were Indians. Rhodes made some attempt to open her facilities to non-Europeans in 1947, before she obtained university status. A decision was taken to admit African post-graduate students and one was actually admitted. On her attainment of university status, however, Rhodes became an all-white university with an affiliated Native College at Fort Hare.

In 1947 there were just under a thousand non-European students receiving full-time university education. There was no full equality of opportunity for the different races, but on the other hand the African was not debarred from the best university facilities which the country could provide on grounds of race alone. Economic inequality between the races was the fundamental cause of the relatively small number of non-European university students. The effect of closing the doors of the Universities of the Witwatersrand and Capetown to African students, in accordance with the Government's wishes, would be to introduce a serious element of inequality, since Fort Hare and Sastri cannot as yet provide the same range of courses or standards of tuition as the larger universities can.

But the issues raised by the apartheid question go beyond that of equality of educational opportunity. In the first place, a university which excludes certain sections of the community is likely to be a poorer place as the result of the exclusion. The effect of studying together on white and black students alike is undoubtedly a healthy one, both for the students themselves and for their country. Prejudiced minds cannot attain that freedom of thought which is so vitally necessary for a university student. The experience of many of the best students in the mixed universities suggests that release from race prejudice means the release of a student's full intellectual powers, and a new vision of the social purpose of education. Moreover, one felt very strongly in the period following the war that something very valuable for South Africa was happening as black and white students began to find that a common intellectual interest was a more important social bond than pigmentation.

These benefits of mixed education were to be seen most clearly at Witwatersrand and Capetown. At both universities non-European students have been elected to the Student Representative Council, and there is surely no finer interracial action on record in South Africa than that of the white Witwatersrand students, who, when the Government stopped giving State Scholarships to African medical students at their university, imposed a levy on themselves to continue the scholarship.

But the Universities of Natal and Rhodes are not entirely lacking in this liberal atmosphere either. Inter-college activities such as debates and symposia on social questions, and even an occasional sports meeting, help to bridge the gap created by separate teaching. Rhodes had particularly valuable opportunities of arranging meetings with African students and staff at Fort Hare, who undoubtedly will continue to provide the black population of Southern Africa with their leaders as they have done in the past. In the period after the war dozens of Rhodes students made valuable contacts with leading black South Africans like Professor Matthews and Jabavu, with men like Samkange and Hlabangana, who were to become acknowledged African leaders in Southern Rhodesia, or Manoah Chirwa, who was to represent Nyasaland in the Federal Legislature of Central Africa. It is difficult to overestimate the effect on future racial co-operation of meetings like these.

One of the principal agencies encouraging this co-operation between students was the National Union of South African Students. NUSAS, as it is familiarly known, worked hard and usually with considerable political commonsense to keep open the channels of interracial co-operation by bringing all students into one organization where common academic problems could be discussed. Unfortunately, the affiliation of Fort Hare and Sastri led to the refusal of the Afrikaans universities to join. NUSAS wisely kept out of politics, and even went so far as to ban interracial socials and dances in areas where these conflicted with local custom. It did this in the belief that more valuable work could be done by encouraging students of different races to meet and discuss their subjects of study. Thus it became something of a university in itself, rather than a humdrum students' trade union. Its greatest achievement, perhaps, was an interracial research expedition to a village in a Native reserve by senior students from different faculties and different universities. There future doctors, architects, sociologists, economists, educationalists and agriculturalists were able to grasp the social purpose of their studies and to realize that their common vocation was a bridge between racial differences.

NUSAS is attacked from many sides. It is a natural target for attack by those who are opposed to interracial co-operation. The leaders of the Nationalist Party have long demanded that it should be banned, but as yet nothing has been done to implement this. Secondly, it finds itself attacked by African nationalists, and tragically enough, the Fort Hare students withdrew from the Union in 1950, owing to its refusal to engage in political agitation. Thirdly, it is attacked by the more timid members of university senates who fear that its interracial activities may lead to Government action against the universities.

The presence of black students at two English-speaking universities, and the interracial co-operation that goes on in all of them and in NUSAS, are the main targets at which Government criticism is directed. On the first question the governing bodies of Witwatersrand and Capetown have taken a firm, though not unanimous, stand. On the second question the authorities at the Universities of the Witwatersrand, Natal and Rhodes, at least, have shown signs of wanting to discourage mixing wherever possible. No one should underrate the difficulties with which they are faced, or imagine that the heads of these universities are not liberal-minded men. But they fear that, if the Government is provoked by continued examples of intermixing, the consequences for the universities might be very serious indeed. For important though the advantages of contact between university students of different races may be, a still greater danger lies in Government control of the universities.

There are on record many statements by leading supporters and allies of the Nationalist Party which suggest that the ultimate direction of Nationalist policy will be towards a corporate state on the Fascist model. In fairness it should be said that Dr. Malan himself does not support such plans, but if extremists within the Nationalist Party were to try to put them into effect, then the universities, like the trade unions, would be converted into mere agencies of the State and the 'Volkswil'.

There is a real danger that, with this threat in mind, the universities will adopt a policy of appeasement towards the Government. Dr. Davey, the Principal of Capetown, was surely right in opposing the exclusion of non-European students, on the ground that to do so would be to admit the right of the Government to interfere in the internal affairs of the universities. Instead of buying off the Government, appeasement on the apartheid issue might lead to even greater interference. The apartheid question could easily be the first round in a long battle between the State and the universities, and in this battle the universities cannot afford to make concessions at all.

But there is an even more fundamental danger to the universities, arising from the attempt to provide a different sort of education for Africans at the lower levels. To put this in its proper perspective it is necessary to say something of the doctrine of Christian National Education, expounded by some Afrikaans professors, particularly at Potchefstroom, which is largely a religious seminary.

The fundamental point made by these theorists is that God calls each nation to a particular destiny. This is a perversion of the Calvinist view of a 'calling', but once it is granted, it is said to follow that each nation, race or linguistic group should receive an education appropriate to its divinely appointed purpose. No universal system of education can provide for this need in a mixed community, like that of South Africa. Therefore there must be Jewish education, English education, Afrikaner education, and so on. The doctrine draws force from the fact that the Afrikaans community have always felt quite rightly that textbooks in subjects like history tended to be biased against the Afrikaans people, and also from the protests of religious fundamentalists common in Afrikaner religious traditions against the teaching of modern science.

But where does the African figure in the schemes of the Christian National educationalists? The answer is equivocal. On the one hand he must be educated in accordance with the calling to which God has assigned him, but on the other the missionary spirit of Christianity demanded his conversion to Christianity. His education must therefore take place under European guidance and in particular under the guidance of the Boer nation.

This doctrine has for some time been taken quite seriously by the Transvaal Provincial Council. Meanwhile the Government, which is not directly responsible for education, has been working on parallel lines, at least as far as the education of the African is concerned. Nationalists have always held that the African should not be turned into 'a second-rate European' but should be educated 'along his own lines'. In 1948 the Government appointed a commission to determine what exactly these lines were. The Commission has reported, and, as a consequence, the Government has transferred responsibility for African education from the Provincial authorities to the Native Affairs Department. The aim of this new authority will not be to increase the number of African children in schools, but to change the nature of the education provided. It appears that the standard of ordinary education provided will be very low indeed, and that thereafter emphasis will be on practical subjects. At present the new authority is attempting to buy out some of the missions in order to implement this policy fully.

From these trends two dangers for the universities arise. One is that the supply of African students will be cut off at its source. The other is that, by direct Government intervention, or by infiltration, the doctrine of Christian National education may get a hold on the universities, other than Potchefstroom where it has a hold already. University people in South Africa are well aware of the second danger and much good counter-propaganda work has been done. As to the first danger, it remains to be seen whether the policy can be implemented. There can be little doubt that African teachers, missionaries and university lecturers and students will do all that they can to see that African education is carried on. But they may need financial assistance from overseas if this proves necessary.

We may then summarize the principal points of the challenge which the apartheid ideology makes to the universities. In the first place, it challenges the view that education is a single process involving a search after truth. Secondly, it challenges the view that universities should be able to choose their students on academic grounds, free from outside interference. Thirdly, it seeks to inhibit the free interchange of experience and information between students and, finally, it seeks to limit educational opportunities for one section of the community.

All that university people overseas are in a position to do for the South African universities in this situation is to advise, encourage and warn. But part of advising consists in giving an example. An example of a truly interracial university can be provided in Central Africa. The future of this new university is not yet fully decided. It has been said that it will be truly interracial. But what interracial means has given rise to argument. In view of the dangers of compromise on this question it would be well if the view of the African members of the Federal legislature of Central Africa were given due weight. One of them writes:

> The students of the University should study under the same roof, eat, play and sleep under the same roof. Any form of discrimination would not be acceptable to the people we represent, would not give enough opportunity to the young generation of growing up without a false sense of superiority, and would undermine the spirit of the federal constitution . . . lecturers and professors should be drawn from all races and should receive equal pay for equal work.

In demanding common hostels, this goes further than the example of the Universities of the Witwatersrand and of Capetown, but there is no doubt that the existence of the additional opportunities provided by a common place of eating and sleeping would help to carry even further the process of co-operation which they exemplify. Those who are concerned about the dangers of apartheid to university life in general should watch this experiment carefully and see that it provides an alternative way of dealing with the problems of the university in a mixed society.